AF731995

SHADOW ECONOMIES IN THE GLOBALISING WORLD

From West Indian sugar and bottles of Southeast Asian arrack to French red wines, English felt cloth, and Mediterranean lemons, many global wares ended up in the Scandinavian borderlands during the late eighteenth century. This book explores how and why these goods came to be there and analyses what smuggling can reveal about the emergence of global trade, the formation of the nation state, and the development of consumer society in Europe's northernmost outskirts.

This book shows that the global underground was ubiquitous in the Nordic countries and fundamentally altered them, politically, economically, socially, and culturally. Through re-evaluating the role of smuggling the book complements and challenges established historical accounts about state building, market dynamics, consumer culture, and ideas and identity. It also offers a roadmap for how to think about illegal global trade and how to approach this notoriously difficult research field. By integrating illegality, the book aims to show how an illicit web entangled often overlooked 'peripheral' territories with traditional 'portals of globalisation' and proposes a novel take on early modern globalisation and the paths to modernity in the European hinterlands. To achieve this a wide variety of sources are used including court records, administrative sources, diaries, ambassadorial correspondence, and maps in various languages including Swedish, Finnish, Norwegian, English, and French.

This book makes a significant contribution to the literature on economic history, the first wave of globalisation, the study of shadow economies, and Scandinavian history more broadly.

Anna Knutsson graduated with a PhD in history at the European University Institute in 2019 after writing a thesis about smuggling in Sweden during the eighteenth century. Since then, she has taken up an international postdoctoral fellowship at Uppsala University, Cambridge University, and NTNU and is currently researching illegal trade and its impact on northern European peripheries.

'This innovative book reconceives smuggling not just as a national phenomenon but as both global and globalizing. At the same time, it shows how smugglers and smuggled commodities – such as coffee – profoundly influenced Nordic culture, politics, cultural mores, and even foreign policy.'

Margaret R. Hunt, *Professor of History, Uppsala University*

Perspectives in Economic and Social History
Series Editors: Andrew August and Jari Eloranta

Luxury, Fashion and the Early Modern Idea of Credit
Edited by Klas Nyberg and Håkan Jakobsson

The Nordic Economic, Social and Political Model
Challenges in the 21st Century
Edited by Anu Koivunen, Jari Ojala and Janne Holmén

North Eurasian Trade in World History, 1660–1860
The Economic and Political Importance of the Baltic Sea
Werner Scheltjens

A History of Cold War Industrialisation
Finnish Shipbuilding between East and West
Saara Matala

Social Cohesion and Welfare States
From Fragmentation to Social Peace
Edited by Christopher Lloyd and Matti Hannikainen

Agriculture and the Great Depression
The Rural Crisis of the 1930s in Europe and the Americas
Edited by Gérard Béaur and Francesco Chiapparino

Shadow Economies in the Globalising World
Smuggling in Scandinavia, 1766–1806
Anna Knutsson

For more information about this series, please visit: www.routledge.com/series/PESH

SHADOW ECONOMIES IN THE GLOBALISING WORLD

Smuggling in Scandinavia, 1766–1806

Anna Knutsson

Routledge
Taylor & Francis Group
LONDON AND NEW YORK

First published 2023
by Routledge
4 Park Square, Milton Park, Abingdon, Oxon OX14 4RN

and by Routledge
605 Third Avenue, New York, NY 10158

Routledge is an imprint of the Taylor & Francis Group, an informa business

© 2023 Anna Knutsson

The right of Anna Knutsson to be identified as author of this work has been asserted in accordance with sections 77 and 78 of the Copyright, Designs and Patents Act 1988.

All rights reserved. No part of this book may be reprinted or reproduced or utilised in any form or by any electronic, mechanical, or other means, now known or hereafter invented, including photocopying and recording, or in any information storage or retrieval system, without permission in writing from the publishers.

Trademark notice: Product or corporate names may be trademarks or registered trademarks, and are used only for identification and explanation without intent to infringe.

British Library Cataloguing-in-Publication Data
A catalogue record for this book is available from the British Library

Library of Congress Cataloging-in-Publication Data
Names: Knutsson, Anna, author.
Title: Shadow economies in the globalising world : smuggling in Scandinavia, 1766–1806 / Anna Knutsson.
Description: New York, NY : Routledge, 2023. |
Series: Perspectives in economic and social history |
Includes bibliographical references and index. |
Identifiers: LCCN 2022034017 | ISBN 9781032127408 (hardback) |
ISBN 9781032127439 (paperback) | ISBN 9781003226031 (ebook)
Subjects: LCSH: Informal sector (Economics)—Scandinavia—History—18th century.
Classification: LCC HD2346.S29 K69 2023 | DDC 338.720948—dc23/eng/20220812
LC record available at https://lccn.loc.gov/2022034017

ISBN: 978-1-032-12740-8 (hbk)
ISBN: 978-1-032-12743-9 (pbk)
ISBN: 978-1-003-22603-1 (ebk)

DOI: 10.4324/9781003226031

Typeset in Bembo
by codeMantra

To my daughter Alva.

CONTENTS

ILLUSTRATIONS

Figures

Graphs

Tables

ACKNOWLEDGEMENTS

This publication is a revised version of a European University Institute PhD thesis, and I first want to thank the EUI and my supervisor Luca Molá for bestowing me with the freedom to develop my project freely and having faith in me to see it through. I also want to thank those who helped to make this book a reality most importantly, my editor Andy Humphries, the series editors Andrew August and Jari Eloranta, as well as the Swedish Research Council that funded both my doctoral research and the project that allowed me to transform it into a publishable book. Thank you to all the various reviewers, known and unknown, who have shared their knowledge as well as expertise with me and helped to form this project. Your help has enabled me to put together the jigsaw pieces of this research.

To Berit Eldvik for sharing her knowledge of peasant textiles with me. To Anna-Karin Jobs Arnberg for enthusiastic conversations about worsteds. To Michael Nix for his insights into the Norwich worsted manufacturing. To Ulf Åsén for his insider knowledge of the Freemasons in Stockholm. A special thank you to the people working at Riksarkivet in Stockholm who have been very helpful in assisting me with finding all the documents I have asked them for. My warmest thank you to Hanna Hodacs, who played a central role in realising this research project and without whom there would be no book in your hands. And a special thank you to Margaret Hunt who painstakingly helped me perfect the manuscript.

Thank you to all the people who have assisted me with languages and translation. To Charlotte Bellamy, who I could always turn to for help with my French material, it has been a pleasure working with you. To Mikko Toivanen, without whom there would be no Finnish language sources in this book. To Yann Peresse, for his struggles with eighteenth-century trade manual German.

Finally, thank you to my family and friends who have seen me through this process in one piece. To Chloe Scott, who kept checking that I was alive, sent me both dog photos and encouragement throughout the years, and answered more than her fair share of English language questions. To Kirsty Alexander, who pushed me to both insert more commas into the book and more exercise into my day, for standing by me in this process and sharing all my ups and downs during TWs and English language Question Time. To my parents, Björn and Kerstin Knutsson, who since my childhood have supported my schoolwork and have pushed me to pursue higher academic degrees with an unwavering faith in my abilities, and who oversaw two final write-ups under their roof, providing food, shelter, and peace. Finally, thank you to Andreas who, with the greatest degree of patience, has supported my work, had faith in me, pushed me to go further, and helped out with our daughter when I needed some sacred writing time. Thank you for being my sparring partner in work and life, metaphorically as well as literally.

1

INTRODUCTION

It was late in the evening of 23 December 1805 and the Swedish customs officer Hallenborg had been trudging through the snowy forest north of Charlottenberg for hours when he suddenly saw something moving through the darkness. Hallenborg had been patrolling the border between Sweden and Norway for days after receiving an anonymous tip-off. As Hallenborg and his colleagues drew closer to the moving object, they discerned that there were in fact two: a pair of horse-drawn sleighs were making their way through the boreal forest in the midwinter darkness. The customs officers managed to halt the sleighs and found that they were driven by two peasants, Erik Jönsson and Olof Persson. From the sleighs brimming with goods, the customs officers retrieved packing cases stocked with West Indian sugar; bottles of Southeast Asian arrack; red wines presumably from France; English felt; a basket of porcelain; and a dozen Mediterranean lemons.[1]

The diverse richness of the goods seized from the two smuggling peasants reflects the variety and reach of global trade. It also reflects a demand for various foreign goods: manufactured European wares as well as extra-European, exotic products. In response to the arrival of such goods, the Swedish state issued increasingly strict protectionist legislation intended to shut them out of the market. Customs officers, tasked with enforcing this legislation on the ground, came to play a crucial role in the consolidation and economic homogenisation of the early modern state. Yet, despite the state's attempts to enforce uniform economic policy throughout its territory, globally sourced goods continued to find their way in, spurred on by persistent consumer demand. This book, covering the 40-year period 1766–1806, investigates both how smuggling functioned in practice and how it was perceived by a wide range of social actors in contemporary society.

DOI: 10.4324/9781003226031-1

Global Flows and Frictions

In 2014, Michael Kwass published an influential study of the early modern global underground which led to the emergence of a new scholarship on smuggling. This new research, which is discussed at further length below, takes a broad view on smuggling and posits that it was an intricate part of early modern society rather than a fringe phenomenon. Kwass identified the cause of smuggling in the eighteenth century as a convergence of three historical processes: globalisation, state formation, and the consumer revolution.[2] These three factors constitute the point of departure in this book and provide a framework for the individual chapters and the main conclusions drawn from the study.

Most scholars agree that the eighteenth century saw an increased flow of consumer goods all around the globe, a process that had a significant impact on the consumer markets in Europe.[3] This global trade stemmed, at least in part, from the intensifying commercial competition between European states.[4] Recent research on smuggling has revealed that global wares also came to spread through illegal channels, and into states previously thought of as 'immune' to their impact, shielded behind national walls of protectionist legislation.[5] How these illegal channels of globalisation worked depended on the state in question, its legal, geographical, social, and cultural conditions, as well as to some extent its relationship with other states. Trade regulations and smuggling were consequently matters of international interest. The character and impact of globalisation was far from uniform, and as Kenneth Pomeranz and Steven Topik have argued, the process of globalisation should be understood as a dynamic interaction between global and local levels.[6] This was particularly true when it came to illegal transfers of global wares, since this trade was normally organised locally rather than nationally.

The interaction between the global and the local is at the centre of recent approaches to transnational history, which turn the historian's perspective towards the study of connections, circulations, entanglements, interactions, and transfers across borders.[7] Some scholars have pointed out that transnational histories can benefit from 'playing with scales', *jeux d'échelles*, moving between the micro-, meso-, and macro-levels in order to explore transnational actors and the various local and global conditions that affected them.[8] A study of smuggling through the lens of such *jeux d'échelles* could thus include a consideration of transgressive actors, local social conditions, state regulations, and global trade flows. Pierre-Yves Saunier has pointed out that by focusing on the mechanics of circulations and connections, it is possible to observe the unevenness of transnational phenomena and the various levels – local, national, international – conditioning them. This offers historians a way to historicise globalisation and to shed light on its complexities.[9] The study of smuggling, by definition a transnational, border-crossing activity, is a particularly suitable field for investigating the historical processes of globalisation.

Adopting a transnational perspective does not necessarily mean moving away from the state as a unit of analysis, but rather admits the existence of other influences, forces, and movements. A number of historians have thus argued that a history of transnational forces should be used as an accompaniment to national narratives, not as an alternative.[10] It could be argued that due to its strong connection to the concept of nation, the category of transnational history is unsuited to the period before the emergence of the nation state. However, some historians have pointed to the insights that can be gained by adopting a transnational perspective on pre-modern 'nations' or states.[11] Focusing on the transnational and border-crossing activity of smuggling allows for a study of the struggles of the developing state in an international context. As the state tried to consolidate its power and control its territory, the regulation of smuggling became an increasing concern. An examination of the responses to smuggling thus permits a study of the state's attempts to consolidate control over its territory and can offer intriguing insights into state capacity.[12] Smuggling is therefore not merely a transnational story of circulations but also, as Kwass has highlighted, a national story about the consolidation of the state and the enforcement of state authority by blocking the circulation of goods.[13]

The final historical process highlighted by Kwass, the consumer revolution, has been problematised since the term was coined in the seminal work *The Birth of a Consumer Society* in 1982.[14] Following its publication, there has been a race to locate this 'birth' in various corners of Europe and in various time periods.[15] Many scholars locate it in the eighteenth century, although some historians have recently questioned whether there actually was an increase in consumption in this period.[16] Both the terms consumer revolution and consumer society are potentially problematic in their presupposition that consumption was increasing due to an expansion of disposable income. While growing consumption may have increased the impetus for smuggling, the main precondition was a *continuing* rather than an *expanding* demand for foreign goods that persisted despite prohibitions. The study of smuggling allows for an exploration of the social meaning and significance of contraband consumption by looking at the interplay between consumer culture, consumers, and contraband. Such an investigation can reveal how global wares were received, appropriated, and put to use. As explored in the historical literature on cultural transfers, objects moving across national and, more importantly, cultural borders came to be reinterpreted – re-semantised – by new agents in new contexts.[17]

The Swedish Situation

Globalisation and the impact of 'the global' on Sweden in the eighteenth century has so far only received limited attention. However, the work that has been done has suggested that Sweden was part of the global fabric, influencing and being influenced by global processes that also affected large parts of Europe in the eighteenth century.[18] Indeed, Leos Müller has argued that the eighteenth century was Sweden's first global century.[19] Such an understanding stands in stark contrast to research which has argued that Sweden in the eighteenth century became an inward-gazing, protectionist, and isolationist state that withdrew from the international stage as it struggled to regain control of the country following the end of the Age of Greatness (1611–1718).[20] A general conclusion in this book is that these two perspectives on the Swedish eighteenth century are not contradictory, but rather that they are different consequences of the same phenomenon: globalisation. Indeed, the progress of globalisation had a range of effects, some of which contradicted one another. Recent international research on smuggling has shed light on these processes as it takes a broad approach to the phenomenon by combining various perspectives.[21] This new scholarship stands in sharp contrast to previous studies, which can be considered as being divided into three largely separate strands: the economy of smuggling, smuggling as a social crime, and smuggling as a cultural occurrence.[22] So far, there has been a dearth of academic scholarship that engages with this new approach to smuggling in both Sweden and Scandinavia more generally.[23]

Addressing a largely overlooked area of Scandinavian history, the aim of this book is to investigate what the smuggling perspective can add to our understanding of three key processes in late eighteenth-century Sweden, namely globalisation, state formation, and consumption. The book draws on a wide range of research and interacts with several fields of historical enquiry as the history of smuggling, just like economic history at large, is tightly interlinked with several other historical fields of enquiry: history of ideas and politics, territoriality, social and cultural history, and international relations. Drawing on earlier scholarship, five dimensions of smuggling have been identified as particularly worthy of further investigation: economic legislation; limits of state control; illegal retailing; circulating objects; inter-state competition.

The new scholarship on smuggling has stressed that in order to understand smuggling it is crucial to start with the state and the economic legislation it issued.[24] Economic legislation was intended to tackle changing economic conditions by allowing state control mechanisms to influence, stop, or condition trade into the state's economic space. The issuing of economic legislation was thus a way for the state to claim control over its territory and its economic integrity. This legislation reflects the state's objectives, and can be used to study state interests, which changed over time due to altering priorities or conflicts of interest.[25] The eighteenth century, or more specifically the period 1650–1780, has sometimes in the historiography of early modern Europe been referred to as 'The Age of Mercantilism'.[26] While the definition of mercantilism as a coherent ideology has been criticised repeatedly during the last 50 years, recent scholarship has suggested that, rather than discarding mercantilism completely, it should be 'reimagined', and opened up for new interpretations.[27] Mercantilism has consequently been reconsidered as part of a wider political, scientific, and societal context, and the notion itself has been deconstructed and considered in its constituent parts.[28] If we are to understand smuggling, and the state's attempts to suppress it, it is then necessary to dig deeper into why specific protectionist legislation was adopted, and how the offenders were treated, rather than to simply tar all states' legislation with the same brush and presume that it had the same goals and consequences. Meanwhile, the reactions to the legislations also provide an excellent starting point if we want to explore how legislation was perceived, and more specifically how the population viewed and related to smuggling. State legislation, just like other historical phenomena, did not exist in a vacuum but provides insights into how debates changed over time influenced by changing forms of government and ideological patterns. It is therefore a great starting point for the study of smuggling, as it provides crucial insights into how the crime of smuggling was constructed, and how this might have changed over time.

This legislation also had to be enforced on the ground and recent research on smuggling has revealed a great discrepancy between official regulation and lived reality. The limits of state authority have been observed in two different, but interlinked ways: the limits of territorial control and the limits of control over inhabitants and other actors moving in and out of the country.[29] Smuggling research has shown that the state's control over its territories was conditioned by pre-existing traditional, social, and cultural ties and conditions along the borders.[30] The customs officers set to work in these locations had to contend with the local conditions, but often also had their own interests and agendas which affected how they could, and chose to, conduct their duties.[31] Anne Montenach has furthermore highlighted the importance of considering the physical dimensions of maintaining a border, pointing out the need to focus on the geography and physical layout of the border regions, something also stressed in E. R. H. Tesdahl's work.[32] Considering the geographical dimensions of trade is, of course nothing new, but formed an integral part of the work of Fernand Braudel.[33] Surprisingly however, this is a dimension that has been largely overlooked in studies of illegal trade, despite its crucial role in shaping illegal trade and the attempts to quench it. Moreover, short term climatic factors such as reduced harvests and outstanding fish yields undoubtedly also played an important role in motivating individuals to turn to smuggling in times when regular sources of income were wanting, thus playing a part in the makeshift economy of the poor. Indeed, as smuggling became a tool to use in challenging situations several scholars have referred to the 'moral economy of smuggling', drawing on E. P. Thompson's 'moral economy'.[34] Such popular conceptions of smuggling stand alongside official views and can help us understand how smuggling was viewed and treated in practice, both by the perpetrators and the customs officers. Meanwhile, the continued border-crossing activities also challenged state authority and affected its ability to create a uniform national economic unit.

Once the contraband had entered the country the next step was how it reached the consumers. Scholars of eighteenth-century retailing have stressed the need to consider the plurality of retailing channels that co-existed during this period. They included old forms of vending, like fairs, markets, and peddling, but also new ones like shops and postal order.[35] The multiplicity of retailing outlets, both older and newer, has also been observed in studies of smuggling. By focusing on the retailer, scholars have shown that a range of different vendors traded in contraband, often in addition to legal goods.[36] What Kwass defined as parallel economies of legal and illegal wares were thus brought together in the mercer's shop and the pedlar's sack.[37] While contraband was traded by a vast range of retailers serving different clienteles, the conditions under which they conducted trade varied considerably. Some were protected by particular patronages while others, like pedlars and women, were continually pursued by the authorities.[38] Meanwhile, contraband retailing could also play a crucial role for exposed groups as their legal options often were extremely limited.[39] In this way, smuggling became an important survival tool for groups discriminated against by the official legislation. While there were significant differences between the retailers, what united all successful contraband vendors was the support of their clients. Montenach has argued that the desirability of the goods shaped popular perceptions of the retailers, and that the consumers played a crucial role in shielding the traders from the authorities so that they could continue dealing in contraband.[40] Understanding the contraband retailers and their clients can therefore give crucial insights not only into the dispersion of illegal wares but also into the state's attempts to control illegal trade and the social support of smuggling and its enablers.

To understand contraband, why it was prohibited, why it was desired, and the effects it had on culture, politics, and society, it is inevitably also necessary to look closer at the things being smuggled. Objects were far from static but were reinterpreted and redefined throughout their 'lives'. However, their materiality remained fairly fixed although they could be marked by age, usage, and incidents.[41] Frank Trentmann has stressed that this materiality was central in deciding what objects actually *did*: coffee was enlivening, gin intoxicating, silk cooling and shimmering, while cotton was washable and printable.[42] Objects were then not merely 'bundles of meaning', but had crucial inherent qualities which defined them. The state's acceptance or rejection of foreign wares was, in general, also based on the nature of the good in question and whether the state deemed a specific item to be a threat. Meanwhile, the nature of a good also helps to explain not just why it was banned but also why it remained in demand. Studies of contraband have therefore tended to focus on one or a couple types of contraband in one general geographic area.[43] Anne Montenach has, for example, stressed that the French demand for banned Asian calico was related to its durability and the fact that it was easy to wash.[44] Similarly, William Farrell has noted that the demand for French silk in Britain was connected to the desirability of its "material qualities".[45] Certainly, many of these objects also became fashionable, but the fashionable aspect was often interconnected with the materiality of the wares. By focusing on the materiality and the life of specific types of contraband, scholars have been able to ask pointed questions about what role contraband played in culture, politics, and the economy. This has shed crucial light on why specific goods were banned, why a demand persisted, and how specific types of contraband were adopted and adapted in various social and cultural contexts. As Igor Kopytoffs observed, "what is significant about the adoption of alien objects – as of alien ideas – is not the fact that they are adopted, but the way that they are culturally redefined and put to use".[46]

Finally, research has shown that smuggling could also represent a form of inter-state competition, particularly during wartime. Smuggling as a form of inter-state competition is not a new notion. Already back in 1918, in his study of the Napoleonic continental system, the Swedish economic historian Eli Heckscher argued that smuggling played an important role in negating the effects of trade blockades.[47] More recent scholarship has similarly argued that states used smuggling strategically to undermine foreign trade barriers during times of war.[48] Such trade barriers, however, also existed during peacetime, in the shape of protectionist legislation intended to position countries against their trade competitors. Still, the relationship between state and smuggling in peacetime has received considerably less attention in the research literature.[49] Indeed, the new scholarship on smuggling has shown only a limited interest for smuggling as inter-state competition, which is a notable omission as it creates an artificial divide between the state's domestic protectionist goals and the competitive globalism from which these goals emerged. How international smuggling was viewed in different states naturally depended on the information state authorities received. This information was supplied by state actors, primarily ambassadors and consuls, which have been shown to have had complex allegiances that affected the information they chose to convey.[50] While state discussions surrounding international smuggling can offer intriguing insight into the state's international concerns and ambitions, they were also shaped by the individuals on the ground who provided information on international trade, prompting questions about who these individuals were, as well as their concerns, interests, and allegiances.

These five dimensions of the phenomenon of smuggling in late eighteenth-century Sweden help structure the study's Chapters 2–6. In turn, the chapters address views on economic state legislation; the extent of a state's authority over its territory; what smuggling meant for the culprits; attitudes towards contraband retailers, contraband and its effects on society; and international perceptions of smuggling and inter-state competition. While each individual approach listed above cannot cover all three of these processes of globalisation, state formation, and consumption, they can, taken together, offer insights into all of them. At the end of the study, in Chapter 7, I will therefore revisit the three processes and discuss why it is crucial to incorporate illegality into our historical analyses.

Shape and Scope

The timeframe chosen for this study, 1766–1806, is based both on external and internal events which affected the Swedish state's relationship to global trade. The investigation starts after the end of the Seven Years' War (1756–1763) and thus covers a period Sophus Reinert has identified as an era of intensifying international trade competition for many European states.[51] In Sweden more specifically, the late 1760s was also a period marked by economic crisis. As part of the Crown's attempt to handle the crisis it introduced a new anti-smuggling and sumptuary decrees. The study reaches its end just before the introduction of the Continental Blockade in 1806, an event which in the short term critically changed how smuggling was conducted in Sweden, as it drew Scandinavia into the Napoleonic Wars,[52] ultimately resulting in a repartitioning of territories and borders all over Northern Europe. The book's 40-year span allows for a rich study of the continuities and shifts in smuggling, over a period characterised by deep political, cultural, and intellectual change both in Europe and Scandinavia.

Chapter 2 looks at how smuggling was conceived as a crime in Sweden and the subsequent development of anti-smuggling legislation. It studies how the conception and treatment of the smuggler was challenged over time, particularly in the newspapers. The discussions illustrate that smuggling and its management were contested, in a public debate that became a battleground between proponents of diverging notions about rights and loyalties. These clashes were linked to changing legislation but also to the emergence of new ideas of rights and a strengthening of 'citizens' rights'.

Chapter 3 explores how the new anti-smuggling legislation was enforced in practice and investigates some of the challenges involved in the state's enactment of Sweden as a homogenous economic space. The chapter pays particular attention to the persistence of smuggling through a study of its actors, the influence of the landscapes and spaces of smuggling, and the varied practices of smuggling.

Chapter 4 delves into the issue of the retailer to explore how contraband was distributed to Swedish consumers across the realm. The chapter gives particular attention to the retailers' relationships both to each other and to the clients in order to analyse the social aspects of smuggling in urban life and in the countryside.

Chapter 5 explores why certain wares were banned and why prohibitions were unable to hamper the demand for these wares. In order to make such assessments, it is necessary to study single wares and specific consumer groups. The chapter thus focuses its analysis on two specific types of contraband: one skilled manufactured product (worsted) and one exotic raw material (coffee). The investigation considers why consumption of smuggled wares occurred and what social and cultural impact these goods had on the consumer market, including how the goods' illegal status affected their impact.

Chapter 6 shifts the focus away from the domestic perspective on smuggling to consider how Sweden's trading partners viewed smuggling in and out of the country. The chapter discusses two central trading partners in particular, Britain and France, both of which played a crucial role in the competitive globalism of the eighteenth century and remained in conflict, either armed or commercial, for the majority of the century. In this perspective of inter-state competition, the chapter pays attention to the role of transnational state actors tasked with reporting on trade and smuggling, allowing a closer study of them as agents operating across borders, with sometimes shifting personal and professional interests and allegiances.

Sources

Despite the numerous insights that can be gained from studying smuggling, it is also a topic which is notoriously difficult to research. This reputation is in part related to smuggling's clandestine nature, but more specifically it is linked to the issues involved in quantifying smuggling and thus also in comparing it to official trade statistics. Smuggling research is therefore, as already noted, often unsuited for numerical studies of trade, and increases and decreases in consumption. Despite its reputation, there are many other ways to approach smuggling, and a creative foray into the archives reveals a host of sources that can throw light on this 'elusive' phenomenon. A crucial feature of smuggling research is, however, that the archival material available to scholars is almost exclusively derived from failed smuggling attempts; in a way, this book is therefore a history of recorded failures, which naturally conditions its analysis and conclusions.

The book draws on a vast range of sources, but there are two types of sources that deserve more in-depth attention at the outset, namely legislation and the customs court records. Legislation, in particular the anti-smuggling decrees, provides a spine to this book. Three key decrees were effective during the period 1769–1806 to control smuggling. The first was published under Adolph Friedrich in 1757 and provided the bare bones for the later decrees. In the decree it was argued that manufactured goods were produced in the kingdom to such a "complete greatness and beauty" that they must be protected from the dangers brought on by smuggling.[53] It further stipulated that the first time a person was caught smuggling, he or she would lose the goods and be fined half the value of their value, with all subsequent violations resulting in a fine equal to the total value of the goods. The confiscator would in turn receive 60% of the fine and the rest would fall to the state.[54] By 1770, the rules tightened, and a smuggling verdict resulted in the loss of the goods and a fine equal to value of the goods, with all later sentences doubling the fine, although for illegal imports of legal goods the fine was settled at a quarter of the price.[55] Under Gustav IV Adolph (1792–1800 [regency], 1800–1809), the regulations were yet again made more severe. In contrast to his grandfather Adolph Friedrich, the young King justified his measures by referring to the responsibilities of loyal subjects towards their fatherland, defining the *contrabandier* as a traitor to the country. The idea was not new, but rather emerged from longstanding discourses, as will be discussed further on. However, it appears to be the first time that this idea was spelled out in the legal framework. The 1799 decree instructed that the offender would lose the goods and pay a minimum fine of 50 Rdr – which was the equivalent of about a year's salary for a peasant – while for contraband worth more than 50 Rdr, the fine would mirror its full value. For second-time offenders, the minimum fine would be 100 Rdr.[56] These were the key components, although the decrees were continuously developed and debated during the period, as will be discussed in the forthcoming chapter. Further components of the decrees, and addendums to them, will also be discussed in connection to the various court cases that will be presented in the book. The anti-smuggling decrees should be considered together with the Import Regulations and the Sumptuary Laws, which were related to the anti-smuggling decrees. In the second half of the eighteenth century, Import Regulations were issued in 1757, 1771, 1776, 1782, 1794, and 1799, and

Sumptuary Laws appeared in 1766, 1770, and 1794. Sumptuary decrees for coffee specifically were also released in 1756, 1766, 1794, and 1799. A level of convergence can be seen between these various protectionist measures.

In addition, it should be noted that the two Swedish Navigation Acts, from 1724 and 1774, were also influencing the control of contraband.[57] These acts stipulated the captain's tasks and responsibilities and outlined when and where ships could stop and unload their cargoes. For the duration of the period in question, they were only allowed to load and unload international cargoes in staple towns.

The second main body of sources derives from the Customs Court (*Tullrätten*), an institution tasked with prosecuting smuggling crimes, which had both a maritime and an inland branch.[58] The Maritime Customs Courts (*Sjötullsrätten*) were located in all the 33 staple towns in Sweden (two new towns were added in the 1780s: Umeå in 1781 and Kaskö in 1785), and they were responsible for resolving disputes regarding shipments and all cases involving the handling of illicit foreign goods. In addition to the maritime courts, there were Land Customs Offices located along the borders to Norway and Russia, which appear to have housed stand-alone courts. The survival of sources from these courts is patchy, and they are spread out in regional archives, although backup copies of some court records have been submitted to the National Board of Trade, the archive of which is housed at the National Archives (*Riksarkivet*) in Stockholm. A corresponding collection from the Finnish provinces is also kept at the Finnish National Archives (*Kansallisarkisto/Riksarkivet*) in Helsinki. These circumstances make it difficult to gain a precise idea about the extent to which Customs Court records have survived, and this book does not offer a systematic review of the material. Instead, I have selected material from specific locations and time periods that I have deemed representative. These records offer an insight into both the kind of wares which were being illegally imported, the actors who were caught smuggling and how they defended their actions, and what sort of punishments they received. Discussions relating to all of these aspects will reoccur throughout the book, although more detailed presentations of how the courts functioned and the appeal process worked will be offered in Chapter 3.

The Customs Court Records are also, in general, unsuitable for quantitative studies both due to the uneven recording of crimes (see discussion in Chapter 3) and due to discrepancies in the methods of recording contraband. A short survey of the seized contraband recorded in Stockholm Maritime Custom Court between June and December in 1769 and 1800 respectively will serve as an example of the limited use of a quantitative method in relation to smuggling. (Graphs 1.1 and 1.2).

The earlier contraband list from 1769 reveals a concentration on textiles, coffee, and various manufactured metal wares, such as shaving knives and buttons. In the later one these goods are still present but there are also more foodstuffs and a heavier presence of alcohol. However, the tables presented here only record the contraband goods as they occur *per mention* in the Court Records. As they do not record the value of each of the wares in a consistent manner, they can only give a rough idea of the make-up of contraband seizures.[59] Due to inconsistencies and

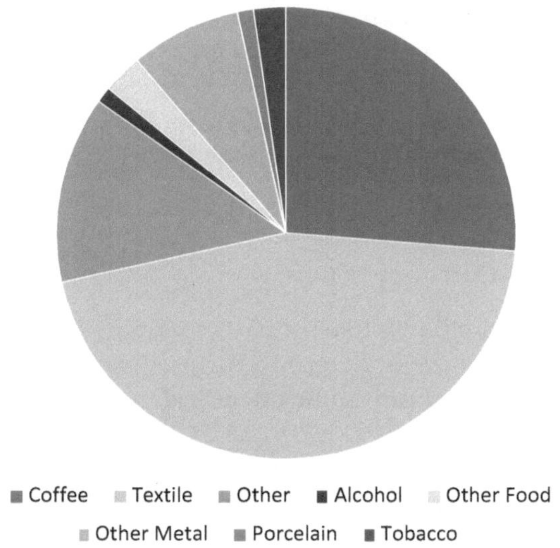

GRAPH 1.1 Contraband seized in June–December 1769 as recorded in the Stockholm Maritime Court Records.

Source: Stockholm City Archive, Stora Siötulls Rättens Dombok, 1769, Stockholms rådhusrätt, Stora Sjötullen, Protokoll, A, vol. 22.

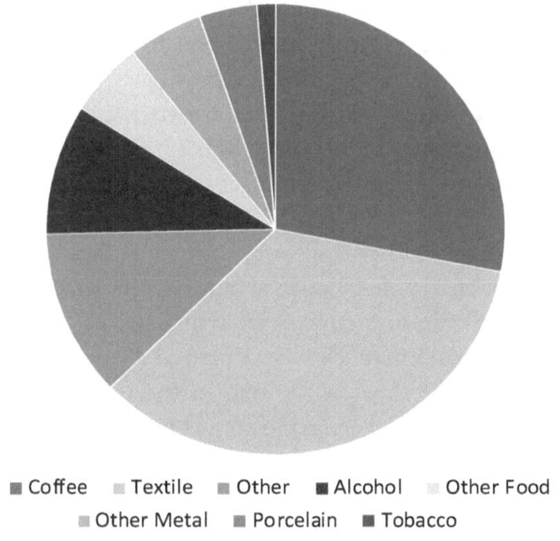

GRAPH 1.2 Contraband seized in June–December 1800 as recorded in the Stockholm Maritime Court Records.

Source: Stockholm City Archive, Stora Siötulls Rättens Dombok, 1800, Stockholms rådhusrätt, Stora Sjötullen, Protokoll, A, vol. 23.

discrepancies in the recordings of contraband, more specific calculations based on price or quantity are difficult to make. However, as quantitative studies of contraband seizures can at best be indicative of trends, extensive studies of this price and quantity data can never be conclusive. The figures that will be discussed in this book should be approached with caution and quantitative discussions will play a subordinate role.

Terminology and Currency

One of the more difficult things to translate for this book were the names of the various institutions involved in the management of smuggling. Whereas some, like *Kommerskollegium,* The National Board of Trade, have their own translations as state institutions still in use, this is not the case with some of the institutions long ago rendered superfluous or reformed, such as *Generaltullarrendesocieteten,* the name of the general customs office during the periods of tax farming, 1777–1782 and 1803–1813. Because the structure and development of the Customs Institution is not a specific focus of this book, some liberties have been taken. *Generaltullarrendesocieteten,* its state counterpart *Generaltulldirektionen* and its subservient arm *Överdirektören för Sjötullen* (also known as *Generalsjötullskontoret*) will for example simply be referred to as the Customs Office or the Maritime Customs Office.

Furthermore, the contemporary Swedish names of towns and cities are given, but with a modernised and standardised spelling. This is to avoid confusion over the many varied spellings which occurred at the time. The Swedish town Varberg is thus rendered as 'Varberg' rather than Warberg, and the Finnish town Kajaani is rendered 'Kajana' rather than the old Swedish spelling 'Cajana'. In some instances, particularly in the Finnish provinces, the Finnish names are also included, as some of the Swedish names are very uncommon apart from in the sources. Finally, quotes in French and English are rendered in their original without alteration, but all Swedish quotes translated into English have been modernised.

One feature that is bound to create some confusion in the present study is the parallel use of different currencies. Four various currencies are referred to in this book (there were also additional currencies which will not be discussed here). From 1766 to 1776, two fiat currencies were primarily used in the court records: daler copper coins (*daler koppar mynt*), which in the text appear as D kmt, and daler silver coins (*daler silver mynt*) referred to as D smt. 3 D kmt equated to 1 D smt. While riksdaler, abbreviated Rdr, were also in use during this period, they rarely appear in the customs records before the coin reform of 1776, when numerous types of currency disappeared. At the time of the reform 1 Rdr equated to 6 D smt or 18 D kmt. The coin reform led to the withdrawal of several types of old silver coins and riksdaler became the primary coin type, with a silver standard replacing the fiat currencies. The two types of currency that appear most readily after this period are *riksdaler (specie)*, in the text referred to as Rdr, and *riksdaler banco*, Rdr bco. The exchange rate between them was constant throughout the period: 1 Rdr = 1 Rdr bco. In 1789, fiat currency was used due to silver shortage, although paper money had also been in use prior to this period. Along with the re-introduction of fiat currency there was also a new currency, *riksdaler riksgälds*, Rdr rgs. While the exchange rates between these various currencies varied over time, in 1795 it was 1 Rdr (specie) = 1 Rdr bco = 1 ½ Rdr rgs. This conversion rate can be seen as a rough guide to the relationship between these various currencies. The fiat currency system was put on hold during the period 1803–1808, when silver coins were re-introduced. The exchange rates remained stable, however. Due to the confusion such a mixture of currencies and exchange rates fluctuating over time can cause, I have occasionally included conversions between the currencies. For example, 100 D kmt in 1767 is equal to 5.5 Rdr in 1777. In order to avoid confusion, the amounts recorded in Rdr riksgäld have been converted into Rdr specie, as this is the predominant currency registered.[60]

Denominations

Daler
1 D kmt = 32 öre kmt
1 D smt = 32 öre smt

Riksdaler
1 Rdr = 48 shillings (skillingar, sk)
1 sk = 12 runstycken

Exchange values
1 D smt = 3 D kmt (1760) - constant
1 Rdr = 3 D smt (1770)
1 Rdr = 6 D smt = 18 D kmt (1777)

Nominal daily earnings for unskilled labourers in Sweden

1766 – 112 öre (or 3.5 D kmt)
1776 – 112 öre (or 3.5 D kmt)
1786 – 9.33 sk specie (roughly 0.19 Rdr specie)
1796 – 10.67 sk rgs (roughly 0.22 Rdr specie)
1806 – 16 sk rgs[61] (roughly 0.33 Rdr specie)

Import Prohibitions

The table below builds on nine different import taxes and import prohibitions, issued 1747–1799 (Table 1.1). Some merely point out new prohibitions or the removal of prohibitions rather than providing a complete list of what was allowed or disallowed. Therefore, there is no data for all years and goods. An empty box

TABLE 1.1 Import prohibitions 1747–1799

Import Prohibitions

○ Free to import

● Prohibited to import

◐ Prohibited to import from anywhere else than the East Indies.

mc – monochrome textiles only

	1747	*1754*	*1756*	*1757*	*1761*	*1771*	*1776*	*1782*	*1794*	*1799*
Silk										
Unpatterned and monochrome		●				●	○	○	◐	○
Patterned		●				●			●	●
Damask		●				●		○	●	●
Taffeta						●	○	(mc) ○	◐	●
Lace						●	○	(mc) ○	●	●
Neckerchieves								●	●	●
Silk gauze						●	○	○	●	●
Crepe						●			○	○
Cotton - undyed										
Cotton, plain, fine				○		○	○	○	○	○
Muslin, plain	○			○				○	○	○
Muslin, striped and checked				○					○	○
Guineas cloth from East India (without print for the manufactories)	○					○				
Cotton - dyed										
East Indian nankin or kitaj						●		●		●
Wool & Worsted	●	●	●	●	●	●	●	●	●	●
Half-wool	●	●	●	●	●	●	●	●	●	●
Linen and hemp										
Cambric, plain, less than 6 quarters wide (anything wider prohibited)	○		●	○	○	○	○	○	○	○
Linen/Hemp (lärft), undyed, plain.				○		○		○	○	○

	1747	1754	1756	1757	1761	1771	1776	1782	1794	1799
Groceries										
Coffee beans	○		●	●	○	○	○	○	●	●
Cocoa beans	○		●	●	○	○	○	○	○	○
Tea			●	○	◐	◐	◐	◐	◐	◐
Arrack			●	◐	◐	●	○	○	○	○
White sugar (powder)	○		●	●		●	○	○	○	○
Sugar candy						●	○	●	●	●
Sugarloaf						●	●	●	●	●
Brown (mascovado, Barbados, or brown raw sugar)	○			○		○	○	○	○	○
Other										
Porcelain			◐			◐	◐	◐	◐	◐i
Tobacco leaves				○		○ii		○iii	○	○
Shaving knives				●	○	○iv		○		○
Trinkets (Nipper)			●			●		●		●
Pins			●	○v		●		●		●
Dyes										
Cochineal						○		○		○
Indigo	○			○		○		○		○

Sources: Taxa, hwarefter, ifrån then 1 September 1747, the på thenne förteckning upförde utrikes ifrån inkommande waror, komma at betala afgift til manufactur fonden (30 Jun 1747), Kongl. maj:ts nådige kundgörelse, angående förbud emot ost-indiske sidentygers införsel och försäljande här i riket, ifrån 1755. års början. (19 Feb 1754), Kongl. maj:ts nådige förordning, angående wiße öfwerflöds wahrors förbiudande til införsel i riket (4 Nov 1756), Kongl. maj:ts nådige förordning, angående wiße utrikes warors så wäl lösgifwande ifrån förbud til införsel, som beläggande med mindre manufactur-fonds och andre afgifter (21 Sep 1761), Kongl. maj:ts taxa, hwarefter stora siö-tullen uppå alla inkommande waror bör erläggas och upbäras (15 Feb 1771), Kongl. maj:ts och riksens kammar-collegii kungörelse, dels angående wisza utrikes waror, hwilka til införsel i riket för thetta warit förbudne, men nu, til underdånigst följe af hans kongl. maj:ts nådige bref under then 14 i thenna månad, til införande hädanefter blifwa låfgifne; dels ock sådane waror the uti 1771 års siö-tulls-taxa utsatte afgifter, i wisza delar härmedelst blifwa ändrade (24 Sep 1776), Kongl. maj:ts taxa, hwarefter stora siö-tullen uppå alla inkommande waror beräknas och erlägges (6 Jun 1782), Kongl. maj:ts nådiga kungörelse, angående dels förbud emot införsel af wiße utländske waror, dels ock högre tull-afgifter derå (1 Jan 1794), Kongl. maj:ts taxa, hwarefter stora sjö-tullen uppå alla inkommande waror beräknas och erläggas (17 Apr 1799).

indicates that no information is available. In these instances it is possible that the wares previous legal status was unchanged; however, as this is not a complete list of *all* import regulations, it is possible that the legal status had changed in the interim. Furthermore, this list is simplified as there are many qualities that have been left out – the import lists usually ran over several hundred pages. For textiles, the general rule was that undyed, unprinted textiles could be imported while any processed cloths were prohibited. Finally, this list is only meant to give an idea of the evolving nature of the prohibitions and does not give a comprehensive view of the legislation as companies and individuals could also be awarded exemptions to import certain 'illegal' wares. This is particularly the case with the Swedish East India Company, which could import certain prohibited wares from Asia. Some of these exemptions are registered in the table above. It is therefore very difficult to establish a comprehensive view of what could legally be imported into Sweden in the eighteenth century and the list above should be considered indicatory rather than exhaustive.

In addition, it should be noted that even if a good could legally be imported it did not follow that it could be consumed by everyone, but sumptuary legislations (such as those from 1766, 1770, and 1794) stipulated who could consume what. For example, the sumptuary decree of 1766 specified that silk could only be consumed by the middling and higher sorts, apart from silk caps which could be used by female servants but not by unemployed women. Women of the lower sorts were also prohibited from using foreign linen, cambric, and muslin. Meanwhile, all men were prohibited from using silk velvet and silk clothing apart from for various adornments including, but not limited to, silk stockings, pocket watch bands, karpus hats, scarves, trousers, and winter hats. East Indian porcelain was prohibited for use, apart from tea sets, while tobacco could only be legally consumed by people over the age of 21.[62] The 1770 decree was very similar, although it did liberate the use of East India porcelain.[63] By contrast, the 1794 did not make a direct hierarchical division of consumption, as silk clothing was to be banned for everyone; however, there were some exceptions for court and gala dress and for the national costume. Just like in the earlier decrees, silk could still be used for certain accoutrements which in effect meant that the ban was not universal.[64] All this complementary and overlapping legislation means that it can be quite difficult to establish what was legal and what was not, not just for historians today but also for those who had to interact with the legislation in the eighteenth century.

Notes

1 'Berättelse, Wärmelands Gräntsen Norraby, 25 Dec 1805, Hallenborg' (1806), Äldre centrala tullarkiv, Generaltullarrendesocieteternas fullmäktige, m. fl., kansliet, Resefiskaler, E9, vol.5.

2 Michael Kwass, *Contraband: Louis Mandrin and the Making of a Global Underground* (Cambridge, MA: Harvard University Press, 2014), 6.

3 For a discussion on the development of the global market space and the global circulation of consumer goods see for example: Kenneth Pomeranz and Steven Topik, *The World That Trade Created. Society, Culture, and the World Economy 1400 to the Present*, 2nd ed. (Armonk, NY; London: M.E Sharpe, 2006); Ina Baghdiantz McCabe, *A History of Global Consumption 1500–1800* (London; New York: Routledge, 2015); Maxine Berg, Hanna Hodacs, and Chris Nierstrasz, eds., *Goods from the East, 1600–1800 Trading Eurasia* (Basingstoke, Hampshire; New York: Palgrave Macmillan, 2015); Anne Gerritsen and Giorgio Riello, eds., *The Global Lives of Things: The Material Culture of Connections in the Early Modern World* (Abingdon-on-Thames: Routledge, 2015). For studies about the spread of specific goods see: Sidney Wilfred Mintz, *Sweetness*

and Power: The Place of Sugar in Modern History (New York; London: Penguin Books, 1986); Macy Norton, 'Tasting Empire: Chocolate and the European Internalization of Mesoamerican Aesthetics,' *The American Historical Review* 111, no. 3 (2006): 2006; Robert Finlay, *The Pilgrim Art: Cultures of Porcelain in World History* (Berkley; Los Angeles; London: University of California Press, 2010); Beverly Lemire, *Fashion's Favourite: The Cotton Trade and the Consumer in Britain, 1660–1800* (Oxford: Oxford University Press, 1991); Beverly Lemire, *Cotton* (Berg Publishers, 2011); Giorgio Riello, *Cotton: The Fabric That Made the Modern World* (Cambridge: Cambridge University Press, 2013).

4 David Ormrod, *The Rise of Commercial Empires. England and the Netherlands in the Age of Mercantilism, 1650–1770* (Cambridge: Cambridge University Press, 2003); Global historians have challenged this approach arguing that it is much too simplistic and that it is necessary to understand globalisation as a process informed by developments both in Europe and in other regions of the world, see: Jan Nederveen Pieterse, 'Oriental Globalization', *Theory, Culture & Society* 23, no. 2–3 (May 2006), 412.

5 Kwass, *Contraband*, 358; Felicia Gottmann, *Global Trade, Smuggling, and the Making of Economic Liberalism, Asian Textiles in France 1680–1760* (Basingstoke, Hampshire; New York: Palgrave Macmillan, 2016), 170; Beverly Lemire, *Global Trade and the Transformation of Consumer Cultures* (Cambridge: Cambridge University Press, 2018), 291.

6 Pomeranz and Topik, *The World That Trade Created*, xii.

7 For a good introduction see: Pierre-Yves Saunier, 'Circulations, connexions et espaces transnationaux', *Genèses* 57, no. 4 (2004).

8 Bernhard Struck, Kate Ferris, and Jacques Revel, 'Introduction: Space and Scale in Transnational History', *The International History Review* 33, no. 4 (2011), 574 & 576.

9 Saunier, 'Circulations, connexions et espaces transnationaux', 111.

10 Struck, Ferris, and Revel, 'Introduction: Space and Scale in Transnational History', 576; Pierre-Yves Saunier, *Transnational History* (New York: Palgrave Macmillan, 2013), 9–11; Patricia Clavin, 'Defining Transnationalism', *Contemporary European History* 14, no. 4 (November 2005), 432.

11 Bartollomé Yun Casalilla, 'Transnational History. What Lies behind the Label? Some Reflections from the Early Modernist's Point of View.', *Culture & History Digital Journal* 3, no. 2 (December 2014).

12 Istvan Hont, *Jealousy of Trade* (Cambridge, MA; London: Harvard University Press, 2005), 460.

13 Kwass, *Contraband*, 6.

14 Neil McKendrick, J. H. Plumb, and John Brewer, *The Birth of a Consumer Society: The Commercialization of Eighteenth-century England* (London: Europa Publications Limited, 1982).

15 See for example: Renaissance Italy Richard A. Goldthwaite, *Wealth and the Demand for Art in Italy: 1300–1600* (Baltimore: Johns Hopkins University Press, 1993); Seventeenth Century Dutch Republic: Jan de Vries, 'Luxury in the Dutch Golden Age in Theory and Practice', in *Luxury in the Eighteenth Century: Debates, Desires and Delectable Goods*, ed. Maxine Berg and Elizabeth Eger (Basingstoke, Hampshire; New York: Palgrave Macmillan, 2003). For a longer discussion see: Wouter Ryckbosch, 'Early Modern Consumption History. Current Challenges and Future Perspectives', *Low Countries Historical Review* 130, no. 1 (2015), 65–71.

16 Ryckbosch, 'Early Modern Consumption History. Current Challenges and Future Perspectives'. For scholars who have questioned the consumer revolution see: 'John Brewer: Was the First Consumer Society Born in 18th Century Britain?', *The Independent*, 30 September 2003; Gregory Clark, 'The Consumer Revolution: Turning Point in Human History, or Statistical Artifact?' (Munich Personal RePEc Archive, 2010).

17 Anna Veronika Wendland, 'Cultural Transfer', in *Travelling Concepts for the Study of Culture*, ed. Birgit Neumann and Ansgar Nünning (Berlin: Walter de Gruyter, 2012), 51.

18 Stefan Eklöf Amirell, 'Den världshistoriska vändningen. Möjligheter och problem i relation till svensk historisk forskning', *Historisk Tidskrift* 128, no. 4 (2008); Leos

Müller, Göran Rydén, and Holger Weiss, 'Global historia - Något för nordiska historiker?', in *Global historia från periferin. Norden 1600–1850*, ed. Leos Müller, Göran Rydén, and Holger Weiss (Lund: Studentlitteratur, 2009); Arne Jarrick and Janken Myrdal, 'Globalhistoria och forkning om långa förlopp', *Historisk Tidskrift* 130, no. 4 (2010); Leos Müller, Holger Weiss, and Göran Rydén, eds., *Global historia från periferin. Norden 1600–1850* (Lund: Studentlitteratur, 2010); Göran Rydén, ed., *Sweden in the Eighteenth-Century World: Provincial Cosmopolitans* (Farnham: Ashgate, 2013).

19 Leos Müller, *Sveriges Första globala århundrade. En 1700-talshistoria* (Stockholm: Dialogos, 2018).

20 Eli Filip Heckscher, *Sveriges ekonomiska historia från Gustav Vasa: Det moderna sveriges grundläggning, 1720–1815*, vol. 2:2 (Stockholm: Albert Bonniers förlag, 1949), 649–652; Lars Magnusson, 'Mercantilism and "Reform" Mercantilism: The Rise of Economic Discourse in Sweden during the Eighteenth Century', *History of Political Economy* 19, no. 3 (1987).

21 Kwass, *Contraband*; Gottmann, *Global Trade*; Lemire, *Global Trade*; Jesse Cromwell, *The Smugglers' World. Illicit Trade and Atlantic Communities in Eighteenth-Century Venezuela* (Chapel Hill: The University of North Carolina Press, 2018).

22 For a longer discussion on this see: Renaud Morieux, *The Channel: England, France and the Construction of a Maritime Border in the Eighteenth Century* (Cambridge: Cambridge University Press, 2016), 250. For examples of economy of smuggling see: W. A. Cole, 'Trends in Eighteenth-Century Smuggling', *The Economic History Review* 10, no. 3 (1958); Hoh-Cheung Mui and Lorna H. Mui, 'Trends in Eighteenth-Century Smuggling Reconsidered', *The Economic History Review* 28 (1975); Smuggling as a social crime: Cal Winslow, 'Sussex Smugglers', in *Albion's Fatal Tree. Crime and Society in Eighteenth-Century England*, First American Edition (New York: Pantheon Books, 1975).

23 So far only two short texts have been published: Pia Lundqvist, 'Förbjudna tyger – textilsmuggling till Sverige under 1700- och 1800-talen', in *Dolda innovationer. Textila produkter och ny teknik under 1800-talet*, ed. Klas Nyberg and Pia Lundqvist (Stockholm: Kulturhistoriska Bokförlaget, 2013); Anna Knutsson, 'Clandestine Commerce. Retailing Contraband Textiles in Late Eighteenth-Century Sweden', *History of Retailing and Consumption*, 5, no. 3 (2019), 261–275, DOI: 10.1080/2373518X.2019.1703323.

24 Kwass, *Contraband*, Chapter 2; William Farrell, 'Smuggling Silks into Eighteenth-Century Britain: Geography, Perpetrators, and Consumers', *Journal of British Studies* 55, no. 2 (2016), 269; Gottmann, *Global Trade*, 54.

25 Annie Tock Morrisette, '"They Would Have a Law of Their Own": The Discourse on Smuggling at the Old Bailey, 1736–1814' (MA thesis, East Carolina University, 2013), Chapter 4; Kwass, *Contraband*, See Chapter 11 'Smuggling in the Enlightenment'; Felicia Gottmann, *Global Trade*, See Chapter 5 'Enlightenment Campaigning'.

26 Roland Findlay and Kevin H. O'Rourke, *Power and Plenty, Trade, War, and the World Economy in the Second Millenium* (Princeton: Princeton University Press, 2007), 227; In the Swedish context Henric Häggqvist has suggested that this mercantilist period lasted until 1815 see: Henric Häggqvist, 'On the Ocean of Protectionism. The Structure of Swedish Tariffs and Trade 1780–1830' (PhD thesis, Uppsala University, 2015), 47.

27 For critics of 'mercantilism' as a useful label see: Coleman, 'Eli Heckscher and the Idea of Mercantilism,' in *Revisions in Mercantilism*, ed. Coleman (London: Methuen, 1969), 117; Joyce Appleby, *Economic Thought and Ideology in Seventeenth-Century England* (Princeton, NJ: Princeton University Press, 1987).

28 Philip J. Stern och Carl Wennerlind, 'Introduction', in *Mercantilism Reimagined: Political Economy in Early Modern Britain and Its Empire* (Oxford: Oxford University Press, 2013).

29 Joshua M. Smith, *Borderland Smuggling: Patriots, Loyalists, and Illicit Trade in the Northeast, 1783–1820* (Gainesville: University Press of Florida, 2006), Kwass, *Contraband*, 87; Farrell, 'Smuggling Silks into Eighteenth-Century Britain', 274; Gottmann, *Global Trade*, 55–59.

30 Eugene Richard Henry Tesdahl, 'The Price of Empire: Smuggling between New York and New France, 1700–1754' (PhD thesis, University of Colorado, 2012), chapter 1, particularly 20–29; Anne Montenach, *Femmes, pouvoir et contrebande dans les alpes au xviiie siècle* (Grenoble: Presses Universitaires de Grenoble, 2017), chapter 1 'Sel de la mer et hautes terres, les enjeux d'un économie montagnarde', particularly 25–31.

31 Maria Ågren, *The State as Master: Gender, State Formation and Commercialisation in Urban Sweden, 1650–1780* (Oxford: Oxford University Press, 2017), 4; Maria Cavallin, 'I kungen och folkets tjänst. Synen på den svenske ämbetsmannen 1750–1780' (PhD thesis, Göteborgs Universitet, 2003). See particularly her discussion about customs officers, 222–226.

32 Montenach, *Femmes, pouvoir et contrebande dans les alpes au xviiie siècle.* See Chapter 1 'Sel de la mer et hautes terres, les enjeux d'un économie montagnarde', particularly 25–31; Tesdahl, 'The Price of Empire'. See Chapter 1, particularly, 14–20.

33 Fernand Braudel, *The Mediterranean: And the Mediterranean World in the Age of Philip II*, trans. Siân Reynolds (Berkley: University of California Press, 1972).

34 Some of the authors that write about moral economy of smuggling are: Kwass, *Contraband*; Gottmann, *Global Trade*; Jesse Cromwell, 'Illicit Ideologies: Moral Economies of Venezuelan Smuggling and Autonomy in the Rebellion of Juan Francisco de Leon, 1749–1751', *THE AMERICAS* 74, no. 3 (July 2017)., 267–297; Cromwell, *The Smugglers' World*, 15–16; Juan José Ponce Vàzquez, *Islanders and Empire: Smuggling and Political Defiance in Hispaniola, 1580–1690* (Cambridge: Cambridge University Press, 2020), 2; David Chan Smith, 'Fair Trade and the Political Economy of Brandy Smuggling in Early Eighteenth-Century Britain', *Past & Present* 251, no. 1 (May 2021), https://doi.org/10.1093/pastj/gtaa008.

35 Bruno Blondé et al., 'Introduction,' in *Buyers & Sellers : Retail Circuits and Practices in Mediaeval and Early Modern Europe* (Turnhout: Brepols, 2006), 8–9.

36 Gottmann, *Global Trade,* 84–89; Montenach, *Femmes, pouvoit et contrebande,* 227–244, see particularly 243; Anna Knutsson, 'Clandestine Commerce'.

37 Kwass, *Contraband*, 114.

38 For protected vendors see: Gottmann, *Global Trade,* 83. For regular shop keepers see: Anne Montenach, 'Une économie du secret. Le commerce clandesitin de viande en Carême', *Rives Méditerranéennes* 17 (2004). For pedlars see: Pia Lundqvist, *Marknad på väg. Den västgöta gårdfarihandeln 1790–1864* (Göteborg: Göteborg Universitet, 2008), 208, 211, 228; Lundqvist, 'Förbjudna tyger. Textilsmuggling till Sverige under 1700- och 1800-talen', 204. For women see: Montenach, *Femmes, pouvoit et contrebande,* 227–244, see particularly 243; Anna Knutsson & Hanna Hodacs, 'When coffee was banned: strategies of labour and leisure among Stockholm's poor women, 1794–1796 and 1799–1802' *Scandinavian Economic History Review* (2021), doi: 10.1080/03585522.2021.2000489, 6–11.

39 Gottmann, *Global Trade,* 84–89; Montenach, *Femmes, pouvoit et contrebande,* 227–244, see particularly 243.

40 Montenach, 272, 270. See also: Gottmann, *Global Trade*, 89

41 On the lives of objects see: Arjun Appadurai, 'Introduction: Commodities and the Politics of Value', in *The Social Life of Things: Commodities in Cultural Perspective*, First published 1986 (Cambridge: Cambridge University Press, 2013). On the centrality of materiality see: Frank Trentmann, 'Materiality in the Future of History: Things, Practices, and Politics', *Journal of British Studies* 48, no. 2 (April 2009), 288–289. For a discussion about how materiality could change see: Anne Gerritsen and Giorgio Riello (eds.), *The Global Lives of Things: The Material Culture of Connections in the Early Modern World* (Abingdon-on-Thames: Routledge, 2015), 14.

42 Frank Trentmann, 'Materiality in the Future of History', 288–289.

43 For studies focused on tea see: H.-C. Mui and Lorna H. Mui, 'Smuggling and the British Tea Trade before 1784', *The American Historical Review* 74, no. 1 (October 1968); H.-C. Mui and Lorna H. Mui, 'The Commutation Act and the Tea Trade in Britain 1784–1793', *The Economic History Review* 16, no. 2 (1963); Leos Müller, 'The

Swedish East India Trade and International Markets: Re-Exports of Teas, 1731–1813', *Scandinavian Economic History Review* 51, no. 3 (2003). For silk see: Farrell, 'Smuggling Silks into Eighteenth-Century Britain'. For calico see Gottmann, *Global Trade*, and for a selection of contrabands see Kwass, *Contraband* (tobacco, salt, and calico) and Montenach, *Femmes, pouvoit et contrebande* (salt and calico).

44 Montenach, *Femmes, pouvoit et contrebande*, 260.

45 Farrell, 'Smuggling Silks into Eighteenth-Century Britain', 286.

46 Igor Kopytoff, 'The Cultural Biography of Things', in *The Social Life of Things. Commodities in Cultural Perspective*, ed. Arjun Appadurai (Cambridge: Cambridge University Press, 1986), 67.

47 Eli Filip Heckscher, *Kontinentalsystemet. Den stora handelsafspärrningen för hundra år sedan* (Stockholm: Handelshögskolan, 1918), 51. An English version was published in 1922 and those page references will here be used: Eli Filip Heckscher, *The Continental System*, trans. Harald Westergaard (Oxford: Clarendon Press, 1922).

48 See for example: Silvia Marzagalli, *Boulevards de la fraude: Le negoce maritime et le blocus continental, 1806–1813: Bordeaux, Hambourg, Livourne* (Villeneuve-d'Ascq: Presses Univ. Septentrion, 1999); Gavin Daly, 'Napoleon and the 'City of Smugglers', 1810–1814', *The Historical Journal* 50, no. 2 (2007); Gavin Daly, 'English Smugglers, the Channel, and the Napoleonic Wars, 1800–1814', *Journal of British Studies* 46 (2007).

49 For some studies dealing with this issue see for example: Ernst Pijning, 'Passive Resistance: Portuguese Diplomacy of Contraband Trade during King John V's Reign (1706–1750)', *Arquipélago História* 2, no. II (1997); G.V. Scammell, 'British Smuggling in the Iberian Americas Circa 1500–1750', *Itinerario* 24, no. 3/4 (2000).

50 See for example: Samuel Fettah, 'Frontières et fraudes. Les consuls de France et la contrebande dans le port franc de Livourne à l'époque du risorgimento', *Revue d'histoire moderne et contemporaine* 2, no. 48 (2001); M. Aglietti, M. Herrero Sánchez, F. Zamora Rodríguez (eds), *Los cónsules de extranjeros en la Edad Moderna y a principios de la Edad Contemporanea*, Ediciones Doce Calles, Madrid 2013; S. Marzagalli (ed), *Les consuls en Méditerranée, agents d'information* (Garnier, Paris, 2015); Oliver Le Gouic, 'Le consulat de France à Cadix face aux réformes carolines (1765–1788)', in *De l'utilité commerciale des consuls. L'institution consulaire et les marchands dans le monde méditerranéen (XVIIe–XXe Siècle)*, ed. Arnaud Bartolomei et al., Collection de l'École Française de Rome (Rome: Publications de l'École française de Rome, 2017). For Sweden see Leos Müller, *Consuls, Corsairs, and Commerce. The Swedish Consular Service and Long-Distance Shipping, 1720–1815*, Acta Universitatis Upsaliensis 213 (Uppsala: Uppsala University, 2004); Aryo Makko and Leos Müller, eds., *I främmande hamn. den svenska och svensk-norska konsultjänsten 1700–1985* (Malmö: Universus Academic Press, 2015).

51 Sophus A. Reinert and Jani Marjanen, 'Patriotism, Cosmopolitanism, and Political Economy in the Accademia Dei Pugni in Austrian Lombardy, 1760–1780', in *The Rise of Economic Societies in the Eighteenth Century: Patriotic Refom in Europe and North America*, ed. Koen Stapelbroek and Jani Marjanen (Basingstoke, Hampshire; New York: Palgrave Macmillan, 2012), 137–139.

52 Some studies that deal with this (if only briefly) include: Marzagalli, *Boulevards de la fraude*, 164–170, but no extensive investigation of smuggling in Gothenburg during the continental blockade has yet been conducted. For changing trade relations with Britain see also Häggqvist, 'On the Ocean of Protectionism', 155 & 157.

53 'Kongl. maj:ts ytterligare nådige förordning, angående lurendrägeriers uptäckande och hämmande' (1757).

54 Ibid.

55 'Kongl. maj:ts förordning emot lurendrägerier eller förbudne utrikes warors införsel i riket' (1770).

56 'Kongl. maj:ts nådiga förordning, til förekommande af lurendrägeri och tullförsnilln-ing. Gifwen Haga slott den 6 april 1799' (1799).

57 'Kongl. seglations-ordningen af d. 28 julii 1724' (1724); 'Kongl. maj:ts förnyade nådiga seglations-ordning 15 juni 1774' (1774).

58 An introduction to the customs archives can be gained from works like: Karin Wikberg, *Alla dessa tullar. En arkivguide. En vägledning till tullarkiv och tullhandlingar i riksarkivet* (Stockholm: Riksarkivet, 2006) which only deals with the collections at Riksarkivet in Stockholm;.Åsa Strandberg, "650 stycken citroner, 120 stycken påmerantzer, 200 stycken apellisiner. Vägledning till tullarkiven på landsarkivet i Uppsala" (Uppsala University, 2011), which gives a similar review of the customs records in the Regional Archives in Uppsala.

59 Although in some instances quantities can be extracted: see for example Chapter 5 for coffee. This was due to more consistent measuring techniques and consistent descriptions compared to for example textiles.

60 Lars O. Lagerqvist, *Vad kostade det? Priser och löner från medeltid till våra dagar* (Lund: Historisk Media, 2015), 129–134; For a very extensive discussion see also Rodney Edvinsson et al., 'The Multiple Currencies of Sweden-Finland 1534–1803', in *Exchange Rates, Prices, and Wages, 1277–2008* (Stockholm: Ekerlids Förlag, 2010), 179–188; All conversions in this study have been conducted through Rodney Edvinsson, 'Prisomräknare från medeltiden till 2100', http://www.historicalstatistics.org/Jamforelsepris.htm.

61 The statistics are collected from Johan Söderberg, 'Long-Term Trends in Real Wages of Labourers', in *Exchange Rates, Prices, and Wages, 1277–2008*, ed. Rodney Edvinsson, Tor Jacobson, and Daniel Waldenström (Stockholm: Ekerlids Förlag, 2010) , table A9.1, 474.

62 'Kongl. maj:ts nådige förordning, emot yppighet och öfwerflöd, gifwen stockholm i råd-cammaren then 26 junii 1766' (1766).

63 'Kongl. maj:ts förnyade förordning emot yppighet och öfwerflöd. 15 martii 1770' (1770).

64 'Kongl. maj:ts nådiga förordning, til hämmande af yppighet och öfwerflöd. gifwen stockholms slott den 1 januarii 1794' (1794).

2

TRADE IN CONFLICT

During the eighteenth century, smuggling was becoming a politically charged issue all across Europe. This was partly related to the threat it posed to the protectionist state and partly due to the introduction of new ideas about the rights and liberties of citizens.[1] The Swedish state was during this time undergoing several changes. Between the 1760s and the early nineteenth century, Sweden's governmental structure was changing from a form of proto-parliamentarianism, to enlightenment absolutism, to regency government, shifts that resulted in alternating state objectives. Ideas of citizenship and rights were also developing and expanding, both in practical and conceptual terms, as a result of the shifting governmental structures.[2] This affected the perceived relationship between the state and its inhabitants, which were increasingly seen as free citizens rather than subjects in the public debate. Meanwhile, new economic threats were looming on the horizon.

Global trade was on the rise in the early eighteenth century. Europe was flooded with wares from newly established colonies in the West and older trade connections in the East. Around the same time, Sweden was withdrawing from the international stage, licking its wounds and lamenting the loss of its Baltic Empire which had fallen in 1718. According to Carl Wennerlind, the loss of the empire inspired a crisis of confidence in Sweden's competitive ability.[3] Not wishing to be at the mercy of the great trading nations, Sweden attempted to distance itself from the global trade by introducing more and stricter protectionist legislation. The goal was to create a self-sufficient and independent country safeguarded from aggressive foreign trading efforts.[4] As the focus turned inward, attention turned to supporting and boosting the domestic manufacturing industry, which, it was hoped, would provide the country with everything it needed. The manufacturing industry was only in its infancy but the manufacturing zealots saw it as a driving force for the entire economy.[5] With the newly won enthusiasm for the Swedish manufactories, the manufactory workers came to be seen increasingly as

DOI: 10.4324/9781003226031-2

a resource in need of public and popular care and attention.[6] In various ways, the state encouraged the augmentation of patriotic feeling to ensure a greater support for the manufactories.[7] This newly developed patriotism was a form of economic patriotism, or protectionist patriotism, which sought to encourage individuals to prioritise the good of the country over private gain.[8]

The ideas and associations related to smuggling were not fixed but varied between different interest groups within the state and over time. Drawing on debates in the riksdag, royal decrees, and newspaper discussions, this chapter explores the various ideas and interpretations of smuggling that existed in a range of arenas, ideas that clashed, altered, merged and eventually resulted in new legislation. This helps to set the scene for the practical consequences of smuggling, discussed in later chapters.

Eliciting the Smuggling Crime

Smuggling in Early Economic Literature

The first noteworthy economic writer to deal with the issue of smuggling in the eighteenth century was Anders Berch (1711–1774), Sweden's first professor in economy. While he awarded the topic limited attention, he labelled it one of the most severe crimes as it undermined legitimate trade and injured all members of society.[9] In his description of smuggling, he pointed to two particular features: the import of permitted wares without paying duty (*tullförsnillning*), which injured the honest merchant who had to contend with higher import costs, and the import of prohibited wares (*lurendrägeri*), which injured the manufacturers. The latter was particularly lamentable to Berch as the damage done to the manufacturers resulted in the suffering of the manufactory workers and by extension the entire nation. Berch was a strong advocate for the advancement of the manufacturing industry, which he saw as a fundamental cog in the development of the country. He was also one of the first writers to advance the idea that the citizens of a society should be considered as an economic resource which needed to be cared for.[10] In regard to smuggling, he linked the consumption of contraband to the suffering, or even starvation, of the Swedish workers.[11] The idea of the suffering or starving worker became a frequently used rhetorical device in the smuggling discussions throughout the eighteenth century, as it efficiently aligned smuggling with suffering.[12] By doing so, Berch created a tangible victim to the crime of smuggling. The injury done to the workers could be understood in two ways: either as detrimental for the workforce at large and thus Sweden's ability to manufacture, or as an abuse of fellow subjects. Against this background, Berch argued that smuggling was not only a crime against the crown, defrauding revenue, but also against the nation and fellow citizens. Meanwhile, he had little faith in the voluntary co-operation of the population but believed that as long as people had access to illegally imported foreign manufactures they would consume these, instead of the domestically produced manufactures, thus undermining Swedish industry.[13]

In order to deal with such threats, Berch argued for a tighter regulation of trade and increased prohibitions.[14] He refuted the idea that taxes and prohibitions were useless or led to temptations to run contraband. Berch was not an isolationist, however, and he stressed the importance of continued international trade. The competition with foreign merchants he saw as vital to avoid the development of monopolies within Swedish trade, which would also be damaging.[15] His ideas would have a great influence on Swedish academic economic thought throughout the eighteenth century and beyond.[16] The same can be said for his ideas about smuggling, which persisted in later discussions about illegal imports and protectionism.

In Berch's writings, he relies primarily on the effectiveness of prohibition and regulation, citizen co-operation in safeguarding the manufactories play a subservient role. By contrast, citizen co-operation and commitment are central in the work of the economic writer and public official Johan Fredrik Kryger (1707–1777). In *Tankar vid lediga stunder* (1761), Kryger dedicated a whole chapter to the issue of smuggling, which he argued could be resolved through increased patriotism and education. He saw himself as having a double responsibility to spread awareness about the dangers of smuggling, both as a member of society and as a public official.[17] Kryger saw the social contract and a limitation of certain natural freedoms as crucial features of a successful state.[18] In *Tankar*, he explained that a well-functioning state demanded not only a contract between state and citizens but also certain virtues among the citizens, including a reverence for religion, love of the fatherland, law-abidingness, and common agreement among the citizens.[19] In his book, Kryger attacked what he perceived as the general laxity or leniency towards smuggling, which he saw as an expression of lacking patriotism. Just like Berch, Kryger placed domestic manufacturing at the core of his argument. The continued survival of the Swedish manufacturing industry was crucial; without it, Sweden's whole future would be jeopardised.

> Smuggling alone can eventually ruin not only the factories, but also all other businesses; so that Sweden, in a short while, must find itself in the same condition as it did shortly after the [biblical] great flood.[20]

In order to avoid such a catastrophe, Kryger highlighted the importance of high import duties and prohibitions, which would protect the domestic industry against unsolicited competition.[21] This was not enough, however, as the continued access to foreign manufactures through the contraband trade allowed consumers to continue to undermine the industry. In his attacks on smuggling, Kryger appealed to people's patriotism, arguing that the consumption of contraband was incompatible with patriotism.

> ...such a mischievous people [the smugglers] must apparently be divorced from those, whose love for the fatherland and reverence for the Laws make them abhor these misfits, or those who err from ignorance: thus, I must undress the Smuggler his fig leaf, and show him in his nude horrendous form.[22]

In treating smuggling, Kryger was careful to note that leniency towards it might not just be due to a wickedness of character, but could also derive from ignorance and a lack of information. He therefore saw it as his duty to inform his readers of the dangers of smuggling.[23] First, Kryger pointed to the religious motivations for obeying authority.[24] Thereafter, he addressed the various apologies for smuggling that he had encountered.

In response to the idea that Swedish industry was less developed and produced poorer products than that of other countries, Kryger replied that patience was needed as the industry was still in its infancy and that love for the fatherland should enable people to support the industry despite its temporary limitations.[25] He then addressed the question of why high exchange rates affected domestic productions and foreign imports differently; why foreign goods were cheaper. Kryger explained that as salaries in Sweden were higher due to a lack of workers, the retail prices for the goods were also higher. He argued that despite this, patriotic sentiment should lead consumers to want to feed Swedish, rather than foreign, workers.[26] Another argument was that everything not produced in Sweden must be acquired from abroad. In response, Kryger maintained that the range of Swedish produce was limited due to both a lack of workers and smuggling itself. These factors prevented the sale of domestic productions and limited their turnover, leading to lower profits which hindered the expansion of the manufacturing industry. Discussing the production of textiles, Kryger pointed out that it took time to produce new designs and that the desire for everything new and foreign was a childish notion which made it impossible for the Swedish manufacturers to be competitive.[27] Finally, he challenged the idea that Sweden was ill-suited for the manufacturing industry due to its small and deficient population and cold climate. This was a particularly objectionable idea to Kryger, who insisted that while there were obstacles to the development of industry, they were political and economic rather than climatic or related to the population's physical inability to engage in manufacturing.[28] This section of *Tankar* sets out Kryger's approach to the manufacturing industry but it also gives an insight into the most common objections to 'buying Swedish'.

Kryger recognised that the survival of the manufactories depended not only on the correct protectionist legislation but also on the behaviour of the country's inhabitants. For Kryger, this meant that the issues posed by smuggling could not be overcome through focusing solely on protectionism; rather, it was necessary to also gain the co-operation of the public. Consumption, he argued, should be a patriotic act: "[F]oreign dress bears witness of the fact that the heart which beats within, must be foreign, rather than Swedish".[29] No true patriot, Kryger argued, could ever engage with contraband.[30]

In both Berch and Kryger's economic writings, there is a focus on manufacturing as the most important aspect of Sweden's economic development. In this context, smuggling was depicted as a looming threat to the survival of Swedish industry and by extension to the welfare of the entire nation. While Berch argued that regulation was the main tool with which to eradicate the threat posed by smuggling, Kryger stressed that the successful enforcement of regulation also required the co-operation of the population. For Kryger, mobilising the population's patriotic sense of duty was a necessary step in the successful implementation of protectionist policy.

While patriotic protectionism held a powerful sway over the smuggling debates in the second half of the century, it did not go unchallenged. Moving away from the belief in the supremacy of regulation, economic writers like Anders Nordencrantz (1697–1772) and Anders Chydenius (1729–1803) instead argued for the centrality of self-interest and natural law. As historian Lars Magnusson has highlighted, these writers believed that the market thrived on freedom rather than control.[31] They rejected the idea of the social contract, which involved individuals abandoning part of their freedom and their natural rights to become full members of society. Instead, they favoured a 'natural' system, where trade as well as society were self-regulating, without the need for either state regulation or individual sacrifice. The focus on natural rights stood in sharp contrast to patriotic protectionism and entailed a very different relationship between state and population, based on the state's obligation towards its citizens rather than the subjects' duties towards the state. Such a divergent worldview also resulted in a very different approach to smuggling.

This new approach to smuggling was first developed by Anders Nordencrantz. He had travelled widely in the British Isles in the 1720s, where he became fascinated by Scottish enlightenment thought, English mercantilism, and particularly Bernard de Mandeville's *Fable of the Bees.*[32] Upon his return to Sweden, Nordencrantz developed a criticism of Swedish protectionism which drew heavily on the ideas he had encountered in Britain. Nordencrantz argued that self-interest (in the vein of Mandeville) together with the right to engage freely in trade were crucial components in sustaining and developing trade. According to Nordencrantz, trade was governed by certain independent and uncontrollable forces and should be left to 'naturally' self-regulate.[33] Regulation only served to contort trade into unnatural and damaging forms.

Smuggling was one expression of this damaging trade. Nordencrantz agreed with Berch and Kryger that "[smugglers] are the bread thieves of the kingdom, of the poor, yes, of the whole nation".[34] However, in order to eliminate this damaging form of trade, he insisted that it was necessary to investigate its foundations.[35] Whereas Berch and Kryger saw smuggling as a consequence of unpatriotic or ignorant behaviour, Nordencrantz argued that smuggling was rooted in the natural desire for sumptuousness ingrained in all men. Sumptuousness and self-interest were in their unconstrained form seen as driving forces in the economy, but could turn destructive when fettered. The demand for foreign goods was not merely due to their novelty value but also their cheap price and good quality, which appealed to men's self-serving nature. By contrast, Swedish consumer wares were seen as expensive and of poor quality, something Nordencrantz identified as being related to "the monopolies, the guild- and stamp-decrees and that all Industry is restricted to certain locations and societies, in addition to the population scarcity and the expensive food stuffs".[36] It should be noted, that some historians have suggested that the high price of domestic products might have been a notion rather than a reality.[37] For Nordencrantz, however, the weakness of Swedish wares was a real issue and the solution was not to shut out all foreign alternatives with rules and regulation and to suffocate invention and creativity in rigid guild systems. Such efforts would merely serve to push the trade underground. Instead, he suggested that increased freedom and competition would motivate the development of production and design, which in time, would make the Swedish products competitive and naturally strengthen the manufactories.

Anders Chydenius, an economic thinker from the Finnish provinces, took a similar approach. Following Nordencrantz's ideas about the importance of self-interest and the uncontrollable nature of trade, Chydenius agreed that the Swedish trade regulations ought to be dismantled in order to safeguard future prosperity.[38] Such actions would also help to resolve the smuggling problem. Chydenius suggested that more staple towns should be established, particularly in the Finnish provinces, which would prevent lengthy and troublesome detours for the legal trade. He saw the hassle involved in the legal trade as a crucial incentive in the smuggling trade.[39]

Both Nordencrantz and Chydenius supported a deregulated trade, with as little state interference as possible, which they not only saw as crucial to Sweden's financial recovery but the solution to the smuggling problem. In contrast to earlier writers who blamed the contraband trade on individual protagonists, the smugglers and the consumers, Nordencrantz and Chydenius blamed the restrictive economic system itself. Consequently, their proposed solution was legislative and institutional reform rather than the rehabilitation of patriotic sentiment.

The early economic writers discussed here, Berch, Kryger, Nordencrantz, and Chydenius, laid the foundation for the debates about smuggling that would continue throughout the rest of the century. The two camps, which can roughly be labelled patriotic protectionism and deregulation, would prove remarkably tenacious. These ideas did not exist in a vacuum, but the discussions about smuggling also came to be affected by political turmoil and shifting economic conditions.

Economic Crisis and the Rise of Protectionism

Kryger, Nordencrantz, and Chydenius were not just engaged in writing on economic issues, they were also politically active during the proto-parliamentary period leading up to 1772. Two main parties, the Hats and the Caps, were during this period fighting for control over the Swedish government. Kryger was a long time a supporter of the Hat Party, although he eventually lost faith in them, something that coincided with a shift in his economic ideas towards a more liberal approach.[40] Nordencrantz and Chydenius, by contrast, were backers of the Cap party. In his early days, Chydenius was part of the more 'fanatical' wing of the Cap party, and during the Riksdag of 1765/66 he managed to gain free export rights for the harbours in *Ostrobothnia*, in the Finnish provinces.[41] These successes with deregulating the Swedish trade were short-lived, however.

By the late 1760s, the economic situation was becoming increasingly problematic. Sweden had been supported by French subsides throughout the Hat Party reign (1738–1764), and during the Seven Years' War (1757–1762) they were pressured to sending troops to Prussia to aid their French benefactors. This constituted a considerable setback for the Swedish finances, which were still struggling to recover from the wars conducted earlier in the century. The Swedish state bank started printing more paper money to deal with the situation, leading to inflation and a reduction in the international value of the Swedish currency.[42] In 1765/66, the Cap Party replaced the Hats in government after nearly 30 years in control. The new governing party introduced disinflation and saving measures which led to other problems in the shape of capital shortage and price hikes.[43] Chydenius, who had been instrumental in the deregulation of trade in *Ostrobothnia* during the Cap take over, soon became disenchanted with the Cap Party following these measures, and instead started backing King Gustav III's coup d'état, which in 1772 put an end to parliamentary dominance.[44] Around this time, the link between the struggling manufactories and smuggling appears to have been firmly re-established in economic as well as political debates, and the political discussions came to be increasingly dominated by protectionism. As the financial crisis escalated so did the attempts to protect the factories, which also meant that smuggling became a hot topic for debate.

Anti-Smuggling Decrees

Decrees against smuggling were nothing new: they had been in use at least since the reign of Charles XI (1660–1697). During the eighteenth century, four main decrees were issued: 1739, 1757, 1770 and 1799, along with several additions, explanations, and amendments. The 1739 decree had been particularly strict and was intended to safeguard the Swedish infant manufactories in a protectionist spirit. It allowed house searches for contraband (known as house-visitations) and prescribed severe punishments.[45] This strict anti-smuggling decree was in 1757 replaced by a much more lenient decree. Many of the old regulations were lifted and the punitive punishments transformed to fairly low fines. Five years later house-visitations were also banned.[46] Such moderate measures were, however, no longer deemed tenable in the increasingly challenging economic climate after 1765. In 1766 the ban on some visitations was lifted, and soon afterwards a new anti-smuggling decree was released.[47] The ongoing economic crisis and its perceived connection to smuggling prompted the riksdag in 1769 to appoint a committee to look into the issue of smuggling and to assess the need for a new anti-smuggling decree to safeguard the manufactories.

The first action of the Trade, Manufacture and Customs Committee was to establish how serious the smuggling threat was to the manufacturers. In order to answer this question, it was first deemed necessary to assess the current state of

Swedish manufacturing. An investigation into the development of the industry between 1764 and 1768 was therefore conducted, and the subsequent report posited that smuggling was one of the main threats to the subsistence of the industry. Pointing to the effects of the 1762 prohibition against house-visitations, the investigation argued that only three months after its introduction the silk manufacturers were feeling the effects. The industry, which had been experiencing its highest growth yet, had suddenly found itself struggling to find buyers for its wares.[48] It was argued that Swedish-made products were particularly at risk due to their poor quality and high price. The high price was believed to originate in part from the expensiveness of food in Sweden, which led to hikes in workers' salaries. If these issues could be addressed, the committee hoped that Swedish-made goods would be easier to sell on the domestic market and that the consumers would prefer these to illegal alternatives. According to the report, such improvements could possibly even make Swedish goods competitive on an international market. The report concluded that the difficulties encountered by Swedish manufacturers, particularly in competition with foreign wares, could be alleviated through support and regulation, embodied by a new stricter anti-smuggling decree.[49]

A few months after the report was issued, in January 1770, member of the riksdag Jonas Björnsson presented a memorandum to the Trade and Manufacture and Customs Committee. In it, Björnsson outlined a 12-point strategy to deal with the smuggling problem.[50] Apart from suggestions to increase the speed of the criminal proceedings and expand surveillance, the most significant suggestions were the re-introduction of universal house-searches, the call to burn all contraband seized and *not* to release it for sale abroad, along with the publication of the names of all convicted smugglers in the newspapers. While the committee remained unconvinced of the necessity of all of Björnsson's suggested measures, they did agree that something had to be done in order to bring the situation under control.

Spurred on by the 1769 report and lobbying efforts, the committee released a new anti-smuggling decree in 1770. The core of the decree was comprised of previously issued decrees. By consolidating and renewing previous regulations, it was hoped that it would be easier to apply and enforce the regulations.[51] The explicit purpose of the decree was to limit the consumption of illegal foreign goods. The attack on contraband was launched on two fronts. Along with the new anti-smuggling decree, a new sumptuary decree was also issued. It was hoped that these two decrees together would allow the state to control both smugglers and consumers.[52] The 1770 anti-smuggling decree, the sumptuary decree, and a new prohibitive import tariff issued in 1771, that banned a total of 871 different wares, show how a unified protectionist legislative front emerged during the economic crisis.[53]

Punishment and Amelioration

The punishments for smuggling prescribed in the decrees were tightly linked to perceptions of smuggling as a crime but also to the evolution of Swedish legal code. Retributivism and deterrence had been common features of punishments in Europe for a long time. While they originated in the Church Law and were based on interpretations of the Bible, they later came to be transferred into regional and state law.[54] Retributivism and deterrence were therefore common in early modern legislation. Swedish punishments, while to some degree rooted in retributivist tendencies, were generally less severe than in other European countries like France and England. According to the legal historian Erik Anners, this was related to the fact that subjects, and in particular peasants, had a stronger social standing in Sweden than in many other countries.[55] The peasant estate was both represented in the riksdag and partook in the creation of legislation.[56]

Another particularly noteworthy feature of the Swedish legal tradition was the relatively early introduction of the idea of improvement. In contrast to deterrence, the idea of improvement stipulated that the offender might be 'rehabilitated' and turned into a healthy member of society. This idea was present already in Olaus Petri's rules for judges (*Domarregler*), developed around the 1540s.[57] The idea of improvement was also popular among the proponents of natural law, such as Samuel von Pufendorf (1632–1694), whose writings were highly influential in Sweden.[58] Likewise, David Nehrman Ehrenstråle (1695–1769), the great authority on Swedish Law in the first half of the eighteenth century, maintained that improvement was one of the main functions of punishment.[59] Nevertheless, the Civil Code of 1734 – the first nationwide collection of laws in Sweden – was still to a significant extent focused on deterrence and retributivism.[60]

Meanwhile, growing attention was paid to foreign enlightenment legal theorists like Charles-Louis de Secondat Montesquieu (1689–1755) and Cesare Beccaria (1738–1794), whose focus lay on discounting retributivism in favour of more efficient deterrence punishments. These deterrence punishments focused particularly on presenting the offender as a warning example; within this context punishments such as the death sentence or deportation were seen as less suitable.[61] As Beccaria observed in his 1764 *Dei delitti e delle pene,* translated to Swedish in 1770 as *Afhandling om brott och straff*, however, deterrence and infamy must be used tactically.[62]

> Smuggling is a real offence against the sovereign and the nation; but the punishment should not brand the offender with infamy, because this crime is not infamous in the public opinion. By inflicting infamous punishments, for crimes that are not reputed so, we destroy that idea where it may be useful.[63]

Instead, Beccaria suggested that the most suitable punishment for smugglers would be labour in the public works in order to repay the crown.[64] This idea, that the punishment should aim to repair, or in the case of smuggling, repay, the damage done by the offence, became a guiding light in Swedish anti-smuggling legislation.

Anti-smuggling legislation in the second half of the eighteenth century was lenient. The 1757 legislation merely stipulated that sentenced smugglers were required to give up their contraband and were fined half the value of the contraband. If the person was unable to pay, the punishment would be converted to a month's prison sentence on water and bread. By 1770, the fine had increased to the full value of the contraband, but it must still be considered mild when compared to the punishments issued in other countries.[65] In France, for example, the punishments ranged from reprimands and fines to exiling, execution, condemnation to the galleys and – reserved for the most dangerous smugglers – drawing and quartering.[66] The leniency of the Swedish legislation was probably related to an unwillingness to introduce draconian and oppressive legislation, which would be difficult to enforce and would fail to gain support among a population used to fairly lenient legislation and who did not necessarily conceive of smuggling as a serious crime.

The Triumph of Patriotic Protectionism

The protectionist efforts launched in the 1770s were expanded into the 1790s. They peaked in 1799, when the future King Gustav IV Adolph, yet again tasked the National Board of Trade with exploring how the Swedish manufactories could be improved and what support they needed.[67] Just as in the 1760s, the Board reported that the Swedish manufactories were lagging behind as a consequence of falling exchange rates and the failure to suppress smuggling. The Board admitted that duty reductions and the lifting of prohibitions could reduce the illegal introduction of foreign goods, but emphasised that this was only the correct course of action *if* smuggling surveillance was as good and extensive as it ought to be. This, the Board argued, was not the case.[68] A new push was needed; the report prompted the release of the most extensive anti-smuggling decree to date. While the 1770 legislation took up 12 pages, the 1799 decree spanned over 36.

A committee with members from the National Board of Trade was tasked with designing the decree. The committee developed a first draft, but it was marred by disagreement as the committee members struggled to agree on two issues in particular: house-visitations and the appropriate punishments for smugglers. The Assistant Judge Samuel Johan Chierlin (1742–1828) was one of the first to comment on the proposed legislation. He agreed that the country needed to find a solution to the issue of smuggling but maintained that the suggested punishments were too severe. He particularly criticised the suggested punishment for third-time offenders: being tied with a metal collar to a pillory. Instead, Chierlin maintained that the focus should be on monetary punishments, as this targeted the smuggler's main motivation: profit. Chierlin argued that this was not just the best way to get through to the smugglers but also because "[l]aws should always aim for the correction and improvement of people...".[69] Condemning people to the pillory, he believed, might do more harm than good, suggesting that others would interpret the smuggler as a victim, a conclusion which would undermine order. Chierlin's arguments thus both pick up on Beccaria's idea that smugglers should not be treated with infamy, and fall back on ideas of improvement. One of the heads of the Justice Division, Count Lars Rosenborg (1728–1807), and the Assistant Judge Leonard Pahl (1733–1804) agreed that the punishments needed to be eased.[70] Another head of the Justice Division, Count Carl David Gyllenborg (1734–1811) had several reservations about the new legislation and argued that experience had shown that neither severe nor light punishments affected the incidence of smuggling.[71] He argued that pillory punishments should be reserved for convicts with sentences for life; for lesser crimes, as pillories risked convicts being severely stigmatised, turning them into useless and harmful members of society after their punishment. Gyllenborg thus saw proportional monetary punishment as a better solution.[72] Assistant Judge Johan Israel Osangius (1741–1810) was not equally convinced of the harm of the pillory, but suggested an update to this old-fashioned penance. Picking up on an idea suggested by Björnsson during the 1769/70 riksdag, Osangius proposed that the name of convicted smugglers ought to be announced in the newspapers, allowing their misdeeds to be known in the entire kingdom rather than just in the city – a pillory in print.[73] The committee eventually managed to reach a compromise and the resulting legislation was published on 6 April 1799.

The new anti-smuggling decree set out to 'cure' smuggling – the "wasting disease in the national body".[74] Punishments were more severe than they had been in both the 1757 and 1770 decrees through the introduction of a minimum fine of 50 rdr for smuggling. Osangius' idea about naming smugglers in the newspapers was adopted along with the notion that they should be stripped of civic trust (*förlust av medborgerligt förtroende*). Whereas the names of all smugglers should be exposed in the newspapers, the loss of civic trust was a punishment reserved for those caught smuggling goods worth more than 50 rdr, and all second-time offenders who had burgher rights to conduct trade. This punishment was thus intended to target individuals who partook in regular and large-scale smuggling – those who actively worked to undermine the protectionist policy rather than small-scale one-time offenders. One physical punishment was also introduced, third-time offenders would be taken to a pole in a public square and put on display for a period of two hours.[75] While the decree of 1799 clearly represented an escalation of the measures to regulate smuggling, including increasingly severe punishments, as we shall see, it was still far removed from what was called for in newspapers. It reflects the legislators' attempts to find a middle way between patriotic protectionism and the lenient laws, which were a distinctive feature of the Swedish legal tradition.

Sweden's increasingly severe anti-smuggling legislation around the turn of the century was related both to the emergence of a new absolutist monarch, Gustav IV Adolph, and to the triumph of patriotic protectionism in the final years of the eighteenth century – two closely interlinked occurrences.

'Blood sucker' or Victim? The Smuggler in the Press

The smuggling debates in the newspapers first gained momentum in the early 1770s after the introduction of the Freedom of the Press Act in 1766, during a period of economic turmoil.[76] These debates were usually incited by new legislation or rumours thereof.

A typical entry to the debate can be observed in 1775 when a certain Arimaspus (potentially the Hat protectionist Abraham Magni Sahlstedt, 1716–1776) sent in a suggestion for a new financial plan for the kingdom to *Dagligt Allehanda,* a Stockholm-based burgher newspaper with a high circulation. The plan was intended to alleviate the current money shortage and to set out a new economic path.[77] The improvement of the domestic manufacturing industry was a central tenet of the plan. According to Arimaspus it required increased regulation, and it was also necessary for the population to refrain from the consumption of foreign luxuries, choosing instead to channel capital into the domestic industry. Such actions, he argued, would lead not only to a self-sufficient Sweden but with time would also allow the country to produce enough for export. To achieve this goal, and to reduce unpatriotic temptation and distractions, smuggling needed to be stamped out through the strengthening of the customs. Arimaspus suggested that in order to achieve this, one part of the manufacturing support fund's (*Manufakturfonden)* budget ought to be earmarked for projects that aimed to root out smuggling.[78] Arimaspus' patriotic protectionist arguments are strongly reminiscent of those used by Berch, Kryger, and later by the National Board of Trade. However, anonymous writers in the press often went considerably further, than their named counterparts. Consequently, in the newspapers, the smuggler was denounced as an economic leech, as a "blood sucker", "traitor", and "drainer" of the country, who threatened the survival of the Swedish manufactories.[79]

Not everyone agreed that the manufacturers needed protection and unequivocal support, however. Others suggested that it put the Swedish manufacturers in an unfairly advantageous position which might negatively impact the consumers.[80] One anonymous writer argued that the lack of competition enabled the manufacturers to keep their prices high and production costs low, which resulted in significant profit for the manufacturers and poor and expensive goods for the consumers. Smuggling occurred, the author argued, because foreign goods were better and cheaper than the domestic productions. "[I]s it strange", he asked, "if I strive to get the best that can be had for the cheapest price, particularly if I am poor".[81] He argued that patriotic protectionism, instead of helping the country, simply concealed individual vice. Like other commentators of his conviction, he maintained that protectionism was problematic as it prioritised the manufacturers and the manufactory workers above the rest of the population, something which in turn could actually result in more smuggling. In the public press, protectionism was thus not univocally seen as a solution to Sweden's economic issues. The newspapers indicate that far from a united protectionist front to bolster and support the manufactories, public opinion in the late eighteenth century Sweden was divided. There was an ongoing tug of war between patriotic protectionists and deregulators, and things were getting infected.

In 1776, a fierce debate broke out in *Dagligt Allehanda* about the abolition of the customs office. It started with the publication of a letter with the title

"Suggestion about the abolition of the land and maritime customs" in May of that year. Its anonymous author argued that the abolition of the customs would advance the 'natural rights' of the citizens and would be profitable for them and for the state at large. Arguing for the importance of laws that combined the interests of the subject and society, the letter strongly opposed exclusive privileges. By contrast, the author suggested that laws should be designed to protect the subjects and their rights, particularly their natural right to conduct the trade or business of their choice, which was hindered by overregulation. According to the author, regulations and prohibitions also squeezed the life out of Swedish manufacturing through reducing competition and thus robbing it of its momentum. "Prohibitions against the importation of foreign manufactures, are in themselves nothing other than a Privilege for native workers: to be as lazy, as superfluous as they want, but still be justified to demand a high wage".[82] There was no reason, the author claimed, that Swedish workers could not produce products equally as good as their foreign counterparts. In order to improve Swedish manufacturing, increased competition was needed. This, the letter argued, would motivate the workers to raise their game. Competition would lead to an improvement in quality and a decrease in price, which would reduce the incentive to smuggle. Regulation and prohibition must therefore be removed, and the surest way to do that, the author argued, was to abolish the customs.[83] While the author revived ideas found in Nordencrantz' and Chydenius' writings, of smuggling as a natural symptom of a protectionist regime, he also took it further by arguing for a full-scale removal of *all* customs controls.

Such a controversial proposal would not go unchallenged, and a month later, a response appeared in *Dagligt Allehanda*. It opposed the dissolution of the customs office and argued that the author of this idea had an erroneous notion of the role of exclusive privilege and lacked insight into the conditions of Swedish manufacturing. Instead of being damaging for Sweden's trade, privileges and monopolies on certain trades protected manufacturers from unfair competition which would otherwise force them to compete with cheaper (foreign) copies. The article suggested that Swedish manufacturers could not compete in price and quality with foreign manufacturers as Swedish workers had to be paid higher wages than foreign workers due to their need for more and better food than in warmer countries. Was this need reason enough to "exterminate" the Swedish workers?[84] The author concluded that no patriot could see the benefits of removing the customs, a move which would compromise the manufacturing process as it would make it unprofitable to produce good-quality products. This in turn would lead to the destruction of the citizens and the country itself. Pointing to the decline in Christian ideals and what the author saw as individual rather than community priorities, he concluded that "our Freethinkers have forgotten the Catechism".[85] The newspaper discussions thus expanded the reach and scope of the smuggling debates and further polarised the two camps.

They represent two radically different interpretations of smuggling: a betrayal of the country or a natural occurrence that counteracted distortions brought about through over-regulation. Both of these interpretations derive from the early economic literature, but in the newspaper discussions, they appear to have been mobilised in a fierce debate about the economic future of the country, which intensified during the recurring financial crises. Which side of the debate the commentators were on seems to have corresponded to their opinions on the role of Swedish manufactories: whether they provided a service for the country; or were at the service of the country.

To an extent, this discussion can also be considered a debate between different factions within the burghership. Roughly speaking, manufacturers argued for protectionism and vendors for an open market.[86] Many manufacturers argued for protectionism by relating to the welfare of the workers, with attacks on protectionism being framed as direct attacks on the Swedish workers.[87] This juxtaposition is particularly evident in a 1771 article titled ‘A word to the Smuggler’.

> Forgive me d[ear] neighbour.... I am as entitled as you to defend my Property and business as you yours, but the difference is that I do it directly and openly, and you through others and secretively.....[y]ou are thus a thief, who steals the Bread from many thousands of your honest and skilled Countrymen, and makes their eyes water, when they cannot earn their bread. You are an unworthy Citizen, who profanely transgresses the Law, and thus neither fears God, nor honours the King.[88]

The manufacturers thus located themselves on the side of their workers in opposition to self-serving interests, portraying themselves as fatherly benefactors and contributors to the common good.

By contrast, the vendors often referred to the nation’s will or taste in their defence of a deregulated trade. When wares were requested that were not produced in the country, or when there was a shortage, they were caught in a vice between the demands of the consumers and the lack of sufficiently attractive domestic products.[89] One anonymous author particularly highlighted the significance of the “Nation’s taste” as a major force in trade.[90] Once the common taste had established, the superiority of foreign goods over domestic ones the former would be in demand. “What happens then? Well, the merchant has to supply both or he will stand idle in his shop”.[91] If the regular merchants did not supply the public there were many unlicensed traders who were happy to oblige. Providing wares in demand was a question of survival for the retailers, but it was also a recognition of the unquenchable power of popular demand. Furthermore, the author argued, it lay within human nature to choose cheaper and better goods, whenever available.

In essence, the two vantage points, protectionism vs. deregulated trade, came to be adopted by two different burgher professions. The first was the manufacturers, who saw themselves as the heartbeat of the country, in need of protection as they worked to secure Sweden’s financial stability. The second was the vendors, who felt the need to adapt to the citizens and their demands. The question thus boiled down to rights and loyalties: did the consumers have the right to consume as they desired, particularly to choose less expensive and better-quality goods? Or should this right be trumped by the consumers' loyalties to the state? The blame for the contraband trade was thus shifted back and forth, from being an issue of lacking loyalty and patriotism, to being an issue of the deficiency of the Swedish manufacturing industry. While these discussions were clearly linked to ideas about protectionism and natural rights, in the newspapers they were also connected to the more mundane conflicts between various business interests. The manufacturers strove to secure the best possible conditions for themselves and to ensure a continued demand for their wares while the vendors were more interested in being able to supply wares to a changing and competitive market.

Punishment in the Press

In the newspapers, supporters of patriotic protectionism were particularly concerned with the need to make the punishments more severe and to follow in the footsteps of countries like France. The proponents of more draconian legislation saw the smuggler as an enemy of the state. This approach fed off patriotic protectionist ideas about patriotism and loyalty, and the smuggler as a traitor.

One prevalent idea repeatedly voiced in the press was that the smuggler had forfeited the right to citizenship, and that he or she should be punished with the loss of civic standing (*förlust av medborgerligt förtroende*) or even exile for life.[92] Loss of civic standing meant that the person in question was deemed unfit to hold any official post in society, or to run for elections. It was a punishment applied to crimes that were understood to compromise the culprit's judgement and honour. Exile for life was a considerably harsher punishment in the same vein. Proponents of this severe punishment justified it by referring to the smuggler as a traitor beyond salvation.

> In the case of a thief it is possible to hope for improvement; but there is no hope for a Smuggler; he smuggles as long as he lives. What damage is there in losing such a dangerous Member of the Country (*Riks-kroppen*), a thief without return, a traitor, a murderer, who takes the food out of the mouth of the native worker, and with their contemptible trade cause a lack of work (*näringslöshet*), suffering and poverty, so that innocent children die of hunger.[93]

Other commentators were not even content with exile for life, instead seeking inspiration from France and Britain, where smugglers were convicted to the pillory, if not the gallows or the galleys.[94]

Unsurprisingly, the patriotic protectionists were much more vocal on the issue of punishment than those according to whom smuggling was a consequence of a bad system in need of reform. Nevertheless, more moderate views on punishments were also voiced in newspaper debates. In 1773, in response to a letter published in *Dagligt Allehanda* the previous year asking why smugglers were not hanged just like they were in England, the author 'Carolin' argued for humanism and understanding rather than condemnation.

> They are human, the smugglers I mean, and like others want to feed themselves by the quickest means. Since they are good for nothing else, have not learned from youth to provide for themselves honestly, nor had the love of domestic goods implanted in them, they fall on this means of livelihood, to which they are encouraged both by the high and the low, yes even the guardians [against smuggling] themselves.... Therefore it is not strange that many are tempted to smuggle. As many are smugglers, who then has the heart to execute such a harsh conviction?[95]

While this type of statement was rare, it was not unique and appears to have tapped into an alternative view of the offender not as a rotten limb but as a human who can err. In certain cases, this led some to make use of the Swedish tradition of improvement and to conclude that, "[a]lthough [the smuggler] has committed an error, it does not follow, that he cannot improve and yet again become a useful Member of Society".[96]

While Swedish anti-smuggling legislation remained fairly lenient, there were voices in the public sphere calling for tougher punishments. There were also commentators who defended the smuggler as a human being, but they only rarely made their voices heard in discussions on punishments, which were dominated by those calling for more serious measures against smugglers. From the point of view of the patriotic protectionist, the loyalty of the subject or citizen was a central component in realising the protectionist state. This also meant that a crime such as smuggling could be perceived as particularly damaging, as it undermined not only the manufacturing industry but the state project itself, which was so severe that they required a tougher approach to offenders.

In 1796, Gustav IV Adolph issued strict new press regulations and during the subsequent years, which the historian Ingemar Oscarsson has referred to as the "iron years", the debate about smuggling appears to have been replaced by a uniform celebration of patriotic protectionism.[97] In April 1799, the new anti-smuggling decree was published in *Inrikes Tidningar*.[98] While the earlier newspaper debates on smuggling had been multifaceted, the 1799 press response was exclusively celebratory and the authors mainly manufacturers.[99] It was even announced that the Society of Manufacturers had made a commemorative coin for this happy occasion. This coin would depict Gustav IV Adolf on one side and on the other, a young hero in roman dress giving his hand to Pallas, surrounded by the attributes of manufacturing and embossed with the words: Domestic Handicraft Protected 6 April 1799.[100]

The tension between patriotic protectionism and natural deregulation fundamentally shaped the debates about smuggling and its definition during the second half of the eighteenth century. It can be seen in economic literature, debates about new legislation as well as in newspaper discussions where the smuggling problem was an ongoing issue of contention. Although patriotic protectionism triumphed at the end of the century, the debates surrounding it reveal that Sweden was deeply divided in the face of threatening global wares, far from the unified front the protectionists yearned for. While oppositional voices were silenced in the press in the 1790s, as later chapters will explore, it did not mean that smuggling was as easily restrained. Before turning to the smuggling itself, however, it is worth spending a bit of time exploring the other discussions that emerged in the wake of the smuggling problem, as they highlight a society in the process of change.

Revoked Rights & New Rights

An Old Right – Hemfrid and House-Visitation

Sweden had, as Jonas Nordin has pointed out, a long tradition of freedom, which was an important part of the Swedish self-perception. This was a common, rather than individual freedom, and was not handed out unconditionally but tied up with expectations of certain behaviours – based on concerns for godliness and the common good.[101] It included the right to be involved in the creation of laws and regulations but also the duty to be obedient to these laws. As Nordin notes: "[t]o offend against the authorities thus became the same as to offend against the common good – or even against the freedom itself!".[102] Sweden had an established discourse on rights and freedoms which dictated that its inhabitants were not just subservient to the state but also had certain privileges.

A crucial facet of this freedom, the freedom from oppression, did, however, come under increased pressure in the eighteenth century with the rise of the house-visitation. The house-visitation or house search was a crucial tool in the persecution of smugglers and had a prominent role in the Swedish eighteenth-century anti-smuggling legislation. It was also a highly controversial tool as it was seen, by defenders and opponents alike, to infringe upon the old Swedish right of house or home peace (*hus-* or *hemfrid)*. The origins of the *hemfrid* laws – or as it is translated in a 1757 dictionary, 'the King's peace' – can be found in mediaeval legislation. They originate in the mediaeval peace laws: the Anglo-Saxon laws (seventh century), the God's Peace of Saxony (1084), and Barbarossa's Landfrieden (1152) all contain examples of such peace-laws.[103] These laws were all intended to reduce blood feuding and violence and thus ensure peace. The same is also true for the Swedish *Edsöreslagarna*, which can be traced back to the eleventh century but were first ratified by Birger Jarl (c.1210–1266); they included: *hemfrid*, church peace (*kyrkofrid*), assembly peace (*tingsfrid*), and peace for women (*kvinnofrid*) and were first written down in the 1290s, in the provincial law of Östergötland.[104] Freedom from violent assault was central in these peace laws, but their exact scope changed over time.

In 1335, the idea of protection of property was added to the notion of *hemfrid* "for each and every one owns freely their properties and money".[105] Swedish legislation retained the connection between house peace and protection of property. In 1734, a new Civil Code replaced the National Law of Christopher dating back to 1442. The section concerning *hemfrid* (Missgärningsbalken, cap. XX) in this new national legislation also included protection against robbery *(rån)*, which despite its misleading name refers to burglary. By this point the protection of house peace was clearly linked to both the individual within the property and the property itself. While the sanctity of the home in itself was not problematic, a freedom *from* also meant that there could be a freedom *to*; as historian Patricia Meyer Spacks has observed, privacy could constitute a type of enablement.[106]

During the second half of the eighteenth century, the tension between the protection of *hemfrid* and the potential misuses it could inspire came to the fore. The house-visitation was not new; the practice of searching the houses of Swedish subjects for contraband had already been introduced in 1739.[107] In 1762, it was revoked when King Adolph Friedrick prohibited the use of visitations for the protection and safety of his subjects.[108] A mere four years later, following much complaint from the manufacturers, he reinstated the visitation, but only in properties where illegal business was known to occur, particularly in the rooms of lackeys and valets.[109] In 1768, an addendum was issued which sought to encourage more visitations. It stipulated that the fine for pain and suffering normally given to the victims of unsuccessful searches by the visiting officers would be reduced. Furthermore, they dropped the requirement that the officers had to announce the name of the person they intended to search and the reasons for the search before the visitation. Instead, a justification for the search would only be required after a failed visitation, and if the court deemed the grounds to be sufficient, the visiting officer would be released of all responsibility and freed from the payment of the fine. At the same time, the responsibility for judging the appropriateness of the visitations moved from the Common Court to the Customs Court.[110]

Jonas Björnsson and his memorandum on how to combat smuggling presented at the riksdag in 1770 have been touched on previously. In it he particularly focused on the house-visitation, arguing that free, but responsible house-visitations in all open shops as well as storages and hidden rooms were necessary in order to tackle smuggling.[111] Others agreed; a memorandum put forward by the National Board of Trade to the riksdag argued: "House-visitations have been seen as the most powerful means to impede Smuggling and the salvation of the Manufacturer from a threatening destruction".[112] In the subsequent 1770 anti-smuggling decree, the house-visitation featured prominently, although it was no longer to be allowed in the houses of non-traders.[113]

The renewed use of the house-visitation evoked protests, particularly from the Silk and Cloth Trader Society who in 1772 sent a letter to the National Board of Trade. They argued that while the house-visitation was often described as a 'suitable cure' for smuggling, it was merely a distraction that impeded the common freedom and security while the real problem, the dearness and poor quality of the Swedish manufactures, was left unresolved.[114] Just like the debates about patriotic protectionism and natural rights, the discussion about the house-visitation came to focus on the tension between rights and obligations. Whereas protectionism remained in place for the duration of the period studied here, this was not true for the house-visitation, which on numerous occasions was successfully contested, leading to legislative change.

A Press for Privacy?

The house-visitation and its changing legal status also attracted comment in the press. Early on, the house-visitation was described as a possible solution to prevent the 'flood' of contraband wares entering Sweden, but this positive approach was increasingly challenged during the last decades of the century.[115] In 1773, rumours were flying around Stockholm that universal house-searches were to be prohibited, inciting a fierce debate in the newspapers. The debate appears to have been started by the commentator 'Lover of the Country's Wellbeing' (*Älskare af Rikets Wältrefnad*) who urged those alarmed by the house-visitation to think of the benefits to the manufactories.[116] In a terse reply, 'Danaus' argued that while he cared deeply for the manufactories he was not willing to sacrifice common safety and security for their sake. If the visitation only affected the smugglers, 'Danaus' explained, then there would be no problem. He doubted, however, that the officers searching homes would be discerning and mistakes were inevitable. Wrongful searches would inflict fear and infamy on the affected family, whether they were guilty or not.[117] 'Lover of the Country's Wellbeing' dismissed this concern, maintaining that no honest member of society had anything to fear from such a measure.[118] The dangers and benefits of the house-visitation were central aspects in the debates throughout the period. While most commentators could see both sides of the argument, they disagreed on which took precedence: the protection of the economic state or the protection of the subjects' freedom.

Who exactly would suffer or benefit from the house-visitation was also up for debate. Some commentators maintained that the universal house-visitation was necessary since while "[s]mall thieves are hanged, the great go free", a notion based on the perception that great people's homes were protected as private spaces, allowing domestic servants to freely deal in contraband while only the unprotected retailers were punished for their crimes.[119] Other commentators did not see this as a solution. 'Hater of the Use of Smuggling Goods' (*Hatare til Bruk af Lurendrägare=Gods*), for example, maintained that even with house-visitations, small-time criminals would still be convicted while the big remained free, since the 'true' owner would store their illegal goods with others thus distancing themselves from the crime.[120] The house-visitation, they argued, targeted the most vulnerable, those used by the protected elites to hide their contraband but also exposed to the authority of the visitation officers.

In this way, the newspaper debates came to touch upon the usefulness of the visitation as a tool to prevent smuggling, the effects of control and its potential benefits and dangers for the population at large. It was, however, clear to many commentators that the house-visitations were not only difficult to manage but also posed a threat to the common safety and freedom. Voices were thus raised in support of a new approach, which instead focused on reducing the demand for smuggled goods. One such suggestion was the introduction of a mandatory national costume made from Swedish produced cloth, which would eliminate the need and demand for foreign manufactures.[121]

Freedom in the Fold: The National Costume

The idea of a national costume, made exclusively from Swedish textiles, was by no means restricted to the realm of the press; in the 1770s, under the direction of the new King Gustav III, it became perceived as a viable solution to the smuggling problem. Gustav III had ascended to the throne in 1771 and the following year, he performed a coup d'état to take back power from the riksdag. While the King was criticised for his despotism by the Estates, he framed it as a victory for the 'right' or 'true' liberty of the people.[122] In particular, Gustav III stressed that he was restoring old Swedish freedoms and liberating the commoners from the grip of the aristocracy. Patriotism, and returning to the Swedish 'roots', became a particular goal, and it was expressed in various 'nationalistic projects'.[123] Meanwhile, Gustav III also strove to find a solution to the smuggling problem that combined common freedom and patriotism.

Gustav III prohibited the use of house-visitations on 16 July 1776 with the motivation that while visitations might have prevented the trade in contraband to some extent, this was not reason enough for disturbing the domestic peace of his lawful subjects. Indeed, the King maintained that the house-visitations were contrary to his new regime, based on common peace and security. A blanket ban on visitations was therefore introduced for the entire kingdom, a ban which should be accompanied by a rise in the border patrols and an initiative to improve domestic manufactures.[124] The King also approached his newly installed cabinet asking them to investigate new ways to control smuggling in co-operation with the National Board of Trade.[125] It was not the first time that less oppressive techniques to control smuggling had been sought: in 1773 it had already been up for debate without any resolution being found.[126] However, Gustav III identified a potential solution in his own nationalistic projects.

The idea of a national costume was presented in 1773, in the form of an essay competition instigated by the King and administered by the Royal Patriotic Society. Its purpose was to explore the benefits and disadvantages of such a costume.[127] One of the explicit objectives of the essay competition was to explore whether a national costume might root out smuggling.[128] Competition entries identified many benefits, including its usefulness in preventing vanity and extravagance, and how it could help to sustain sartorial hierarchy. It was also hoped that it would inspire nationalism and unify the population while helping to support Swedish industry and preventing the importation of foreign goods.[129] Despite this early start, the costume itself was not launched until 28 April 1778. The costume was designed by the King himself, inspired by the Burgundian costumes of the seventeenth century, and made entirely with Swedish textiles. In conjunction with the release of the costume, Gustav III published his thoughts about it, pointing explicitly to the impossibility of controlling smuggling as one of the main motivations behind its introduction.

> with a glance at the geographical situation of the kingdom, we can see that our coasts are too extensive to defend against bold and enterprising smugglers, encouraged by potential gain. We must cut the evil at its root, and make it impossible for us to be copies…[130]

For the King, the best method for controlling the consumption of contraband was evident. The new consumer practices would be controlled through national normative control, which, he mused, would lead to the salvation of the Swedish manufactures.

> … it is believed that the expected change will be detrimental to the factories; but, I dare say, nothing is more wrong than this objection. Our factories, constantly forced to compete against foreign designs, which they merely imitate after the fashion for them has faded, now confined to producing fabrics of a single colour, will soon be able to perfect them and even match the foreign manufactures in beauty. Hence, contraband will cease, and the ease and cheapness of the domestic stuffs will soon outdo those that according to the interests of the state and the laws are prohibited.[131]

The combination of common freedom and patriotism thus came to be epitomised in the national costume, which enabled Gustav III to cancel the house-visitation and to re-establish house peace while simultaneously ensuring continued support for the Swedish manufactories and a rejection of foreign wares.

Far from everyone found this solution appealing, however, and in December 1778, one newspaper notice by 'Backenbergen dweller and People' (*Bakebergenbo och folk*) noted that forcing people to refrain from foreign goods and to wear a national uniform simply was not good enough for a "free people".[132] Indeed, he argued, smuggling could never be eradicated completely "for Man will be Man". [133]

Freedom Infringed

Eventually, the King also reached this conclusion and in 1785 he was obliged to file a revocation of the 1776 decree with the justification that the freedoms he had awarded to his subjects had been abused. The new 1785 decree only allowed visitations in shops and storage houses belonging to those with the right to sell domestic and foreign goods, which meant that the majority of the population would still be spared the tribulations of a visitation. Such shop and storage visitations would, according to the decree, not be detrimental to the *hemfrid* or public security.[134]

The new decree appears to have resulted in a truce between the two camps and the issue lay dormant until 1793 when the National Board of Trade wrote a letter to the King. This letter was also published in the newspaper *Stockholms Posten* on the initiative of the Society of Manufacturers (*Fabriks Societeten*). It concerned the state of the Swedish industry, which, according to the National Board of Trade, had stagnated. For some time, the letter claimed, the desire for foreign goods had overridden all patriotic feeling, which had led to a considerable increase in the introduction of foreign contraband. This 'acute' situation prompted the Society of Manufacturers to complain to the National Board of Trade and request that universal house-visitations should be reintroduced.[135] The National Board of Trade agreed and maintained that the 1785 decree, which allowed the visitation of shops and storages, was insufficient as it omitted many spaces where goods could be stored and trade conducted. Universal visitations, the National Board of Trade argued, were a necessary precondition, enabling the smuggling decrees to fulfil their purpose.[136]

The letter by the National Board of Trade provoked anger, with one newspaper commenter lamenting: "It is infallible that house and home peace, is one of the first rights a Citizen should enjoy in a free Kingdom".[137] Gustav III's cancellation of the house-visitation, another commentator argued, had been motivated by a desire to avoid confusing the innocent and the guilty, which previously had caused plenty of distrust and ill-will among the population. Improvement of the factories was instead the only sound way to combat smuggling.[138]

Freedom Withdrawn

Despite public concerns over the National Board of Trade's letter, the idea that new measures were required to control smuggling found a supporter in the future King, Gustav IV Adolph. When he installed a committee to investigate the possibilities of creating a new smuggling decree in 1798/99, the house-visitations came to be one of the main issues under discussion. One committee member, Count Gyllenborg, argued that while a new anti-smuggling decree was important in order to safeguard both the citizens' rights and safety as well as the manufactories, it was very difficult, perhaps impossible, to combine these two objectives. Gyllenborg reasoned that all searches of domestic residences should be avoided as the price was too high – too many innocents were affected, including women and children, and even if nothing was ever found a good name and reputation would be irrevocably tainted.[139] However, he was as good as alone on the committee in arguing against the domestic house-visitation. Indeed, both Assistant Judge Chierlin and J. I. Osangius both maintained that the common good should be prioritised over individual freedom.[140] Assistant Judge Brohmmer went one step further and had no reservations about the use of the visitation at all.[141] According to Brohmmer, the visitation was the most important tool for suppressing the "cancerous" spread of smuggling.[142] In other words, while the loss of *hemfrid* was seen as problematic by the majority of the legislators, it was still considered a necessary evil in the fight against smuggling.

The 1799 anti-smuggling decree proved to be the most extensive to date and featured the re-introduction of universal house-visitations.[143] It did not put an end to the controversy surrounding house-visitations, however, which remained a contested tool. In 1800, the riksdag convened and the anti-smuggling decree, particularly the use of house-visitations, was debated. Representatives of the burgher estate opposed the universal visitations and argued that they were suffering at the hands of unscrupulous law enforcers. Consequently, they asked that the visitations should be restricted to places where they would be less taxing, such as in border regions and in specific customs spaces. Furthermore, they asked that houses, roads, and inns should be exempted from the visitation in order to protect the *hemfrid*.[144]

The concept of *hemfrid* belonged to the old rights that constituted a core in the Swedish self-image of a free people, and there existed a more or less common agreement that this right was important.[145] It guaranteed the subjects freedom from oppression and safety in their own homes, along with their property. *Hemfrid* was intended to reinforce peace and harmony in society, but as it allowed people protected by the privacy of their homes to clandestinely act against the interests of the state, it was also highly problematic. While house-peace was supposed to ensure common wellbeing, infringements against it could also undermine the right itself because it no longer protected the common good.

Throughout the period, the National Board of Trade maintained its position as one of the fiercest defenders of protectionism and the use of the house-visitation. However, the influence of the Board varied over time and under different systems of government. King Adolph Fredrick and his son Gustav III both opposed the house-visitation, but while Adolph Fredrick's cancellation of house searches in 1762 lasted only four years before it was overturned by the National Board of Trade, Gustav III, who through his coup d'état had regained some of the power lost by the crown during the preceding proto-parliamentarian period, managed to maintain his 1776 cancellation for nine years before he agreed to re-introduce limited house searches. By contrast, Gustav IV Adolph gave free rein to the National Board of Trade, which led to an increased focus on control and less attention to rights and freedoms. The conflict between the ancient right to *hemfrid* and the desire to control smuggling, together with the shifting political power balance helps to explain why the visitation legislation underwent considerable changes during this period as new political incentives and interests developed.

While the universal visitation was reintroduced towards the end of the period, there was never a satisfactory solution to the issue of *hemfrid*. Indeed, following the Revolution of 1809, which overthrew Gustav IV Adolph, the riksdag would readdress the issue of the visitation and the damage it caused to society.[146]

A New Right: Consumer Choice and Patriotic Consumption

The discourse of patriotic consumption and the right to consume freely came to prominence in the final decade of the eighteenth century. It emerged in the debates because while the creation of a protectionist state and the safeguarding of the manufactories could in theory be achieved through legislation, prohibition, and duty hikes, in reality the continued access to foreign goods on the Swedish black market meant that the consumers played a key role in this process. The consumers had the power to either strengthen or undermine the country's protectionist ambitions through their consumer choices. Meanwhile, a new notion of free consumer choice was on the rise.

Consumption in Sweden had long been regulated through legislation, and the propagation of patriotic consumption had been an ingrained feature of the sumptuary decrees at least since the emergence of the first nationwide decree in 1664. An important aim of the sumptuary laws was to define the Swedes, through dress, as something different to other groups of people.[147] How people consumed, and particularly what they wore, was seen as deeply linked to who they were. The purpose of the sumptuary decrees was thus to reject foreign influences and to re-establish a 'Swedish' mode of dress and, subsequently, 'natural' Swedish inhabitants unspoiled by foreign influences.[148] During the period under consideration in this book, three general sumptuary decrees were issued: 1766, 1770, and 1794. They were intended to reduce foreign influences but also to re-establish a visual hierarchical order, with unique dress codes for each estate. In addition to the sumptuary decrees there were also other attempts to control consumption and ensure patriotic consumption through the introduction of new norms, the most notable being Gustav III's national costume. Such regulatory measures were intended to standardise consumer behaviour by prescribing how Swedish consumers ought to consume. They also suggest that free consumer choice was considered a disorderly and destructive force. This is further supported by previous research on eighteenth-century consumption, which has shown that there existed a contemporary concern with excessive consumer choice, particularly for women, which, it was believed, would lead to a neglect of duty.[149] Such ideas are reminiscent of those of the patriotic protectionists, relying on a belief that the population was in need of regulation to hinder their destructive tendencies. Historian Erik Bodsten has linked this idea to the Christian view of man as flawed, in need of superior control to maintain "normative moral societal order".[150]

Patriotic consumption was not simply something imposed on an unwilling population; it also became fashionable in itself as it was perceived to signal a devotion to duty, the fatherland, and the common good. It became particularly popular among (elite) citizens who saw it as part of their social role to strengthen the nation through their consumer choices.[151]

At the same time, two parallel and partially interconnected shifts were underway. The definition of citizenship expanded to include more groups in society, including peasants and workers, while the right to consume freely gained increasing support.[152] This coincided with a re-evaluation of the state, which went from being conceived as a single organism to being considered as constituting of a multitude of individuals – with certain rights.[153] Individual rights derived from the discourse on natural rights, and it strengthened the individual in relation to the state and highlighted that citizens should enjoy certain rights.[154] In this way, the relationship between citizen and state was being reconfigured in the late eighteenth century, which impacted on the discussions about consumer choice and what obligations individual citizens had in preventing smuggling.

Swimming Against the Tide

In 1793 the Duke Regent Charles, who governed on behalf of his underage nephew, future Gustav IV Adolph, issued a request to all parishes to discuss the potential introduction of a new sumptuary decree as a way to improve the state of Swedish finances and reduce the consumption of foreign goods. Each parish was asked which wares and practices they were willing to give up for this patriotic cause.[155] A committee was charged with evaluating the responses and assessing the potential for a new decree. It noted that foreign wares had long been brought into the country both legally and illegally, and that citizens in general imagined them to be superior in quality and cheaper in price to domestic manufactures. Continued access to illegal wares on the Swedish market: "puts the [citizens'] Patriotism to a test, as it demands the sacrifice of one's own supposed profits, which [their Patriotism] rarely or ever survived".[156] Thus, it was argued, patriotism as such could not trump other consumer concerns, real or imagined, and for this reason, it was necessary to regulate consumer choice through sumptuary law – as it had in earlier times.

Shortly thereafter, in August of 1793, a memorandum handed in to a parish meeting in Örebro earlier in the summer was published in the newspaper *Stockholms Posten*. The text, authored by Johan Bergström, maintained that the common people targeted in the parish discussions were also members of society and as such had right to certain freedoms. He suggested that those who laboured the most should enjoy the possibility of reaping the benefits of their hard work.

> I am therefore of the impossible belief, that the sumptuousness in dress, which has established itself among the working classes has been possibly more beneficial than damaging, and that this Class's so-called luxury in dress should be easier to allow than the extravagancies of the better sorts. … It is not the common people's fault if they use smuggled goods … and it is not their business to distinguish the foreign from the domestic.[157]

Importantly, Bergström pointed out that it was not the (poor) consumer's responsibility to ensure that the goods they bought were legal nor should they be tasked with salvaging the state finances. Instead, he suggested that they deserved the right to make their consumer choices freely. Bergström insisted that the root of the problem was to be found with the middle and upper ranks of society – those who dictated fashions. Their behaviour, he argued, was much more influential than any laws or regulations.[158] Bergström's views stand in stark contrast to those of the higher classes, who according to historian Leif Runefelt, feared egalitarian consumer practices. Runefelt has argued that this concern became gradually more pressing towards the end of the century, because consumption increased and consumer choice expanded, thus challenging the visual hierarchy.[159] Although fears of egalitarian consumption may have existed, particularly within certain circles of society, the sumptuary decree was on its last legs.

Nevertheless, the new regime made one last attempt to introduce a sumptuary decree. When the new sumptuary decree was published in 1794, its proclaimed objective was to address the poor situation of the Swedish finances and to "conquer the prejudice which unfortunately has maintained a regrettable desire for foreign goods within the Nation".[160] In contrast to earlier decrees, this one stipulated that the regulations were the same for all members of society. The decree prohibited men "of all estates" to use silk, apart from for trousers, scarves, knee and shoe roses, and various other adornments. Women were instructed not to wear silk, or make dresses, sweaters, or skirts from cambric, linon, or moll muslin, which were all thin cotton fabrics.[161] While sumptuary legislation for a long time had been used to stabilise social order and hierarchy, as well as to enforce patriotic feeling and unity, it was finally falling out of fashion.[162] According to Runefelt, the end of the sumptuary decree was brought on by the emergence of a new type of self-regulation which distinguished the elite from the lower ranks, through the development of a polite (*bon ton*) urban culture.[163]

While the sumptuary decree was fading from relevance, consumption was expanding to incorporate more groups, including workers and peasants who during this time were also extended the title 'citizen'.[164] The smuggling debates usually did not distinguish between estates, but the state was normally considered one consuming unit. Similarly, the final sumptuary decree issued in 1794 incorporated new ideas of equal, although not free, consumer rights. It legislated that everyone should engage in patriotic consumption but they should do so on equal terms.

Free Choice for the Masses?

It was, however, not certain that the new consumers wanted to engage in patriotic consumption. In the newspaper, voices were raised against consumer regulation. One commentator with the signature 'M ===== S=====' argued that the search for comfort and distinction was natural for human beings and as such, the sumptuary decrees along with the import prohibitions aimed to achieve something impossible, to recast man in a new shape. The fault, the author argued, lay in the laws and not in the consumers; pointing to the ongoing French Revolution, he maintained that the suppression of people's desires and choices could have dangerous consequences.[165] In a reply '---s----m' answered that the former clearly did not understand the population at all. The problem was not restricting consumption per se, but in the consumption of foreign goods. According to this commentator, the higher ranked consumers could abuse the lower estates and consume as they saw fit as long as they consumed Swedish goods. Their loyalty to the nation could thus be measured through their choice to consume Swedish wares. It was the consumption of foreign goods which was the true betrayal of the Swedish workers. Echoing many commentators before him, he concluded, that every ell of smuggled cloth prevented Swedish citizens from being useful, reducing them instead to poverty.[166] A clear disconnect can be observed between these writers, the first recognising that the commoners were also consumers who desired choice and the latter confining the commoners to the role of producers in need of wages.

While consumption motivated by a single desire – to preserve and support Swedish industry – was promoted in the patriotic consumer discourse, consumers themselves had different concerns and priorities. Their behaviour did not fit into a uniform mould. The sanctimoniousness that was frequently expressed by the supporters of patriotic consumption prompted one commentator to observe that such notions were obsolete:

> You are repeating the eternal cry against smuggling; but what does your conscience say? Have you never purchased a for import prohibited manufactured ware from someone, when you have found it better and to a cheaper price, than those of domestic production. The cry is preposterous, as long as you and every Individual do not own the public virtue, to never buy smuggled goods...[167]

Just like the discussions about protectionism, and the house-visitations, the debate about the right to choose also came to centre on the ambiguous relationship between the state and its citizens, and which rights took precedence. Increasing attention was given to the individual right to choose freely based on personal needs. In contrast to the right to house peace, the common right to choose freely was still in its infancy. Rather than being based on thoughts of the common good, it was founded on ideas about the natural rights of individuals to make decisions that benefited themselves and not only the state. As consumption was not only an individual act but also had an effect on the state at large, it could be used either to support the domestic manufactories or to undermine the country's economic integrity. Consequently, the right to make free consumer choices remained a highly contested phenomenon. However, the newspaper discussions do not answer the question of whether commoner consumers themselves only were interested in chasing fashions and a cheaper price, or whether they too were concerned with patriotic consumption. I will return to these questions in Chapter 5.

*****

During the eighteenth century, protectionist policies, import prohibitions, and anti-smuggling legislation were issued at an ever-increasing rate which helped to codify and define the Swedish economic area. This chapter has explored how conceptions of smuggling in Sweden changed under the influence of the various political and conceptual shifts that occurred in the eighteenth and early nineteenth centuries. It has considered how smuggling was defined according to two of the main economic lines of thought at the time, and how tools to control smuggling ran into conflict with pre-existing and developing ideas of rights. More specifically, it has shown that the definitions and perceptions of smuggling, and its associated issues, were created and re-created through an interactive process between theoretical ideas and actual conditions.

Smuggling appears to have been debated in many European countries in the eighteenth century. While these debates might have been born out of a general protectionist fervour and challenged by enlightenment ideas, in each country, they were also shaped by domestic concerns and conditions. In Sweden, smuggling first became a serious issue for scrutiny and debate with the emergence of patriotic protectionism in the early eighteenth century. This patriotic protectionism built on notions of citizen co-operation for the common good, and self-sacrifice for the betterment of the state. It was portrayed as a communal project for the Swedish citizens and within this context smuggling came to be defined not only as a betrayal of the state but also of fellow citizens. Condemnation was not restricted to the smuggler but extended to all Swedish inhabitants who traitorously consumed illegal foreign wares, contrary to the interests of the state. This interpretation of smuggling was, however, challenged by natural rights proponents calling for individual and trade liberties. In contrast to the patriotic protectionists, they understood smuggling as a symptom of an unnatural and oppressive regulatory system. While they did not consider smuggling as a severe threat in and of itself, the proponents of this approach argued that it was a sign of an ineffectual system which could only be corrected through the removal of trade barriers. The discussion between the patriotic protectionists and the natural rights proponents was tightly interlinked with the Swedish proto-parliamentarianism of the first half of the eighteenth century, which encouraged open debate and diverse opinions, particularly after 1766 when the Freedom of the Press Act was passed. The two interpretations of smuggling might have been born during the Age of Liberty (1718–1772) but they remained influential in the newspaper debates throughout the subsequent period of absolutism and the early regency period, lasting into the 'iron years' after 1796.

Despite a diverse debate, the legislation adopted, particularly after 1766, was increasingly protectionist, drawing heavily on the patriotic protectionist discourse. The legislation does, however, also bear marks of the influence of natural right and natural law, which becomes particularly clear when considering the prescribed punishments for smuggling offences. While the legislation indicates that while the state's economic objectives became progressively more protectionist during the second half of the eighteenth century, the state refrained from the punitive actions suggested by hard-line protectionists instead bearing the hallmarks of enlightenment thought.

Sweden was not a blank legislative canvas, however, and the anti-smuggling legislation had to contend with pre-existing ideas of rights and freedoms, some of which had for centuries been protected by law. Such was the case with the house-visitation, which was seen by many as a threat to the old established freedom from oppression and right to house peace that had long been important. The public refutation of the house-visitations resulted in changes in legislation. Legislative changes were not only related to ideological shifts or 'the will of the people' but also depended on how the state was run, and its objectives; something that emerges starkly in Gustav III's 'liberation' of his people from the house-visitation in 1776. In this case, the prohibition of the house-visitations should not be interpreted as diminishing protectionism, but as a new stance on how to enforce it. Indeed, Gustav III's solution to the issue of smuggling, the launch of a national costume, infringed upon another, newer, and arguably less important freedom, the freedom of choice.

While anti-smuggling legislation was running into conflict with pre-existing ideas of freedoms, new ideas of individual rights were also emerging that had a bearing on the discussions about smuggling. In the 1790s in particular, new ideas of rights were emerging, and the definition of citizenship started to expand. While the old patriotic protectionist interpretation saw the workers as producers of wares in need of support, these same workers were now suddenly appearing as consumers in their own right. There was also, in the newspapers and in the legislation, an increased recognition of the population as a uniform consumer mass, which should be induced to engage in patriotic consumption. Around the same time, voices were also raised in support of the right to choose freely, particularly among the poorer sorts, who, it was argued, should be allowed to purchase good quality products cheaply. This meant that state control, while being intended for the 'common good', was by some perceived as an affront to the liberty and freedom of the Swedish population. In this context, the smuggler was seen to cater for the needs and desires of an oppressed population rather than being a traitor. However, while such ideas can be observed in the press, they were quickly stamped out through the increasing of press regulation and replaced with a celebration of patriotic protectionism.

The last years of the regency government saw a crackdown on various rights and liberties as the future King Gustav Adolph became ever more involved in state affairs. After 1796, new and extended censorship legislation put an end to the freedom and smuggling debates in the regular press and in 1799, the harshest anti-smuggling legislation to date was released.

The discourse of smuggling was shaped by competing ideas about economy, rights, and the relationship between the state and its citizens. The laws and legislation changed over time, reflecting both changing ideologies and systems of government. While the general tendency was towards increasing regulation and protectionism under the guidance of various forms of government, committee proceedings, newspapers, and economic literature allow us to observe another vein of thought about natural rights, liberalised trade and citizens' rights, which existed alongside patriotic protectionism. Over time proponents of deregulation found their public platform infringed upon and their voices silenced, but the existence of these ideas suggests that despite increasingly severe anti-smuggling legislation, there existed another interpretation of smuggling – one which might not have been deemed appropriate to express in the newspapers, but which might nevertheless have had an impact on the treatment of smugglers and the consumption of contraband in practice.

Notes

1 Farrell, 'Smuggling Silks into Eighteenth-Century Britain', 269; Gottmann, *Global Trade,* 54.
2 Jakob Christensson, *Lyckoriket: Studier i svensk upplysning* (Stockholm: Atlantis, 1996), 128–158; Carl Wennerlind, 'Atlantis Restored: Natural Knowledge and Political Economy in Early Modern Sweden.' *American Historical Review.* 2022. Vol. 127. No. 4.
3 Wennerlind, 'Atlantis Restored'.
4 Magnusson, 'Den ekonomiska diskussionen under frihetstiden – Ett framlängesperspektiv', in *Riksdag, kaffehus och predikstol. Frihetstidens politiska kultur 1766–1772,* ed. Marie-Christine Skuncke and Henrietta Tandefelt (Stockholm: Atlantis, 2003), 25 & 30; Wennerlind, 'Atlantis Restored'.
5 Sven-Eric Liedman, *Den synliga handen: Anders Berch och ekonomiämnena vid 1700-talets svenska universitet* (Göteborg & Stockholm: Arbetarkultur, 1986), 200.
6 Monika Edgren, *Från rike till nation arbetskraftspolitik, befolkningspolitik och nationell gemenskapsformering i Sverige under 1700-talet* (Lund: Historisk Media, 2001), 33.
7 Edgren, 33.
8 Jani Marjanen, 'Den ekonomiska patriotismens uppgång och fall. Finska hushållningssällskapet i europeisk, svensk och finsk kontext 1720–1840' (PhD thesis, Helsingfors universitet, 2013), 269; Jani Marjanen, 'Moral Economy and Civil Society in Eighteenth Century Europe: The Case of Economic Societies and Business of Improvement', *Journal of Global Ethics* 11, no. 2 (2015), 209. While Jani Marjanen uses the term 'economic patriotism' I will here use the term 'patriotic protectionism' to stress the centrality of protectionism in the Swedish economic policy.
9 Anders Berch, *Inledning til almänna hushålningen, innefattande grunden til politie, oeconomie och cameral wetenskaperne. til deras tiänst, som biwista de almänne föreläsningar inrättad* (Stockholm, 1747), 314–315.
10 Edgren, *Från rike till nation,* 33.
11 Berch, *Inledning til almänna hushålningen*, 314–315.
12 This is something which occurs both sides of the political spectrum, both in the work of Johan Fredrik Kryger, *Tankar wid lediga stunder* (Stockholm: Tryckt på Direct. Lars Salvii förlag, 1761), 301–302; and Anders Nordencrantz, *Bekymmerlösa stunders menlösa och owälduga tankar,* vol. 1 (Stockholm: 1767–70), 35.
13 Berch, *Inledning til almänna hushålningen,* 314–315.
14 Berch, 314.

15 Berch, 315.
16 His textbook remained standard at universities until 1829 when it was replaced by Lars Georg Rabenius' new *Lärobok i nationalekonomien;* see Lars Magnusson, *The Tradition of Free Trade* (Abingdon: Routledge, 2004), 141.
17 Johan Fredrik Kryger, *Tankar wid lediga stunder* (Stockholm: Tryckt på Direct. Lars Salvii förlag, 1761), 288.
18 Magnusson, Äran, Korruptionen Och Den Borgerliga Ordningen, 46.
19 Kryger, *Tankar wid lediga stunder,* 199; this has also been observed by Magnusson, *Äran, korruptionen och den borgerliga ordningen, essäer från svensk ekonomihistoria* (Stockholm: Atlantis, 2001), 48.
20 Kryger, *Tankar wid lediga stunder,* 317–318.
21 Kryger, 292.
22 Kryger, 295.
23 Kryger, 293.
24 Kryger, 289.
25 Kryger, 296–300.
26 Kryger, 301–302.
27 Kryger, 303–307; Kryger also addressed the slightly stranger argument that fishing cost just as much as the import of foreign cloth. This he said was both correct and incorrect; see page 308.
28 Kryger, 311–313.
29 Kryger, 316.
30 Kryger, 288, & 314–315.
31 Magnusson, *The Tradition of Free Trade,* 129 & 134.
32 Lars Hertlitz, 'Anders Nordencrantz', https://sok.riksarkivet.se/sbl/artikel/8203, *Svenskt biografiskt lexikon,* Accessed 1 March 2022; Magnusson, *The Tradition of Free Trade,* 135.
33 Magnusson, *The Tradition of Free Trade,* 129 & 134.
34 Nordencrantz, *Bekymmerlösa stunders menlösa och owälduga tankar,* 35.
35 Nordencrantz, 35.
36 Nordencrantz, 34.
37 Lundqvist, 'Förbjudna Tyger', 203.
38 Magnusson, 'Den ekonomiska diskussionen under frihetstiden', 28.
39 See 'Vederläggning af de skäl, hvarmed man söker bestrida Öster- och Vesterbottniska samt Vesternorrländska städerna fri seglation', in Anders Chydenius, *Politiska Skrifter* (Helsinki, 1880), 87.
40 Tore Frängsmyr, 'Johan Fredrik Kryger', https://sok.riksarkivet.se/sbl/artikel/11836, *Svenskt biografiskt lexikon,* Accessed 1 March 2022.
41 Eli P. Heckscher, 'Anders Chydenius', https://sok.riksarkivet.se/sbl/artikel/14849, *Svenskt biografiskt lexikon,* Accessed 1 March 2022.
42 Patrik Winton, 'Sweden and the Seven Years War, 1757–1762: War, Debt and Politics', *War in History,* 19 (2012), 21–23.
43 Patrik Winton, 'Parliamentary Control, Public Discussion and Royal Autonomy: Sweden, 1750–1780', *Histoire & Mesure* XXX, no. 2 (2015), 66.
44 Magnusson, 'Den ekonomiska diskussionen under frihetstiden', 26.
45 'Kongl. maj:ts ytterligare nådige förordning, til hämmande af lurendrägerier och inpracticeringar af utrikes waror, gifwen Stockholm i råd=cammaren den 21. maji 1739' (1739).
46 'Kongl. maj:ts ytterligare nådige förordning, angående lurendrägeriers uptäckande och hämmande' (1757).; 'Kongl. maj:ts nådige resolution och förklaring, uppå de allmänna beswär, som…städerne i swerige och finland… andragit' (1762), 31§.
47 'Kongl. maj:ts nådige förordning, til lurendrägeriers hämmande' (1766); 'Kongl. maj:ts ytterligare nådiga förordning, till lurendrägeriers hämmande. gifwen i råd-cammaren then 18 april 1768' (1768).

48 *Riksens hoglofl. ständers handels- och manufactur-deputations berättelse, angående de swenske manufacturers tilstånd och beskaffenhet ifrån 1764 til 1768 års slut* (Stockholm: Kongl. Finska Boktryckeriet, 1769), 4–5.
49 '21 Sep 1769', Handels- & Manuf & Tull Deputs Betänkande För Åren 1769–1770,' 1769, Borgareståndets arkiv, R1402, 1769–1770, vol. 6, Riksarkivet.
50 Jonas Biörnsson, *Riksdagsmannens Jonas Biörnssons märkwärdiga memorial* (Stockholm, 1770).
51 All previous anti-smuggling legislation would be included save for the one issued on the 7th of October 1766, which concerned the surveillance of people conducting illicit trade: see 'Riksens ständer handels och manufactur samt tull deputationens betänkande angående en förnyas förordning emot Lurendrägerier och Tullförsnillning given wid Riksdagen i Stockholm den 19 Januarii 1770', Handels- & Manuf & Tull Deputs Betänkande För Åren 1769–1770,' 1769, Borgareståndets arkiv, R1402, 1769–1770, vol. 6, Riksarkivet.
52 'Kongl. maj:ts förnyade förordning emot yppighet och öfwerflöd. 15 martii 1770' (1770). The goods that were prohibited included arrack, French liquors, rum and various wines, 'desserts' apart from those made with Swedish fruits, and the use of silk among commoners.
53 'Kongl. maj:ts taxa, hwarefter stora sjö=tullen uppå alla inommande waror bör erläggas och upbäras, 15 feb 1771' (1771).
54 Erik Anners, 'Straffteorierna i svensk rättshistoria', *Svensk Juristtidning* (1964), 241–242.
55 Anners, 242–243.
56 Jonas Nordin, *Ett fattigt men fritt folk. Nationell och politisk självbild i Sverige från sen stormaktstid till slutet av frihetstiden* (Stockholm: Brutus Östlings Bokförlag Symposium, 2000), 256.
57 Erik Erl. Bodell, 'Letter to P. A. Wallmark, vol 3' (30 maj 1811), Peter Adam Wallmark, KB1/Ep.V 4), Kungliga Biblioteket, 243; Gunnar T. Westin, 'Olavus Petri', https://sok.riksarkivet.se/sbl/artikel/7688, Accessed 1 March 2022.
58 Anners, 'Straffteorierna i svensk rättshistoria', 243.
59 Anners, 244; the idea of improvement and moral education would not come into focus in a European context until Gaetano Filangieri (1752–1788) published his *La Scienza della legislazione* in 1780, a work that would not be translated into Swedish until 1814. See Anners page 245 and Gaetano Filangieri, *Lagstiftningens vetenskap* (Stängnäs: Carl Er. Ekmarck, 1814).
60 Anners, 'Straffteorierna i svensk rättshistoria', 243; David Nehrman Ehrenstråle also came to criticize the Civil Code of 1734 for this focus.
61 Anners, 245.
62 Cesare Cesare Beccaria, *Afhandling om brott och straff* (Stockholm: Wennberg och Nordström, 1770).
63 These quotations are taken from the English translation of *Dei delitti e delle pane* which just like the Swedish was translated from the French: Cesare Beccaria, *An Essay on Crimes and Punishments, Translated from the Italian; with a Commentary Attributed to Mons. de Voltaire, Translated from the French* (London, 1767), 139.
64 Beccaria, 142.
65 'Kongl. maj:ts ytterligare nådige förordning, angående lurendrägeriers uptäckande och hämmande' (1757); 'Kongl. maj:ts förordning emot lurendrägerier eller förbudne utrikes warors införsel i riket' (1770).
66 Kwass, *Contraband*; see for example 218–219, & 232; Gottmann, *Global Trade,* 78.
67 'Letter 16 April 1798' (1798), Kollegiers m fl skrivelser till Kungl Maj:t, skrivelser från Kommerskollegiet, 9, vol. 269, Riksarkivet, 2–3.
68 'Letter 16 April 1798' (1798), Kollegiers m fl skrivelser till Kungl Maj:t, skrivelser från Kommerskollegium, 9, vol. 269, Riksarkivet, 5.
69 'Lurendrägeri förordningen' (1799), Kommerskollegium, Huvudarkivet, Handels- och manufakturdivisionens protokoll, A I fa, vol.42, 1799, Riksarkivet, 246.

70 'Lurendrägeri förordningen' (1799), 260.
71 'Lurendrägeri förordningen' (1799), 263–264.
72 'Lurendrägeri förordningen' (1799), 265–266.
73 'Lurendrägeri förordningen' (1799), 289.
74 'Kongl. maj:ts nådiga förordning, til förekommande af lurendrägeri och tullförsnillning gifwen haga slott den 6 april 1799' (1799).
75 Ibid.
76 A quick search in the digital newspaper records for *lurendrägare* will show that the decade 1750–59 registers 14 articles mentioning 'smuggler', while 1760–1769 has 7. By contrast, the period 1770–1779 records 52 articles mentioning the former word. Just like in the periodicals of the earlier periods, many of the articles dealing with smuggling were published in the shape of letters and many of these letters interacted, propagating the debate. Svenska dagstidningar, http://tidningar.kb.se/, Accessed 2 Feb 2019.
77 Arimaspus, 'Herr Walerius Publicola', *Dagligt Allehanda*, December 29, 1774, no 298.
78 Ibid.
79 'Swar på frågan i Dagligt Allehanda n:o 28 om lurendrägerie generals=hus', *Dagligt Allehanda*, 12 March 1772, no 60; Arimaspus, 'Herr Walerius Publicola', *Dagligt Allehanda*, 29 December 1774, no 298; '-', *Dagligt Allehanda*, 3 March 1775, no 52.
80 '-', *Dagligt Allehanda*, 13 December 1775, no 286.
81 Ibid.
82 'Förslag om landt= och sjö=tullarnes uphäfvande', *Dagligt Allehanda*, 21 May 1776, no 114.
83 Ibid.
84 'Anmärkning wid det i Dagbladet N:o 114 ugifne förslag om landt= och sjö=-tullarnes uphäfwande', *Dagligt Allehanda*, 13 June 1776, no 133.
85 Ibid.
86 For two very evident, albeit slightly later, examples of the manufacturers' support of protectionism in the newspapers see: 'norrköpings manufactur-idkares underdånigst ingifne skrift til hans kongl. maj:t, i anledning af des nådiga förordning til lurendrägeriers hämmande, dat. den 6 april 1799', *inrikes tidningar*, 25 june 1799, no 73; 'fabrikören jacob reinhold bremers från åbo underdånigste tal til hans kongl. maj:t, wid nådigst lewnadt företräde på Drottningholms Slott den 4 i nästl. månad, i anledning af Kongl. förordningen til lurendrägeriers hämmande, dat. den 6 apr 1799', *Inrikes Tidningar*, 7 August 1799, no 92.
87 See for example: 'Anmärkning wid det i Dagbladet N:o 114 ugifne förslag om landt= och sjö=tullarnes uphäfwande', *Dagligt Allehanda*, 13 June 1776, no 133; 'Strödda tankar öfwer swaret på anmärkningarne emot förslaget om landt= och sjötullarnes uphäfwande', *Dagligt Allehanda*, 23 August 1776, no 192.
88 'Et ord til lurendrägaren', *Dagligt Allehanda*, 7 November 1771.
89 'Fortsättning, från gårdags=bladet, af en fabriqueurs bref', *Dagligt Allehanda*, 10 March 1773, no 58; 'Frågas herrar såckerbruks=idkare i Götheborg', *Götheborgs Allehanda*, 17 March 1775, no 22.
90 'Til herr Arimaspus i anledning af Dagbladerne N:Ris 73 Och 74 för innewarande år', *Dagligt Allehanda*, 23 April 1776, no 92.
91 Ibid.
92 '-', *Dagligt Allehanda*, November 20, 1771, no 261, 1; Arimaspus, 'Herr Walerius Publicola.', *Dagligt Allehanda*, 29 December 1774, no 298.
93 '-', *Dagligt Allehanda*, 3 March 1775, no 52.
94 'Pro Memoria för dem som skrifwa i finance', *Dagligt Allehanda*, 17 February 1775, no 40; '-', *Dagligt Allehanda*, 21 February 1775, no 43; For a discussion on the French use of galleys as prisons for smugglers see Kwass, *Contraband,* 234.
95 Carolin, 'Swar på Dagligt Allehanda no 84, den 11 april 1772', *Götheborgska Nyheter*, 30 January 1773, no 5.
96 'Til herr Arimaspus', *Dagligt Allehanda*, 7 February 1775, no 31.

97 Oscarsson, 'Med tryckfrihet som tidig tradition', in *Den svenska pressens historia: I begynnelsen (Tiden före 1830)*, ed. Karl Erik Gustafsson and Per Rydén (Stockholm: Ekerlids Förlag, 2000), 196.
98 '-', *Inrikes Tidningar*, 23 April 1799, no 46; '-', *Inrikes Tidningar*, 24 April 1799, no 47.
99 'Norrköpings manufactur-idkares underdånigst ingifne skrift til Hans Kongl. Maj:t, i anledning af des nådiga förordning til lurendrägeriers hämmande, dat. den 6 april 1799', *Inrikes Tidningar*, 25 June 1799, no 73; 'Fabrikören Jacob Reinhold Bremers från Åbo underdånigste tal til Hans Kongl. Maj:t, wid nådigst lewnadt företräde på Drottningholms Slott den 4 i nästl. månad, i anledning af kongl. förordningen til lurendrägeriers hämmande, dat. den 6 apr 1799', *Inrikes Tidningar*, 7 August 1799, no 92.
100 '-', *Inrikes Tidningar*, 6 November 1799, no 131.
101 Nordin, *Ett fattigt men fritt folk*, 256.
102 Nordin, 257.
103 Lisi Oliver's, *The Beginnings of English Laws* (Toronto: Toronto University Press, 2002); Heikki Pihlaiamäki, *Conquest and the Law in Swedish Livonia* (Leiden: Brill, 2017), 67ff; Warren C. Brown, *Violence in Medieval Europe* (Routledge, 2014), 223–224.
104 Pihlaiamäki, *Conquest and the Law*, 67.
105 'SDHK-Nr: 4197', 1335. Svenskt Diplomatariums huvudkartotek över medeltidsbreven, Skännninge, 30 Nov 1335. Riksarkivet.
106 Patricia Meyer Spacks, *Privacy: Concealing the Eighteenth-Century Self* (Chicago: The University of Chicago Press, 2003), 14.
107 Dan Norberg, *Kongl. commerce collegii underdånige relation om manufacturerne ingifwen wid riksdagen år 1769 Stockholm* (Gävle: Ernst Sundqvist, 1770), 9.
108 Kongl. maj:ts nådige resolution och förklaring, uppå de allmänna beswär, som... städerne i Swerige och Finland... andragit. 1762, 31§.
109 'Kongl. maj:ts nådige förordning, til lurendrägeriers hämmande.' (1766).
110 'Kongl. maj:ts ytterligare nådiga förordning, till lurendrägeriers hämmande. gifwen i råd-cammaren then 18 april 1768.' (1768).
111 Biörnsson, *Riksdagsmannens Jonas Biörnssons Märkwärdiga Memorial*, 5.
112 Norberg, *Kongl. Commerce Collegii*, 10.
113 'Kongl. maj:ts förordning emot lurendrägerier eller förbudne utrikes warors införsel i riket.' (1770).
114 'Til commerce collegium - om husvisitationer och fiscaliska besök i de handelandes gatubodar', 1772. Skråarkiv, Siden- och kramhandelssocieteten, Siden- och kramhandelssocietetens handlingar 1770–1787, F1, vol.2. Stockholms Stadsarkiv.
115 Lurendrägaren (Fictional), 'Swar til fäderneslandets=älskare', *Posten*, 12 April 1769; 'project, til hämmande af lurendrägerier', *Dagligt Allehanda*, 19 June 1770., *Dagligt Allehanda*, 19 Jun 1770.
116 'Swar på frågan i Dagligt Allehanda n:o 28 om lurendrägerie generals=hus'.
117 'Til herr Älskare af Rikets Wältrefnad',*Dagligt Allehanda*, 16 June 1773, no 133.
118 'Til Herr Danaus i Dagligt Allehanda 133', *Dagligt Allehanda*, 1 July 1773, no 145.
119 'Swar på frågan i Dagligt Allehanda n:o 28 om lurendrägerie generals=hus,' *Dagligt Allehanda*, 12 March 1772, no 60.
120 '-', *Dagligt Allehanda*, 8 July 1773, no 151.
121 Ibid; 'Tankar om en wiß stadgad swensk kläde=drägt', *Dagligt Allehanda*, 6 December 1773, no 279.
122 Henrika Tandefelt, 'The Image of Kingship in Sweden, 1772–1809', in *Scandinavia in the Age of Revolution. Nordic Political Cultures, 1740–1820*, ed. Pasi Ihalainen et al. (Farnham: Ashgate Publishing Limited, 2011), 43.
123 Bo Lindberg, 'Introduktion: nationalism och nationell identitet i 1700-talets Sverige', in *Nationalism Och Nationell Identitet i 1700-Talets Sverige*, ed. Åsa Karlsson and Bo Lindberg (Uppsala: Swedish Science Press, 2002), 11–12.
124 'Kongl. maj:ts nådiga förbud emot hus=visitationer, gifwit ekolsund then 16 julii 1776' (1776).

125 '-', 1776. Handels- och finansexpeditionen med finanskontoret (äldre), Råds och konseljprotokoll i renskrift, AI, vol.3. Riksarkivet, 410–412.
126 Åke Essén, *Johan Liljencrantz som handelspolitiker: Studier i Sveriges yttre handelspolitik 1773–1786* (Lund: Gleerup, 1928), 124; (Konseljprot. I handels- och fin. Ärenden, d. 1/12 1773).
127 Lena Rangström, 'Gustaf III's svenska dräktprojekt- en nationell reform i tiden', in *nationalism och nationell identitet i 1700-talets Sverige*, ed. Åsa Karlsson and Bo Lindberg (Uppsala: Swedish Science Press, 2002), 133.
128 The essay question was: If, to avoid the quick changing of fashions, and to hamper smuggling, it might be beneficial to adopt a National Costume in Sweden, suited to the Swedish climate and different from other Nations? (Om, til undvikande af täta ombyten I Moder, samt hämmande af Lurendrägerier, förmånligt kunde blifva, at I Sverige antaga en Nationel Kläde-Drägt, lämpad efter Svenska Climatet, och skiljaktig från andra Nationers?). For further information about the smuggling dimension in the essay competition, see: Eva Bergman, *Nationella dräkten: En studie kring Gustaf III:s dräktreform 1778* (Stockholm: Nordiska museets förlag, 1938), 41–48. Thank you to Sara Ekström for this reference.
129 Mikael Alm, 'Making a Difference: Sartorial Practices and Social Order in Eighteenth-Century Sweden', *Costume* 50, no. 1 (2016), 45.
130 Gustavus III, *Réflexions* (Liege, 1780), 13.
131 Gustavus III, 30–32.
132 'Anmärkning wid hwad i Stockholmske Dagbladet N:o 250 blifwit infördt, rörande banco=lån och handels=balance', *Dagligt Allehanda*, 12 December 1778, no 285; for a longer discussion about the Swedish self-perception of being a free people, see Nordin, *Ett fattigt men fritt folk*.
133 'Anmärkning wid hwad i Stockholmske Dagbladet N:o 250 blifwit infördt, rörande banco=lån och handels=balance', *Dagligt Allehanda*, 12 December 1778, no 285.
134 'Kongl. maj:ts nådiga förordning til hämmande af lurendrägerier, gifwen Stockholms slott then 14 martii 1785' (1785).
135 They particularly wished for the house-visitations to return to how they had been in the 1770 anti-smuggling decree.
136 'Kongl. Commerce Collegii underdåniga betänkande angående fabrikernes tilstånd, och om nödwändigheten af visitationer efter lurendrägade waror. På Fabriks Societeternes anhållan utlemnadt til tryckning', *Stockholms Posten*, 15 February 1793, no 39.
137 'Svar på Stockholms Posten no 39 15 feb 1793', *Extra Posten*, 25 February 1793, no 47.
138 'forsättning', *Extra Posten*, 26 February 1793, no 48.
139 'Protokoll'. Kommerskollegium, Huvudarkivet, Handels- och manufakturdivisionens protokoll, A I fa, vol.42, 1799. Riksarkivet, 262–263 & 270.
140 Ibid., 249 & 296.
141 'Protokoll'. Kommerskollegium, Huvudarkivet, Handels- och manufakturdivisionens protokoll, A I fa, vol.42, 1799. Riksarkivet, 341.
142 'Protokoll'. Kommerskollegium, Huvudarkivet, Handels- och manufakturdivisionens protokoll, A I fa, vol.42, 1799. Riksarkivet, 335.
143 'Kongl. maj:ts nådiga förordning, til förekommande af lurendrägeri och tullförsnillning gifwen Haga slott den 6 april 1799' (1799).
144 Wälloflige borgare-ståndets protocoller wid riksdagen i norrköping år 1800 (Stockholm: C.F. Marquard, 1800), 638.
145 Nordin, *Ett fattigt men fritt folk*, 256–257.
146 *Register till riksdagens protokoll med bihang*, vol. 2 (Stockholm: Central Tryckeriet, 1892), 1046.
147 Eva I. Andersson, 'Foreign Seductions: Sumptuary Laws, Consumption and National Identity in Early Modern Sweden', in *Fashionable Encounters. Perspectives and Trends in Textile and Dress in the Early Modern Nordic World*, ed. Tove Engelhardt Mathiassen et al. (Oxford: Oxbow Books, 2014), 16–17.

148 Andersson, 26 & 28; Jon Johansson, 'Min Ringa Kalminks Väst' (MA thesis, Stockholm University, 2015), 24.
149 Rickard Karlsson, *Svensk-franska förhandlingar. bland sprätthökar och franska flugor i svenskt 1700-tal* (Linköping: LiU Tryck, 2007); Agneta Helmius, 'Mode och moral. Begär och hushållning i svenska 1700-talspublikationer,' *Tidskrift för genusvetenskap* 1 (2011); Leif Runefelt, *Att hasta mot undergången. Anspråk, flyktighet, föreställning i debatten om konsumtion i Sverige 1730–1830* (Lund: Nordic Academic Press, 2015), 99–141; Agneta Helmius, 'Sprätthöken. En manlig livsstil i svensk debatt under 1700-talet,' in *À la mode : mode mellan konst, kultur och kommers*, vol. S. 128–145 (Göteborg: Makadam i samarbete med Centrum för Öresundsstudier vid Lunds universitet, 2016).
150 Erik Bodsten, *Politikens drivfjäder: Frihetstidens partiberättelser och den moralpolitiska logiken* (Lund: Historiska Institutionen, 2016), 96.
151 Johanna Ilmakunnas, 'Ståndsmässig konsumtion: högadelns penningbruk och konsumtionsvanor i Sverige under senare delen av 1700-talet', *Historisk Tidskrift för Finland* 86, no. 2 (2001), 94; Leif Runefelt, *Att hasta mot undergången,* 277. For the increased role of equality between citizens after 1792, see: Christensson, *Lyckoriket,* 128–158.
152 Christensson, *Lyckoriket,* 128–158.
153 Martin Melkersson, "Staten, ordningen och friheten. En studie av den styrande elitens syn på statens roll mellan stormaktstiden och 1800-talet" (Uppsala University, 1997), 78–79; Nordin, *Ett fattigt men fritt folk,* 334.
154 Nordin, *Ett fattigt men fritt folk,* 334.
155 Kollegiers m fl skrivelser till Kungl. Maj:t, Skrivelser från landshövdingar, ämnesordnade handlingar, ang. Överflöd och yppighet, C: 25–29, Riksarkivet; the protocols from the discussions are extensive, dealing with everything from the local dress and wedding practices to ideas about what they were willing to give up and the nature of a harmful good. This rich source material will be returned to in Chapter 5 in relation to the consumption of contraband.
156 'Kommittée Ang Förordning Mot Yppighet Och Överflöd, 1793', 1793, ÄK 817, vol. 1, Riksarkivet.
157 'Ödmjuk memorial', *Stockholms Posten*, 6 August 1793, no 176.
158 Ibid.
159 Runefelt, *Att hasta mot undergången*, 259–268.
160 'Protokoll', 1794, Kommerskollegium, Huvudarkivet, Handels- och manufaktur divisionens protokoll, A I fa, vol. 37a. Riksarkivet, 134.
161 'Kongl. maj:ts nådiga förordning, til hämmande af yppighet och öfwerflöd. gifwen Stockholms slott den 1 januarii 1794' (1794). §1–3. However, some caveats were made for gala dress and for the national costume, which still allowed for some limited use of silk.
162 Alexander Maxwell, *Patriots against Fashion: Clothing and Nationalism in Europe's Age of Revolutions*, Palgrave Connect (Houndmills, Basingstoke, Hampshire New York: Palgrave Macmillan, 2014), 47 & 57.
163 Runefelt, *Att hasta mot undergången*, 212–214.
164 Christensson, *Lyckoriket,* 144.
165 'Til ---s----m n:o 41 d. 19 febr.', *Stockholms Posten*, 5 March 1794, no 53.
166 'Til Herr M.---S--- i Stockholms Posten N:o 53 d 5 martii', *Stockholms Posten*, 28 April 1794, no 95.
167 'Anmärkningar öfwer det, som rörande swenske fabrikerne', *Inrikes Tidningar*, 29 August 1797, no 101.

3

POROUS BORDERS

The Swedish state was, like many other European states, undergoing a consolidation process during the eighteenth century. This consolidation process entailed increased legislative and economic homogenisation, which, according to Istvan Hont, contributed to transforming composite states into competitive 'commercial nation states'.[1] For Sweden, this consolidation process included the introduction of protectionist policies, import prohibitions, high import duties on many wares, and anti-smuggling legislation, which were all intended to keep global trade at bay and transform the delineated Swedish territory into a homogenised economic space. However, as Lauren Benton points out for empires, legal sovereignty was "not at all consistent with the image produced by monochrome shadings of imperial maps".[2] This was also true for many emerging nation states where turning legislation into reality depended on irregular enforcement on the ground. Research on state capacity and frontiers has shown that border areas were particularly complex regions with limited and uneven sovereignty which depended on the delegation of power to remote state agents.[3] Such research has suggested that in terms of state building, the government visions were conditioned by the realities on the ground.[4] In regard to the economic legislation, it depended extensively on customs officers with divided loyalties and private interests.[5] Control of these areas was also affected by the geography, climate, culture, and history of the borderlands.[6] In other words, the enforcement of economic policy and anti-smuggling legislation was intimately conditioned by the state's representatives on the ground, their intentions and interests, as well as the physical shape of the territory and the conditions prevailing along the border.

Meanwhile, the smugglers who traversed these borders were go-betweens that tied together spaces with different legislation and allowed goods to circulate between distinctive economical areas.[7] Intermediaries have increasingly been appreciated for their role in interconnecting the world through their abilities to

DOI: 10.4324/9781003226031-3

surpass boundaries and rules separating various regions, enabling cross-cultural trade and the circulation of knowledge, people, goods, and capital.[8] These go-betweens came in many shapes and sizes and their reasons for smuggling varied. Previous research on smuggling has suggested that smuggling could be viewed as a type of 'popular illegalism' and smuggling as moral economy in the vein of E.P. Thompson.[9] Although financial reward certainly was a prime incentive for smuggling, due to the multitude and variety of individuals involved

FIGURE 3.1 Map of Sweden and Finland. G. Biurman, 66, 'Svea och Göta riken med Finland och Norland afritade i Stockholm år 1747'.

Source: National Library of Sweden, MS, Generaltullarrendesocietetens svenska tullatlas, 66.

in smuggling, it is necessary to consider their specific contexts and situations in order to understand what function smuggling had in their (economic) lives. A closer study of these go-betweens enables an exploration of their incentives for smuggling and the effects of their transgressive movements.

This chapter investigates court records to try to establish how the country's challenging geography, limited state authority, and the movements of go-betweens affected the state's ability to create a uniform economic unit as well as how the perpetrators perceived smuggling and whether it was considered an alternative source of revenue in times of need.

Defining Space, Drawing Borders

The area that will be discussed here is the Swedish core area, as rendered in Georg Burman's 1747 map of Sweden, sourced from the Customs Office Atlas (Figure 3.1). It corresponds roughly to present-day Sweden and Finland, a space of 780,000 km2 and inhabited by 3 million inhabitants, a vast but sparsely populated area at the edge of Europe. While Sweden was a reasonably stable territory for the duration of the time period, 1766 to 1806, it still bore the marks of more or less recent territorial changes. During the period 1611–1721, sometimes referred to as the Age of Greatness, Sweden had gained several areas from Denmark-Norway. As a result of the Second Treaty of Brömsebro in 1645, the regions Jämtland and Härjedalen, as well as the islands Gotland and Ösel, had been conceded to the Swedes, along with the county of Halland, which was granted on a 30-year loan. Thirteen years later, in the 1658 Treaty of Roskilde, further territories were added to Sweden as Denmark conceded the provinces of Skåne, Blekinge, Halland (permanently), Norwegian Tröndelag, and the island of Bornholm.[10] In the eastern half of the country, in the Grand Duchy of Finland, territorial changes had taken place even more recently. As a consequence of Swedish losses in the Great Northern War (1700–1721), several territories along the eastern shore of the Baltic Sea were lost, including Livonia, Estonia, Ingria, and Viborg. Not long after that, another war was fought against Russia (1741–43), which aimed to retake control of the areas lost some 20 years previously. Instead, the war resulted in further Swedish territorial losses and in the subsequent Treaty of Åbo in 1743 the southern part of the province of Karelia was also conceded to Russia. The borders surrounding Sweden were thus both of the older and the younger variety. New borders redrew the official maps, but older borders also came to be redefined over time – hardening as they were militarised and softening as to become virtually invisible. It is therefore crucial to consider the border not merely as a line on a map but as an ever changing, malleable entity.

At the same time, Sweden was also undergoing a gradual shift towards increased homogenisation. One crucial feature of this development was the creation of a unified legal code for its core territory in 1734. This legal code covered the core areas, as seen in Figure 3.1, and played a crucial role in creating a homogenised legislative territory. This core territory also became synonymous with Sweden's economic space as it was covered by uniform customs legislation.[11] This economic and legal core territory later came to form the base of the emerging nation states Sweden and Finland.

It should be noted, however, that while the western and eastern halves of the kingdom were the same legislative space, not all inhabitants appear to have been treated equally.[12] One crucial difference pertained to language. Finnish speakers, in contrast to those with Swedish as their mother tongue, were not allowed to defend themselves in court in their own language. In addition, not all decrees were communicated to them in Finnish, which raises the question of whether they were even aware of all the new legislation that came to be issued by the Swedish state.[13] This is worth bearing in mind as it establishes a distinctly different power dynamic between the Swedish speaking establishment and the Swedish speaking inhabitants in the West and Finnish speaking in the East.

If we return to the map, it is evident that the territory was surrounded not only by borders with different historical contexts, but by borderlands with very different geographical characters, ranging from maritime borders, archipelagos, and beaches, to extensive land borders, stretching across mountains ranges and trekking through vast forests, features that, as Fernand Braudel reminds us, conditioned human activity.[14] The changing of the seasons also dramatically changed the living conditions, in terms of weather, temperature, and hours of daylight, particularly in the north and the inland. These factors not only dictated the cycle of employment, conditioning when seeds could be sown, when houses could be built, and when fish visited the shorelines, but also the practical conditions for travel and surveillance.[15]

Sweden also acquired territories along the southern shore of the Baltic: often referred to as Swedish dominions, they were under Swedish control but were never fully incorporated into Sweden's core lands. While many of these dominions were lost during the final years of the Swedish empire, 1718–1720, some areas seized under the old empire remained under Swedish control throughout the eighteenth century. The important trading centre Wismar remained a Swedish dominion until 1803 and Swedish Pomerania until 1815. Along with these European dominions, Sweden also gained the Caribbean colony Saint Barthélemy from France in 1784; it would remain in Swedish hands until 1878.[16] One year after the Swedish acquisition, Saint Barthélemy was declared a free port and became an important transit port in the West Indies as a neutral, commercial harbour serving both French and British interests. Over time, it also became a critical smuggling hub.[17] The Swedish dominions and its colony provided important opportunities for the exchange of knowledge and skill, as officials moved between Pomerania, Sweden, and Saint Barthélemy. Customs officers born in Pomerania could thus find themselves coming head-to-head with smugglers from the same area along the Swedish coast, while economic theorists like the Rügen-born Johan Fredrick Kryger penned supports of Swedish patriotism.[18] While there was a lot of exchange between the dominions, the colony, and the Swedish core territory, they were also all distinctly different on a fundamental level.

These continental dominions were never fully incorporated into the Swedish state and were legally distinct territories.[19] The discrepancy in economic legislation between the Swedish core territories and its dominions meant that for the duration of the eighteenth century, the dominions were treated as foreign territories in terms of trade. While the role of the dominions was redefined through the century, as we will see, they continued to play an important role for the economic development of Sweden's core territory. This general tour of the Swedish territories serves as a stepping stone when we now turn to look at a few different key areas, the legislation meant to regulate and control them, and the people who challenged them.

Stockholm Archipelago

We will start out in the middle of the Swedish kingdom, by the Baltic Sea, where the capital, Stockholm, is located. The surrounding archipelago, consisting of around 30,000 islands and islets, played a crucial role in shaping smuggling in the region around the capital (see Figure 3.2). At this time, Stockholm also housed Sweden's largest harbour and a significant part of all official foreign trade ran through the city. Large numbers of trading vessels and a wide-stretched archipelago created a conundrum for the authorities set to survey foreign trade. The geography of the archipelago was difficult to control. In order to try to get around this issue, a customs chamber was built on Dalarö, an island further out in the archipelago. At Dalarö, all trading vessels should be searched before they entered the main body of the archipelago. More measures were needed, however, and the 1757 anti-smuggling degree stipulated that ships coming from foreign territories should be met in the archipelago by a customs officer who would seal all the openings on the vessel in anticipation of it being thoroughly searched (7§, 1757). Enforcing this decree was nearly impossible, however, due to the expanse of the archipelago. In an attempt to rectify the situation, the 1770 anti-smuggling legislation prohibited all unloading of goods in the archipelago, whether to another ship, a beach, a house, or a hiding place. All such unloading would from now on be classified as smuggling (5 Art, 1§, 1770).

Legislating against it was one thing, enforcing it quite another. Even for the most diligent customs officers, overseeing all the crags, islets, and islands would have been a near impossible task. In addition, there was some doubt among the legislators concerning the officers' loyalties. Consequently, the 1770 anti-smuggling legislation stipulated that servants of the crown, such as the pilot at sea, who usually resided out in the archipelago, and customs officers, would be declared infamous if they engaged in or encouraged smuggling. They would also be condemned to forced labour for a minimum of three years to life for their crimes (2 Art, 1§, 1770). While this was a harsh punishment, it is unclear how effective it was in controlling the behaviours of state servants on remote islands.[20]

As Sweden's capital and most important harbour, Stockholm had a prominent customs presence.[21] Management of the archipelago fell to the Maritime

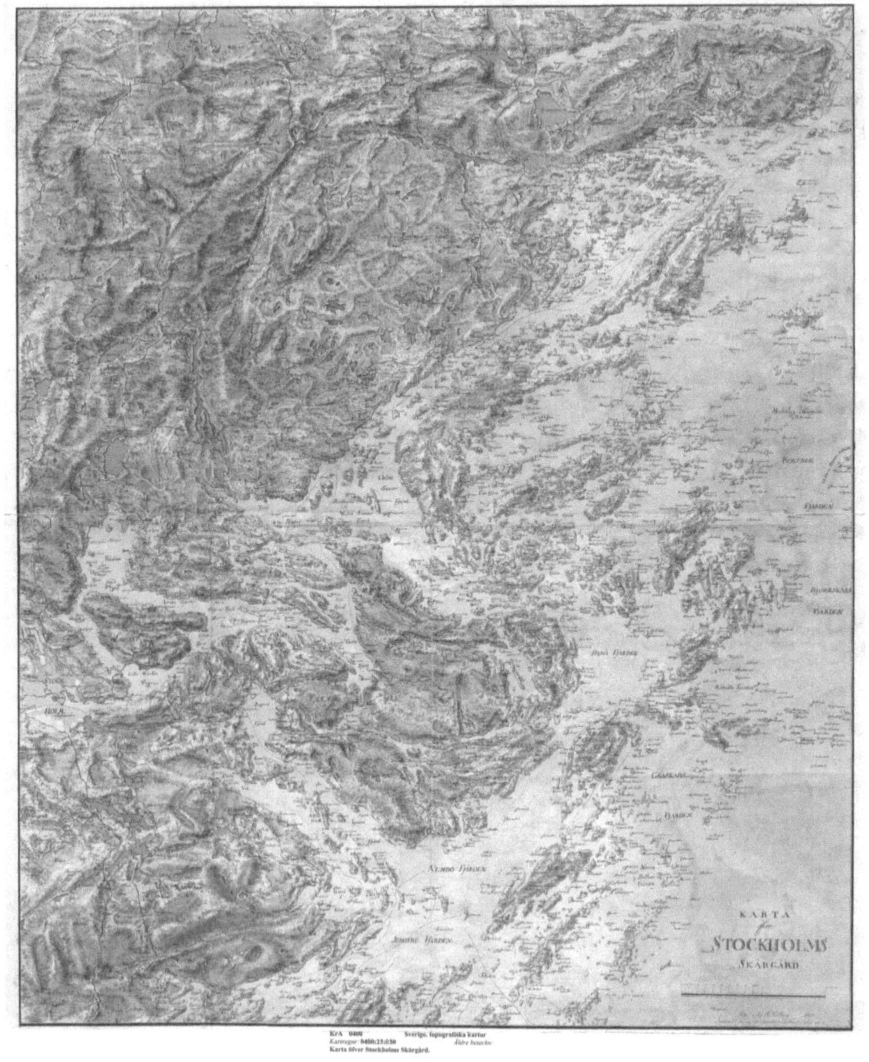

FIGURE 3.2 Map of Stockholm Archipelago. 'Östersjön, Öresund och Bälten. Karta öfver Stockholms Skärgård' (1809).

Source: Swedish Military Archives, Sveriges Topografiska kartor 1580–1990, 23:30.

Customs Office in Stockholm. By 1770, around 350 people were employed by the various branches of the customs around Stockholm alone. It was thus the largest government department in terms of personnel.[22] First housed in the Argus neighbourhood in the Old Town of Stockholm, the Maritime Customs Office was later moved as the old venue could not deal with the increasing demands smuggling placed on it – particularly in regard to the storage space required for seized contraband. A new customs office was built in the 1780s.

The large majority of the cases before the Maritime Customs Court related to seizures of contraband in incoming shipping vessels. The records from 1769, for example, report that 95 smuggling trials were held during the six-month period from June to December. Out of these, 84 concerned confiscations made on board ships (88.42%).[23] Delving into the court records produced by the Maritime Customs Court, we can start to get an idea of who engaged in smuggling and why, as well as what was done to prevent it.

The Captain's Burden

The ship captain, or skipper, is one of the most frequently occurring defendants in the Stockholm Maritime Customs Court. A primary reason for this was the anti-smuggling legislations' definition of accountability, which came to focus increasingly on the captain. In the 1739 and 1741 anti-smuggling decrees, it had been sufficient for the captain to swear an oath upon the ship's arrival that the manifest, the list containing all goods on board the ship, was correct. From 1757, this was no longer deemed sufficient and searches on arriving ships became the norm. The content of the ship's manifest was also transformed, from a list of 'packs', 'baskets', and 'barrels' to an exhaustive inventory of each package, giving the quality and the quantity of each good (2§, 1757). The customs officers checked the manifest against the contents of the ship upon arrival, and if anything was out of order the captain was held personally responsible.[24] At the same time, it was prohibited to enlarge the ship or add any hidden compartments (1§, 1757). Incidentally, the captain was also tasked with controlling all clothes brought on board, by the crew and passengers, ensuring that they did not bring more than necessary for their personal needs while on board the ship (6§, 1757; 5 Art, 4§, 1770).[25] If illegal goods belonging to the crewmembers were found the captain was issued with a fine of 10–100 D smt for negligence.[26] By 1799, this sum was raised to 5–50 Rdr.[27] In 1799, it was highlighted that 'forgetfulness' was not an acceptable excuse for omitting objects in the manifest.[28] In this way, the captain was early identified as ultimately responsible for any smuggling that went on aboard his ship, and over time his responsibilities for controlling cargo and crew were extended, limiting his ability to claim ignorance. By focusing on the duties of the captain, the legislators tried to distinguish a responsible party over whom the customs officers could exert control.

Additionally, it helped them get around the issue of trying to identify the 'real' culprit: the illusive individual(s) who organised and financed the operations. An illustrative example is the 1769 case of Captain Michael Lefverentz from Danzig whose ship was found to contain illegal red silk atlas, flowered silk taffeta, and five socks filled with coffee beans. The captain explained that he had received the wares in Danzig to take them across the Baltic Sea to Sweden. Lefverentz denied being the owner of the goods, but he was unable to prove it. As it was impossible to trace the consigner, Lefverentz recognised that the burden of the crime fell on him. He admitted that he was aware of the decrees and that he was willing to take responsibility for his cargo as stipulated by the 1757 decree. Lefverentz consequently accepted his fine, which equated to half the value of the goods and lost possession of the contraband.[29]

Not every captain was so easily convinced to bite the bullet, and some absconded when they found themselves forced to take responsibility for their cargoes.[30] Faced with this, the anti-smuggling decrees introduced measures to deal with escaping smugglers. From the second half of the century, the anti-smuggling decrees demanded that an announcement should be made in the church pulpits when a smuggler was on the run, so as to alert the population, (5§, 1757), (Art 5. 2§, 1770) and (Art 5. 2§, 1799); this was later also followed up by advertisements in the newspapers.[31]

An important reason for appointing responsibility to the captain was that as the head of the ship he should have been in possession of up-to-date trading information. This information, derived from consular or chargé d'affaires reports, allowed the captain to know what was currently legal and illegal in each destination country and what specific rules governed various facets of trade there, including what could legally be imported, how to unload the ship, and what to report to the customs office and so on.[32] Regardless, captains often tried to claim ignorance of the laws when they were caught with an illegal cargo. One of the most blatant examples of this were the Wallis brothers, who independently of each other stood trial for smuggling in 1769. It is possible that the first brother, Captain Alberg Wallis, made a mistake when he arrived in Stockholm from London along with a chest of illegal wares, bearing the inscription 'Zu Barth'. Wallis explained that the chest in question was not destined for Sweden, but had been purchased for his brother Martin Wallis who lived in Barth, Pomerania – where Alberg Wallis would return after his visit to Sweden. After swearing an oath to the accuracy of his statement, Wallis was freed from all fines.[33] Five months later, Martin Wallis arrived in Stockholm from Stralsund. During the visitation of his ship, the customs officers found two loose planks underneath the captain's bunk. Hidden beneath were rugs stuffed with various goods such as damask tablecloth and Dutch linen sheets. While Martin Wallis claimed to be unaware of the prohibitions, the elaborate concealment along with his brother's recent run in with the law convinced the court that he was lying and he was sentenced to pay his fines.[34] Claims of ignorance were only accepted so far.[35]

Where did these smuggling vessels originate and how can the smuggling activities be understood? A survey of the origins of the smuggling vessels caught by the Maritime Customs in Stockholm between June and December 1769 reveals the outlines of a pattern. The majority of the ships came from Pomerania, the Swedish enclave. Of the 84 ships caught smuggling, 16 arrived from Wismar alone, which makes it the most common origin for contraband during this period. The prevalence of vessels originating in Wismar indicates that this was an important contraband route into Sweden and there is reason to believe that

Pomerania's role as a transit hub for contraband to Sweden became more pronounced with time. The protectionist policies in Pomerania were eased in 1786, and its near- and long-distance trade boomed from the late 1770s, peaking in the 1790s.[36] At the same time, the ties between Sweden and Pomerania were strengthened.[37] These developments would have improved the possibilities for ships from Pomerania to engage in the lucrative contraband trade.[38] The regular trade between the two territories remained strong and by 1800, 10–25% of all boats arriving in Stockholm originated in Swedish Pomerania.[39] Similarly, in the smuggling statistics, 12 out of 110 cases at the Maritime Customs Court in 1803 involved ships from Pomerania, the subsequent year the numbers were 12 out of 111.[40]

The second most common origin for smuggling vessels, 13 ships, was the British Isles.[41] Sweden had an extensive trade with Britain throughout the period, and Nordic exports such as iron, timber, and tar were crucial ingredients in the running of the British empire and its industrialisation.[42] This ensured a heavy traffic of vessels sailing between Sweden and Britain. While a large part of the ships sailed to Gothenburg on the more accessible western shore, some also sailed to Stockholm.

From the British point of view, engaging in trade with Sweden was no easy task. A tariff which favoured the export of iron in Swedish ships had been introduced in 1722. It caused British ships to pay up to 70% more in taxes for exporting iron from Sweden. Two years later, a Commodity Act was released which further limited what goods could be brought into Sweden on foreign ships.[43] Additional import restrictions were launched throughout the century, which forced many ships to travel to Sweden with ballast alone. In this situation, a small extra profit brought about through smuggling could have been significant for the skipper.[44] The contraband trade from Britain will be returned to in later chapters for now it is enough to point out that the country was the origin of a noteworthy amount of smuggling vessels.

The trading vessel, moving between various legal zones, provided a challenge for the customs office as it did not just facilitate the movement of people and legal goods, but could also be used to conceal contraband. Legislation and regulation were meant to impose increased transparency upon the trade, and to pin responsibility on one individual, the captain. However, enforcing the legislation was no simple matter. As long as the protectionist state was connected to more liberal markets by trade, maintaining its economic integrity was a challenge. A country under restrictive trade legislation was thus a renegotiated space, where foreign goods could still enter, albeit on new premises.

The Crew's Ambition

While the captain was ultimately responsible of the ship, he was certainly not the only one aboard the ship that could engage in smuggling. A range of crewmembers appear in the Maritime Customs Court records, from the able seaman to the kitchen boy. How they organised their illegal ventures differed. In some instances, crewmembers appear to have worked together in a model of organisation where each member invested in illegal goods according to personal capability, but then worked together with the loading and unloading of the goods.[45] Another model was for one or more individuals, crewmembers or others, to own the goods, remunerating the rest of the crew for their silence and assistance.[46] These two models of organisation affected the perceived culpability of the various crewmembers but also their potential profits. While the owner of the goods could expect the highest profits, he also took the largest risks and would bear the brunt of the fines if caught. By contrast, those aiding and abetting could expect smaller returns but also lesser punishments for their involvement.

How such a work division could manifest can be seen in the case of cook Joachim Hindric Hinnes, able seaman Peter Michelsson, and first mate Johan Lorentz. They arrived into the Stockholm archipelago in April 1769 aboard Captain Johan Mathias Schmidt's ship from Wismar. While out in the archipelago, Hinnes and Michelsson secretly managed to leave the ship with their contraband. They split up, but were ultimately caught, Hinnes by Gälna gård and Michelsson, together with first mate Johan Lorentz, by Kodjupet. Hinnes and Michelsson confessed to being the owners of the goods seized from them but Lorentz claimed not to own any contraband. He did, however, admit that he had been bribing customs officials on Michelsson's request.[47] In this way, crewmembers co-operated, splitting various tasks between them. For the customs, this meant that it was difficult to tie down personal responsibility as it was muddied through the sharing of responsibilities and tasks. While there were dangers in including multiple people in smuggling ventures, it also meant that blame could be negotiated and greater contraband hoards could be moved.

Meanwhile, the reward for information leading to a seizure of contraband was high, probably much higher than the crew could have expected for their assistance in the crime. In the 1757 decree, the reward for a person who exposed a smuggling venture was 60% of the value of the confiscated goods.[48] This was an illustrious prize for a disgruntled crewmember, and tip-offs certainly do appear in the records. It was, for example, a tip-off that led the customs to search Captain Wilhelm Dahl's ship from Danzig out in the archipelago in the autumn of 1769. Onboard the ship, they found a large amount of coffee and cloth hidden away. Interviews with the crewmembers revealed that the goods belonged to first mate Peter Mattsson and another able seaman, who had absconded when the customs officers arrived.[49] However, tip-offs are not as common as you might expect. Whether this is an indication of loyalty among the crewmembers or fear is uncertain.

Why then did these crewmembers want to participate, either directly or indirectly, in smuggling? The short answer is simple, profit. In Sweden, the monthly salary of the average able seaman was around 10 Rdr rgs and a first mate 15 Rdr rgs.[50] These salaries were fairly stable until the summer of 1808, when they started to rise.[51] The same cannot be said for consumer prices, which increased from the 1770s and increased steeply after 1790.[52] Trading in contraband could therefore have been used to extend an income which was not keeping pace with the costs of living. Many of the small-scale culprits probably fall into this category.[53] It is also worth pointing out that sailor wives are overrepresented as contraband retailers in Stockholm, which further underlines the role of sailors in the contraband trade.

Considering the high values of some of the contraband caches and the modest salaries of the crewmembers, it begs the question how the larger smuggling operations were financed. Some appear to have been financed by credit.[54] Certain foreign vendors extended credit to smugglers in order to reach Swedish consumers.[55] In addition, there were certainly traders who also took a more active role in the smuggling and who hired sailors to run their contraband. Unfortunately, this type of information is rarely divulged in the customs records and more research of merchants' account books is needed to understand how this trade might have worked. Large-scale smuggling ventures organised by crewmembers recede in the later court records.[56] This might have been related to the fact that the captain was gradually assigned more responsibility for checking his vessel and crew. A situation that would have made it necessary to involve the captain of the ship in any smuggling operation.

The new regulations also show a clear trend towards pursuing higher level offenders in order to stamp out the instigator. Together with the previously mentioned harshening punishments for the able mates, sailors, and the captain in 1770, a new tip-off system was also introduced in 1799.[57] According to the new system, an able seaman or captain unable to pay the fines would be spared hard labour if he could prove that the ship-owner or another commissioner had been responsible for, or known about, the smuggling. In that case, the fines would instead be converted to prison on water and bread.[58] It has not been possible to identify any such cases in the court records, however. Whether this is due to the fact that such cases were processed differently or whether the sailors never divulged the principal smuggler, either out of ignorance or due to other reasons, is uncertain.

Towards the end of the eighteenth century, attention moved from the vessels bringing in contraband to the vendors selling it, resulting in a proportional drop in trials against both captains and crewmembers. During the six-month period from June to December 1800, the Maritime Customs Court in Stockholm oversaw 46 trials, out of which only 25 concerned confiscations on board ships (54.34%): a definite drop from 1769.[59] This was related to the emergence of a new surveillance tactic. The late eighteenth century saw a shift in focus with the introduction of new anti-smuggling legislation and the reintroduction of shop searches in 1785 and universal house searches in 1799.[60] Such a tendency can also be discerned in the customs records, where confiscations on ships decreased while shop confiscations increased, which we will return to in Chapter 4.

Finally, virtually all of the ship confiscations were made during the period between March and (early) December, and there were hardly any seizures between late January and March. This was most likely due to the climatic conditions, as

Stockholm during this period came to be surrounded by an ice sheet, which immobilised trade for some months at the start of the year.[61]

Throughout the eighteenth and into the nineteenth-century transgressing vessels caused much concern for the authorities and despite ample legislative attempts to control them, they were never fully able to secure the archipelago around Stockholm, which is reflected in the changing legislation. Continuous movements of people, vessels, and illegal goods between Sweden and its trading partners undermined Sweden's protectionist economic policy and space. At the same time, the sources indicate that smuggling played an important role for those who sailed to Sweden, increasing meagre trade profits and boosting private income.

Boreal Borderlands

After this foray into the smuggling around the capital, the smuggling of professional sailors and shippers, attention turns to some more peripheral borderlands, which were populated by different kinds of smugglers. Three types of border spaces will be considered here: a maritime border, an older land border (established prior to 1700), and a newer land border (established after 1700). In addition, we will look at a singular space, a free port, that was located within the Swedish kingdom but which was not bound by regular laws. While all areas analysed were defined by cross-border exchange, they were also characterised by attempts to detach and distinguish Sweden in relation to its neighbouring territories and to restrict cross-border movement.

Maritime Borders: Crags, Salting-Houses, and Sand

The West Coast

Sweden's west coast offers a varied landscape, from extensive sandy beaches in the south to inhospitable, craggy archipelagos in the north. The varied geography presented an assortment of problems for the customs officers, at the same time as the anti-smuggling legislations posited that the people living and working along the coast were seen as particularly suspect and in need of surveillance.[62] Suspicion of the coastal dwellers was related to the fact that many of them were involved in maritime transport and fishing and therefore equipped with boats – boats that could easily be used to transport contraband into Sweden, particularly from Denmark, which, at its closest, could be reached with just over an hour's rowing in fair weather.[63]

The south-west and west coasts were prominent areas for shipping. Since becoming Swedish in 1645, peasants, particularly in Skåne, Halland, and Bohuslän, had enjoyed special rights to complement their farming with shipping. Peasant shipping (*allmogesjöfart*) primarily focused on exporting timber to Denmark was a continuation of a trade established while these territories were Danish. However, over time the trade diversified and also came to include iron and herring. By the 1770s herring had become the dominant export good. It was exchanged for different types of consumer goods, including spices and dyes. The Danish trade remained strong, but the peasant sailors also travelled to England, France, and even as far as the Mediterranean as the demand for salt started to increase.[64] The peasants' free navigation rights aggravated traders in Gothenburg which led to increased pressures to control trade from the mid-seventeenth century, to limit the peasants' free navigation rights and weaken peasant shipping.[65] At the same time, this trade played an important role for these coastal areas, which were still dependent on a makeshift economy for their survival, and would not become agriculturally self-sufficient until the nineteenth century.[66] The exact character of peasant navigation varied between regions, however. In Halland, the sailing was dominated by a few villages, while in the northerly west coast province of Bohuslän, the practice was common all along the coastline.[67] Peasant shipping, in different shapes, thus had a long tradition along the west coast and contributed to the local economy.[68] It also faced increasing calls for regulation, and one important argument against it was that as it enabled smuggling.[69]

Peasant sailors also appear in the court records. The case we know most about is that of Olaf Jonsson, which will serve to illustrate how this trade could work in practice. Jonsson was living on the island Vrångö, in the archipelago south of Gothenburg. In the 1780s, Vrångö became an important stopping point for peasant sailors, but they are known to have resided on the island even earlier.[70] In April 1776, custom officers searched a boathouse on the island, reputedly belonging to the peasant shipper Jon Nilsson. From "Nilsson's boathouse", the officers retrieved 19 boxes of contraband.[71] Upon further enquiry, the boathouse was found to belong to another peasant shipper, Olaf Jonsson. Jonsson had been missing since the seizure and interviews with his neighbours failed to provide any information about his whereabouts. When comparing the accounts of neighbours and witnesses, it became clear that some of them were lying. After extended questioning, one witness finally revealed that Olof Jonsson had left for Helsingör in Denmark.[72] The contraband, mainly British textile imports, was valued at 6968 D smt and Jonsson was convicted in abstentia.[73] This case reveals not merely the role of a peasant shipper in bringing in a considerable amount of British consumer wares into Sweden but also the customs officers' unusually thorough investigation reveals Jonsson's connection to Helsingör. It is highly possible that he acquired the wares there before hiding them in his boathouse. Furthermore, we find that the general community of Vrångö attempted to deter the investigation and stonewall the custom officers to shield Jonsson. This case highlights not merely the role that peasant sailors could play in connecting the Swedish and foreign markets, but the difficulties faced by the customs officers working in hostile environments.

Shipping was not the only activity that came to shape life on the west coast; there was also the fishing. In Bohuslän in particular, herring fishing became an important source of income from the middle of the eighteenth century, but fish was in flux and provided booms of employment in certain regions during limited periods.[74] The fish boom led to the establishment of *sillsalterier* and *trankokerier* in the archipelago where herring was salted and train oil extracted.[75] Due to the bad odour emanating from these processes, the establishments were often remotely located. In this way, the fishing and transport industry supplied the coast with an extensive network of boathouses, storage houses, and refineries along the coast, particularly along the northwestern coast. These remote storage buildings came to be used as hiding places for contraband, and they could hold considerable caches. During a 1768 search of *sillsalteriet* at Långedrag, south of Gothenburg a contraband cache was found containing illegal wares worth an impressive 6394 D smt. The goods were confiscated but as the owner could not be established, the case was left open awaiting further information.[76] The following year another confiscation was made in the salt houses at *sillsalteriet* Barna Bratten on an island south of Gothenburg. This time the goods were valued at 3454 D smt and the owner of Barna Bratten, merchant Peter Bagge, was issued with the fines despite attempts to redirect the blame onto 'two unknown sailors'.[77] It was common for the owners to claim ignorance of the activities taking place in these remote buildings, but it rarely shielded them from fines.

The ten-year period 1766–1776 offers a window into how these buildings were used to facilitate smuggling. During this period searches were legal and have left behind piles of customs records.[78] In July 1776 the searches came to an abrupt end, however, when Gustav III banned the use of the house-visitation, which included all sorts of privately-owned structures, including boathouses and *sillsalterier*.[79] The ban on searches of coastal storage houses was only lifted in 1798, following a grace period of more than 20 years.[80] The new legislation "Prohibition against the illegal trade and storage of smuggled goods in the Country's archipelagos" revoked the special privileges that the *sillsalteri* had been enjoying, privileges that included the right to import and store provisions for their business free from surveillance. A right, it was argued, that had been misused to store illegal foreign goods, "which often with an open boat, from foreign places, are smuggled in directly to the *Salteri*".[81] Visitations and searches were reintroduced in all structures in the archipelago and along the coastline, anywhere people were trading without permission. Anyone conducting illegal trade along the coast would be fined 200 Rdr each time they were caught regardless of the value of the goods.[82] Both the regulation and the customs protocols bear witness to the role played by these coastal storage houses in enabling the contraband trade. However, the visitation prohibitions, 1762–1766 and 1776–1798, meant that these buildings lay beyond the reach of the customs officers for extended periods during the second half of the eighteenth century and could then safely be used for storing contraband (Figure 3.3).

In the final years of the eighteenth century, the tides were turning. A month after the reintroduction of the visitation of the coastal storage houses, another decree was issued intended to prevent open boats from sailing across to foreign territories. Open boats were much easier and faster to unload without proper mooring.[83] According to the decree, this also made them suitable for smuggling and their use should be hampered. The following year a new anti-smuggling decree increased the scope of visitations again, and the fiscal officers gained the right to also search private homes along the coast in search of contraband. Although fiscals were fined 20 to 100 Rdr for an unwarranted search, it is clear that the spotlight had now been turned on the coastal dwellers (8 Art. 8§, 1799).

Despite these attempts to strengthen the anti-smuggling legislation and to extend the reach of the customs officers, the west coast was still difficult to manage. In a memorandum submitted in 1804 by travelling fiscal B. E. Hjelm from the fishing community Råå, a community with a population of 100 people located along the north-west coast of Skåne, Hjelm observed that the residents of Råå and the surrounding areas still travelled to Denmark for illegal trade, and co-operated with foreign trading vessels under the pretence of fishing.

Why did this smuggling trade continue despite increasing legislation and expanded customs officer authority? Hjelm noted that the geography of the area, in particular its extensive beaches, made it possible to offload contraband anywhere, which proved an immense challenge for the local customs officers.[84] During the spring and summer, these long beaches were patrolled by mounted officers, but patrolling the beaches was not an easy task. In 1797, mounted officers Olof Granbom and A. J. Tanson in Helsingborg, just north of Råå, reflected on their own lack of seizures from the previous year. "The Smuggler has through many years' training and experience become more careful and difficult to get

FIGURE 3.3 Author's own photograph of house used for the storage of contraband in Edenryd, Skåne.

Source: © A. M. C. Knutsson 2017.

to...[and] the officer on horseback is not able to be in all places at the same time".[85] While the extensive beaches enabled smugglers to land anywhere along the coast, for the mounted officers success depended on being in the right place at the right time. Although they got some information through tip-offs, more often than not the mounted officers appear to have been dependent on luck.

The beach surveillance was limited to the spring and summer months and largely absent during the winter months.[86] As this southern region would not have been suffering from winter ice, the exact reason for this short 'surveillance season' is uncertain.[87] Indeed, we know from other Nordic peripheries that a lot of smuggling occurred during the winter due to the bad weather, as fewer customs cutters were patrolling the seas.

Further north along the coast in the craggy archipelago of Bohuslän, there were issues of a different nature. An endless number of cliffs, crags, and other hiding places turned surveillance into a game of hide-and-seek between customs officers and smugglers.[88] Local knowledge was crucial as the archipelago was difficult to navigate, but due to the rotation schedule practised by the customs office, this type of local knowledge could be difficult to acquire. Some customs officers posted along the coast appear to have had no nautical knowledge at all. The most extreme case is probably that of Jacob Parell, a customs officer from Stockholm who had been posted in the Bohus archipelago in 1791. Unable to row, Parell could not even interfere when he saw a boat with contraband pass by just outside his office.[89] Geography and skill were thus crucial both for the smugglers and the customs officers. For the customs officers, it was vital that they were able to adapt to their local conditions and to gather the same local knowledge which most of the perpetrators already possessed. Indeed, as we shall see, the need for local knowledge was vital for all surveillance actions.

Despite attempts to control the coastline, smuggling continued, and it came to receive particular attention during the riksdag of 1800, where one member noted:

> It is a too well-known truth, that the so-called fishing villages in Skåne... have now been transformed to loading and unloading places for contraband goods... This abuse, so harmful for the Kingdom and for both common and individual safety, cannot, due to the expanse of the coastline, through any possible surveillance be stopped; and Your Royal Highness' wise and gracious decree for the prevention of smuggling will not be effective due to the ease with which smuggling can be conducted in these fishing villages.[90]

The activities in these fishing communities and along the coast were part of a makeshift economy which came to be increasingly controlled and regulated as a part of the government's consolidation of the borders and the increased focus on the economic integrity of the Kingdom. However, in practice, a challenging geography and shifting regulations made it difficult to exert the desired control over these spaces. For the customs officers, this varied geography presented an assortment of problems while offering many opportunities for the smugglers.

The Free Port

Marstrand, an isolated island in the southern part of the Bohus archipelago, was an altogether different type of maritime space. As a free port, it enjoyed a particular economic standing, and was not covered by the same protectionist legislation as the rest of the country. In Marstrand goods could be brought in, stored, consumed, and re-exported duty-free, but it was also a free-town with religious freedom, where the guild-system had been abolished and some criminals even were absolved of their crimes.[91] The island thus conforms to Francesco Somaini's definition of an *emboîtement* territory – a small space encapsuled in a larger space.[92] This emboîtement territory was meant to secure the benefits of free trade in Sweden while maintaining the protectionist legislation in the main body of the Kingdom.

The creation of the free port was announced by Gustav III on 15 August 1775.[93] It was the result of the efforts of Johan Liljencrantz, State Secretary of the Trade and Finance Office, who had been lobbying for transit trade since a tour of the Netherlands in the 1750s.[94] Liljencrantz had studied both Marseille and Livorno as models for the Swedish free port, and particularly found inspiration in the multi-cultural and multi-religious Livorno.[95] The idea of a free port was not met with universal approval, however, and one of the most significant objections to the free port was that it encouraged smuggling. In order to avoid this undesirable side effect, it was important to find a location which could be easily monitored and surveyed. Several locations were up for discussion, but Liljencrantz favoured Marstrand as he thought that it would be easy to monitor but also because as a former staple town it contained all the related infrastructure, which would make the *porto franco* cheaper to build.[96]

Twelve years after the initiation of the free port at Marstrand, an unimpressed visitor approaching Tjuvkil, the ferry terminal to Marstrand, observed:

> The walking path there went between rocks and over marshland: and the customs cabin by the beach is located between cliffs with a lonesome view of the sea. All of the islands and islets that can be seen are rock; and these are all barren...[97]

While the island had been chosen for its seclusion and limited access, it quickly became apparent that these were features that also encouraged smuggling. As early as 1776, new reinforced controls were required. Military units were stationed on Marstrand, and a guard boat patrolled the Mittsund, the water between Marstrand and Koön. In addition, several other patrol boats circulated in the surrounding archipelago.[98] By 1782, it was deemed necessary to publish a particular decree relating to the movement around Marstrand. It stipulated that it was forbidden to sail around in the archipelago and that all vessels must exit to Kattegat through the quickest route available. In addition, all open auctions also had to be attended by a magistrate to make sure that they were conducted lawfully.[99]

A few years after the introduction of the free port, a defeated Johan Liljencrantz admitted that its establishment had led to an increase in smuggling. It was too difficult to prevent goods leaving the island surreptitiously due to the difficult terrain, which made surveillance a continuous struggle.[100] Marstrand's reputation as a smuggling hotspot even reached foreign merchant manuals, which described how

> ...the inhabitants of that town receive many commodities, as entrepôt-goods, and they are later smuggled to Denmark, Scotland and domestic locations for distribution.[101]

Goods bound for export thus leaked into the Swedish territory, something that is also visible in the customs records. In 1776, a large hoard of contraband was seized at Lahall Inn, on the road between Marstrand and Gothenburg. The goods had just arrived from Canton on the ship *Terra Nova* and had been stored in Marstrand officially awaiting re-export, before they suddenly turned up at an inn in the Swedish countryside in the middle of the night.[102] The customs records contain many such examples of how goods intended for re-export instead entered the Swedish market surreptitiously.[103] While Marstrand's particular legal status was limited to the island, the goods brought in could not be so easily confined.

In 1794, this experimental extra-legal space finally lost its free port rights.[104] While the free port had been founded to serve as an extra-legal space to allow Sweden to participate in free trade while maintaining its protectionist policy, Marstrand's geographical conditions and its proximity to the Swedish mainland made it impossible to create a barrier between the free port and the protectionist mainland. This did not just undermine the Swedish economic space but also the integrity of the free port.

In both of these coastal examples, the general case of the west coast and the specific case of Marstrand, legislation and regulations were used to define the spaces as part, or not, of the Swedish economic space. Through creating set standards of acceptable behaviour, these legislations also helped to define smuggling as a crime. Meanwhile, the coastal areas were highly exposed to smuggling and were difficult to control and manage. The coast thus became a contested geopolitical space, as the Swedish legal dominion was simultaneously challenged and defined by criminality in these areas. The continued existence of smuggling and the struggle to control these challenging spaces meant that there was a continual interaction between the legislation and the crime – which in part depended on political developments, as discussed in the last chapter, but which were also related to the geographical space itself, its possibilities, and limitations.

Land Borders: Mountains, Woods, and Snow

As the investigation turns from maritime to overland smuggling, it is important to address the geographical and climatic conditions that came to shape this smuggling. The topography of Sweden, particularly the northern two-thirds, is dominated by the taiga, the primeval evergreen forest which spans most of the subarctic, or boreal, climate region. It is a forest that together with the mountainous regions along the Swedish north-west border makes the area vastly difficult to oversee and control to this day. For this reason, these territories have throughout history been used to conceal secret and forbidden movements. Meanwhile, the region's subarctic climate has ensured regular and heavy snowfall throughout the winter period, along with frozen rivers and lakes. The eighteenth century, which falls under the period sometimes referred to as the Little Ice Age, saw low average temperatures and an increased risk of crop failure.[105] Snow and ice, as well as the absence of agricultural chores, made winter into a time of travel and transport. It was also a period when many seasonal workers found themselves without regular employment. At the same time, short and dry summers, resulting in poor crop yields, could increase the need to resort to alternative sources of income in the autumn. Indeed, the perceived link between smuggling and the winter was such that one defendant even argued that he could not possibly have committed the smuggling crime he stood accused of because it had not yet been winter, claiming that smuggling in the summer was hardly an option as it necessitated the use of regular roads which passed by the customs chambers.[106]

Topography and climate not only conditioned movements in the terrain but also influenced the location of customs chambers, which were rarely located at the actual border. For example, Duved, the main customs chamber in Jämtland, was constructed in a location, below the tree line, where several roads across the mountains converged (see Figure 3.6). Consequently, there existed a stretch of land along the border which did not, in practice, require the importers to pass by a customs chamber to sell their wares on Swedish land, creating a type of economic no man's land. Duved was located around 50 km from the border, Härjedalen's customs chamber in Funäsdalen around 30 km away and Dalarna's Idre about the same (see Figure 3.4). While mounted officers were supposed to oversee these areas, it is clear from the customs reports that they struggled due to understaffing and vast distances.[107] In practice, this meant that the effective economic border was located further into the country than the border delineation on maps. Nor was the economic border a continuous line but rather a series of disconnected outposts with limited staff in their employ. Some customs chambers were even run by a single officer.

A similar situation can also be observed along the border to Russia. Just like along the Norwegian border there appears to have been a corridor between the border and the customs offices. In Figure 3.5, we can see the locations of the customs offices along the border. What is noticeable is not just the distance from the border but their distance from each other. The northernmost customs chamber, Kusamo, not covered by this map, was located even further away.

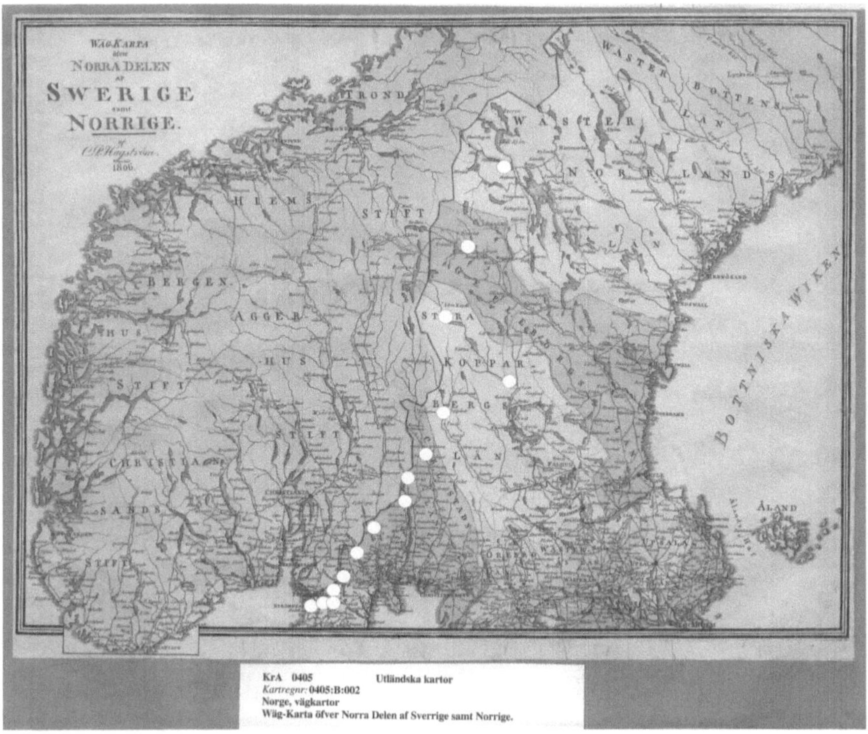

FIGURE 3.4 Road Map of Northern Sweden. The white circles represent customs chambers along the border. Duved, Funäsdalen, and Idre are the three most northern circles. As can be seen, they leave a mostly unsupervised corridor along the Norwegian border. While this area was not heavily populated, it allowed enough space to find alternative routes into the Swedish economic space that did not pass a customs office. C.P. Hagström, 'Wäg-Karta öfver norra delen af Swerige samt Norrige', 1806.

Source: Swedish Military Archives, Utländska kartor, 405, Norge, B:2.

Jämtland and Härjedalen

The areas of Jämtland and Härjedalen had become Swedish in 1645 after previously belonging to the Kingdom of Denmark-Norway. Throughout the eighteenth century, they maintained a strong regional identity with extra-Swedish ties, particularly to the Norwegian province Tröndelag. Trondheim, the regional capital of Tröndelag, has been referred to as the Hamburg of the North. It enjoyed an ice-free harbour and was an important trading centre for central Scandinavia, attracting settlers both from Norway and Sweden.[108] After the separation in 1645, trade played a key role in tying together the regions and their populations.[109] However, as ideas of a unified economic space with a common agenda started to emerge in Sweden, this cross-border trade became increasingly uncomfortable for the authorities who sought to control and regulate it.

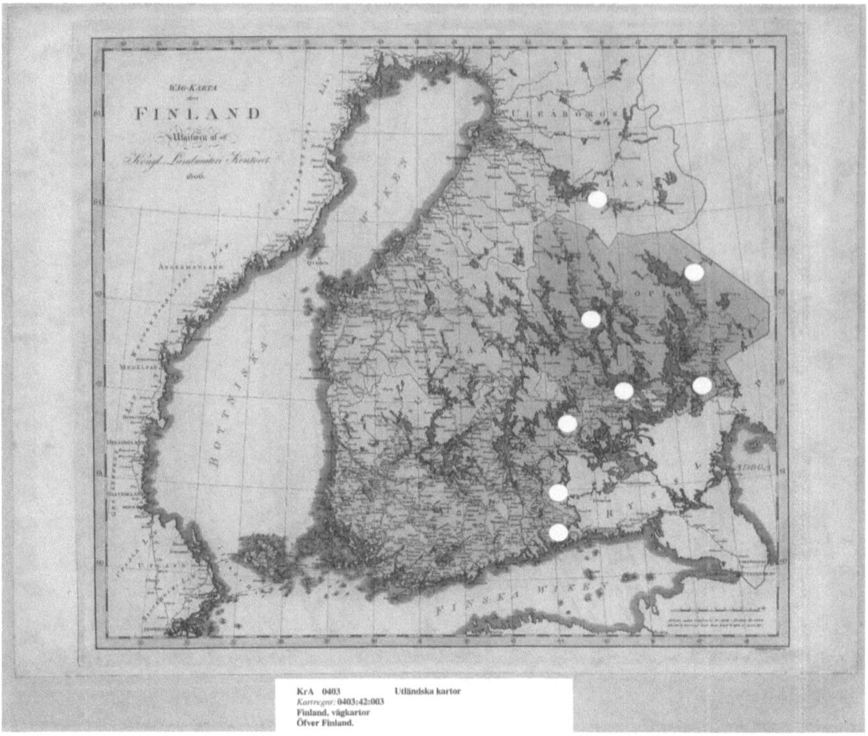

FIGURE 3.5 Road Map of Finland. 'Wäg-karta öfver Finland', 1806. The white circles represent customs chambers along the border.

Source: Swedish Military Archives, Utländska kartor, 403, Finland, 42:3.

From a Swedish perspective, Jämtland and Härjedalen were remote provinces, far from any substantial towns. They were characterised by a mountainous terrain which peaked along the Norwegian border. The institution of a border through these highlands in 1645 was followed by the establishment of several strategic customs chambers in the 1690s, two of which will be considered here: Duved in Jämtland and Funäsdalen in Härjedalen. The customs chambers were located along old roads crossing the mountains, but far from all roads were covered by customs chambers. Skarvdörren, a passage to Norway on the border between Jämtland and Härjedalen, was, for example, left completely unguarded. For all roads across the mountains, see Figure 3.6. The use of that road was consequently prohibited, but it proved impossible to ensure that this prohibition was respected.[110] By 1769, Funäsdalen and Duved customs chambers employed four people each, a negligible workforce considering the need to continuously man the customs chamber and patrol vast mountainous areas and multiple by-roads.

The first yearly report from the customs chamber in Härjedalen dates from 1766. Its author, the customs officer Petter Cerling, observed that the customs officers were unable to impede transgressions that took place in the villages and

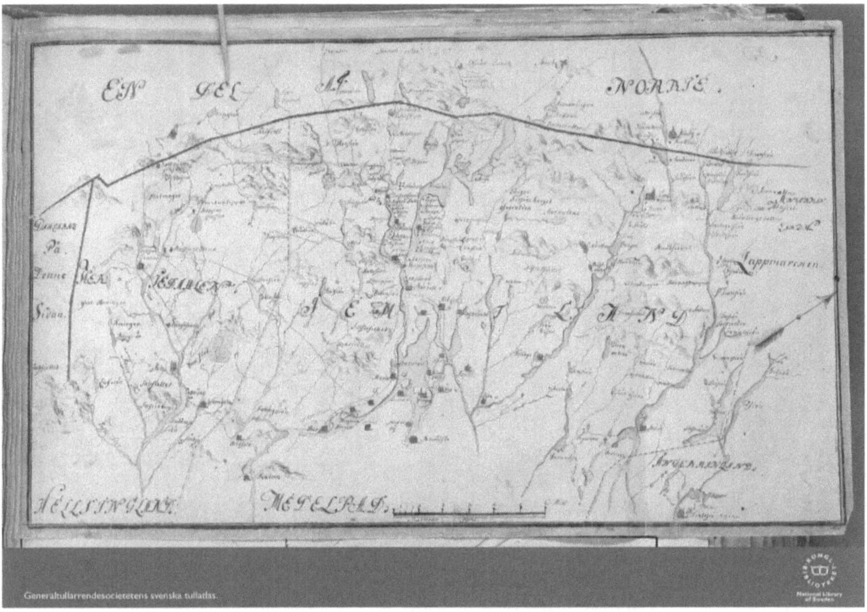

FIGURE 3.6 Map of the Jämtland and Härjedalen border towards Norway. Skarvdörren is the passage furthest to the left on this map. 'Karta över Jämtland, Härjedalen och Ångermanland vid gränsen mot Norge', undated.

Source: National Library of Sweden, MS, Generaltullarrendesocietetens svenska tullatlas, Vol 5, 151.

cottages located along the Norwegian border.[111] Their old paths predated the border and daily chores such as fishing, farming, and taking animals up to the mountains for pasture brought the inhabitants in and out of Norway. In addition, local people travelled on Norwegian roads to Ljusnedal iron works where some of them were employed. The border crossings were thus a regular occurrence and crucial to the economy of the mountain dwellers. By trying to harden the border and to safeguard the Swedish economic territory, the customs officers efficiently attempted to drive a wedge between Sweden and Norway, interfering with the daily lives of the border dwellers. However, instructing the border dwellers not to use their ancient routes was quite a different thing to enforcing it and the quotidian passages into Norway continued by necessity and nonconformity.

Trade was naturally the most troubling cross-border activity for the customs. Pehr Lind, a customs officer in Duved, emphasised the continuous and unstoppable exchanges with Norway.[112] In particular, he stressed the centrality of the market in the Norwegian town of Levanger. The Levanger Market was of particular importance for the people of Jämtland and Härjedalen and was a longstanding feature of the trade in the region. The earliest documentary evidence of the market dates back to the 1530s, although there is reason to believe that it had been in existence since the twelfth century.[113] It was held twice a year, in March

FIGURE 3.7 Map over Sweden's Provinces. 'Underlagskarta för Sveriges indelning i landskap', 1810.

Source: Swedish Military Archives, Sveriges topografiska kartor, 1A:19b.

and December, and was timed to correspond with the snow season, which made journeys across the mountains considerably easier as visitors could travel by ski or sleigh.[114] Levanger was ideally located beside the ice-free Trondheim fjord and could be accessed by trading ships in both the winter and summer. At its peak in the middle of the eighteenth century, about 2,000 Swedes attended the market each year. Foodstuffs had always been a main trading good but during the eighteenth century various other wares started to be sold, including manufactured goods many of which were prohibited to import into the Swedish realm.[115]

One such manufactured good was worsted, a British wool textile prohibited for import to Sweden for the duration of the eighteenth century, which is discussed at length in Chapter 5.[116] Customs protocols from Funäsdalen stretching back to the 1770s show that worsteds played an important role among the contraband seized in Härjedalen. In a typical seizure from 1772, an unknown man was found carrying, among many other things, red striped calamancoes, black, yellow and red striped taboret, blue, white and red flowered taboret, satins in white, red and blue, and kersey, along with snuff boxes and brass and horsehair buttons, adding up to a full value of 19 Rdr 13 sk specie (c. 182 D kmt).[117] The textiles might have been smuggled either from one of the markets in Norway or potentially from the mining town Röros only 70 kilometres from Funäsdalen.

From Duved, no customs protocols have survived prior to 1805 (Figure 3.8). The protocols that have survived, however, indicate that most of the trade journeys were timed to coincide with the biannual market in Levanger in March and December. In 1806, customs officers at Duved made six major confiscations, four between the 10th and 12th March and the last two on the 18th and 21st December, dates corresponding to the Levanger Market.[118] Just like the confiscations from Funäsdalen, these mainly involved textiles. Along with the worsteds common in the 1770s records, there was also a large proportion of cotton, particularly handkerchiefs and children's neckerchiefs along with calico cloth of various colours and prints. The customs records give an idea of what types of goods were smuggled, and how they changed over time, but they also highlight the consistently prominent role of the Levanger Market in the consumer life of Jämtland and Härjedalen.

While the customs protocols show that some goods were seized upon their arrival in Sweden, a closer examination of the circumstances and conditions in the customs chambers indicates that these seizures were made despite severe deficiencies in the running of the regional customs. In 1784, the then customs officer at Funäsdalen, Anders Lund, reported that confiscation cases were waiting 6–8 years to be prosecuted as they currently had no regular Customs Court chairman. The customs personnel consequently also missed out on their confiscation bonuses, something that undermined their incentive to perform their duties.[119] Meanwhile, the lack of prosecutions further encouraged border dwellers to ignore the regulations.

Although reports of smuggling dwindle after 1789, when Fredrich Björkebaum was appointed chief customs officer at Funäsdalen, a close investigation reveals that it was not due to a decrease in illegal trade.[120] When travel fiscal Magnus Hammer came to inspect the customs chamber in late autumn 1803, he quickly started to suspect that something was awry after two arrested Norwegian farmhands were released in return for bribes. Two weeks later, Hammer uncovered another indiscretion, when he caught Björkebaum returning eight

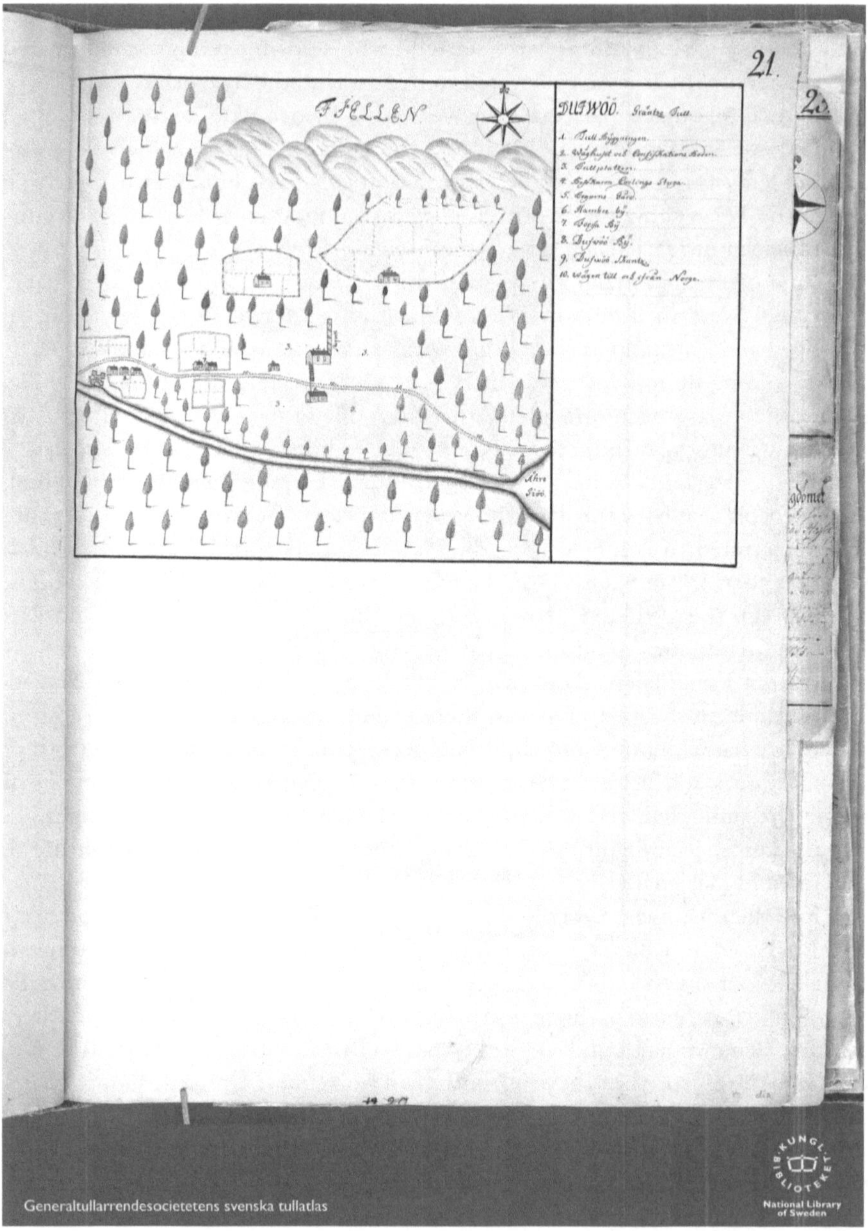

FIGURE 3.8 Duved Customs Chamber. 'Dufwöö [Duved] Gräntze Tull', undated. *Source*: National Library of Sweden, MS, Generaltullarrendesocietetens svenska tullatlas, Vol 5, 21.

sacks of coffee beans, and a sleigh load of other contraband, to Johan Linde, a peasant caught smuggling. These occasions proved to be part of an established pattern. Indeed, Björkebaum had even participated in smuggling himself when he transported gunpowder out of Sweden from Ljusnedal's iron works to Norway on behalf of the foundry proprietor Zacharias Wiklund. The two men had deceived both the neighbouring population and the other customs employees into believing that Wiklund had been given a license to conduct toll-free trade. When Hammer discovered the irregularities, he demanded to see the customs records, which he was denied. In his subsequent report, Hammer relates that he was exposed to threats of violence and eventually fled to Duved customs chamber. From there, he was finally able to report back to the central offices in Stockholm. During Hammer's stay in Funäsdalen, Björkebaum had repeatedly denied him the use of the customs office's own postal services, so this was the first time Hammer could reach his superiors in the capital.[121] The Björkebaum case does not merely illustrate the presence of corruption in the customs chambers, and how enforcers could become enablers but it also reminds us to approach the customs office records with caution, a lack of reports does not necessarily mean an absence of smuggling. It shows that enforcers cannot simply be seen as an extension of the state but were individuals with private interests and concerns. The efficient maintenance of the borders thus relied on aligning the objectives of the state and its enforcers.

Smuggling did not endure only because of the shortcomings of the customs surveillance, but it continued due to permanent shortages in the border regions. These areas had few alternatives to the illegal cross-border trade. Visiting Jämtland in 1804 the Pomeranian traveller Ernst Moritz Arndt commented:

> Trondheim is not located far off...Both the pleasure and profit of a legal and illegal mutual trade are so great, that many are enticed to seize such a profitable trade... In the houses of many peasants it is possible to buy wine, coffee, silk and cotton cloth, along with many other fripperies...[122]

Most of these goods would not have been available through Swedish channels. In 1806, Björkebaum's successor C. G. Lundberg noted that the local population still chose to buy and sell goods in Norway. He explained that "the introduction of illegal goods, seems to be a consequence of the remoteness of [Swedish] Cities".[123] Lundberg makes clear that the transgressions against Swedish legislation should be understood both as a continuation of old traditions to sell and source goods in Norway but also as a lack of a feasible alternative. For most border dwellers, it would not have been possible to source consumer wares in Sweden without great difficulty, travel, and expense, sacrifices few consumers were willing to make when well stocked markets awaited them on the other side of the border. As a result of the difficult geography and the limited reach of state authority, smuggling continued as long as the local population favoured it and found it economically beneficial.

Karelia and Ostrobothnia

While the western border dated back to the previous century, the eastern border towards Russia was relatively recent. A new border through Karelia had been drawn up in the Treaty of Nystad (1721), which marked the end of the Great Northern War. More recently still, Sweden had lost parts of southern Karelia to Russia following the Treaty of Åbo in 1743. These new borders cut through previously established villages, which meant that the inhabitants of these areas suddenly needed to cross into Russia to get to their parish church or the local mill.[124] Similar to their compatriots in the west, their lives were fragmented by the border, and their quotidian movements across it became politically charged as they were seen to enable smuggling and to undermine the integrity of the new border.[125]

Just like Jämtland and Härjedalen, the eastern Finnish provinces Karelia, eastern Ostrobothnia, and Savolax were far removed from the central powers in Stockholm. They had no considerable towns or industries, particularly after 1743 when the eastern towns Villmanstrand, Nyslott, and Fredrickshamn were lost to Russia. In contrast to the mountainous region along the western border, the eastern terrain was reasonably flat but dominated by the taiga, the boreal forest that covers most of the northern latitudes. The inland climate ensured freezing winters and heavy snowfalls.

The economic state of these border regions can in part be derived from early academic treatises. In a treatise about the œconomy of Karelia from 1756, the Karelian native Johan Kraftman noted that there were only two customs chambers along the border and that a sole mounted officer was stationed in all of Karelia. This was woefully insufficient according to Kraftman, who pointed to the extensive border, the difficult terrain, and the many secret paths and byroads known only to the Karelians themselves.[126] Kraftman was also altogether negative towards the 'Russian trade' that was common along the border and which according to Kraftman undermined the Swedish industry.[127] There were, however, several other commentators who took a different approach. One of them was Ostrobothnian Eric Carstén, who in his 1754 academic treatise about the county of Kajanaborg, in the province of Ostrobothnia just north of Karelia, described the biannual markets at Kajana and the accompanying Russian trade as integral to the town's development (Figure 3.9). Markets like the one at Kajana had been set up to attempt to regulate and standardise the Russian trade to Sweden-Finland.[128] They became important in these porous border areas, as they were intended to create order and to control the movements of goods in and out of the country. Kajana was at this time a town with a mere 135 inhabitants but Carstén described the market as well attended, both by peasants from Karelia and Savolax as well as by burghers from Uleåborg, Brahestad, Gamla and Nya Karleby, along with a multitude of Russians from Repola, Pyhaniemi, Vuokkiniemi, Russian Kemi, and Sordawalla Kargapol, and an increasing number of people from Arkhangelsk.[129] In this way, Carstén argued, the market was a meeting point between people from Finland and Russia, stimulating trade and local development in areas otherwise far removed from any major town.

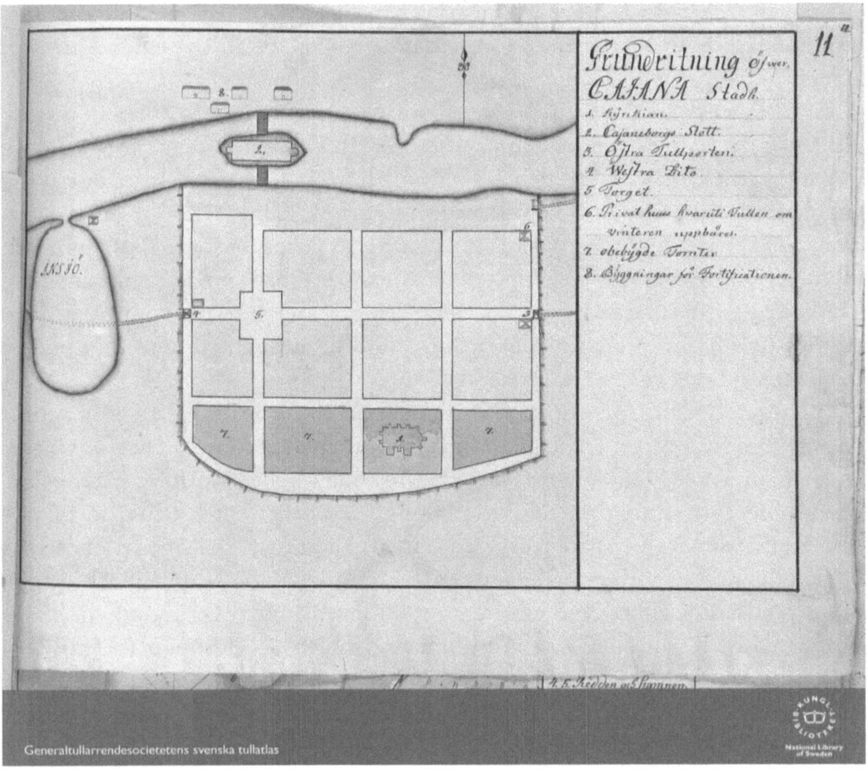

FIGURE 3.9 Customs office drawing of Kajana along with its two tollgates, no. 3 to the east and no. 4 to the west, along with a fence around the town, undated but originating from the 1760s or 1770s. 'Grundritning öfwer Cajana Stadh', undated.

Source: National Library of Sweden, MS, Generaltullarrendesocietetens svenska tullatlas, Vol 5, 11.

Just like the academic accounts, the first yearly reports from the customs stress the porousness of the Karelian border, and a general support for smuggling among the border population. In the first report from the customs at St Mickel, located in southern Savolax and tasked with surveying the customs chambers in Karelia, it was noted that Karelian and Savolaxian peasants were often involved in smuggling from Russia.[130] Even those that were not directly involved were still unwilling to assist the officers. Widespread support for smuggling, as well as the smugglers' propensity for violence, caused some officers to observe that they could not make any real difference without military support. Violent smugglers were nothing new but Kraftman had concluded that if an honest customs officer wanted to make a confiscation he had to prepare for a violent encounter.[131] Because of this, requests have been made to the King to arm the customs officers and give them military assistance.[132] The need for military assistance was not unique to Karelia, but it does appear to have been particularly pressing there.[133] Accounts like these bear witness to the dangers involved in the enforcement of borders.

Vast distances and the countless by-roads were prominent features in the reports from the eastern border. Long distances do not, however, appear to have had a deterrent effect on the people who inhabited these areas. In one striking example from February 1771, a peasant from Torneå, Henric Larsson (or Laurinpaika), had travelled to Kajana market by sleigh to purchase some Russian cloth, an expedition of roughly 600 km.[134] Such vast distances made comprehensive surveillance as good as impossible. These remote and sparsely populated areas made up transit zones where contraband could be brought in and transported into the main body of the country.

Despite early calls for military assistance, military postings did not appear along the border until the late 1780s and only then as a consequence of Gustav III's Russian War (1788–1790). They do, however, appear to have had an immediate effect on smuggling activities along the border. At Kajana, an official observed that smuggling had decreased due to the presence of military postings all along the border through all seasons.[135] The military postings appear to have had a long-lasting effect, and as late as 1806 it was noted that smuggling was still limited in Kajana due to the military postings.[136] Although the military postings did not eliminate smuggling completely, they certainly added a level of complexity. Meanwhile, the relentless smuggling was probably aided by shortcomings at the regional customs chambers, where reports describe aged and incapacitated mounted officers, and customs chambers that were too few and far between.[137]

This smuggling trade relied, as in earlier times, on the co-operation of the border dwellers who both housed contraband and later transported it further into the country.[138] What then motivated the border population to get involved in the contraband trade despite the dangers? One of the common aspects reported upon by the customs officials, both from the Norwegian and the Russian border, was the economic situation in the region. In reports from various border regions, customs officers observed that smuggling *into* the country decreased in times of economic hardship, while smuggling *out* increased as the foreign markets offered higher returns for sales.[139] Such observations serve to connect smuggling to the makeshift economy and highlight how it could be used as a tool to cope with economically challenging situations. The proximity to the border was used as an asset to navigate and offset, at least in part, the hardships caused by the state of the national or local economy.

Another intriguing feature that emerges from the Finnish customs protocols is how the culprits actually viewed their own crimes. In particular, how they defined the criminal act of smuggling. In the early 1780s, Simon Sisonen was caught with contraband by the village Megrijervi, in Libelitz (now: Merkijärvi). While he recognised the wares as foreign he maintained that as he had not brought them to the Swedish side of the border, he had not committed any crime. To Sisonen, the criminal act had been to introduce the wares into Sweden in the first place, but once they had entered they were 'legal'.[140] This popular definition of smuggling reoccurs in several protocols.[141] There appears to have existed an idea that once the goods were in the country, they were no longer illegal and that the crime of smuggling was defined as bringing prohibited wares across a border. As we will see, this definition did not match the legal reality.

All the provinces considered here, whether on the coast, in the mountains, or in the woods, were located along the edges of the kingdom and were characterised by cross-border movement and exchange. While the borders were created at different dates, they came to be increasingly enforced during the eighteenth century as the protectionist agenda developed. Eighteenth-century anti-smuggling legislation also reflects an increasing concern with the borderlands. Legislation became more prevalent and detailed throughout the second half of the century and even began to target specific types of border territories such as the archipelago. The attempts to control the border regions, along with the people and goods featuring in them, became a quest not only to define Sweden's economic boundaries but also what was fitting and acceptable within the Swedish economic space. Hardening borders and new legislation defined existing patterns of movement and trade as illegal and criminalised common behaviours within these borderlands. At the same time, the continuation of old border-defying movements challenged the state's attempts to ensure territorial control and standardised economic borders.

On the Road – Smuggling within the Dominions

The crime of smuggling was, despite what some defendants argued, not legally restricted to the movement of goods over a national border but included all handling of contraband within the Swedish economic space. Domestic contraband transport can also be considered in terms of borders, between regions (i.e. where customs officers had their jurisdictional power), and across the borders separating towns from the countryside. In contrast to the regional border which was often marked but unguarded, the town border often consisted of physical restrictions such as fences, gates, and, crucially, tollgates.

Regulating and Surveying the Countryside

As Sweden's external borders were far from impervious to smuggling, it became necessary to extend the surveillance of smuggling into the country. Since the sixteenth century, there had been an official requirement to apply for domestic passports for all journeys within Sweden. The passport ordinance was meant to limit drifting and transiency among the peasantry, but the lack of surveillance meant that it could easily be circumvented. Unregulated travelling appears to have continued, and in 1799, a crackdown on travelling without passports was deemed necessary.[142]

Along with the crackdown on domestic travelling, there were also new directives regulating the movement of goods intended to make it easier for the customs officers to distinguish between legal and illegal manufactures. This was particularly the case for cloth, which when it was purchased normally was cut from a bolt of cloth that bore hall- or customs stamps. A cut piece of fabric would thus not be attached with a stamp, and without these stamps, it was difficult to establish whether the cloth was legal or not. In order to rectify this situation, the 1770 anti-smuggling decree stipulated that any piece of textile sent from one destination to another must be accompanied by a written proof that the fabric derived from a legal, stamped, bolt of cloth. If larger collections of textiles were to be transported, it was necessary to apply for a new hall-stamp in the town from which it was sent (8 Art, 2§, 1770).[143] The 1776 Country Customs Regulations Act (*Land-Accis*) developed these directives even further: wares in transit now had to be accompanied by two identical slips stating the origin and destination of the consignment along with exact details regarding weight, numbers, and measurements, proof of having been stamped, and if applicable, where and when the appropriate duties had been paid on imported wares.[144] This stipulation reoccurred in the 1799 decree with two notable additions.[145] Firstly, if forbidden wares were discovered in transit, no warrant or witnesses were needed for their confiscation, and secondly, any fiscal was allowed to make a seizure. The increased regulation and strengthened authority of the customs officers and other state officials tasked with surveying the countryside were intended to expand the state's reach into the countryside, a place notoriously difficult to control due to its sparse population and significant distances.

Nevertheless, surveillance of roads was scant and irregular. Road patrols were usually issued on a temporary basis on the command of a particularly vigilant customs officer, such as Customs Fiscal Hjelm, who in 1801 issued several patrols in the countryside around the town of Kristianstad, an undertaking that resulted in numerous arrests.[146] Confiscations 'on the road' generally referred to roads just outside towns, roads connecting towns, or along exposed coastlines. There are, however, some exceptions to this general rule, such as in the case of farmhand Torsten Jönsson, who happened to encounter the Super Inspector of the Customs Court W. Ramelius in Markaryd, Småland, as the latter was travelling from Stockholm to Kristianstad (Figure 3.10). Jönsson, who at the time was carrying a trunk containing 697 Rdr Specie of contraband, found his cargo unceremoniously seized.[147]

In addition to the main roads, there was a multitude of by-roads, of which most officers at best had a limited knowledge. One travel fiscal thus complained in 1791 that it was necessary to gather more knowledge about the by-roads in order to keep up to date with the commonly used smuggling paths.[148] Another travel fiscal recommended himself to the job of surveying the border between Dalsland and Norway on the grounds that he grew up locally and thus had an intimate knowledge of the roads since childhood.[149] Local knowledge was a crucial tool in the surveillance of the countryside.

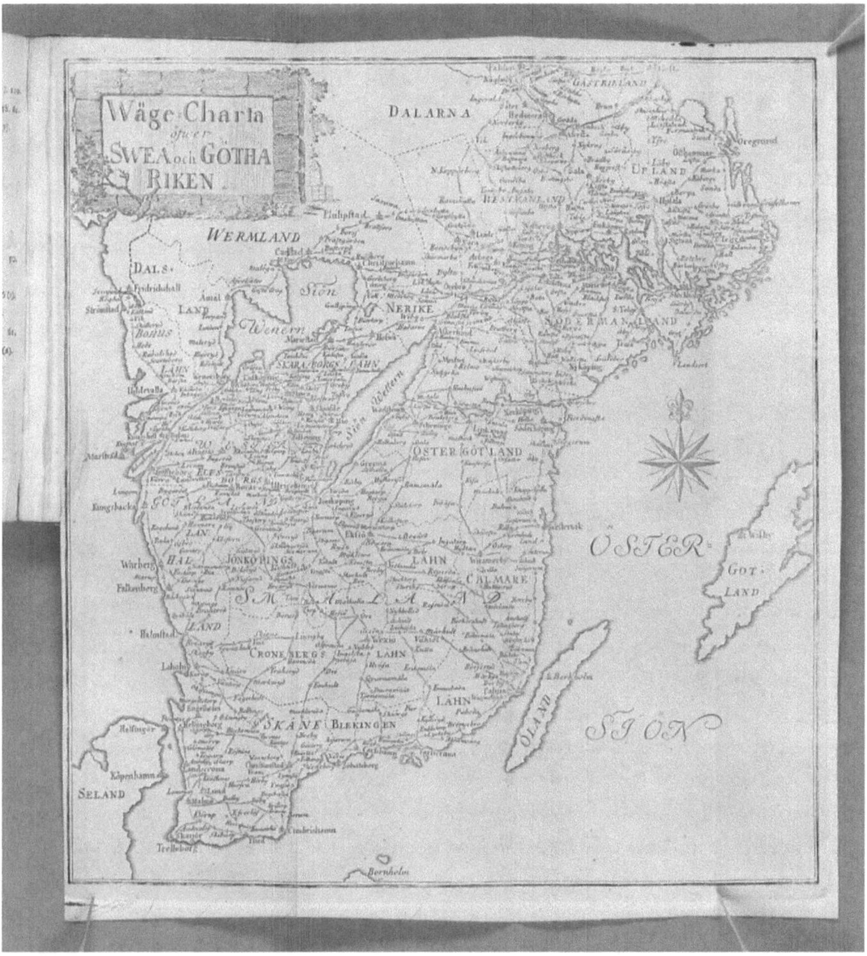

FIGURE 3.10 Road networks in southern Sweden. G. Biurman, 'Wäge Charta öfver Swea och Götha Riken', 1742.

Source: G. Biurman, *Vägvisare uti Svea- och Göta Riken samt Stor-Förstendömet Finland*, Stockholm, 1742.

Effective surveillance was not only an issue of intelligence and local knowledge, however; it was also an issue of practical skill and authority. While the issue for customs officers along the coast was sea mobility, for the officers along the land borders, it was snow mobility, in particular skiing. From the Norwegian border, Customs Officer C.G. Borre reported that "most of the subjects of both Countries, who conduct smuggling, run during the wintertime over mountain and valley on skis, and thus they can come in all over the border and through the forests".[150] By contrast, the local patrolling officers, not natives to the snow ridden inlands, were unable to ski properly. To Borre, this made them unsuited for their positions as they were unable to keep up with the smugglers through the snow. A further hindrance to the efficient surveillance of the countryside was the limited authority of the customs officers, who only held power in their respective jurisdictions.[151] Even if they could ski, they still would not be able to pursue smugglers across district lines. In turn, smugglers could escape persecution by using these borders strategically.

Although there were attempts to increase the regulation of the countryside and extend further powers to the customs officers, the efficient enforcement of this control was irregular at best, something that is also reflected in the customs court records, which feature few roadside confiscations.

The Inn and the Tavern

While the countryside was a vast and fairly unmanageable space for the customs personnel, there nevertheless existed certain fixed sites where travellers, including smugglers, would come together for shelter and provisions. The inns (*gästgiverier*) provided an important reference point for travellers of various distinctions. Located at regular intervals along the public highways, they aimed to ease travelling and to shift the burden of housing visitors from the peasants, who had previously been responsible for supplying shelter, to formal establishments.[152] Travelling salesmen, as well as peasants frequenting markets, were common visitors.[153] The tavern (*krogen*) was a similar establishment to the inn, but cheaper and possibly rougher in character.[154] These establishments were spread out across most of the Swedish countryside but were particularly common in the areas around cities as they provided shelter for people who were unwilling, or could not afford, to stay *in* the city.[155] The inns were transit points as well as meeting points, spaces for social exchange and an intersection between the local and the outside world.[156] They played a crucial role for transaction and exchange.[157]

The authorities did not condone trade in these spaces, however, and regulations were issued to try to control it. In 1783, a prohibition was issued against secret trading, which particularly focused on inns due to their role as sites of contraband exchange.[158] The 1799 anti-smuggling legislation further stipulated that if a person in possession of contraband stopped at an inn or another resting place, any fiscal could immediately seize the goods. The goods would then immediately be listed in the presence of a witness.[159] Despite attempts to control the inn and the tavern through increasing regulation, evidence from Europe indicates that this was to a large extent unsuccessful.[160] This was partly due to the absence of regulatory authorities and partly to the nature of these places as social spaces shaped by popular demand.

The customs court records reveal that smugglers used inns and taverns just like all other travellers. For example, in 1776, while moving a hoard of Cantonese contraband worth a staggering 20,037 D smt (47 years of work for an unskilled labourer), the smugglers stopped at Lahall Inn, 20 km north of Gothenburg to change horses,[161] something the inn-keeper diligently recorded in his 'Inn diary'.[162] Inns were also used as sites of exchange and acquisition.[163] It was thus at Östorp Inn in Småland that the farmhand Hans Dahlberg had acquired the illegal cups, tea caddies, microscope glasses, knives, and various metal buttons, confiscated from him in 1803.[164] Dahlberg's account, along with similar statements, illustrate that the inn was a site where contraband changed hands, where it could be sold, or where travellers could be found who were willing to transport it for a fee. Whether it was always clear that the goods in question were contraband is, however, uncertain.

How involved, then, were the inn-keepers in this clandestine trade? Beat Kümin has noted that the inn-keeper profession had excellent contacts, and the ability to bring people together, resources favourable to clandestine networking.[165] Due to their central position at the inn, it would have been difficult to run, particularly large scale, smuggling operations without their knowledge and in some instances active participation.[166] This is illustrated by the case of tavern-keeper Enström, whose establishment on Stora Hissingen, just outside of Stockholm, was scouted out by a group of customs officers one night in December 1803. In the middle of the night, three people came rowing to the tavern, and as one of them went to the tavern to announce their arrival, the other two were arrested by the customs officers. During the ensuing commotion, the rowers escaped and Enström was apprehended as he was thought to be involved in the enterprise. However, from the first moment of his arrest, he worked with the customs officers. He explained that people often smuggled wares past his tavern and even gave them a tour around his grounds, explaining that he often found suspicious-looking boxes there. After a lengthy trial, it was still impossible to tie Enström to the crime and he was eventually cleared of all charges.[167] Innkeepers thus had an ambivalent role; they could both enable smuggling and assist the prosecution and, in the customs records, they appear both as defendants and as witnesses.

While the inn played a prominent role as a site for smuggling, it could also spell danger as it was a space that attracted particular attention from the authorities. This was something that Achima Purmunen got to experience when he was stopped by officers at Louhivara Inn in Kavi Kapell in northern Savolax. The customs officers who were staying at the inn noticed Purmunen as he was 'dressed suspiciously like a Russian'. Purmunen, from the border village Nehavaniemi (now Nehvonniemi), had been arrested for smuggling the previous winter and let out on bail. At the meeting at Louhivara Inn, he was actually on his way to the Customs Court in Uleåborg to stand trial, but he was also carrying new Russian contraband. While the customs officers attempted to apprehend Purmunen, he managed to flee.[168]

The inn and tavern thus provided not just a meeting place for smugglers; they also enabled smuggling, continuing the transit of illegal goods across the country and between intermediaries. Many inns and taverns were also located near towns, providing poorly regulated spaces just outside of the town limits. While it might have been possible to acquire contraband in these spaces, getting it into the towns was considerably riskier and many smugglers only got as far as the tollgate.

Controlling the Town

The most substantial customs surveillance was reserved for towns and cities, which were often surrounded by fences and walls, interspersed by tollgates that, in theory, any visitor would have to pass through. Due to the high level of surveillance in place, town-based customs officials have generated plentiful records and in order to make it manageable we shall here focus on Gothenburg, and specifically the tollgate Carl's Gate.

Gothenburg

In the eighteenth century, Gothenburg became Sweden's second largest city, much due to its international harbour. While the city grew, it retained its old fortifications, which is significant as it meant that getting into the town, without passing through a tollgate, was considerably harder than in most other towns. Gothenburg thus makes an excellent case study as it highlights the tensions between international trade and protectionist attempts at regulation.

In the customs office map of Gothenburg (Figure 3.11), three tollgates can be seen: (from north to south) Queen's Gate (*Drottnings porten*), King's Gate (*Kungs porten*), and Carl's Gate (*Carls porten*). Carl's Gate was the smallest and least impressive tollgate and was the only one not featured in the work *Suecia antiqua et hodierna* for its architectural elegance (Figure 3.12).[169] It was also the tollgate that generated the majority of all contraband seizures in the city. For instance, in 1785 there were 13 contraband seizures were recorded at Carl's Gate.[170] By comparison, there were five at King's Gate and four at Queen's Gate.

Carl's Gate faced south west towards the area Masthugget, which had previously had the character of a suburban shantytown. In the late eighteenth century, the area was on the rise, however, and the population doubled between 1765 and 1816.[171] Masthugget stretched along the coast and had two main streets, the Broad and the Narrow Way. The properties that lined the seaside were called harbours and stretched out into the water on stilts and could be used as storage spaces as well as loading docks.[172] Masthugget was intrinsically shaped both by the proximity of the sea and Gothenburg, which contributed to transforming it into a smuggling centre.

The customs records from Carl's Gate give the image of Masthugget as an area where contraband was in continuous circulation, passing between individuals who attempted to inconspicuously introduce it into the city. For instance, the records relate that a coachman by the name of Nils Lieberg was stopped with two barrels of contraband tobacco driving down the Narrow Way in February 1791. Lieberg explained that he had encountered a boy by the Spa house (*Kurhus)* down by the quay who had asked him to drive the two barrels into Gothenburg.[173]

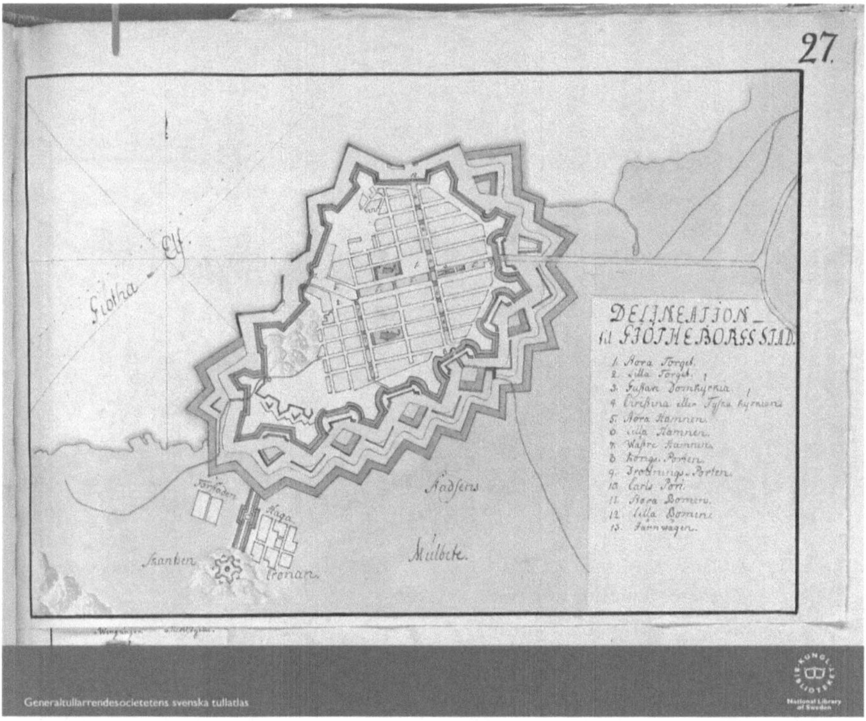

FIGURE 3.11 Gothenburg Town Map. 'Delineation af Giötheborgs stad', 1760s.
Source: National Library of Sweden, MS, Generaltullarrendesocietetens svenska tullatlas, Vol 5, 27.

Similarly, the maid Catharina Andersdotter described how she had been walking down the Narrow Way one summer evening when she suddenly had been asked to bring cotton cloth, striped cotton nightcaps, and worsted socks into the city, where she would be met by the owners of the contraband.[174] Contraband appears to have been fairly prominent in Masthugget and accounts like these suggest that it passed relatively unreservedly between various individuals, known and unknown.

The preponderance of cases at Carl's Gate might also have been linked, at least partially, to how the customs officials managed their duties. A disproportionate number of smuggling offenders were caught through body searches at Carl's Gate. Out of the 17 cases of contraband hidden under clothes reported in Gothenburg in 1785, all but three were found by or near Carl's Gate.[175] It is, however, difficult to determine whether the frequency of these cases was due to increased rates of body searches, or because the practice of concealing contraband under clothes was particularly common at Carl's Gate.

High rates of body searches did not guarantee an impeccably managed tollgate, however. In 1804, travelling fiscal Olof Bellander visited Masthugget and

FIGURE 3.12 Artist's rendition of Carl's Gate. Unknown artist after Elias Martin, 'Karlsporten från stadssidan'. 1787.
Source: Gothenburg City Museum, GhmB:3245.

Carl's Gate, submitting a damning report about conditions at the tollgate, a customs barrier that Bellander himself noted was of great importance to the town. In particular, he recounted an incident with the customs officer Lundblad, who was supposed to have been on duty but had gone missing from his post. Following some investigations, Bellander discovered that Lundblad's absences were a regular occurrence and that he could normally be found at a nearby tavern. The drunk and violent Lundblad was subsequently brought back to his post, where he stayed only a few minutes before disappearing again. Meanwhile, another customs officer, Sven Hagman, albeit not on duty, was found lying passed out drunk in the middle of the street.[176] While the surveillance in the towns, with its fences, gates, and many officers, stands in sharp relief to the unmanageable countryside it was far from optimal, and as will become clear in the next chapter, a lot of contraband still managed to get past the tollgates.

Women and Children as Smugglers

The Gothenburg case study also highlights something virtually absent in other customs material, namely women and children's involvement in the contraband trade. Female defendants are particularly frequent in the Gothenburg records, making up nearly a third of all people caught smuggling in 1785.[177] A significant proportion of the smuggling women were identified through body searches. Out of the 15 women caught smuggling in 1785, ten had undergone body searches. By contrast, among the 37 cases involving men from the same year, only seven were caught through body searches.[178] There are some likely reasons for this difference. Firstly, men had more options in relation to how to smuggle inconspicuously, as they often drove carriages in and out of the city while women often came on foot. Secondly, the female costume allowed more possibilities for hiding goods, particularly with the wide skirt and large pockets that remained in fashion for most of the period. Without routine body searches, female smuggling would thus have gone largely undetected.

Other differences can also be observed between female and male offenders, particularly in regard to how they acquired their goods. The major difference between the sexes lay in whether they had *bought* the goods and intended to introduce them into the city, or if they had been *given* the goods to bring into the city. In a survey of ten cases, from 1785 and 1791, where the defendants expanded on how they had acquired the goods, there were five cases of bought goods, and five of commissioned goods. Out of the five cases of purchased goods, four of the smugglers were female, whereas all of the people introducing commissioned goods to Gothenburg were male.[179] It is possible that men were seen as preferable for commissioned smuggling and that the women were simply buying for their own consumption. However, the two did not have to be mutually exclusive; private consumption could be combined with commissioned smuggling, as a customs official noted for a later period:

> ...the goods are smuggled to the shop, shirting piece by shirting piece, hidden under the trading peasant woman's clothes. In this manner... a merchant in Gothenburg, who has ordered 500 shirting pieces from England, will have his wares within a week free of charge, smuggled into his shop by all the peasant women who visit his shop to buy coffee, sugar and pepper. [180]

Women thus appear to have played an important role in bringing contraband into towns, whether it was for personal enjoyment, profit, or both. It also agrees with earlier European scholarship, which has highlighted that women used smuggling, as well as other illegal activities, to generate additional income.[181]

Children also played an important role in the contraband trade into Gothenburg.[182] Children younger than 15 had not yet reached the age of criminal responsibility and were, normally, not punishment. It could, however, sometimes be a struggle to assert the age of the children. In a case from 1785, the father of a girl caught smuggling chocolate into Gothenburg was called to testify to the age of his daughter. The father explained that his daughter was only 13, a statement "which was confirmed by the girl's weight and appearance".[183] In this instant, the court freed the girl as she was considered too young and ignorant to be deemed culpable.

This situation was used strategically and children were used as buffers to protect the true identities of the smugglers. One such example has already been noted in the case of Nils Lieberg, who received a commission to drive contraband into the city from a boy he thought was a servant.[184] An unknown boy also approached the peasant Eric Larsson in 1791 and engaged him to come to the Nordre river to collect a contraband commission destined for Gothenburg.[185] While not all children avoided punishment, they do appear to have been a partially protected group, which could be used to enable and disguise smuggling ventures.[186] In addition to communicating and commissioning, children were used as lookouts during smuggling operations.[187] Children thus came to hold quite a specific role, as diversions and buffers between the various links in the contraband chain.

Despite being limited in scope, this case study of Gothenburg's tollgates reveals the multitude of people involved in the contraband trade. Men, women, and children all seem to have found their part to play in the movement of illicit goods, and to many it was probably a welcome addition to their finances. While contraband transporters could come in all shapes and sizes, they often played different roles in the transit of contraband. The material from Gothenburg indicates that children often served as intermediaries to control and direct larger smuggling ventures, while women often appear to have smuggled for their own consumption. Adult male smuggling was, as discussed throughout this chapter, more multifaceted. One thing, however, united practically all of these actors: their relative poverty. It played a part in motivating the smuggling of fishing communities along the coast, of borderland dwellers, as well as of women and children in Gothenburg. While the cause and extent of their financial strain varied, many different actors appear to have used smuggling to bolster earnings, as part of a makeshift economy, and this smuggling can in this way be conceived of as a type of popular illegalism with widespread support.

Poverty as a Redeeming Feature?

Smuggling might have been seen as a coping mechanism by the perpetrators, but was poverty also seen as a redeeming circumstance by the customs court? Before turning to this question, it is necessary to consider what a contraband-runner could actually hope to gain from their involvement in the contraband trade. Most of the smugglers discussed in this chapter did not own the contraband they transported but it had been given to them on credit or commission. The potential rewards appear to have been very limited. The earliest mention of a reimbursement for contraband transport is from Gothenburg in 1785 and appears to be referring to some type of drink.[188] Seven years later, the peasant Sven Andersson explained to the court that he had been paid 1 *plåt* (probably 2 D smt) to hold a box containing contraband until its owner returned.[189] Meanwhile, in 1803, the crofter Anders Jonsson in Stockholm was offered 32 shillings by the peasant Per Jansson and the churchwarden Jan Ersson for his help in transporting some smuggled goods by boat. For Jonsson, this sum might have been significant. However, during the subsequent trial, he was facing fines reaching up to 815 Rdr bco for his involvement (1 Rdr bco was equal to 48 shilling). Eventually, Jonsson was cleared of all charges as it proved impossible to ascertain that he knew that the goods were illegal.[190] While it is difficult to attain any precise knowledge about how much a runner could hope to gain from their involvement in a smuggling venture, which probably varied considerably, it is nevertheless clear that the compensation was eclipsed by the potential fines attached to the crime.

For the people motivated by poverty, the fines for smuggling were frequently impossible to pay. This was also recognised in the anti-smuggling legislation of 1757, which settled that if the culprit was unable to pay the fines for the crime the sentence would be converted into a prison sentence on water and bread, a clause that reappeared again in (1 Art. 6§, 1770) and (9 Art, 1§, 1799). However, according to the customs court protocols, poverty, particularly in conjunction with poor health, could also lead to an alleviated punishment, and in some instances the punishment was completely scrapped. One such incidence from May 1776 features the fire watchman widow Helena Lundbeck. During a search of her home in Gothenburg, some 50 ells of forbidden cloth had been found. While Lundbeck explained that the cloth belonged to the surgeon's apprentice Johan Arnhold Schoner, Schoner denied any involvement and stated that he had never set his foot in her house. As Lundbeck was unable to provide any witnesses to back up her story, she was landed with the full responsibility for the contraband. Unable to pay the fines, the punishment was converted to 28 days in prison on bread and water. However, the punishment was suspended, most likely due to Lundbeck's age and poor health.[191] Other similar cases show that this was not a unique occurrence, but punishments were occasionally dropped due to poverty, ill health, and having many dependants.[192] It shows that there was room for some negotiation within the legal framework and that poverty could be a redeeming feature. Moreover, before the cases ever came to court, poverty might have helped to dissuade the customs officers from making an arrest.

Such leniency towards poor smugglers was not universal, however. Within the Finnish material from the border customs chamber at Kides, there is a case from 1787 which contained an appeal to convert a multitude of smuggling fines into jail sentences. The nine convicted criminals in question were all too poor to pay off their fines, and the customs office requested the court to convert their sentences into jail sentences on water and bread stretching from 8 to 20 days, which the court also agreed to.[193] Poverty was thus not always seen as a redeeming factor and whether it was or was not most likely came down to local conditions, such as the prevalence of smuggling in the area and whether leniency could be seen to encourage more smuggling or if it could be construed as a single act of mercy.

*****

How smuggling functioned depended on the border in question. Neither maritime nor land borders offered much of a barrier, but the tactics required to smuggle wares across them differed and so did the possibilities for their surveillance. The border dwellers, who were particularly likely to smuggle in their own region, possessed both the skills and equipment to trespass against 'their' border: the peasant sailors on the west coast had both boats and navigation skills, the mountain and forest dwellers skis, sledges, and knowledge of their local terrain. They thus had the necessary skillset to cross the borders, which, as we have seen, was not always true for the people set to prevent them. The integrity of maritime borders, and to a lesser extent the land borders, could also be threatened by go-betweens not local to the region. The situation was particularly challenging along the maritime borders, as passing vessels could fairly quickly dispose of contraband along the extensive coast. Trading vessels, with their large freight volume, were seen as especially problematic and various attempts were made to control them. Subsequently, the responsibility for the ship's contents was delegated to the captains. These attempts at control aimed to make the captain a stand-in for the customs officers, and consequently the state, on board the ship, a responsibility that most captains did not want and tried to distance themselves from. The maritime and land borders were also affected in varying ways by the changing of the seasons, which influenced both surveillance and smuggling. Particularly noteworthy is the shift between snow, ice, and darkness in the winter, and the long, bright, and relatively warm days of summer. The winter was prime time for overland smuggling, as it enabled long journeys by sledge, and was simultaneously a period when many other types of employment, such as agricultural labour, were unavailable. Maritime smuggling, by contrast, appears to have followed a different schedule, particularly along the Baltic Sea, which often froze in winter.

Smuggling across maritime and land borders thus presented a fundamentally different set of challenges and advantages for both smugglers and surveillance officers. By contrast, whether borders were of a recent or an older date appears to have had little bearing on smuggling. Cross-border trade does not appear to have diminished or perished with time. Instead, trade continued as long as it was meaningful to the people living in these border regions. More important than the age of the border was how it was maintained. When a reduction in smuggling was eventually recorded, it was in conjunction with the militarisation of the Finnish-Russian border in the 1780s. The arrival of military postings appears to have achieved what the customs chambers could not: impeding cross-border movements and smuggling. At the same time, as the customs officers themselves noted, while the military postings reduced smuggling, they did not extinguish it.

It is therefore crucial to consider the effectiveness of the protectionist legislation in terms of its enforcement, which depended upon the level of surveillance present in various spaces. While the level of enforcement was particularly high around customs chambers, and in towns, it was less systematic along the border between customs chambers and in the Swedish countryside. The Swedish economic space thus benefits from being considered in terms of 'hotspots' of protectionist enforcement rather than as a uniform economic space. One such hotspot was the town: limited in scope, and with a large customs force, it was relatively easy to survey and manage. And yet, as discussed in this chapter, and as will become even more evident in the next, even the town was far from impervious to contraband.

While most of the go-betweens travelling between Sweden and extranational areas were male, the go-betweens who moved locally, for example in and out of the cities, were considerably more diverse and included women and children. Most likely, this reflected women and children's movement patterns, as they were less likely to travel great distances independently, as most of the long-distance transporters did. It does not, however, indicate that smuggling into towns was less dangerous than across state borders. Instead, the opposite appears to have been the case due to strict surveillance at the tollgates, and few alternative entry points into towns. Diverse groups of people thus engaged in the transport of contraband, despite the potential dangers. They were motivated by the prospect of profit, as one crucial, unwanted, consequence of the protectionist legislation was that it increased the incentive to smuggle, by limiting the potential to conduct trade legally and making traditional trade patterns illegal. An array of various perpetrators has been discussed in this chapter: many of them poor, marginalised, and sharing a common need to extend their income. As the restrictions on trade increased, the people who had previously depended on it, to add a bonus onto a meagre salary or as a crucial part of a makeshift economy, chose to maintain their trading activities even though these were redefined as illegal. In particular, smuggling out of the country seems to have been adopted to increase earnings during periods of crisis. In this way, smuggling appears to have been used as a popular way to negotiate the adverse effects of protectionism on the private economy.

Sweden was undergoing a process of legislative homogenisation during the eighteenth century. This chapter has shown that economic standardisation in law was not necessarily accompanied by the development of a state apparatus able to provide the level of surveillance required to enforce the legislation and to make Sweden into a homogenised economic space. In effect, the early modern Swedish state experienced numerous difficulties when it came to controlling its territory, including a vast and challenging geography, a shortage of resources, and limited authority over its own customs personnel. A spontaneous de facto provincial autonomy was thus reigning despite the development of de jure sovereignty. While customs surveillance appears to have improved in the early nineteenth century, mainly through the introduction of the travelling fiscals tasked with overseeing the regional customs chambers, the period was marked by uneven and unreliable customs enforcement. Sweden's borders must thus be understood as porous, enabling people and illegal global goods to enter surreptitiously, which made it challenging to impose protectionism in practice. The porousness of the borders also challenges our understanding of Sweden's globalisation process in the eighteenth century. Protectionist attempts to control and limit the impact of global trade on the Swedish market resulted in this trade being pushed underground, with wares from other economic jurisdictions still able to enter secretly via more liberal markets and entrepôts in surrounding territories. Such markets included

Sweden's largest trading partner Great Britain, its own dominions in Wismar and Pomerania, and its neighbouring territories Denmark-Norway and Russia. In practice, it is thus difficult to efficiently distinguish Sweden's economic space from that of the surrounding territories; and wares located in these territories, prohibited in Sweden, could easily cross the border.

Notes

1 Istvan Hont, *Jealousy of Trade* (Cambridge, MA; London: Harvard University Press, 2005), 459–461.
2 Lauren Benton, *A Search for Sovereignty: Law and Geography in European Empires, 1400–1900* (Cambridge: Cambridge University Press, 2009), 2.
3 Peter Sahlin, *Boundaries. The Making of France and Spain in the Pyrenees* (Berkley; Los Angeles; London: University of California Press, 1989); Morieux, *The Channel.*
4 Marjolein 't Hart, 'The People and the State. Nordic Paths in State Formation, 1500–1800', *Bringing the People Back in. State Building from Below in the Nordic Countries ca. 1500–1800*, ed. Knut Dørum, Mats Hallenberg, Kimmo Katajala (Routledge, 2021).
5 Maria Cavallin, 'I kungen och folkets tjänst. Synen på den svenske ämbetsmannen 1750–1780' (PhD thesis, Göteborgs Universitet, 2003). See particularly her discussion about customs officers pages 222–226; Ågren, *The State as Master*, 17–20. See also Magnus Linnarsson, 'Contested Customs. Swedish Towns and the Private Customs Company, 1726–1762', *Bringing the People back in. State Building from Below in the Nordic Countries ca. 1500–1800*, ed. Knut Dørum, Mats Hallenberg, Kimmo Katajala (Abingdon-on-Thames: Routledge, 2021).
6 Tesdahl, 'The Price of Empire', 14–20: Anne Montenach, *Femmes, pouvoir et contrebande*, 25–31.
7 Recent studies of go-betweens, or intermediaries, have highlighted their crucial role in the spread of knowledge and goods between countries as well as continents. See for example: Sanjay Subrahmanyam, ed., *Merchant Networks in the Early Modern World* (London; New York: Routledge, 1996); Simon Schaffer et al., eds., *The Brokered World. Go-Betweens and Global Intelligence, 1770–1820* (Sagamore Beach: Science History Publications, U.S.A., 2009). For a Swedish study, see Lisa Hellman, 'Ett ensamt skepp på öppet hav? Kopplingar, kontakter och utbyten ombord svenska ostindiefarare [A Lone Ship at Open Sea? Connections, Contacts and Exchanges on Swedish East Indiamen]', *Historisk Tidsskrift* 3 (2014).
8 Francesca Trivellato, 'The Historical and Comparative Study of Cross-Cultural Trade', in *Religion and Trade: Cross-Cultural Exchange in World History*, ed. Francesca Trivellato, Leor Halevi, and Catia Antunes (Oxford: Oxford University Press, 2014).
9 Niklas Frykman, 'Pirates and Smugglers: Political Economy in the Red Atlantic', in *Mercantilism Reimagined: Political Economy in Early Modern Britain and Its Empire*, ed. Philip J. Stern and Carl Wennerlind (Oxford: Oxford University Press, 2013); Kwass, *Contraband*; Gottmann, *Global Trade*; Cromwell, 'Illicit Ideologies'; Vázquez, *Islanders and Empire*, 2.
10 The last two were quickly returned to Denmark-Norway in 1660 under the Treaty of Copenhagen.
11 For a brief discussion about custom legislations, see Nordin, *Ett fattigt men fritt folk*, 91 & 323.
12 Nordin, *Ett fattigt men fritt folk*, 325 & 438; Marjanen, 'Den ekonomiska patriotismens uppgång och fall', 156.
13 Nordin, *Ett fattigt men fritt folk*, 327.
14 Braudel, *The Mediterranean.*
15 On the seasonality of work, see: Carl-Johan Gadd, 'The Agricultural Revolution in Sweden', in *The Agrarian History of Sweden 4000 BC to AD 2000*, ed. Janken Myrdal

and Mats Morell, (Lund: Nordic Academic Press, 2011), 131; Kathryn E. Gary, 'The Distinct Seasonality of Early Modern Causal Labour and the Short Durations of the Working Years: Sweden 1500–1800', *Lund Papers in Economic History* 189 (2019). For a general discussion on the economic effects of fish migration, see: Lars Nilsson and Erik Lönnroth, 'Det stora sillfisket 1752–1808', in *Bohusläns Historia* (Stockholm: Almqvist & Wiksells, 1963).

16 Pierrick Pourchasse, 'Trade between France and Sweden in the Eighteenth Century', *Forum Navale* 67 (2011), 110; Eric Schnakenbourg, 'Sweden and the Atlantic: The Dynamism of Sweden's Colonial Projects in the Eighteenth Century', in *Scandinavian Colonialism and the Rise of Modernity. Contributions To Global Historical Archaeology*, ed. Naum M. Nordin and et al. (New York: Springer, 2013), 239.

17 Victor Wilson, *Commerce in Disguise: War and Trade in the Caribbean Free Port of Gustavia, 1793–1815* (Åbo: Åbo Akademis förlag, 2015); Han Jordaan and Victor Wilson, 'The Eighteenth-Century Danish Dutch, and Swedish Free Ports in the Northeastern Caribbean: Continuity and Change', in *Dutch Atlantic Connections, 1680–1800: Linking Empires, Bridging Borders*, ed. Gert Oostindie and Jessica V. Roitman, vol. 29 Atlantic World: Europe, Africa and the Americas, 1500–1830 (Leiden: Brill, 2014); Leos Müller, 'Sweden's Neutral Trade under Gustav III: The Ideal of Commercial Independence under the Predicament of Political Isolation', in *Trade and War: The Neutrality of Commerce in the Inter-State System*, ed. Koen Stapelbroek (Helsinki: Helsinki Collegium for Advanced Studies, 2011).

18 For a discussion about J. F. Kryger's writings about protectionism and patriotism, see Chapter 2.

19 Andreas Önnerfors, *Svenska Pommern: Kulturmöten och identifikation 1720–1815* (Lund: Lund University, 2003), 369; Andreas Önnerfors, 'Gränser och gemenskaper. Hur svenskt var svenska Pommern?', in *Vid gränsen. Integration och identitet i det förnationella Norden*, ed. Harald Gustafsson and Hanne Sanders (Göteborg & Stockholm: Makadam Förlag, 2006), 251.

20 One example of a pilot at sea reporting a smuggling venture has been encountered, which, however, predates the new legislation. On 28 July 1768, Captain Johan Martin Smitt's crew anchored their ship in headwind outside of Herrhamra (*Härhamra*), some way south of Dalarö, and three of the able seaman had thrown two sacks into a boat, preparing to row off, when pilot at sea Hans Hansson enquired about their actions. They responded that the sacks contained goods they wanted to transport ashore, asked if Hansson could help them and promised that in return he would be remunerated. According to his own account in court, Hansson was wary and unsure about how to act as he wanted to "conserve himself" and thus be able to expose the offence to the authorities. Finally, he decided that he would go along with it and took the sacks to his home on the isle of Krok. Shortly thereafter, Hansson revealed the offence to the Inspector at Herrhamra, Johan Westman, and handed over the goods. As these events show, smugglers could be bold and brazen in their activities and unfaced by coastal dwellers, who could be seen as an asset rather than a threat. Furthermore, it illustrates which type of enticements state officials could be faced with if they chose to aid rather than prevent the smuggling. Hansson did, however, find himself well rewarded for his report and received 60% of the value of the seized contraband as stipulated in the 1757 decree. See: 5 July 1769, 'Stora Siötulls Rättens Dombok' 1769, Stockholms rådhusrätt, Stora Sjötullen, Protokoll, A, vol.22, Stockholms Stadsarkiv.

21 Gothenburg took over as Sweden's most important harbour in 1860: 'Stockholms Hamnar'. Accessed 1 March 2022, https://www.stockholmshamnar.se/historia/epoker/1850–1899/.

22 Jan Berggren, *Tullsnok - Öppna bommen! Carl Michael Bellman och tullen* (Stockholm: Carlsson Bokförlag, 2003), 24–28.

23 'Stora Siötulls Rättens Dombok', 1769, Stockholms rådhusrätt, Stora Sjötullen, Protokoll, A, vol.22, Stockholms Stadsarkiv.

24 'Kongl. maj:ts ytterligare nådige förordning, angående lurendrägeriers uptäckande och hämmande' (1757). 1§ & 2§.
25 Modée, 'Kongl. maj:ts förordning emot lurendrägerier eller förbudne utrikes warors införsel i riket, 22 martii 1770' (1770). 5 Art., 1§ & 3§.
26 'Kongl. maj:ts förordning emot lurendrägerier eller förbudne utrikes warors införsel i riket, 22 martii 1770' (1770). 5 art., 3§; an example of this new legislation in action can be seen in 1776 when Captain M. Lannes' ship arrived in Gothenburg from Aberdeen. 25 illegal items were found on board belonging to the able seaman Jon Stephens. Stephens confessed that he had brought the items onto the ship without the captain's knowledge. Jon Stephens was fined 177 D smt for his offence, while his captain had to pay 10 D smt for negligence (5 art. 3§, 1770). 30 April 1776, in 'Dombok' 1776, A1, vol.10, Göteborgs Sjötullsrätt, Göteborgs Landsarkiv.
27 'Kongl. maj:ts nådiga förordning, til förekommande af lurendrägeri och tullförsnillning gifwen haga slott den 6 april 1799' (1799). 5 art. 3§.
28 Ibid. 5 art., 2§.
29 20 Dec 1769, 'Stora Siötulls Rättens Dombok' 1769, Stockholms rådhusrätt, Stora Sjötullen, Protokoll, A, vol.22, Stockholms Stadsarkiv.
30 One example of this is the captain Petter Östlund who absconded following a visitation on his ship. An arrest order was featured in the newspaper *Stockholms Posttidningar* on the 3rd of January 1801, no 1.
31 See for example *Stockholms Posttidningar*, 4 December 1800, no 137, *Inrikes Tidningar*, 10 September 1802.
32 Müller, *Consuls, Corsairs, and Commerce*. See for example: 'Publication sur les privileges du port franc de la ville de Marstrand, du 19 avril 1776', Mémoires et Documents, Suède, vol.6, 1632–1814, Centre des Archives diplomatiques de la Courneuve; 'David Hailes to Lord Grenville, Stockholm, 16 Apr 1799', 1799, FO 73, vol.27, British National Archives.
33 20 Juni 1769, 'Stora Siötulls Rättens Dombok' 1769, Stockholms rådhusrätt, Stora Sjötullen, Protokoll, A, vol.22, Stockholms Stadsarkiv.
34 24 Nov 1769, 'Stora Siötulls Rättens Dombok' 1769, Stockholms rådhusrätt, Stora Sjötullen, Protokoll, A, vol.22, Stockholms Stadsarkiv.
35 See also the case of Captain John Harrison who had sailed between Britain and Sweden for five years when he was caught smuggling in 1803 and claimed to be ignorant of the Swedish legislation, which, unsurprisingly, was not deemed a suitable defence. 20 June 1776, 'Dombok' 1776, A1, vol.10, Göteborgs Sjötullsrätt, Göteborgs Landsarkiv.
36 Magnus Ressel, 'Swedish Pomeranian Shipping in the Revolutionary Age (1776–1815)', *Forum Navale* 68 (2012), 74–75, & 83.
37 Önnerfors, *Svenska Pommern,* 269–484.
38 Unfortunately, no records from the Stockholm Maritime Customs have survived from the period 1770 to 1799, which makes it difficult to make any calculations for this period.
39 Thomas Lundén, *Pommern ett gränsfall i tid och rum*, Slavica Lundensia 27 (Lund: Lund University, 2016), 44.
40 'Confiscationer i Stockholm', 1803, Äldre centrala tullarkiv, Överdirektören vid Sjötullen, Advokatfiskalen, Liggare, D3, vol. 1–2, Riksarkivet.
41 As the arrivals either refer to distinct origins London (4), Hull (2), Colchester (1), Lancaster (1), or more generally as 'England' (5) I have standardised all these under 'England' as they all refer to the same legislative and economic space.
42 Bertil Andersson, *Göteborgs historia. Näringsliv och samhällsutveckling* (Göteborg: Nerenius & Santérus, 1996), 196.
43 The Swedish Produktplakatwas modelled on earlier British Navigation Acts: Michael Roberts, *British Diplomacy and Swedish Politics, 1758–1773* (Minneapolis: University of Minnesota Press, 1980), 126.

44 Louis Sicking, 'A Wider Spread of Risk: A Key to Understanding Holland's Domination of Eastward and Westward Seafaring', in *The Dynamics of Economic Culture in the North Sea- and Baltic Regions*, ed. Hanno Brand and Leos Müller (Hilversum: Verloren, 2007), 128.
45 30 May 1769, 'Stora Siötulls Rättens Dombok' 1769, Stockholms rådhusrätt, Stora Sjötullen, Protokoll, A, vol.22, Stockholms Stadsarkiv.
46 28 April 1769, 'Stora Siötulls Rättens Dombok' 1769, Stockholms rådhusrätt, Stora Sjötullen, Protokoll, A, vol.22, Stockholms Stadsarkiv, 5 July 1769, 'Stora Siötulls Rättens Dombok' 1769, Stockholms rådhusrätt, Stora Sjötullen, Protokoll, A, vol.22, Stockholms Stadsarkiv.
47 28 Apr 1769, 'Stora Siötulls Rättens Dombok' 1769, Stockholms rådhusrätt, Stora Sjötullen, Protokoll, A, vol.22, Stockholms Stadsarkiv.
48 'Kongl. maj:ts ytterligare nådige förordning, angående lurendrägeriers uptäckande och hämmande' (1757).
49 15 Sep 1769, 'Stora Siötulls Rättens Dombok' 1769, Stockholms rådhusrätt, Stora Sjötullen, Protokoll, A, vol.22, Stockholms Stadsarkiv.
50 Jens Ahlfors, 'Sjöfolkslöner i Göteborg 1808–1810. Presentation av ett lönehistoriskt material', in *Handel och sjöfart under gustaviansk Tid*, Meddelanden från historiska institutionen i Göteborg 4 (Göteborg: Historiska Institutionen, 1971), 78.
51 Ahlfors, 78.
52 Rodney Edvinsson and Johan Söderberg, 'The Evolution of Swedish Consumer Prices 1290–2088', in *Exchange Rates, Prices, and Wages, 1277–2008*, ed. Tor Jacobson, Daniel Waldenström, and Rodney Edvinsson (Stockholm: Ekerlids Förlag, 2010), 432, see figure 8.1.
53 For examples of smaller contraband seizures, see for example: 6 June 1769, First mate Carl Kron with 20 chocolate cakes from Pernaw; Able seaman Sune Edlund with 20 small silk cloths and 12 ribbons from Riga; 23 June 1769, First mate Johan Sidin 16 pounds coffee beans from Arensburg; 5 July 1769, Able seamen Dahlman and Bertel Hindricsson 2 pounds coffee, silk ribbons, women's worsted socks from Danzig; 7 July 1769, Able seaman Eric Böttcher 48 pounds coffee from Wismar (escaped); 8 July 1769, First mate Eric Ström, Russian soap, 11 pounds of coffee, Russian linen cloth, from St Petersburg; 28 July 1769; Able seaman Peter Rosing, 4 pounds of coffee, 7 ells of blue cloth, in 'Stora Siötulls Rättens Dombok', 1769.
54 1 Dec 1769, 'Stora Siötulls Rättens Dombok', 1769, Stockholms rådhusrätt, Stora Sjötullen, Protokoll, A, vol.22, Stockholms Stadsarkiv.
55 This use of credit is for example mentioned in an account of the trade between Trondheim and Sweden, see: Pehr Lind, '37. Dufwed', 1766, Äldre centrala tullarkiv, Överdirektören vid Sjötullen, Kansliet, Personella berättelser och anmärkningspunkter, E1, vol.2, Riksarkivet.
56 'Stora Siötulls Rättens Dombok', 1800, Stockholms rådhusrätt, Stora Sjötullen, Protokoll, A, vol.23, Stockholms Stadsarkiv; 'Confiscationer i Stockholm'.
57 'Kongl. maj:ts förordning emot lurendrägerier eller förbudne utrikes warors införsel i riket, 22 martii 1770' (1770). 1 art., 6§.
58 'Kongl. maj:ts nådiga förordning, til förekommande af lurendrägeri och tullförsnillning gifwen Haga slott den 6 april 1799' (1799). 1 art. 1§.
59 'Stora Siötulls Rättens Dombok', 1769; 'Stora Siötulls Rättens Dombok', 1800.; a similar trend can also be observed in the newspapers – out of the 126 people announced as smugglers in Inrikes Tidningar in 1807, 26 were captains, 9 of them British. '-', *Inrikes Tidningar*, 7 July 1807, no 72; See also 'Confiscationer I Stockholm', 1803, Överdirektören vid Sjötullen, Advokatfiskalen, Liggare, D3, vol. 1–2, Riksarkivet.
60 Kongl. maj:ts nådiga förordning til hämmande af lurendrägerier, gifwen stockholms slott then 14 martii 1785 (1785); Kongl. maj:ts nådiga förordning, til förekommande af lurendrägeri och tullförsnillning gifwen Haga slott den 6 april 1799 (1799).

61 Leos Müller, 'Under svensk flagg i medelhavet. Algeriska söpass 1770–1800', in *Från Afrikakompaniet till Tokyo. En vänbok till György Nováky*, ed. Marie Lennersand and Leos Müller (Exkurs, 2017), 53–56.
62 'Kongl. maj:ts ytterligare nådige förordning, angående lurendrägeriers uptäckande och hämmande.' (1757); 'Kongl. maj:ts nådige förordning, til lurendrägeriers hämmande.' (1766).
63 This time approximation is solely intended to give an indication of the distance between the two countries and is taken from Erik Palmstedt, *Resedagbok 1778–1780* (Uppsala: Almqvist & Wiksells A.B., 1927), 25.
64 Albert Sandklef, *Allmogesjöfart på Sveriges västkust 1575–1850* (Lund: C. W. K. Gleerup, 1973), 328.
65 Sandklef, 109–111.
66 For the Halland example, see Pablo Wiking-Faria, 'Freden, friköpen och järnplogarna. drivkrafter och förändringsprocesser under den agrara revolutionen i Halland 1700–1900' (Göteborg: Göteborgs Universitet, 2009), 54.
67 Sandklef, 17–18.
68 Sandklef, 373.
69 Wiking-Faria, 55; Pia Lundqvist, *Marknad på väg*, 146.
70 Albert Sandklef, *Allmogesjöfart*, 39.
71 11 April 1776, 'Dombok' 1776, A1, vol.10, Göteborgs Sjötullsrätt, Göteborgs Landsarkiv.
72 2 May 1776, Ibid.
73 6 May 1776, Ibid.
74 Arne Carlsson, 'Marstrand under frihamnstiden 1775–1794', in *Handel och sjöfart under gustaviansk tid*, Meddelanden från historiska institutionen i Göteborg 4 (Göteborg: Historiska Institutionen, 1971); See also: 'Consular Report, Gothenburg 2 March 1781', 1781, FO 73, vol.1, British National Archives; 'Consular Report, Gothenburg 21 Jan 1786', 1786, FO 73, vol.5, British National Archives; 'Consular Report, Gothenburg 10 Feb 1787', 1787, FO 73, vol.6, British National Archives; 'Consular Report, Gothenburg 27 Nov 1787', 1787, FO 73, vol.6, British National Archives.
75 Fish oil or whale oil.
76 11 Aug 1768 & 26 Aug 1768, 'Dombok' 1768, A1, vol.7, Göteborgs Sjötullsrätt, Göteborgs Landsarkiv.
77 20 Feb 1769, Kommerskollegiet, Advokatfiskalskontoret, D3a, Rättsprotokoll, Göteborgs Sjötullsrätt.; This island, later renamed Styrsö Bratten, would continue to figure as a site for smuggling well into the 1820s and 1830s. See: C.R.A. Fredberg, *Det gamla Göteborg. Lokalhistoriska skildringar personalia och kulturdrag*, vol. 3 (Göteborg: Bröderna Weiss, 1922), 876–877.
78 The house-visitation was banned between 1762 and 1766, see, 'Kongl. maj:ts nådige förordning, til lurendrägeriers hämmande.' (1766); for a longer discussion about the visitation see chapter 2.
79 'Kongl. maj:ts nådiga förbud emot hus=visitationer, gifwit Ekolsund then 16 julii 1776' (1776).
80 'Kongl. maj:ts nådiga kungörelse, angående förbud emot oloflig handel och uplag af lurendrägade waror i rikets skärgårdar. gifwen Stockholms slott den 19 junii 1798.' (1798).
81 Ibid.
82 Ibid.
83 'Kongl. maj:ts och rikets commerce-collegii kungörelse, angående segelfarten på utländske orter ifrån Götheborgs och Bohus, samt Hallands=läns skärgårdar.' (1798).
84 'Memorial 13 Juni 1804, B. E. Hjelm', 1804, Äldre centrala tullarkivet, Generaltullarrendesocieteternas fullmäktige, mfl, Kansliet, Resefiskaler, E9, vol.4, Riksarkivet.

85 '17. Helsingborg', 1797, Äldre centrala tullarkiv, Överdirektören vid Sjötullen, Kansliet, Personella berättelser och anmärkningspunkter, E1, vol.26, Riksarkivet.

86 Summer confiscations by mounted officers all along the west coast are registered June-September in: '1795 Berättelse' May 1794, Äldre centrala arkiv, Överdirektören vid sjötullen, Huvudarkiv Liggare över föredragna mål D1, vol.7, Riksarkivet, 40, 45b, 58.

87 During the Little Ice Age, the sea to Denmark did freeze over on some occasions but this does not appear to have been a regular occurrence. S. Lindgrén and J. Neumann, 'Crossings of Ice-Bound Sea Surfaces in History', *Climatic Change* 4, no. 1 (1 March 1982).

88 'Ankomna Skrivelser Från Kungl. Maj:T m. Fl.', 1776, Landskansliets för Göteborgs och Bohus län arkiv, Göteborgs Landsarkiv; Gustaf Johan Ehrensvärd, *Dagboksanteckningar förda vid Gustaf III:s hof af friherre Gustaf Johan Ehrensvärd*, 2nd ed., vol. 1, 2 vols (Stockholm: P.A. Norstedt & Söners förlag, 1878); Magnus Hollertz, *Resa omkring en mycket liten bit av jorden* (Stockholm: Albert Bonniers Förlag, 1949), 228.

89 Nicolaus Källberg, 'Memorial, Marstrand, Bewakning, 9 Aug 1791', 1791, Äldre centrala tullarkiv, Generaltullarrendesocieteternas fullmäktige, m. fl., kansliet, Skrivelser från tullfiskaler E8, vol.1, Riksarkivet.

90 Various, *Wälloflige borgare=ståndets protocoller wid riksdagen i Norrköping år 1800* (Stockholm: C. F. Marquard, 1800), 655–656.

91 Arne Carlsson, 'Marstrand under frihamnstiden 1775–1794', 27–28.

92 Francesco Somaini, 'Territory, Territoralisation, Territoriality: Problems of Definition and Historical Interpretation', *Plurimondi* 10 (2012), 35.

93 'Kongl. majts kungörelse, angående inrättandet af en så kallad porto-franco uti Marstrand. Den 15 augusti 1775' (1775).

94 Essén, *Johan Liljencrantz som handelspolitiker*, 64.

95 Essén, 94.

96 Essén, 100 & 111.

97 Jonas Carl Linnerhjelm, *Brev under resor i Sverige* (Stockholm: Wahlström & Widstrand, 1932), 236.

98 'Ankomna Skrivelser Från Kungl. Maj:t M. Fl.', 1776, Landskansliets för Göteborgs och Bohus län arkiv, Göteborgs Landsarkiv.

99 'Kongl. maj:ts och riksens commerce-collegii kungörelse, angående wißa omständigheter rörande Marstrands fri=hamn; gifwen Stockholm then 20 junii 1782' (1782).

100 Ehrensvärd, *Dagboksanteckningar*, 283.

101 Gottfried Christian Bohn, *Gottfried Christian Bohns Wohlerfahrner Kaufmann Herausgegeben von C.D. Ebeling, Professor Am Gymnasium Zu Hamburg Und Mitvorsteber Der Handlungsakademie, Und P. H. C. Brodhagen, Lehrer Vei Der Handlungsakademie*, 5th ed. (Hamburg: Carl Ernst Bohn, 1789), 723–724.

102 22–30 Oct 1776 ' Dombok' 1776, A1, vol.10, Göteborgs Sjötullsrätt, Göteborgs Landsarkiv.

103 25 July 1791, 'Dombok' 1791, A1, vol.19, Göteborgs Sjötullsrätt, Göteborgs Landsarkiv; '1795 Berättelse' May 1794, Äldre centrala arkiv, Överdirektören vid sjötullen, Huvudarkiv Liggare över föredragna mål D1, vol.7, Riksarkivet.

104 Arne Carlsson, 'Marstrand under Frihamnstiden 1775–1794', 58.

105 Mann, 'Little Ice Age', 504.

106 4 Jan 1792, 'Kuopio, N:o 333', 1792, Routsin kauppakollegion tuomiokirja-arkistoa, Rajatullioikeuksien tuomiokirjat, RTO, vol.1, Kansallisarkisto (Finska riksarkivet).

107 See for example: C.G. Borre, '40. Fahlun', 1786, Äldre centrala tullarkiv, Överdirektören vid Sjötullen, Kansliet, Personella berättelser och anmärkningspunkter, E1,vol.11, Riksarkivet.

108 Sven Olofsson, 'Till ömsesidig nytta. entreprenörer, framgång och sociala relationer i centrala Jämtland ca 1810–1850' (Uppsala University, 2011), 75.

109 Erik Opsahl, 'Jemtland fra dansk til svensk i 1645? Staten, riket og nasjonen som identitets- og lojalitetsgrunnlag i norden i tidlig nytid', in *Jämtland och den jämtländska*

världen 1000–1645, ed. Olof Holm (Stockholm: Kungl. Vitterhets Historie och Antikvitets Akademien, 2011), 193.

110 Abraham Hülper, *Samlingar till en beskrivning öfwer Norrland, andra och tredje samlingen, Jämtland och Herjedalen*, 1775. Andra samlingen 132–135; tredje samlingen, 90–91.

111 Petter Cerling, '36. Herjedalen', 1766, Äldre centrala tullarkiv, Överdirektören vid Sjötullen, Kansliet, Personella berättelser och anmärkningspunkter, E1, vol.2, Riksarkivet.

112 Lind, '37. Dufwed', 1766.

113 Einar Sandvik, 'Levangermartnan', 93 1992, http://www.marsimartnan.no/Marsimartnan%202008/DKS/LEVANGERMARTNAN.pdf., Accessed 1 March 2022.

114 Many markets were held in the wintertime as this was a time that allowed easier travel. Another example of such a winter market is the Hindersmässo market in Örebro – see for example Birger Wennberg, *Hindersmässan i dikt och verklighet*. Nerikes Allehandas förlag (1995).

115 Lars Waggen, 'Gamaltids marknadsliv i Inntrøndelag,' *Årbok for 1952, Nord-Trøndelag historielag* (1952), 39–40.

116 See chapter 5 for a longer discussion on worsteds and why they were prohibited.

117 §4, 'Funäsdalen', Kommerskollegiet, Advokatfiskalskontoret, Rättsprotokoll, D, Gränstullsrätten norr om Värmland (1736–1824), Riksarkivet. See also §14, 'Funäsdalen'.

118 1806, 'Duved', Ibid. See cases 2, 3, 4, 5, 6, and 7.

119 'Brev Från Herjedalens Tullkammare, 3 Marti 1784, Anders Lund, Ankom 7 April 1784', (1784), Äldre centrala tullarkiv, Generaltullarrendesocieteternas fullmäktige, mfl, Kansliet, Skrivelser från land- och sjötullkamrarna, E10, vol.4, Riksarkivet.

120 '31. Herjedalen', 1789, Äldre centrala tullarkiv, Överdirektören vid Sjötullen, Kansliet, Personella berättelser och anmärkningspunkter, E1, vol.16, Riksarkivet.

121 Magnus Hammer, 'Memorial, No 23, Dufveds Gränse Tull, 30 Dec 1803', 1803, Äldre centrala tullarkiv, Generaltullarrendesocieteternas fullmäktige, m. fl., kansliet, Resefiskaler, E9, vol.2, Riksarkivet. See also, Letter Funäsdalen, 19 Dec 1803; Memorial, Funesdalen 19 Oct 1803, in the same volume.

122 Ernst Moritz Arndt, *Resa genom Sverige år 1804*, trans. J. M. Stjernstolpe, vol. 3 (Carlstad, 1808), 108.

123 C.G. Lundberg, '29. Herjedalen', 1806, Äldre centrala tullarkiv, Överdirektören vid Sjötullen, Kansliet, Personella berättelser och anmärkningspunkter, E1, vol. 38, Riksarkivet.

124 For more on how bordering worked in practice and the role of the clergy, see: Jenni Merovuo, 'Local Space Building as State Building? Mediating Clergy on the Russo-Swedish Borderland.' (2021), *Bringing the People back in. State Building from Below in the Nordic Countries ca. 1500–1800*, ed. Knut Dørum, Mats Hallenberg, Kimmo Katajala (Routledge, 2021).

125 Arno Rafael Cederberg, *Pohjois-Karjalan kauppaolot vuosina 1721–1775* (Helsinki, 1911), 107–108.

126 Johan Kraftman and Johan Lagus, 'Tankar om hushållningens uphjelpande i Carelen' (Åbo Academy, 1756), 9–10.

127 Kraftman and Lagus, 12.

128 'Taxa för Wilmanstrand, Cajana, Kides- och Pelis tull-Kamrar wid ryska gränsen' (1738).

129 Eric Carstèn and Pehr Kalm, 'I Jesu namn! Historisk och œconomisk beskrifning öfwer Cajanaborgslän' (Åbo Academy, 1754), 28.

130 Lars Shürer, '41. St. Michels', 1766, Äldre centrala tullarkiv, Överdirektören vid Sjötullen, Kansliet, Personella berättelser och anmärkningspunkter, E1, vol.2, Riksarkivet. See also the entry for St Michels in 1767, Äldre centrala tullarkiv, Överdirektören vid Sjötullen, Kansliet, Personella berättelser och anmärkningspunkter, E1, vol. 3, Riksarkivet.

131 Kraftman and Lagus, 'Tankar om hushållningens uphjelpande i Carelen', 9–10.

132 Cederberg, *Pohjois-Karjalan kauppaolot vuosina 1721–1775*, 110.
133 Joh. Ol. Lund, '39. Dufwed', 1786, Äldre centrala tullarkiv, Överdirektören vid Sjötullen, Kansliet, Personella berättelser och anmärkningspunkter, E1, vol.11, Riksarkivet.
134 12 Feb 1771, 'Sjötullen Uleåborg', 1771, Kommerskollegium, Advokatfiskalskontoret, D. Rättsprotokoll, Uleåborg 1769–1794, Riksarkivet.
135 Abraham Strand, '34. Kajana', 1787, Äldre centrala tullarkiv, Överdirektören vid Sjötullen, Kansliet, Personella berättelser och anmärkningspunkter, E1, vol. 12, Riksarkivet.
136 And. Westman, '35. Cajana', 1806, Äldre centrala tullarkiv, Överdirektören vid Sjötullen, Kansliet, Personella berättelser och anmärkningspunkter, E1, vol. 38, Riksarkivet. See also similar statements for Kajana and Savolax: Hindrich Forshaell, '43. St. Michels', 1796, Äldre centrala tullarkiv, Överdirektören vid Sjötullen, Kansliet, Personella berättelser och anmärkningspunkter, E1, vol. 25, Riksarkivet.
137 Hindrich Forshaell, '43. St. Michels', 1796, Äldre centrala tullarkiv, Överdirektören vid Sjötullen, Kansliet, Personella berättelser och anmärkningspunkter, E1, vol. 26, Riksarkivet.
138 J. J. Göös, 'Rapport Från Kuopio, Haukivuori, 23 Maj 1804', 1804, Äldre centrala tullarkiv, Generaltullarrendesocieteternas fullmäktige, mfl, Kansliet, Resefiskaler, E9, vol.4, Riksarkivet.
139 Eric Noréen, '23. Wärmland', 1796, Äldre centrala tullarkiv, Överdirektören vid Sjötullen, Kansliet, Personella berättelser och anmärkningspunkter, E1, vol.25, Riksarkivet; G. Kranck, '35. Kusamo', 1806, Äldre centrala tullarkiv, Överdirektören vid Sjötullen, Kansliet, Personella berättelser och anmärkningspunkter, E1, vol.38, Riksarkivet.
140 19 June 1785, 'Mikkeli No 649', 1785, Routsin kauppakollegion tuomiokirja-arkistoa, Rajatullioikeuksien tuomiokirjat, RTO, vol.1, Kansallisarkisto (Finska riksarkivet).
141 See for example the case of Anders Waris who referred to previous cases of domestic contraband transport which he argued ended with acquittals: 4 Jan 1792, 'Kuopio, No. 333'. Routsin kauppakollegion tuomiokirja-arkistoa, Rajatullioikeuksien tuomiokirjat, RTO, vol. 1, Kansallisarkisto (Finska riksarkivet).
142 'Öfwer=ståthållare-embetets förnyade kungörelse om resandes skyldighet at med rese-pass sig förse. 1799.' (1799).
143 'Kongl. maj:ts förordning emot lurendrägerier eller förbudne utrikes warors införsel i riket, 22 martii 1770' (1770).
144 'Kongl. Maj:ts Förnyade Land-Tulls Och Accis Stadga, 19 Sep 1776' (1776).
145 'Kongl. maj:ts nådiga förordning, til förekommande af lurendrägeri och tullförsnillning gifwen Haga slott den 6 april 1799' (1799).
146 One of these seizures on the road between Ulls Inn and Bälinge was particularly significant. The wares, mainly silks, were valued at 1693 Rdr: 19 Maj 1804, Nr 1163, 'Christianstad', Kommmerskollegium, Advokatfiskalskontoret, Årsberättelser Lurendrejerimål (1803–1804) Cb4, vol. 2, Riksarkivet.
147 Ibid.
148 Sparre, 'Memorial, No 178, Helsingborg, 17 Maj 1791', 1791, Äldre centrala tullarkiv, Generaltullarrendesocieteternas fullmäktige, m. fl., kansliet, Skrivelser från tullfiskaler E8, vol.1, Riksarkivet.
149 Hellbom, 'Brev 595, 4 Augusti 1804' 1804, Äldre centrala tullarkiv, Generaltullarrendesocieteternas fullmäktige, mfl, Kansliet, Resefiskaler, E9, vol.4, Riksarkivet.
150 Borre, '40. Fahlun', 1786, Äldre centrala tullarkiv, Överdirektören vid Sjötullen, Kansliet, Personella berättelser och anmärkningspunkter, E1, vol.11.
151 Sparre, 'Memorial, No 178, Helsingborg, 17 Maj 1791', 1791, Äldre centrala tullarkiv, Generaltullarrendesocieteternas fullmäktige, m. fl., kansliet, Skrivelser från tullfiskaler E8, vol.1, Riksarkivet.
152 Lars Levander, *Landsväg, krog & marknad* (Mörklinta: Gidlunds Förlag, 1976).

153 This is for example explored in the play 'Värdshuset', *Carl Michael Bellmans skrifter VI, dramatiska arbeten* (Stockholm: Albert Bonniers Förlag, 1936), 201.
154 Giuseppe Acerbi, *Travels through Sweden, Finland, and Lapland, to the North Cape: In the Years 1798 and 1799* (London: Joseph Mawman, 1802), 364.
155 Allan Sjöding, 'Gästgivargården i svensk 1700-talslitteratur', *Svensk litteraturtidskrift* 42, no. 1 (1978), 33; Lars Levander, *Landsväg, krog & marknad*, 90–91.
156 Beat Kümin, 'Useful to Have, but Difficult to Govern. Inns and Taverns in Early Modern Bern and Vaud', *Journal of Early Modern History* 3, no. 2 (1999), 157 & 163; Sjöding, 33.
157 Lars Magnusson, 'Försnillning, smyghandel och fusk. Förlagssystem och hantverkskultur i Eskilstuna vid början av 1800-talet', *Historisk Tidskrift*, no. 2 (1986), 179–182.
158 'Öfwer=ståthålare embetets kungöresle och förbud, emot handels= manufactur- och handtwerkeri warora obehöriga afsalu, gifwen Stockholm then 12 september 1783' (1783).
159 'Kongl. Maj:ts Nådiga Förordning, Til Förekommande af Lurendrägeri och Tullförsnillning Gifwen Haga Slott den 6 April 1799' (1799), 8 Art. 3§.
160 Kümin, 174.
161 22–30 Oct 1776 'Dombok' 1776, A1, vol.10, Göteborgs Sjötullsrätt, Göteborgs Landsarkiv; Bror A. Andersson, *Skepplanda socken: Från forntid till nutid i ord och bild*, ed. Sven Forsæus (Skepplanda kommunfullmäktige, 1972), 24.
162 As seen in this account, the inn-keeper was tasked with2z committing the names and destinations of all travellers staying at the inn to a particular 'Inn Diary', according to the 1734 Inn-decree. 'Kongl. maj. giästgifware=ordning, öfwersedd, förnyad och förbättrad wid riksdagen uti Stockholm' (1734), §22; For another similar case see also 2 Oct 1805 & 11 Dec 1805, Catharina Hesse, 'Stockholms Stora Sjötulls Rätt', 1805, Stockholms rådhusrätt, Stora Sjötullen, Protokoll, A, vol.27, Stockholms Stadsarkiv.
163 23 Jun 1791, 'Dombok' 1791, A1, vol.19, Göteborgs Sjötullsrätt, Göteborgs Landsarkiv.
164 19 Jan 1803, 'Stora Siötulls Rättens Dombok' 1803, Stockholms rådhusrätt, Stora Sjötullen, Protokoll, A, vol.26, Stockholms Stadsarkiv. Östorp Inn was strategically located between Wimmerby and Westerwik, only 5 Swedish miles (henceforth referred to as *miles*) from the sea. Taking the road north from Östorp would take the traveller towards Stockholm; it seems likely that Dahlberg would have taken this route. Travelling from Östorp to Stockholm he would have covered 349 km with his wares before being stopped by Hornstull, a tollgate southwest of Stockholm. 1 Swedish mile = 10 689 m, until 1889 when the unit was standardised as 1 mile = 10 000 m. For further information see Nils-Erik Winther, Rolf Wändel, and Matz Jörgensen, *Gästgifwerier, krogar och skjutshåll* (Löddeköpinge: Harjager härads fornminnes- och hembygdsförening, 2003). All distances are calculated based on Georg Biurman, *Vägvisare, til och ifrån alla städer och namnkunniga orter, uti Svea- och Göta-riken, samt stor-förstendömet Finland; jämte tvänne uti koppar stuckne väg-chartor, efter skedde vägmätningar uprättad, af Georg Biurman. Med Kongl. maj:ts allernådigste privil*, 4th ed. (Stockholm: Johan Georg Lange, 1776), 87.
165 Beat Kümin, 'Useful to Have', 164.
166 See the complicated case of inn-keeper Johan Lindbom: 6 April 1799, 'Mikkeli No 655', 1799, Routsin kauppakollegion tuomiokirja-arkistoa, Rajatullioikeuksien tuomiokirjat, RTO, vol. 2, Kansallisarkisto (Finska riksarkivet); 6 April 1799, 'Mikkeli No 655', 1799, Routsin kauppakollegion tuomiokirja-arkistoa, Rajatullioikeuksien tuomiokirjat, RTO, vol. 2, Kansallisarkisto (Finska riksarkivet).
167 5 Oct–16 Nov 1803, 'Stora Siötulls Rättens Dombok', 1803, Stockholms rådhusrätt, Stora Sjötullen, Protokoll, A, vol.26, Stockholms Stadsarkiv.

168 28 Mars 1797, 'Mikkeli No. 653', 1797, Routsin kauppakollegion tuomiokirja-arkistoa, Rajatullioikeuksien tuomiokirjat, RTO, vol.2, Kansallisarkisto (Finska riksarkivet).
169 Erik Dahlberg, 'Suecia Antiqua et Hodierna', https://suecia.kb.se/F/?func=find-b&local_base=sah, Accessed 13 February 2019.
170 This number excludes people caught before they reached the tollgate. 1785, 'Inneliggande Handlingar' 1786–1781, F, vol.7, Göteborgs Sjötullsrätt, Göteborgs Landsarkiv.
171 Andersson, *Göteborgs Historia,* 182.
172 Per Adolf Granberg, *Staden Göteborgs historia och beskrifning*, vol. 1 (Stockholm: Elmén och Granberg, 1814), 207.
173 21 Feb 1791, 'Dombok' 1791, A1, vol.19, Göteborgs Sjötullsrätt, Göteborgs Landsarkiv.
174 4 Aug 1791, 'Dombok' 179), A1, vol.19, Göteborgs Sjötullsrätt, Göteborgs Landsarkiv. There is also another, nearly identical, case from the same day involving the farmhand Anders Lundström.
175 1785, 'Inneliggande Handlingar' 1786–1781, F, vol. 7, Göteborgs Sjötullsrätt, Göteborgs Landsarkiv.
176 Olof Bellander, 'Raport [sic], Göteborg 23 Juni 1804' 1804, Äldre Centrala tullarkiv, Generaltullarrendesocieteternas fullmäktige, mfl, Kansliet, Resefiskaler, E9, vol.4.
177 There were 51 cases this year involving 15 women and 37 men: 1785, 'Inneliggande Handlingar', 1786–1781, F, vol.7, Göteborgs Sjötullsrätt, Göteborgs Landsarkiv.
178 1785, 'Inneliggande Handlingar' 1786–1781, F, vol.7, Göteborgs Sjötullsrätt, Göteborgs Landsarkiv.
179 13 Jan 1785, 31 Jan 1785, 17 Feb 1785, 7 July 1785, 1 Sep 1785, 7 Nov 1785, 'Dombok' 1785, A1, vol.18, Göteborgs Sjötullsrätt, Göteborgs Landsarkiv.; 7 March 1791, 23 June 1791, 4 Aug 1791, 29 Dec 1791, 'Dombok' 1791, A1, vol.19, Göteborgs Sjötullsrätt, Göteborgs Landsarkiv.
180 Magnus Hollertz, *Resa omkring en mycket liten bit av jorden* (Stockholm: Albert Bonniers Förlag, 1949), 228.
181 Margaret Hunt, *Women in Eighteenth-Century Europe.* Harlow (New York: Pearson Longman, 2009), 170.
182 See for example: 26 Aug 1768, 'Dombok' 1768, A1, vol.7, Göteborgs Sjötullsrätt, Göteborgs Landsarkiv.
183 17 Feb 1785, 'Dombok' 1785, A1, vol.18, Göteborgs Sjötullsrätt, Göteborgs Landsarkiv.
184 21 Feb 1791, 'Dombok' 1791, A1, vol.19, Göteborgs Sjötullsrätt, Göteborgs Landsarkiv.
185 29 Dec 1791, 'Dombok' 1791, A1, vol.19, Göteborgs Sjötullsrätt, Göteborgs Landsarkiv.
186 Some examples of children convicted of smuggling can be found: 'Till Underdånigste Följe Af Kongl. Maj:ts Nådiga Förordning till Förekommande Af Lurendrägerier Och Tullförsnillning Af D N 6 April 1799', *Inrikes Tidningar,* 26 November 1805, no 133; 'Confiscationer I Stockholm' 1803 -1807, Överdirektören vid Sjötullen, Advokatfiskalen, Liggare, D3, vol. 1–2, Riksarkivet, 12.
187 5 July 1769, 'Stora Siötulls Rättens Dombok' 1769, Stockholms rådhusrätt, Stora Sjötullen, Protokoll, A, vol.22, Stockholms Stadsarkiv.
188 7 Nov 1785, 'Dombok' 1785, A1, vol.18, Göteborgs Sjötullsrätt, Göteborgs Landsarkiv.
189 26 Mar 1792, 'Dombok' 1792, A1, vol.19, Göteborgs Sjötullsrätt, Göteborgs Landsarkiv.
190 5 Oct–16 Nov 1803, 'Stora Siötulls Rättens Dombok' 1803, Stockholms rådhusrätt, Stora Sjötullen, Protokoll, A, vol.26, Stockholms Stadsarkiv.

191 6 May 1776, 'Dombok' 1776, A1, vol.10, Göteborgs Sjötullsrätt, Göteborgs Landsarkiv.

192 17 Feb 1785, 'Dombok' 1785, Göteborgs Sjötullsrätt, A1, vol.18, Göteborgs Landsarkiv; 5 Oct 1803, 'Stora Siötulls Rättens Dombok' 1803, Stockholms rådhusrätt, Stora Sjötullen, Protokoll, A, vol.26, Stockholms Stadsarkiv; 7 Maj 1804, Nr 1078, 'Carlshamn', 1803–4, Kommerskollegium, Advokatfiskalskontoret, Årsberättelser Lurendrejerimål, Cb4, vol 2, Riksarkivet, Stockholm.

193 16 April 1787, 'Kitee No. 578', 1787, Routsin kauppakollegion tuomiokirja-arkistoa, Rajatullioikeuksien tuomiokirjat, RTO, vol 1, Kansallisarkisto (Finska riksarkivet).

4

RACKETEERING RETAILERS

During the eighteenth century, retailing in Sweden was performed by a multitude of various actors, but it was also strictly regulated according to the reigning protectionist norms. Who could trade, what, and where were issues closely guarded by societies and guilds. As the previous chapter showed, however, control in theory and in practice were two different things and certain places were under considerably tighter control than others. This was equally true for retailing as it was for the movement of contraband. Trade in the countryside and the towns was thus fundamentally different, which naturally also affected the retailing of contraband, as the vendors needed to adopt varying techniques not only to conduct illicit trade but also to escape, or minimise the effects of, their punishment.

Contraband retailing was not merely shaped by state control mechanisms but also by consumer attitudes. As discussed in Chapter 2, the debates around smuggling were dominated by a conflict between patriotic protectionism and a more tolerant approach to foreign wares. While the latter only had a limited impact on the legislation, it had a more direct impact on consumer attitudes, as revealed by research into the consumer habits of the Swedish elite. Johanna Ilmakunnas has shown that the consumption of the aristocracy was driven by two impulses: an ideal of frugality, which demanded moderation in consumption and habits, but encouraged 'acceptable' consumption that supported Swedish industry, and conspicuous luxury consumption in line with their international counterparts.[1] The elite's double role of being both protectors of the fatherland and its economy, *and* members of a cosmopolitan community meant that they were both actively supporting the protectionist project while illegally importing foreign luxuries for their own consumption.[2] Tolerance for smuggled foreign goods was not unique to the elite, however, but traversed all social levels.[3] Consumer attitudes towards contraband also reflected on the retailers who provided these illicit desirables. Indeed, in order to understand how the retailing in illegal wares worked, it is

DOI: 10.4324/9781003226031-4

necessary to consider not merely legislation and enforcement but also the relationship between consumer and retailer.

Research on the relationship between consumer and retailer has pointed to a symbiotic relationship, where traders became popular by selling to the fashionable, while people of fashion retained their status through buying from modish retailers.[4] Between them, the consumers and the retailers created and maintained the concept of fashionableness, but it was ultimately dependent on the continuation of a supply of fashionable wares. As long as foreign wares remained in fashion securing access to these goods was key for retailers who wanted to make a mark. Studies from France have suggested that the symbiotic relationship between consumer and retailer was particularly important in relation to smuggling. Anne Montenach has even gone so far as to argue that the risks the merchants took to involve themselves in the contraband trade might have increased their respectability and heroism in the eyes of their consumers.[5] In order to explore the retailing of contraband, it is therefore necessary to consider not merely the legislative trading conditions, and enforcement thereof, but also the social structures around the retailers, in particular the relationship between retailer and client.

Four retailing groups in particular appear to have been involved in the distribution of contraband in Sweden at this time. A member of the committee tasked with developing a new sumptuary legislation in 1793 listed them as "the smuggling Trader in the Town… the Jews and the so called Westgothians (*Skål-wästgöthar*) and certain privileged People who can provide richly".[6] These various retailers served under distinct licences and legislations that shaped their trade, and were active in different environments and will therefore be dealt with separately, although as will become clear there were connections between them.

Just like the previous chapter, this one builds predominantly on customs records and strives to understand the retailing of contraband in Sweden and to explore how it was affected by two facets in particular: regulation and its irregular enforcement, and the social relationships between the retailers of smuggled wares and their consumers. The chapter asks how the retailers responded to the prohibition against, condemnation of, and continued demand for illegal wares, and how their response was influenced by their inter-personal relationships to customers and other traders.

The Wandering Pedlar

In the eighteenth century, the vast majority of the Swedish population lived in the countryside; by 1810, less than 10% of the population resided in towns.[7] While the bulk of the population lived in rural areas, the countryside presented few purchasing opportunities. Shops were prohibited in the countryside until 1846, which meant that rural consumers had to rely on markets and travelling salesmen for their supply of legal as well as illegal wares.[8] Two main groups of travelling salesmen, or pedlars, came to play an important role in the distribution of goods within the Swedish dominions in the eighteenth century – in the west, the Westgothian pedlars (*westgöta gårdfarihandlare*) and in the east the Trading Russians (*kiöpryssar*). While these were not the only pedlars active in the kingdom, the prominence of these two groups in the customs records suggests that they were particularly involved in the retailing of contraband and in need of further investigation.

Ever since the publication of Laurence Fontaine's *History of Pedlars in Europe*, there has been a developing appreciation of the crucial role that pedlars played in the development of early modern consumption.[9] Pedlars, a group often considered unorganised and vagrant, appeared in various forms, often making up complex and sophisticated networks. Many pedlar groups were not confined to a single country but capitalised on cross-border trade.[10] In Sweden, pedlars played a crucial role in the development of consumption, they were an integral part of the distribution networks of manufactured goods, and used established trading tools such as credit to reach new consumers.[11]

Westgothian Pedlars

The Westgothian pedlars originated in Sjuhäradsbygden, Småland, and had long been trading across the country under special privileges, which were only officially ratified in 1776.[12] Although their trade was supposed to be restricted to the sale of handicrafts from Sjuhäradsbygden, the traders came to play an important role as conveyors of minor conveniences and luxuries, including manufactured goods.[13] In her extensive study of the Westgothian pedlars, Pia Lundqvist notes that their varied range of stock, legal and illegal, was an important contributing factor to their success, as they were able to cater for changing tastes quickly.[14]

Due to their involvement with the contraband trade, the Westgothian pedlars were regarded with a certain level of concern by both the government and fellow merchants, and attempts were made to infringe upon their trading freedoms, particularly in order to prevent the distribution of contraband. A Royal Decree from 15 August 1792 prohibited the pedlars from entering any foreign country for trade, except for Norway. It was hoped that this would hamper the introduction of illicit foreign goods into the country.[15] The exception of Norway was possibly related to the longstanding trade links important for both pedlars and border dwellers, particularly in the Jämtland and Härjedalen provinces.[16] Despite this, the ban was extended to Norway only a few years later, as the government strove to shut down all contraband channels.[17] While the regulations were intended to keep foreign contraband out of the Westgothian pedlars' reach, the customs court records indicate that the transgressions continued.

There were many pedlar routes out of the country, two of the most prominent ones were through the provinces of Skåne and Halland, on the south and southwest coast of Sweden. Due to the peasant shipping discussed in the previous chapter, these areas were interconnected with various countries including Denmark, England, and France. This enabled pedlars to travel out of Sweden, but it also turned these provinces into acquisition sites in their own right. In Halland, pedlars could, for example, purchase manufactured textiles such as wool, silk, and cotton directly.[18] Skåne and Halland were thus both transport and acquisition sites.

The customs material from these areas contains a growing number of reports of pedlar smuggling from the 1790s onwards, which coincides with the increasing regulation of, and prohibitions against, their foreign travels. The customs in Malmö, Skåne, reported that many pedlars passed by the customs. Groups of pedlars spread out over vast distances making it nearly impossible for the customs officers to seize them all.[19] Similar situations were reported from other customs chambers along the coast, such as in Helsingborg.[20] The 1792 ban on foreign travel appears to, at best, have had a limited effect on the pedlars, a testament not merely to the difficulty of controlling the mobility of the pedlars, but also to the important role foreign goods played in their business activities.

The practice of travelling in groups was particularly irksome for the customs office, not just because they scattered but also because they caused a more substantial threat to the customs officers. In July 1795, Royal Constable Gyllberg reported coming across a group of five pedlars on the border between Halland and Älvsborg counties, in Marks Härad. The constable was initially able to confiscate 16 packages of contraband from the tradesmen who took flight. However, as Gyllberg attempted to transport the contraband back to the confiscation warehouse, he was surrounded "by numerous pedlars" intent on reclaiming the goods and, unable to resist, was forced to abandon the confiscated items. Six of the packages were eventually recovered in a pile of manure and were soon after auctioned off for export, fetching the significant price of 942 Rdr 35 sk.[21] Moving in larger groups made it possible for the pedlars to not only transport greater quantities of goods but also to defend themselves if they came under threat, or split up in order to avoid capture. Pedlar caravans were increasingly seen as a problem by the authorities, who in 1803 tried to limit the number of pedlars in each travelling group to six in order to avoid disturbances.[22] How effective this rule was is hard to establish, but there are indications that smuggling pedlar caravans persisted.[23]

As the traders travelled into the country, single pedlars split off from the group to attend their destination markets. Together, the pedlars created a distribution network which spanned the whole country, but single traders usually had their own distinct markets, whether in the sparsely populated countryside or in a city.[24] Having established markets allowed the pedlars to develop a trust and credit network which made it possible to trade with a larger range of customers.[25] Contraband could thus spread in areas where ready money was scarce and among people living remotely in the countryside.

Over time, pedlars became increasingly associated with the dissemination of illegal and, at least according the power holders, inappropriate, luxury. Already in 1775, Baron Silfverhem of Jönköping noted that the Westgothian retailing of foreign textiles in his region had led to an "increased luxury among the commoners, whose children buy such wares".[26] Two decades later, similar reports were made in numerous Swedish provinces. In the parish discussions about rural luxury from 1793, the parishioners in the mining region Norrbärke observed that "the Westgothian pedlars, visiting every farm, come stocked with ample, and probably illegal goods".[27] Indeed, such were the attractions of the pedlar's stock that, in the neighbouring parishes of Ludvika and Grangärde just to the north of Norrbärke, it was suggested that the parish men needed the help of the state to reduce their wives' luxury consumption. They proposed that a royal decree should be issued that forbade the pedlars from selling textiles to the commoners, as they themselves were unable to prevent their wives from buying the pedlars' attractive wares.[28] While Pia Lundqvist has pointed out that the pedlars had some support from local governors, the reigning attitude among the decision-makers was that the pedlars were a destructive force.[29] Attempts to limit the pedlars' trading activities and to introduce new control mechanisms were probably linked to their popularity among rural consumers, a feature that emerges even more distinctly in the Finnish material.

Russian Traders

In Finland, pedlars often referred to as 'Trading Russians' or 'Rucksack Russians' (but usually of East Karelian origin) came to play a similar role to that of the Westgothians traders in the western part of the kingdom. The peddling activities of the East Karelians can be traced back at least to the seventeenth century. They mainly traded with manufactured goods, including textiles – many of which were illegal for import into Sweden.[30] East Karelia was plagued by barren soil and poor framing conditions which made it difficult for the peasants of the area to survive on farming alone. Instead, they were able to use peddling as a way to increase their funds as they, despite their relative isolation, were within reach of important Russian trading centres such as St Petersburg, established in 1703 after the Swedish loss of Ingria, and Arkhangelsk, where an English trading company had existed since the sixteenth century. From these centres, they acquired goods that they peddled in the Finnish countryside. The trading language was a mixture of Karelian, Finnish, and Swedish, depending on where the pedlars worked and how far they travelled.[31] Most of their peddling activities broke with the Swedish regulations, which in the standardised national law of 1734 severely limited the right to peddle in the countryside.[32] In contrast to the Westgothian pedlars, the Russian Traders were never exempted from this rule, and their peddling thus remained illegal for the duration of the eighteenth and into the nineteenth century.

According to Johan Kraftman's 1756 academic treatise on the œconomy of Karelia, these pedlars smuggled manufactured cloth, including calico, satin, damask, silk, and various linens, neckerchiefs and caps into Sweden-Finland, where they sold them to eager peasants.[33] Kraftman argued that the erratic nature of the trade made it difficult to find a cure for this "smuggling plague".[34]

As discussed in the previous chapter, the conditions along the extensive Russian border, with its vast distances and sparse population, made the border difficult to control, which clearly worked in the pedlars' favour. A customs official in Torneå observed that:

> the Russian subjects tend to smuggle when they cross the border to Torneå with their wares, which is facilitated by the fact that Farms are located everywhere along the road, where they can sell their goods safely.[35]

Just like the Westgothian pedlars in the western part of the country, the Russian traders caused anxiety among those in charge. This is reflected by a report submitted by vice-governor Roos of Umeå on the state of trade in Torneå. In his report, Roos noted that the Russian traders were highly damaging to the region, travelling to Torneå in groups throughout the winter with a great assortment of legal and illegal goods.[36]

One of the key objections to the Russian traders was their mobility, which made it difficult for the customs office to oversee what they sold. One popular solution to the problem was that Trading Russians should be obliged to sell their wares exclusively at markets.[37] Occasions fixed in time and space that could be surveyed. These markets, the proponents suggested, should be held close to the borders in places with established customs chambers such as Kajana and Kusamo, to prevent the 'Russians' from entering too far into the Swedish-Finnish territory.[38] While this suggestion was repeated by academics, vice-governors, and customs officers alike, it was never viable as the pedlars refused to be contained. Mobility offered traders an opportunity to acquire and distribute lucrative contraband goods, at the same time as it made them harder to oversee and control, ensuring a higher profit.

Finnish customs court protocols bear witness to the difficulties involved in identifying and controlling the smuggling pedlars. Many of the individuals who smuggled foreign wares escaped capture and were never identified, and the most common sentence in the customs records concerning these pedlars is "confiscated from unknown Russians". The assumption that the escaped offenders were Russian appears to have been based on their dress, but presumably also language.[39] The culprits that do appear with name and origin, usually derived from East Karelia, which supports the idea that most of the Trading Russians came from this region.[40] However, these named individuals belong to a minority and are vastly outnumbered by "unknown Russians". This anonymity was also a consequence of the pedlars' mobility, as they covered significant distances and would have been unfamiliar to the local customs authorities.

Mobility was not the only problem with the Trading Russians, however, and in 1777 vice-governor Roos made another troubling observation. According to Roos, the peasants living on the Swedish-Finnish side of the border appeared to be in cahoots with the Russians.[41] Roos suggested that Swedish-Finnish subjects were not only friendly with the Russian pedlars but that they also supported them in various ways. How this support could manifest can be observed in the customs records. One night in 1787, the customs officer Johan Strandeen found the Russian trader Onto Jänis hiding in the house of the peasant Jöran Pesani in Ilmantz parish (now Illomantsi). Strandeen seized Jänis' bag of contraband, which contained blue wool cloth, red/white silk cloth, calico, ribbons in red silk and blue, along combs, ribbons with red pearls, pins and striped belts. Upon the seizure, a violent brawl erupted and Jänis hit the customs officer over the head with a halberd, leaving Strandeen with a significant cut in his forehead.[42] Similarly, a decade later, the customs officer Johan Pellgren was travelling along the remote roads of Kideslax. At 3 o'clock in the morning, he arrived at the home of the peasant Lukas Machonen (later referred to as Maikoses) in the village of Jama in the parish of Kides. When he entered the house of Machonen, three unknown men "dressed like Russians" ran out of a room, carrying leather bags. Pellgren managed to seize the bags, but despite his best efforts, he was unable to identify the Russian men.[43] Such observations were made along most of the border and indicate that the local border population aided the pedlars, assisting them by shielding them and providing housing. It is also notable that most of these seizures took place in the middle of the night. A general antipathy towards the customs officials can be observed among the border population, which is likely linked to the cross-border lives common among the border dwellers, as discussed in the last chapter.

Scholars have argued that the presence of contraband in the pedlar's sack was an important part of their success as it allowed them to offer everyday luxuries to the common people, in the countryside as well as in the city.[44] As this examination of pedlars in the customs records has shown, they managed to acquire contraband in Sweden's neighbouring countries and distribute it widely through the co-operation, mobility, and anonymity that characterised the pedlars' trade. Meanwhile, the desirability of their wares landed them with protection from the rural population, who shielded them from the customs officers and enabled them to surreptitiously conduct trade in the countryside without risking exposure. The pedlars' illegal trade was thus dependent on the co-operation of their consumers, who supported them in their endeavours to circumvent the Swedish legislation.

The Mercers

Retailing in Stockholm had, since the seventeenth century, been divided between different trade societies that controlled who was allowed to sell particular wares.[45] In order to acquire burghership and membership in a society, it was necessary to go through an apprenticeship with a registered merchant, after which they could apply to the city magistrate and the trade societies for burghership.[46] If awarded burghership they were required to take a burgher oath (*borgared*); this was an oath of fidelity to the King and included a promise not to deal in illicit goods.[47] One of these trade societies was the Silk and Cloth Trader Society (*Siden och klädeskramhandels societeten*), which was tasked with the trade in finer fabrics, such as wool, worsted, silk, halfsilk, and finer cotton textiles, both domestically produced and whatever could be legally imported (see Table 1.1.).[48] The Silk and Cloth Trader Society was a crucial tool in supporting the domestic manufacturers through yearly stock-purchases from the Swedish manufacturers.[49] While outsiders might have viewed the mercers in the society as a support mechanism for the protectionist industries, this was not how they viewed themselves. The Silk and Cloth Trader Society was one of the most vocal opponents of the protectionist legislation and stricter anti-smuggling legislation. Many mercers saw it as their task to cater for the demands of the consumers, rather than simply being an outlet for Swedish manufacturers. This created a conflict between mercers and manufacturers, which came to the fore in the discussions on smuggling. In line with the proponents of deregulated trade, the Silk and Cloth Trader Society maintained that smuggling was merely a natural consequence of an unviable system.[50] "[S]muggling", they argued, "is founded in man's covetousness… [which is] planted in all men…".[51] As custom court records reveal, this position was not merely a rhetorical device but also translated into an active engagement with the contraband trade.

Shop-Owners Under Surveillance

In contrast to the mobile pedlars, the mercers were fixed in the townscape. They were known members of the trade society and conducted their business from established shop premises. It is symptomatic of the nature of their trade that the vast majority of all mercers who appeared before the customs court had been caught with contraband during shop-visitations. As discussed in Chapter 2, the visitation legislation changed several times during the eighteenth and nineteenth centuries, which altered the conditions for illegal trade.[52] Between 1769 and 1776, universal visitations were allowed in shops and storages. In 1776, a royal decree prohibited the use of all visitations due to public safety issues, a prohibition that lasted until 1785, when visitations were reintroduced for selected properties used by registered merchants, most prominently shops and storage houses.[53] This created a decade long unintended grace period for smuggling shop-keepers, which is reflected in the customs records in the shape of a nearly total absence of mercers. During the periods when shop searches were allowed mercers often appear in the customs records, but the illegal trade that they conducted looked very different to that of the wandering pedlars.

Shop searches were usually attended both by customs officers and the shop-keeper and they could be tense affairs. The shop-keepers in question were not merely well known to the customs officers due to their prominence in town but also because many of them were called into work for the customs office, to provide valuations following contraband seizures.[54] Valuations were crucial in the customs office's work, and they helped to establish the culprit's fines, which should be the median between the foreign retail and domestic wholesale price of the illegal wares.[55] As the work also included separating domestic and foreign manufactures, fines could be significantly reduced or increased by the valuators. It was not unproblematic that the individuals with the expertise to value the textiles also occurred as defendants. In order to counteract any ulterior motives in the valuations, the valuators often consisted of both retailers and manufacturers. However, the valuation was usually one of the most contested issues during mercer smuggling trials.[56] The value of the goods was crucial as it could involve considerable sums.[57] In 1773, Samuel Bruse (or Burce) (1732–1800), a merchant in Gothenburg was sentenced to pay 10,658 D smt.[58] For comparison, Bruse had purchased his estate Rossared a few years earlier for 10,383 D smt.[59] This considerable fine appears to have put a strain on Bruse's finances, as he shortly after his smuggling conviction published an advertisement calling for anyone who had pawned anything to him to immediately buy it back.[60] Although Bruse suffered a financial setback, it appears to have been of short duration.

One important reason that mercers were able to recover relatively quickly was their continued support of their clients. Indeed, most mercers do not appear to have suffered a loss of customers following a smuggling conviction, even a very public one. In 1769, the Stockholm-based mercer Johan Sundbeck (173?–1800) was convicted of smuggling an assortment of foreign textiles into the city. Due to the spectacular nature of his case, he disguised himself as a trading assistant by the name of Carl Holm and his case was published as a pamphlet, which was advertised in Stockholm's newspapers.[61] With such exposure, Sundbeck's crime appears to have become common knowledge in Stockholm. However, while a prominent retailer's transgressions might have been of public interest, it did not automatically follow that the consequences were negative. Similar to Samuel Bruse, Johan Sundbeck appears to have suffered no longstanding financial difficulties following his conviction but enjoyed a thriving business at least until 1785.[62] Around 1785, Sundbeck's business appears to have suffered a setback, and he was forced to leave his house on Stortorget and move to a poorer area of the city, where he stayed until his death in 1800.[63] It would, however, be a stretch to link this to his smuggling activities which had taken place 16 years previously.

Although a conviction of smuggling does not appear to have been detrimental to their business, it did not mean that the shop-keepers did not fight their attackers. This particularly played out in the court where mercers sought to question the validity of the search and the valuations, while in various ways attempting to distance themselves from the crime. After contraband was retrieved from Samuel Bruse's shop, he repeatedly refused to turn up to court claiming illness while simultaneously launching his own complaint against the customs prosecutor Hoffgardh, who had performed the confiscations in his shop.[64] Bruse expressed a concern that Hoffgardh had used his absence and "the fear of his assistants" to "break in", an idea that quickly was dismissed by the court. When Bruse finally appeared at court, he explained that he could "impossibly imagine or believe that any contraband had been in his shop", and offered to swear an oath to the effect that no one had brought in illegal wares to his shop.[65] Despite insisting on the "illegality of the search", Bruse's attempts to have his case overturned by claiming professional misconduct on the part of Hoffgardh eventually proved unsuccessful. Bruse was one in a line of mercers who actively used the court system in order to save themselves after a contraband seizure. Mercers were particularly likely to appeal their crimes, especially on technicalities.[66] Their willingness to challenge the court, and to use it for their own purposes was probably related to their social position: as prominent burghers who had previously assisted the customs office with valuations, they were familiar with, and unintimidated by, the customs court world.

However, the attack on the customs office did not always take on such bureaucratic forms and was not necessarily led by the mercers. In 1786, the year after the re-introduction of the house-visitation, there was a search of the shop of Gothenburg-based merchant Erick Linderoth (1750–1790).[67] The search was overseen by Samuel Bruse's adversary, Hoffgardh, who by now had been appointed Super-Inspector. During the search a crowd gathered outside of the shop. At first, they were merely shouting abuse but matters escalated and the crowd started attacking Hoffgardh and his guards with stones, forcing them to flee with the seized goods. Surrounded, the customs officers had to seek refuge in several houses, including a pharmacy, where they were trapped for hours while a stone-throwing mob smashed all the lower floor windows.[68] Hoffgardh described the mob as consisting of "several 100 people...among whom there were many traders and people of note".[69] While the size and composition of the crowd might be a matter of debate, it is clear that the confiscations at Linderoth's shop triggered some sort of riot. It led to the cancellation of two other shop-visitations scheduled to take place that day, buying some time for the surrounding merchants. For Linderoth, the chaotic nature of the search, resulting in several errors on the part of the customs officers, gave fodder for negotiations in the courtroom. Meanwhile, the attack on Hoffgardh and his officers indicates that the public was not want of showing their displeasure for the reintroduced house-visitations which they perceived as attacks on their merchants.

These features, the large scale of the contraband hoards, the renown of the mercers both to customs officers and clients, their tendency to negotiate in court, and particularly the unflinching support of their clients, were crucial in shaping how the mercers conducted their illegal trade and why, despite intense surveillance, they were able to persevere. With these general features in mind, we shall now turn to a more detailed investigation of one mercer, which offers deeper insights into the world of the urban smuggling merchants.

A Case Study – Johan Abraham Théel (1765–1811)

Setting the Scene

In 1799, the anti-smuggling legislation was expanded further to include extended visitation rights, and more severe punishments. The visitations should be overseen by fiscal officers; these included the city fiscals, the country fiscals, and the industry fiscals, and in particular the trade and manufacturing fiscal (*Handels och Slögde Fiskal*). As responsible parties, they would be charged a fine if they launched a search on a house which presented no, or only negligible amounts of contraband.[70] It was therefore important that they had reasonable suspicion before they applied to the mayor, the King's official, or the head of the enforcement office, to conduct a visitation.[71] In order to guide the fiscal officers in their duties, a manual for the trade and manufacturing fiscal was issued in August 1803. The manual stressed the need for diligence and severity in the line of duty.[72] At the time of the publication, the position of trade and manufacturing fiscal in Stockholm was held by Petrus Jonas Junbeck (1761–1820) commonly referred to as P. J. Junbeck. According to his own memoirs, published between 1815 and 1817, he performed his work zealously without consideration for personal relationships, something that would later come back to haunt him.[73] Junbeck calculated that during his career, he had overseen the confiscation of 9451 Rdr 38 sk worth of goods and brought in some 2289 Rdr worth of fines to Stockholm.[74]

In 1803, Johan Abraham Théel happened to come to P. J. Junbeck's attention. Starting with Junbeck's contraband seizures at Théel's premises, this chapter will in turn examine Théel's career, his networks, and connections, allowing a deeper exploration both of what role contraband played in the mercery business but also what effect the contraband convictions had upon reputations. Comparing the result of the study of Théel and his social networks with material from the customs court protocols offers insight into the close ties that connected the Silk and Cloth Traders' Society members, as well as other burghers. It also illustrates the prevalence of contraband convictions among the retailers in this Society in particular, and among the burghers more generally and shows how the customs officer, rather than the smuggling merchant, was the outlier.

The Crime

On 7 December 1803, the Trade and Manufacturing Fiscal P. J. Junbeck conducted a search of the premises of silk-mercer Johan Abraham Théel on Mynttorget 4 in central Stockholm. Three sealed sacks of wares were confiscated containing unstamped textile goods. Junbeck brought Théel before the Customs Court where the 135 types of textiles were valued and assessed by silk manufacturers Lindström and Distlein, and textile merchant Sundin. While it was easy to establish Théel's guilt, it was considerably more complicated to determine the extent of the crime. Both parties announced their dissatisfaction with the valuations and requested a re-examination of the wares.[75] A fresh valuation followed. The prosecution called on textile merchant Björkman, who was deemed to be trustworthy and possessed a good knowledge of the goods concerned. Théel agreed but reserved the right to call upon another, according to him, reliable merchant by the name of Juggström.[76] Following a guilty verdict in the Maritime Customs Court, Théel appealed to the Court of the National Board of Trade on the grounds that many of the wares identified as contraband were actually domestic productions. After some deliberations and additional valuations, the National Board of Trade eventually agreed with the verdict of the Maritime Customs Court. It was decided that Théel should pay the full fines for the wares deemed to be foreign manufactures and to lose the right to stand for election for any post that required civic trust. This last punishment was stipulated in (1 Art, 1§, 1799) and should have been imposed on anyone in possession of more than 50 Rdr worth of contraband. Théel was released on bail after the mercers A. H. Norin and C. Wiberg had signed his security.[77] In a ledger of confiscation cases, Théel's contraband was valued at approximately 217 Rdr bco worth of legal but unstamped textiles, and 657 Rdr bco worth of foreign contraband. Théel was fined a total of 754 Rdr bco, but the contraband alone would later fetch 934 Rdr bco at auction, as it was sold for export.[78] Despite his misfortune, Théel appears to have been let off rather lightly. His name never appeared in the newspapers as the 1799 decree stipulated, and the loss of the right to stand for election for posts that required civic trust seems never to have been enacted, as Théel was elected as an assessor (*taxeringsman*) for Stockholm City in 1810.[79] The lack of public exposure of Théel's crimes and his later election are likely linked. Without a public announcement, it was easier to overlook other features of the punishment as well, which would have been more difficult to ignore if he had been publicly exposed as a smuggler.

Networks, Contacts, and Career

Théel had started his career in Stockholm in the shop of Carl Wiberg (1751–1821) and Abraham Elfving (?–?), a fact that appears to have shaped a lot of his later career. The shop was located in the Rosenadler house (*Rosenadlerskahuset*) on Mynttorget in the 1780s, on premises that Théel would later take over.[80] Mynttorget and the Rosenadler house have been described as a mercantile centre in Stockholm in the 1780s and housed several shops and cafés.[81] By the time Théel arrived in Stockholm from the mining town Falun around 1790, Wiberg and Elfving had moved to the property just across the street from the Rosenadler house, where Wiberg would remain until his death in 1821. Théel probably benefitted from the merchants' extensive connections and it was also here that Théel met his future business partner, the shop assistant Carl Fredrick Hasselquist. Hasselquist was at the time working for the merchant Ek, who kept a shop in the same building.[82] It is unclear exactly how Wiberg and Elfving conducted their business as they shared shop premises but were not officially partners. What is evident, however, is that Théel found himself in a highly favourable position upon entering Wiberg and Elfving's service. Both were successful tradesmen in their own right. In 1778, Wiberg had been one of the members of the Burgher Estates Economic Committee (*Borgare Ståndets Oecomonie utskott*).[83] Abraham Elfving was also a successful burgher. Sometime in the 1790s, Elfving left Wiberg and the retailing business to become a wholesale dealer, entering into a partnership with another wholesale dealer and head of division at the National Board of Trade

(Kommersråd), Eric Zetterstén, whose daughter Johanna he later married. Despite this, Elfving's contact with Théel remained strong, and in 1803, he became godfather to Théel's third daughter Erica Wilhelmina.[84]

Notably, Ek, Wiberg, Elfving, and Zetterstén all appear in the customs court records. Ek and Wiberg both had contraband textiles seized in their respective shops.[85] Elfving, on the other hand, was involved in hiding 1000 kg of coffee beans on Zetterstén property on Djurgården, an island in Stockholm.[86] It should be noted that the burden of the crime landed on Johanna Elfving, Elfving's wife, and Zetterstén's daughter, who claimed accountability as her father was ignorant of the crime and her husband was abroad. Understanding Théel's background and acquaintances is important both because it illustrates how common business illegalities of various descriptions were among this group of traders, and because it illustrates the interconnectivity of the retailers active in Stockholm.

After training under Wiberg and Elfving, Johan Abraham Théel was awarded burghership in the Silk and Cloth Trader Society in December 1791 at the age of 26.[87] His first company was Joh. Abr. Théel & Comp, which he ran together with C. F. Hasselqwist.[88] Already by 1796, Théel appears in the list of board members of the Silk and Cloth Trader Society along with his former employer Carl Wiberg.[89] Three years later, in October 1799, the City Fiscal Teuchler conducted a raid on Hasselquist and Théel's establishment in the Rosenadler house where he confiscated a few wares. Just before his visit, Teuchler had made some confiscations in the shop of Carl Wiberg.[90] Théel protested that the seized wares had been Swedish productions and during the later trial, the manufacturer J. M. Ahlberg offered to pay the fines, as he claimed that he had produced the unstamped wares.[91] Both Théel and Ahlberg were landed with fines, the former for selling unstamped goods in his shop and the latter for not stamping his productions.[92]

A few months after this incident, in December 1799, Théel was involved in purchasing and exporting contraband wares to Wismar.[93] This practice was legal and part of the effort to cleanse the country of illegal foreign goods. However, suspicion was raised that some of the goods were reintroduced to Sweden, and in 1799, an investigation was launched. Several people known to be dealing in smuggled goods appear in this investigation, including Théel, who appears three times, once shipping textiles worth 1487 Rdr with Captain M. Nilsson (or Nelson) to Copenhagen, a second time shipping etamin, flowered wool satins and chalons among other things worth 465 Rdr to Wismar with the Captain H.J. Schmid, and the third time when Théel shipped 2472 Rdr worth of textiles with C. Mattson, again to Copenhagen.[94] At least one of the captains, Captain Schmid, is known to have smuggled goods to Sweden around the same time.[95] It is not impossible that Théel acquired some of the contraband found in his shop a few years later from this type of sham 're-export' business.

Théel's presence in the Rosenadler house can be observed from 1800.[96] However, it is only in 1801 that Théel was noted as the tenant of the shop space on the corner of Mynttorget and Smedjegatan (later Västerlånggatan). The following year he also decided to move in there with his family, renting all three floors above, as well as the basement and the attics.[97] In 1802, the year before the contraband seizure, his and Hasselqwist's company was dissolved and Théel set up on his own.[98] Théel appears to have been very active in these years and frequently appears in bankruptcy cases as a creditor.[99] During Théel's early years in Stockholm, he was introduced to many merchants with whom he would maintain contact for the duration of his career. This appears to have been a small close-knit community of traders – by 1797, there were a total of 53 mercers in Stockholm.[100] While the Silk and Cloth Trader Society was relatively small, many of its members appear to have been involved in the contraband trade, as their names appear in the customs court records.

After December 1803, when Junbeck made the large contraband confiscation in Théel's shop at Mynttorget, Théel suddenly disappears from the Silk and Cloth Trader society proceedings. His name reoccurs again in 1806 once the debacle had been resolved and forgotten.[101] This indicates that while the society was treating smuggling offenders with care they also had an institutional tolerance for the crime.

According to the 1799 anti-smuggling legislation anyone caught with more than 50 Rdr of contraband should have their name published in the newspapers. Théel, along with other mercers, appear to have fought this punishment in particular.[102] This raises the question: if there was a general acceptance of smuggling, then why did the contraband retailers seemingly object to having their names appearing in the newspapers? Most likely, this was due to the fact that honour and integrity remained important virtues, particularly for public individuals such as the trading burghers. While the mercers in practice could support the contraband trade, they were unwilling to be publicly labelled 'unpatriotic' smugglers who had betrayed their nation. Being denounced as an unpatriotic smuggler in the press was something quite different to the day-to-day practice of selling contraband to encouraging consumers. Several of the convicted retailers, including Théel, also appear to have fought such public shaming.[103] Having never been publicly denounced in the newspapers, Théel was able to return to his old position once the dust had settled.

During his absence from the society, he appears to have directed his efforts elsewhere. Théel had joined the Freemasonic lodge *St Jean Auxiliaire* back in 1795 and quickly rose through the ranks. In 1799, St Jean Auxiliaire found itself with a new grand master with Duke Carl, the crown prince's uncle and later King, Carl XIII, who initiated a merger of his old lodge St Johannis and St Jean, under the name *Den Nordiska Första*.[104] This also coincides roughly with Duke Carl's first recorded purchases in Théel's shop. At some point, Théel came to be moved from *Den Nordiska Första* to *St Andreas Nordiska Cirkeln* where he continued his rise through the ranks. Between 1804 and 1805 he was Treasurer (*skattemästare*) and in 1805 he became Junior Warden rising to Senior Warden in 1810. His career as a Freemason appears to have taken off at the same time as his mercer career ran into some difficulty. It thus appears that he shifted his focus during this period. However, according to §10 of the Masonic rules introduced by Duke Carl in 1800 (*Ordens Allmänna Lagar*), any brother who had been condemned by a court of law should also be condemned by his brothers and lose the right to bear the Freemasonic name and decorations as well as be crossed out of the lodge's cadastral and forever be condemned to exclusion from the community of the Order.[105] This clearly did not happen in the case of Théel; rather, it seems that he could continue to progress there while his opportunities in regular society had been temporarily put on hold.

High-Ranking Clients and Social Rise

During the 1790s, Théel had established himself as a merchant of fine textiles. At the same time as he was moving into the Rosenadler house, his bills turn up in the most prominent accounts. An early customer was the crown prince, future King Gustav IV Adolph. His earliest purchase was made in May 1792, which was the first of at least 37 separate purchases made up until April 1794.[106] Other prominent customers followed his lead, such as Hans Axel von Fersen and Duke Carl, who made numerous purchases from Théel.[107] These are only a few examples of the type of accounts in which Théel's bills turn up but they give an indication of the social make-up of his customer base. An elite clientele of this type was extremely important and helped both to boost the social standing of the trader and promote his business.[108] Notably, these bills stem from the same period in which Théel is known to have traded in contraband.

Other material also indicates that Théel's customers were not deterred by his smuggling activities. To get an idea of the customer response, it is helpful to consult the diary of Märta Helena Reenstierna, who was a longstanding client of Théel's. Reenstierna lived at Årsta just outside of Stockholm and was married to Cavalry Captain Christian Henrik von Schnell. Her first purchase from Théel's shop was recorded in 1794: a grey silk shawl.[109] A few months before the confiscations in his shop, on 12 August 1803, she recorded, "[f]rom Merchant Théel I let Nyström collect Sitz 9 3/4 ells for a dress".[110] Of course, it is impossible to say whether this 'sitz' or chintz was of the type later confiscated, but many of her purchases were similar to the contraband cloth seized in 1803. Six months after the raid on his premises, she was back, buying a muslin neckerchief for her brother. In her diary, Reenstierna relates purchasing goods from Théel on at least 11 occasions between 1794 and 1804.[111] If she knew about the court case against him, Reenstierna, who was acquainted with several high-ranking customs officers, seems to have paid it little heed.[112] As Reenstierna herself is known to have bought illegal wares elsewhere and assisted escaping smugglers, she would probably not have abandoned her long-term shop.[113]

Théel turned out to be a successful merchant despite the 1803 conviction. By 1810, he had eight people in his employ, a tobacco plantation in the parish Adolph Fredrick, and a yearly income of 2500 Rdr.[114] The tobacco plantation had been purchased the previous year, and the manor attached to it also contained a silk weaving-mill, which added an additional branch to his business activities.[115] Théel's career was cut short when he died in 1811 at only 46 years old from consumption, leaving behind a wife and six daughters.[116] At this final point in Théel's life, the wholesale dealer Anders Emanuel Maulström makes an appearance. According to Théel's will, Maulström was to take over his business and care for his wife and children. In Théel's estate inventory, the warehouse stock, mainly containing silks and cottons, was valued at 61,682 Rdr bco. The lists of outstanding payments from customers lists an array of notable people, from King Carl XIII, previously Duke Carl, and the Dowager Queen's favourite Gustav Badin, to the Duchess and Excellency Armfeldt, Baron Höpken, Fabian von Fersen, and Axel Adolph Piper along with many other prominent individuals, including the Super-Inspector at the Customs Office A. Muhr.[117]

One final note should be made about Maulström, the person charged with taking over Théel's estate. He also appears in the customs court records and in the newspapers, where he was exposed as a smuggler. Almost exactly a year after the confiscations in Théel's shop, in 1804, P. J. Junbeck visited Maulström in his warehouse on Götgatan where he confiscated 896 Rdr worth of various goods.[118] The exact relationship between Maulström and Théel is so far unknown, beyond the fact that they had both been members of the Freemasonic lodge *St Jean Auxiliaire* in the late 1790s.[119] While it is not always possible to get to the bottom of the nature of each relationship, it seems clear that the constellations that Théel and the other mercers and wholesale dealers worked within were tightknit social networks which meant that they could be allied both in business, and through societies such as the Freemasons. Conversely, any comparison between Théel's customer lists and the Freemasonic lodge memberships show great overlaps. This does not mean that they were clients because of their associations with the Freemasons, but rather that many burghers, officials, and aristocrats joined because they saw the social and professional benefits of such connections. However, it still resulted in numerous entanglements and social connections between various traders, and between customers and vendors. Going into a Stockholm shop in the late eighteenth century was thus not an encounter between anonymous individuals but a meeting between actors interconnected in various ways through the social fabric of the town.

As this survey illustrates, Théel – while clearly using illegal means to expand his trade, particularly in the early years – nevertheless managed not only to keep his clients and become an important member of his trade society but also to expand his trade, bolstered by an extensive network both of members from the Silk and Cloth Traders Society and wholesale dealers. Another intriguing feature which will be returned to later in the chapter is how interconnected Théel's trade appears to have been, not merely with members of his own trade but also with other types of retailers, including pedlars and Jewish merchants. Théel's case thus helps to highlight several features of the mercer's contraband trade; moreover, this case study expands upon some of the trends which were observed in earlier cases where less information was available about the mercers, their lives and their contacts. It also suggests that while control and surveillance expanded over time, the social acceptance of this contraband trade persevered.

Meanwhile, for the prosecuting officers, diligence in the line of duty could prove disadvantageous over time, when the offenders retained power and influence.[120] This was something P.J. Junbeck got to experience at the end of his career as trade and manufacturing fiscal. His job had landed him with powerful enemies who thwarted his attempts to set up a business and excluded him from the burgher community.[121]

While this case study primarily has focused on J. A. Théel, it has also shown the intricately intertwined nature of the burgher community and how many of its members were involved in underground trade. This notion is further backed up by the customs records. In Stockholm alone, the court records show that in 1804, 11 out of the 110 convicted smugglers were titled either merchant or wholesale dealer, and the following year the numbers were 8 out of 80.[122] Shop-keepers thus made up roughly 10% of convicted offenders towards the end of the research period, a significant number in relation to their relatively low number.

Mercer smuggling was very different from that of the pedlars: it was conducted under higher levels of surveillance and the culprits themselves had a very different social position. The urban mercers made ample use of what can be described as their social capital – their contacts and networks, good name and reputation – in order to shield themselves from any of the adverse effects of their crimes. As members of the burgher estate, they were also equipped with the confidence, skill and know-how to 're-negotiate' their crime in the courtroom. The mercers were at home in the world of courtrooms, administration, and state servants. Most often their re-negotiations, through oaths and appeals, did not lead to a reduction of the monetary fines, but rather an escape from the other features of the punishment such as the public announcement of their crime. The mercers' involvement in the contraband trade was also, crucially, interlinked with their customers, their wants, and patronage. Without the customers' demand for contraband textiles, it would not have been profitable for the mercers to engage in this risky trade, and without their continued visits to the shop following a conviction, the mercers would most likely have suffered a reduction in their business, potentially even bankruptcy. There are, however, no signs that the mercers were ever 'punished' by their clients following a smuggling offence. It suggests that while a patriotic protectionist discourse was dominating newspapers and legislation, consumers both supported and benefitted from the mercers' contraband trade. This mutually beneficial relationship enabled smuggling to continue, something that will become even more evident as the investigation moves on to look at other types of urban retailers.

The Jewish Trader – A New Nemesis

Jewish traders were first invited to settle in Sweden in 1775. Gustav III played a pivotal role in opening up the Swedish realm as part of an attempt to improve Swedish trade and manufacturing. It was hoped that this influx would help to regenerate the Swedish market by bringing in new money and competency.[123] The move was only possible for a select few, as becoming a protected Jew involved a considerable financial investment.[124] The King also took similar measures in Pomerania, where Jewish traders were offered protection in 1776.[125] Most of the Jews who eventually settled in Sweden came via Mecklenburg, which indicates that the Swedish dominions functioned as an entrance to the Swedish territories. In addition to the arrivals from Mecklenburg and the German lands, there were arrivals from Denmark, Galicia, and to a lesser extent, from Britain and the Netherlands.[126]

Francesca Trivellato has done much to shed light on the role of protected Jewish communities in generating dynamic trade areas in Europe and in her research, she has pointed to the importance of family ties in building up trust and creating reliable networks of exchange.[127] Even more recently, Nuala Zahedieh has argued that the Sephardic diasporas played a central role in the maintenance of global illicit trade, particularly in high-risk environments. She posits that as these smugglers were acting outside of the realms of legal protection and state support, they had better prospects of surviving if they operated in close-knit communities based on trust and social discipline.[128]

The first Jewish traders to settle in Sweden, settled in the free port of Marstrand. The first area in Sweden to enjoy freedom of religion.[129] The same year Aaron Isaac, an engraver from Mecklenburg, along with his brother Marcus Isaac and their business associate Abraham Pach, became the first protected Jews to settle in Stockholm without having to convert.[130] A Bill for Religious Freedom was issued in 1779, which formally extended religious toleration to the Jews. However, it was not until 1782 that the Jewish Regulation Act (*Judereglementet*) was issued, which fully explained and regulated their rights and limitations. The act established that Jews, despite being part of the Jewish rather than the Swedish Nation, would be allowed to settle in three towns in addition to Marstrand: Stockholm, Gothenburg, and Norrköping, and after 1785 the port town Karlskrona.[131] The Jewish Regulation Act drew on foreign examples and embodied a compromise between two opposing political interests, protectionism, which was anchored in the guild system, and the government's pro-business factions.[132] Consequently, while the 1782 decree established some rights, to trade wholesale and retail and to set up manufacturing businesses, it also set up firm boundaries for the Jewish settlers. They had to restrict their trade to open shops and were not allowed to trade in alcohol, medicine, or any guild controlled craft.[133] This led to a disproportionate representation of Jews in wholesale dealing and manufacturing; historian Bertil Andersson has shown that, between 1782 and 1838, 85% of the protected Jews in Gothenburg were involved in trade.[134] Meanwhile, immigration numbers remained small.[135] Throughout the eighteenth century, the Jewish community in Sweden was thus a fairly small group of strictly controlled traders and manufacturers.

The Jews held a contradictory position in Sweden. While they had been invited to stimulate and open up trade, they soon found themselves bogged down by regulation, even more so than other Swedish burghers.[136] The Jewish experience in Sweden was marked by a struggle between the controlling guilds and the proponents of free trade, where one side saw them as a threat and the other as playing an important role in liberalising trade.[137] Their situation is similar to that of the mercers, but more extreme. Just like in the case of the mercers, the Jewish traders also came to be trapped between regulations and the realities of trade. Despite their relatively small numbers, however, Jewish merchants started to appear relatively frequently in the customs court records from the 1780s onwards.[138] While there was clearly some Jewish involvement in the contraband trade from early on, there were also other reasons as to why they repeatedly appear in the customs material.

Accusations of Smuggling from Outside of the Jewish Community

The Jewish traders were, just like the mercers, affected by the patriotic protectionist discourse. However, their distinctive status as Jewish rather than Swedish merchants exposed them to even harsher criticism and accusation. Accusations of smuggling often drew on the idea that as Jewish emigrants the traders lacked a genuine loyalty towards the Swedish state. Such accusations were, to a large extent, based on self-interest and were often used to challenge and discredit those who were seen to pose unwanted competition.

One case from 1792 will serve to illustrate this phenomenon. It concerns the Jewish trader and manufacturer Fabian Philip (1761, Mecklenburg – 1832), who had been granted protection to stay in Karlskrona and to set up a sailcloth factory to cater to the needs of naval base housed in the city, and the Super-Inspector and Customs Manager Mathias Fredrich Strübing (1753–1816). In October 1792, Strübing sent a letter to the Customs Board in Stockholm explaining that he suspected that Fabian Philip was using his warehouses to conceal significant repositories of forbidden and unstamped goods, which were used to conduct "the most extensive trade" in illicit goods.[139] According to Strübing, he was unable to properly investigate Philip as the anti-smuggling decree of 1785 only allowed visitations in open shops and storages owned by those practising retailing. He therefore requested for the decree to be extended to include the homes of Jews. As they, according to Strübing, conducted the majority of their trade "[in their] living chambers, which are furnished with shelves and counters as shops and stores" enabling them to hide away their forbidden goods out of reach of the customs office.[140] In order to rectify this situation, Strübing asked for an extension of his powers so that he could search the homes of the trading Jews inhabiting Karlskrona, which would have effectively divested Jewish traders of the right to house peace.[141] While the discriminatory regulations were never introduced, Strübing's request highlights that some officers within the customs office believed that the Jews passed under the radar of the anti-smuggling surveillance and control mechanisms. Strübing argued that this made the Jewish merchants particularly suspect and dangerous. Meanwhile, their 'suspiciousness' was used as an argument against the Jewish settlers and a justification for why they should not enjoy the same liberties as other Swedish citizens.

In order to fully understand the alleged threat posed by Fabian Philip, it is necessary to consider the conditions for his settlement in Karlskrona. Philip had arrived in Sweden in 1780 together with Emanuel Samuel and had been granted the right to stay in Karlskrona by the town council. Through the introduction of the Jewish Regulation Act in 1782, it became illegal for Jews to live anywhere other than Stockholm, Gothenburg and Norrköping. In order to stay on in Karlskrona, Philip approached Henrik af Trolle, the Admiral of the Fleet, and offered to set up a sailcloth manufacturing business that would serve the Royal Navy that was based in the town. Seeing the need for such a business, af Trolle applied to the King for a special permission for Philip to remain in Karlskrona, which was granted.[142] However, Philip seems to have been slow in taking up his new line of business, which angered the other burghers in Karlskrona. In 1783, the Karlskrona trade society raised objections to Philip's privilege to remain in the town, claiming that instead of producing sailcloth, Philip and his Jewish employees spent their time dealing in illegal merchandise.[143]

Philip was not the only one targeted with this sort of slander, however. In the 1790s, the newly settled Karlskrona Jews attracted a lot of attention from the established trading community. Historian Janrik Bromé has labelled this a "hunt for black market traders, soldiers and 'cheaters'".[144] However, this should probably be seen more as a discrediting campaign by the already established burghers, many of whom had themselves arrived in Karlskrona from the Swedish dominions in the first half of the eighteenth century and had financial motives for keeping Jewish traders at bay. It is worthwhile to point out that Super-Inspector Strübing derived from one of these established merchant families and it is possible that his background and connections might have played into his persecution of Philip.[145]

While the trade society engaged in a discrediting campaign against Philip, others defended him against the assault, and for every letter against him, the admiralty received one in his favour.[146] Philip never lost the support of the admiralty and no evidence of the alleged smuggling ever came to light.[147]

The Jewish traders found themselves in a difficult situation as they, by legal definition, were part of the Jewish rather than the Swedish Nation, with different rights and obligations.[148] This distinction made them vulnerable to attack as they did not fit into the regular Swedish patriotic merchant narrative. Harry Svensson argues that the animosity towards Philip should be understood not as an expression of antisemitism but as a response by the Karlskrona guild board to a perceived increase in competition.[149] However, while the competition argument might not in and of itself have been an expression of antisemitism, the expression it took is considerably more problematic as it specifically targeted Jewish trading techniques and the perceived lack of loyalty evidenced by the "unpatriotic crime" of smuggling.

Accusations of Smuggling from Inside the Jewish Community

The accusation of smuggling did not only come from people outside of the Jewish community but also from within. Although the Jewish community in Stockholm was tightknit and reasonably small – by 1807, it contained 333 members, including women and children – this did not mean that it was devoid of internal conflict.[150] In the 1790s, a schism developed between Aaron Isaac, the leader of the Jewish community in Stockholm, and David Hirsch (c. 1752–1811). In his memoirs, Isaac, who had a longstanding conflict with Hirsch, suggested that Hirsch had started out as a poor itinerant tobacco-seller in the Swedish countryside. According to Isaac, Hirsch acquired his tobacco on credit from Elias Magnus, one of Isaac's close acquaintances.[151] Over time, the relationship between Magnus and Hirsch deteriorated, and most of the Jewish community of Stockholm sided with Magnus. To their annoyance, Hirsch progressed in his trade and in 1793 he received a licence to conduct trade in trinkets (*nipperhandel*). Meanwhile, the ostracism of Hirsch continued and in a letter to the Governor-General in Stockholm, he complained that he was being persecuted by two Jewish traders, Josef Marcus and Levin Isaac.[152]

It is unclear what conflict between Aaron Isaac and David Hirsh was rooted in but in his memoirs, Aaron Isaac noted that David Hirsch was untrustworthy in trade, and was giving the Jewish traders a bad name.[153] David Hirsch, meanwhile, appears to have disliked Aaron Isaac's dominance in Stockholm and suggested that the longstanding conflict was caused by a power struggle between the two merchants.[154] Over time, the conflict grew increasingly infected and eventually resulted in accusations of smuggling.

In 1799, a letter sent by David Hirsch to the King was published in *Dagligt Allehanda*. In the letter, Hirsch demanded that the accusations of smuggling launched against him by the Jews Gumpert Hirch and Isaac Michaelson, Aaron Isaac's son-in-law, should be investigated and challenged. Contrary to the statements issued by his 'enemies', David Hirsch argued that his trade was and would remain 'untainted'. In his letter Hirsch noted, "the command of morality and the deep obedience of the subject are the objects which guide me...".[155] Accusations of smuggling were thus also used within the Jewish community itself to reject undesirable traders. It shows how these traders used prejudicial accusations directed at themselves to achieve their own goals.

Entanglements and Contrabands

Meanwhile, there is little doubt that there were Jewish merchants who engaged in the contraband trade to bolster and expand their businesses, just like the mercers. Incidentally, several of the people said to have persecuted David Hirsch appear themselves in the customs records after receiving illegal cargos.[156]

One of these was Josef Marcus (1750 Schwaan – 1838), a wholesale dealer and manufacturer, who had arrived in Stockholm in 1777 under the protection of Aaron Isaac. Josef Marcus had made his fortune during Gustav III's Russian Wars by delivering provisions to the Swedish army in Finland, which might also have helped secure his wholesale license in 1790.[157] In 1804, Marcus also set up a calico printing manufacture in Stockholm.[158] One of Marcus' known clients was the, by now familiar, mercer J. A. Théel. Indeed, upon Théel's death in 1811, his largest unpaid debt was owed to Marcus.[159] While Théel likely used Marcus' services to stock his shop with textiles, it is uncertain whether Théel acquired cloth from him as a wholesale dealer or as a calico printer, or, indeed, both. It is nevertheless clear that they engaged in extensive trade with one another.

Théel's second largest debt was owed to the brothers Jacob Moses Jacobsson (1773 Karlsruhe – 1827) and Abraham Moses Jacobsson (1776 Karlsruhe – 1838).[160] J. M. Jacobsson had arrived in 1798 and gained a wholesale dealer license in 1801. The same year his brother A. M. Jacobsson also joined him in Stockholm. Just like Marcus, A. M. Jacobsson frequently appears in the customs records. The first mention of A. M. Jacobsson dates from 1803 when 318 Rdr worth of contraband was seized at the premises of his glass shop.[161] It is notable that despite two contraband convictions and one unproved suspicion of smuggling,[162] A. M. Jacobsson was awarded with a wholesale license.[163] The interconnectivity between Théel and these Jewish wholesale dealers was not unique, but other similar cases suggest that mercers and the Jewish traders engaged in extensive trade with one another.[164] As earlier noted, many Jewish merchants worked either with the import of foreign goods or with the manufacture of calico cloth and the mercers, who dealt mainly in imported fabrics or finer domestic productions, would have wanted their shops well-stocked with both types of cloth. It is thus likely that at least some of the contraband textiles found in the mercer shops had been imported by Jewish wholesale dealers, who had extensive foreign networks that could aid them to organise illicit operations.

How this could work in practice can be seen in a case from 1803, which also involves some by now familiar names. That year, a contraband hoard consisting of various goldwares and precious stones worth 1404 Rdr 32 sk was seized in Helsingborg from ferry boatman Bengt Persson. Persson had travelled from Helsingör in Denmark and brought with him a package addressed to the apothecary Berkenmeijer. Further investigation revealed that the package was actually destined for Stockholm and the Jewish merchants Isaak Michaelson, Aaron Isaac and M. M. Bendix.[165] This was proved by a letter submitted to the Maritime Customs Court by the ferryman. The letter in question had been given to him along with the wares by the Jewish trader Ruben in Helsingör.[166] As this case shows, domestic and foreign networks helped to organise and shield illicit shipments through the use of intermediaries and via dummy recipients.

Increasing Restriction and Blame

Around the turn of the century, support for patriotic protectionism was at its peak. Regulations intended to keep retailers in check expanded, and at the same time the slurs made against Jewish traders were becoming increasingly severe. This escalation became particularly visible in the conflict between the jewellery and goldsmith guilds and the Jews. It came to a fore in 1809 when the court-jeweller Bengt Sander published the antisemitic lampoon, "Some evidence, that the Jews contribute to the common distress in Sweden", blaming the Jews for the miserable state of Swedish trade.[167] A strong reaction followed its publication and several rejections of Sander's text appeared in print. In one of them, an anonymous writer argued that the Jews had been labouring under "severe laws and the attention of jealous rivals", and that they could not be blamed for the destruction of Swedish finances – by contrast, they had played an important role in developing domestic manufacturing.[168] The writer went on to note:

> ...search without violence and partiality, the public evidence that exists of the shameful actions of the pursuit of profit, and it shall easily be revealed, whether the Country's own Sons always and without exception can be congratulated on their law-abiding and civic mind-set; judge also the Stranger without prejudice and resentment, and some few examples of illegal pursuits, which the Law have prosecuted, will not make us unjustly proceed against an entire communion of honest and worthy Members, who deserve our reverence and respect.[169]

Despite such defences of the Jewish traders, they were facing an increasingly hostile environment. On 19 December 1806, Jews were prohibited from entering Sweden. Although it was lifted after the revolution in 1809, by 1815, Jewish immigration had stopped completely with the cancellation of the Jewish Regulation Act.

When the Jewish traders arrived in Sweden, they entered into a pre-existing conflict between those who favoured a rejection of international trade in favour of protectionist policy and those who advocated a more liberal approach to trade, in other words, between those who benefitted from and those who suffered under restrictive guild and protectionist rules. This meant that the Jewish traders and the international goods they brought along with them were embraced by some, as a boost for Swedish trade, and rejected by others, as damaging and threatening to Swedish interests. Within this framework, the accusation of smuggling came to play a prominent role, as it was seen as evidence of conflicting loyalties. It is an amplified version of the diverging views on smuggling discussed in Chapter 2, where the protectionists saw smuggling as an expression of failing loyalty, whereas natural rights defenders saw it as a natural consequence of an oppressive economic system.

Jewish traders were under particular pressure, as they were both under the scrutiny of the customs office and the target of accusations of smuggling from both outside and inside the Jewish community. At the same time, they also appear to have been able to negotiate this situation, as the vast majority of the individuals studied in this section appear to have been successful in their trades despite accusations of smuggling and/or actual involvement in the contraband trade. The Jewish traders are similar to the mercers in that, while they were suspected of smuggling, they nevertheless managed, on an individual basis, to maintain a profitable trade. As wholesale dealers, they were also heavily involved in trade with the mercers, and their illegal trade activities might well have been related. The Jewish traders as a group came under increased pressure towards the end of the period as their very presence in Sweden was increasingly seen as damaging, a view which also aligned with a general move towards increased patriotic protectionism in the same period.

The Elite Smuggler – The Case of Marcelin Robert (1753–1832)

In this final section of the chapter, attention turns to an individual hardly visible in the customs court records despite his heavy involvement in contraband retailing, Marcelin Robert. Robert arrived in Stockholm sometime in 1775, although it is uncertain what he did during his early years in the Swedish capital. Originally from Millau in the Occitan region of France, he had prior to his move to Sweden lived in Paris, where according to his own account he trained as a merchant.[170] In 1781, Robert entered the royal household as a second valet, and almost immediately came to be engaged by the young Crown Prince, the future Gustav IV Adolph, who took a liking to him. Not everyone was equally delighted by the Frenchman, however. The Prince's tutor Fredric Sparre described Robert as a "complete stranger" and added that the Prince could not understand a word he said and vice versa, a comment which indicates that Robert at this point was unable to speak Swedish.[171] Despite some initial difficulties, Robert quickly found his footing at court. Only a month and a half after his engagement in the Prince's service, he was selling him lavender water, combs, and various trinkets.[172] Retailing valets were not uncommon at this time, particularly at court, where they often functioned as intermediaries between the court and the outside world. Indeed, the 1766 anti-smuggling decree indicates that they even had a reputation for dealing in contraband, as the decree specified that customs personnel should take extra care with valets and lackeys and search their rooms for illegal goods.[173] Robert was thus not remarkable in retailing at court; however, the reputation he managed to gain through it was.

Robert's business flourished and he quickly became a regular fixture at court. Duchess Charlotte made her first recorded purchase from him in 1787 for 84 Rdr.[174] She was not alone in favouring him with business; several other members of the royal family are known to have purchased goods from Robert, including Duke Carl and Crown Prince Gustav Adolph. All of them came to amass considerable debts to Robert during his time as at court. In 1793, Duchess Charlotte owed Robert at least 1052 Rdr and at the end of 1793, the Crown Prince Gustav Adolph had purchased lace, vases, pomades, and cloth from Robert worth a hefty 4377 Rdr.[175] Such considerable sums indicate Robert's importance as a vendor at court.

Robert the Contrabandier

Robert seems to have gotten involved in contraband trade early on, and his first run-in with the customs authorities occurred as early as September 1788, when one of Robert's clandestine cargoes was confiscated while in transit. The goods, worth 871 Rdr, were seized from an unknown man who escaped capture at Åstorp's Inn, located along the main road between Helsingborg and Stockholm. Immediately following the seizure, the goods were transported to Helsingborg Customs Court, where they were identified as illegal and marked for export. Meanwhile, King Gustav III had penned a letter to the customs authorities explaining that the goods seized belonged to his valet Robert and that they should be released from confiscation in exchange for a 'just' duty on the goods, most of which were prohibited from importation.[176] However, closer inspection of the contraband hoard suggests that the goods were not intended for the King's private consumption but destined for sale to numerous clients. The goods included 324 pairs of various women's and men's silk stockings, 139 pairs of silk gloves, 8 dozen silk neckerchiefs of various design, 12 silk waistcoat fabrics, 128 ells of patterned taffeta, and 819 ells of blue taffeta.[177] The contraband was released, but the customs officers were disgruntled and complained that this meant that they would miss out on their lawful confiscation fees and that the state would also lose out on its fines.[178] As this incident clearly illustrates, Robert received protection and help from the highest quarters, which enabled him to conduct illicit trade without any concern for the Customs Office. However, Robert's activities were not greeted with enthusiasm in all quarters. In 1793, Duchess Charlotte wrote in her diary:

> It has inspired extreme discontentment, that the duke has enjoined the greatest economy, at the same time as he let many wares be introduced into the country for Robert, without paying import duty as the goods arrived in the name of the duke and therefore cannot be searched. This process is far from correct and cannot but awaken resentment. In this, one can yet again see proof of the duke's indiscretion and his inability to refuse a solicitation, for it is impossible for the duke to refuse anyone, whether it is a general or a smuggler, if [the latter] knows how to present his request persuasively. Moreover, [the duke] has a secondary reason to tolerate smuggling since he himself loves to decorate his own apartments with objects in good taste, and gives away Christmas presents of the same type.[179]

While Robert was able to cater for noble tastes with illegal French imports under royal protection, these actions also resulted in increased discontentment with an unfair system. Paying no heed to this, Robert kept using his contacts with the royals to avoid his customs obligations, writing a letter to King Gustav IV Adolph in 1800 asking to be relieved from paying import duty on the importation of a set of porcelain.[180] Robert was not only favoured by the court but the court also actively worked to protect and enable his illegal business activities by deploying its privilege. It is thus maybe not surprising that in 1795 Robert was described as a "by the court protected and tacitly authorised smuggler".[181]

In return for the court protection bestowed on him, Robert was able to offer direct access to the latest fashions from Paris.[182] This can be seen, for example, in the correspondence of Duchess Charlotte, the wife of Duke Carl, and sister-in-law to the King. In August 1791, she wrote an excited letter to her friend Sophie Piper: "Robert has arrived from Paris and has an incredible amount of things with him. There are all kinds of things and more than enough for him to make some money".[183] A few days later, she again addressed a letter to her friend explaining that the King's favourite, Gustav Mauritz Armfelt (1757–1814), had bought almost all of Robert's hats and split them between his wife and his mistress, who was said to have looked magnificent in her new attire.[184] This is reminiscent of how traders and consumers together helped to create and sustain ideas of fashionableness.[185]

Conflict with the Burghers

While Robert was a success at court, his activities were not appreciated by everyone, particularly not his competitors. In 1792, Robert decided to expand his business and applied to become a burgher in Stockholm, which would give him the right to trade officially and to keep a shop. In order to acquire burghership, it was necessary to apply to the City Magistrate and Trade Commission with letters of recommendation and proof of skill and experience. If the magistrates declined the application, it was still possible to appeal to the magistrate, and later to the National Board of Trade, and finally to the King.[186] The first rejection of Robert's application was filed by the Stockholm City Magistrate on 6 December 1792. This was followed by an appeal to the National Board of Trade, which also rejected his application on 22 February 1793. This second rejection was supported by the Silk and Cloth Trader Society, which also added an explanation detailing why they considered Robert to be unsuitable for burghership. In the first rejection, by the city magistrate, it was explained that Robert's lack of official training disqualified him from becoming a burgher.[187] In Robert's answer to the rejection of his application, he argued that he had served the King loyally for 13 years and that he had been relied upon by Gustav III to acquire all sorts of wares to dress and ornament the king as well as the rest of the royal court. He noted, "this involved considerable quantities [of textiles], so that I in this way got to know the mercer trade here in the Country, in all its breadth".[188] Indeed, it appears that it was exactly this that unsettled both the National Trade Board and the Silk and Cloth Trader Society, at least ostensibly. In response to Robert's appeal, the society posited that:

> … the Members, cannot remain silent, there is a rather well known and possibly even verifiable rumour which relates that Robert during many

> years has carried on mercery trade here in the city if not only with foreign and prohibited wares, then at least the main part has been of that kind...[189]

They further maintained that the sort of trade knowledge that Robert possessed was detrimental to the kingdom itself, arguing that Robert's business activities would lead the Swedish finances into disaster. They also voiced the familiar argument that it would leave the children of the kingdom in danger of being thrown into complete poverty.[190] The same arguments had previously been used *against* the Silk and Cloth Trader Society and it is interesting to find them applying them on their own behalf. The intrusion of a foreign, non-guild-affiliated merchant who dominated the trade at court was clearly not looked upon with sympathy. That Robert was competing directly with the Stockholm-based mercers is supported by the account books of the elite, which contain both bills from Robert and from the above-mentioned mercers, including for example J. A. Théel and Carl Wiberg.[191]

Following this onslaught, however, it was decided, perhaps by Duke Regent Carl, that Robert should be awarded the title *contingent-borgare*, a type of position whereby a person who was not part of the bourgeoisie could trade but only as a wholesale dealer, in return for a fee paid to the State.[192] The position, the appointment of which could not be challenged, was commonly used by nobles, or people of the crown, and later also women and others who were unable to gain a regular burghership.[193] In 1797, there were only 18 *contingent-borgare* in Stockholm in comparison to the 128 wholesale dealers and 53 mercers.[194] Very soon after his failed application to become a burgher, Robert could thus nevertheless style himself a valet and merchant.[195] Robert never appears to have been able to officially establish a shop in town, however. This was prevented by the fact that he as a *contingent-borgare* was not legally allowed to sell to private individuals, a rule he clearly ignored. Thus, people kept visiting 'chez Robert' to make unlawful purchases. Robert's continued influence is further indicated by his appointment as consul to Lyon in 1796. Baron af Nordin, in his accounts from court, suggests that the appointment was linked to the huge debts which Duchess Charlotte and her husband, as well as the rest of their circle had run up.[196] Robert never appears to have taken up his position in Lyon but stayed on in Stockholm. He eventually returned to France in 1814, but continued to furnish the Swedish court with the most fashionable wares from Paris. As late as 1818, Robert still functioned as an agent for the Swedish court, tasked with sending wares including vases, candelabras, and a clock to Stockholm.[197]

The case of Marcelin Robert crystallises two observations which have already been made in relation to other retailers. Firstly, it underlines the importance of the relationship between the merchant and the consumer and how it was one of mutual benefits. The symbiotic relationship between Robert and the members of court not only enabled Robert to conduct illegal trade, it also enabled the members of court to wear and consume foreign goods that were officially prohibited. It was this relationship, and the court's protection that sprung from it, that allowed him to become a successful contraband trader despite protectionist legislations and his lack of burghership. In addition, Robert's case clearly illustrates how various retailers were fighting for the same clients and that accusations of smuggling came to be levelled against the competition. The group of traders that came to particularly object to Robert were the mercers, who, as previously discussed, catered for the same clients as Robert. The Silk and Cloth Trader Society, which had a long-standing and well-known tolerance towards contraband retailing, paradoxically came to attack Robert on the grounds of his smuggling activities, with the motive of warding off the 'unfair' competition he posed to its members. While the pedlars, mercers, and Jewish traders all had to contend with the Swedish legal system, Robert was absolved from it. It was not the contraband dealing in itself that vexed the mercers, but rather the conditions under which it was conducted.

*****

Four groups of retailers – pedlars, mercers, Jewish traders, and a trade agent – have been discussed in this chapter. All of them were involved in the distribution of contraband in eighteenth-century Sweden. Together they distributed contraband across the Swedish realm to a variety of different consumers. Contraband could be purchased everywhere, from the forests of Karelia to the streets of Stockholm, including in the royal castle of the capital.

Meanwhile, these retailing groups attracted criticism coloured by patriotic protectionism. The pedlars were dubious because their mobility enabled them contact with foreign markets, and the mercers because they traded in fine textiles, but no trader was as suspicious as the Jewish trader. As outsiders, with extensive international trade networks, the Jewish traders' position was particularly scrutinised by a society in which patriotic duty and a closed market were pitted against the attractions of international trade.

Various kind of legislation and surveillance measures were introduced to control them. While attempts were made to limit the movements of the pedlars to domestic territory, the mercers were exposed to shop-visitations, and the Jewish traders fenced in by restrictions. Discrepancies in regulation, but also in the scope of their retailing activities, meant that the various groups of retailers conducted trade under very different conditions and legal premises. It affected how they went about transgressing the law, in order to engage in smuggling. Three coping strategies have been identified: pedlars physically avoided the customs officers, the mercers negotiated in the courts, and Marcelin Robert relied upon his influential customers to shield him from the law. While the means were different the aim was the same, to circumvent the legislation and profit from the underground trade.

Although the groups were dissimilar in many ways, they were also interconnected. Records of debts suggest that the mercers, the pedlars, and the Jewish merchants conducted trade with each other, and sometimes appear to have been working together. Similarly, consumer account books and bills show that the retailers, to an extent at least, were competing for the same clients, most prominently this was the case for the mercers and Marcelin Robert. Retailing in Stockholm was a small and interconnected world, one that benefits greatly from being studied through its entanglements, which enabled co-operation and the circulation of goods, but could also foment competition and enmity. This is reflected in the fact that accusations of smuggling did not merely come from manufacturers and other protectionists but were also used within and between retailer groups as they tried to eliminate and ostracise competition.

Furthermore, this chapter has highlighted the importance of the relationship between the retailers and the consumers. To a significant extent, it was this relationship, and the support that sprang from it, that enabled the trade in contraband to continue even under the pressure of increasing regulation and control. The shape of this support varied, depending on who the consumers and the retailers were. For example, commoner consumers in the countryside could shield and shelter the pedlars, while urban consumers could financially support the mercers through continued consumption, and at court Robert's privileged clients could bestow legal exemptions upon him. Such support allowed the contraband retailers to continue with their illicit trades and to 'bounce back' if they were convicted for smuggling. Ultimately, the support of the retailers was based in the public's appetite for contraband, which echoes historian Anne Montenach's observation that the risks that the merchants took in catering for the popular demand for illicit goods *might* actually have increased their respectability and valour in the eyes of the general public.[198] In this way, the relationship between the retailers and the consumers can be seen as one of mutual benefits: while the retailers catered for the public demand for contraband, the consumers supported the retailers, enabling them to continue their illicit trade and thus also to expand their stock and their profits. The fact that consumers could turn to their normal retail outlets to procure contraband probably also served to normalise its consumption.

Notes

1 Johanna Ilmakunnas, 'Ståndsmässig Konsumtion: Högadelns Penningbruk Och Konsumtionsvanor i Sverige under Senare Delen Av 1700-Talet', *Historisk Tidskrift För Finland* 86, no. 2 (2001), 391–392, 394; Charlotta Wolff, *Vänskap och makt. Den svenska politiska eliten och upplysningstidens Frankrike* (Helsinki: Svenska litteratursällskapet i Finland, 2005), 336.

2 Wolff, *Vänskap och makt,* 302–303; Johanna Ilmakunnas, 'The Luxury Shopping Experience of the Swedish Aristocracy in Eighteenth-Century Paris', in *Luxury and Gender in European Towns, 1700–1914*, ed. Deborah Simonton, Marjo Kaartinen, and Anne Montenach (Routledge, 2014), 123.

3 See Chapter 5.

4 Sofia Murhem and Göran Ulväng, 'To Buy a Plate: Retail and Shopping for Porcelain and Faience in Stockholm during the Eighteenth Century', in *A Taste for Luxury in Early Modern Europe*, ed. Johanna Ilmakunnas and Jon Stobart (London: Bloomsbury, 2017), 201.

5 Montenach, *Femmes, pouvoir et contrebande,* 272.

6 'Kommittée Ang Förordning Mot Yppighet Och Överflöd, 1793'.

7 http://ortshistoria.se/nedladd/befolkn_txt/befolkning_1570–2000_andel.txt, Accessed 10 Jan. 2019
8 Anna Brismark and Pia Lundqvist, 'Rural Retailing of Textiles in Early Nineteenth-Century Sweden', in *Selling Textiles in the Long Eighteenth Century. Comparative Perspectives from Western Europe*, ed. Jon Stobart and Bruno Blondé (London: Palgrave Macmillan, 2014), 101.
9 Laurence Fontaine, *History of Pedlars in Europe* (Polity Press, 1996).
10 Fontaine, *History of Pedlars in Europe*, 8–11; Johanna Wassholm and Anna Sundelin, 'Emotions, Trading Practices and Communication in Transnational Itinerant Trade: Encounters between 'Rucksack Russians' and Their Customers in the Late Nineteenth- and Early Twentieth-Century Finland,' *Scandinavian Economic History Review* 66, no. 2 (2018), 134.
11 Göran Rosander, *Gårdfarihandel i Norden. En översikt av en gammal handelsform* (LTs förlag i samarbete med Institutet för folklivsforskning, 1980); Jacqueline Stare, ed., *Judiska Gårdfarihandlare i Sverige* (Stockholm: Judiska museet, 1996); Lundqvist, *Marknad På Väg;* Wassholm and Sundelin, 'Emotions, Trading Practices and Communication in Transnational Itinerant Trade: Encounters between "Rucksack Russians" and Their Customers in the Late Nineteenth- and Early Twentieth-Century Finland'. On the use of credit see: Lundqvist, *Marknad på väg* (Göteborg: Göteborgs Universitet, 2008), 183–206.
12 Lundqvist, 68.
13 Anna Brismark and Pia Lundqvist, 'Före lanthandelns tid? förutsättningarna för och förekomsten av handel på den svenska landsbygden före 1846', in *Kommers. historiska handelsformer i norden under 1700- och 1800-talen* (Uppsala: Uppsala University, 2001), 134.
14 Lundqvist, *Marknad På Väg,* 208, 211, 228.
15 Johan Liljencrants, *Kongl. commerce=collegii circulair til samtelige tull=rätter, angående widtagne anstalter emot mißbruk af den allmogen i wißa händer af Elfsborgs län tillåtne gårdfari=handel,* 1792.
16 Karin Wikberg, '"Skogarnas wilda innevånare" Tull och smuggling i 1800-talets Jämtland', *Argus,* no. 8 (1994), 13; Pia Lundqvist, *Marknad På Väg,* 146; According to Stein Tveite, Swedish and *västgöta* textiles had already been prominent in all of Norway by the late 17th century, See Stein Tveite, 'Den norske tekstilmarknaden på 1700-talet', *Historiallinen Arkisto,* 1967, 63.
17 *Kongl. maj:ts och rikets commerce-collegii förnyade kungörelse, angående wästgöthe allmogens gårdfarihandel med hwad derwid i akt tagas bör. gifwen Stockholm den 8 martii 1803* (Stockholm: Kongl. Tryckeriet, 1803). 1§. This same edict also stipulated that it was forbidden for sailors to ferry a commoner across to a foreign shore, or to ship wares across the sea on their behalf. Any transgression would be fined 50 Rdr.
18 Lundqvist, *Marknad på väg,* 146.
19 Sparre, 'Memorial, No143, Alingsås, 29 Apr 1791' 1791, Äldre centrala tullarkiv, Generaltullarrendesocieteternas fullmäktige, m. fl., kansliet, Skrivelser från tullfiskaler E8, vol. 1, Riksarkivet.
20 Sparre, 'Memorial, No 178, Helsingborg, 17 Maj 1791.', Ibid.
21 '1795 Berättelse', Äldre centrala arkiv, Överdirektören vid sjötullen, Huvudarkiv Liggare över föredragna mål D1, vol.7, Riksarkivet, 49–50.
22 Lundqvist, *Marknad på väg,* 146.
23 'Till underdånigste följe af Kongl. maj:ts nådiga förordning till förekommande af lurendrägerier och tullförsnillning af d n 6 april 1799', *Inrikes Tidningar,* 3 May 1805, no 49.
24 Lundqvist, *Marknad På Väg,* 71, 78, 172.
25 Lundqvist, 189–196.
26 'Baron Silfverhielm, Jönköping, 18 Aug 1775' 1775, Kollegiers m fl landshövdingars skrivelser till Kungl. Majt, 15 Skrivelser från landshövdingar, ämnesordnade, A, vol. 13, Ang handelsrörelse mellan städer och landsbygd, 1775–1776, Riksarkivet.

27 'Norrbärke, 7 Juli 1793' 1793 Kollegiers m fl skrivelser till Kungl. Maj:t, Skrivelser från landshövdingar, ämnesordnade handlingar, ang. Överflöd och yppighet, C, vo. 28, Riksarkivet.
28 'Ludvika & Grangärde, 27 Juli 1793' 1793, Kollegiers m fl skrivelser till Kungl. Maj:t, Skrivelser från landshövdingar, ämnesordnade handlingar, ang. Överflöd och yppighet, C, vol.28, Riksarkivet.
29 Lundqvist, *Marknad på väg*, 69.
30 Nils Storå, '"Rucksack Russians" in Finland Peddling and Culture Contact', trans. Michele McNabb, *Ethnologia Scandinavica* 21 (1991), 74.
31 Storå, 78–79.
32 *Sweriges Rikes lag, gillad och antagen på riksdagen 1734* (Stockholm: Historiographi regni, 1736). See (handelsbalken §6 om landskiöp).
33 Kraftman and Lagus, 'Tankar om hushållningens uphjelpande i Carelen', 9.
34 Kraftman and Lagus, 12.
35 Gustaf Lithners (?), '39. Torneå', 1767, Äldre centrala tullarkiv, Överdirektören vid Sjötullen, Kansliet, Personella berättelser och anmärkningspunkter, E1, vol.3, Riksarkivet.
36 'Vice Landshövding Roos, Umeå, 1 Dec 1777' 1777, Kollegiers m fl landshövdingars skrivelser till Kungl. Majt, 15 Skrivelser från landshövdingar, ämnesordnade, A, vol. 13, Ang handelsrörelse mellan städer och landsbygd, 1775–1776, Riksarkivet.
37 Kraftman and Lagus, 12.
38 Kraftman and Lagus, 12; Vice Landshövding Roos, Umeå, 1 Dec 1777' 1777, Kollegiers m fl landshövdingars skrivelser till Kungl. Majt, 15 Skrivelser från landshövdingar, ämnesordnade, A, vol. 13, Ang handelsrörelse mellan städer och landsbygd, 1775–1776, Riksarkivet; Kranck, '35. Kusamo'. 1806, Äldre centrala tullarkiv, Överdirektören vid Sjötullen, Kansliet, Personella berättelser och anmärkningspunkter, E1, vol.38.
39 See for example: 16 April 1787, 'Kitee No. 578', Routsin kauppakollegion tuomiokirja-arkistoa, Rajatullioikeuksien tuomiokirjat, RTO, vol.1, Kansalliarkisto, Finska Riksarkivet; 'Cajana', 1803–1804, Kommmerskollegium, Advokatfiskalskontoret, Årsberättelser Lurendrejerimål, Cb4, vol 2, Riksarkivet.
40 Examples from the sources include the smuggling Russian peasants, Ivan Harrinen and Joseph Mehtonen, stopped on the 29th of February 1804 near Kajana, who identified themselves as originating from Vuokkiniemi, East Karelia. The same day another Russian, Michell Karjanamen, also informed the customs that he was from Vuokkiniemi, after being arrested at the customs chamber at Sotkamo, east of Kajana. 'Uleåborg', 1803–1804, Kommmerskollegium, Advokatfiskalskontoret, Årsberättelser Lurendrejerimål, Cb4, vol. 2, Riksarkivet.; Vuokkiniemi is an area known for peddling, and in the 1830s when the Finnish scald Elias Lönnroth visited the area, he noted that more than 400 men travelled from there to Finland for trade in the autumn, not to return until the following spring. See Storå, '"Rucksack Russians" in Finland Peddling and Culture Contact'. Elias Lönnroth, '-', *Helsingfors Morgonblad*, 28 July 1834.
41 1 Dec 1777, 'Vice Landshövding Roos, Umeå'. Kollegiers m fl landshövdingars skrivelser till Kungl. Majt, 15 Skrivelser från landshövdingar, ämnesordnade, Ang handelsrörelse mellan städer och landsbygd, A, vol. 13, 1775–1776, Riksarkivet.
42 7 Nov 1787, 'Kitee No 578', 1787, Routsin kauppakollegion tuomiokirja-arkistoa, Rajatullioikeuksien tuomiokirjat, RTO, vol. 1, Kansallisarkisto, Finska riksarkivet.
43 5 Feb 1798, 'Kitee No. 580', 1798, Routsin kauppakollegion tuomiokirja-arkistoa, Rajatullioikeuksien tuomiokirjat, RTO, vol. 1, Kansallisarkisto, Finska riksarkivet.
44 Lundqvist, *Marknad på väg,* 228 & 230; Sigfrid Svensson, *Skånes folkdräkter. En dräkthistorisk undersökning 1500–1900,* Nordiska Museets Handlingar 3 (Stockholm, 1935), 292.
45 *Svenskt Konversations-Lexicon*, vol 2 (Stockholm: P. G. Berg, 1847), 46.

46 Erik Lindberg, *Borgerskap och burskap, Om näringsprivilegier och borgerskapets institutioner i Stockholm 1820–1846* (Uppsala: Acta Universitatis Upsaliensis, 2001), 78–81.
47 This can be seen from a comparison of two burgher oaths, one from the early seventeenth century and the other from 1808. The only addition in regard to the wares was that in the earlier oaths, the trader swore not to deal with foreign goods but in the later oaths illicit goods were also included. This was probably a reflection of the developing Swedish manufacturing sector and refers to unstamped, thus untaxed, domestic manufactures. See Borgmästare och råd i Stockholm, Utdrag ur Taxor för år 1620 (ryggtitel), see https://stockholmskallan.stockholm.se/post/7896, Accessed 29 March 2018; 22 September 1808, Borgerskapets gubbhus, Inträdesansökningar, E1, vol. 8, Stockholms Stadsarkiv.
48 Klas Nyberg, 'Stockholms Handlande Borgerskap Och Manufakturister', in *Till salu. Stockholms textila handel och manufaktur 1722–1846*, ed. Klas Nyberg (Stockholm: Stads- och Kommunhistoriska Institutet, 2010), 60–61.
49 Nyberg, 60–61.
50 For more on this, see Chapter 2.
51 'Til Commerce Collegium - Om Husvisitationer Och Fiscaliska Besök I de Handelandes Gatubodar' 1772, Skråarkiv, Siden- och kramhandelssocieteten, Siden- och kramhandelssocietetens handlingar 1770–1787, F1, vol.2, Stockholms Stadsarkiv.
52 For a longer discussion about the visitation see Chapter 2.
53 'Kongl. maj:ts nådiga förbud emot hus=visitationer, gifwit Ekolsund then 16 julii 1776' (1776); 'Kongl. maj:ts nådiga förordning til hämmande af lurendrägerier, gifwen Stockholms slott then 14 martii 1785' (1785).
54 See for example the trader Samuel Bruse: 14 & 24 Nov, 'Dombok', 1768, A1, vol.7, Göteborgs Sjötullsrätt, Göteborgs Landsarkiv. Erick Linderoth: 27 July 1786, 'Dombok' 1786, A1, vol.18, Göteborgs Sjötullsrätt, Göteborgs Landsarkiv.
55 19 May 1769, & 24 May 1769, & 6 June 1769, 'Stora Siötulls Rättens Dombok' 1769, Stockholms rådhusrätt, Stora Sjötullen, Protokoll, A, vol.22, Stockholms Stadsarkiv. This would the following year become the standardised practice (4 Art, 1§, 1770).
56 19 May 1769, & 24 May 1769, & 6 June 1769, 'Stora Siötulls Rättens Dombok' 1769, Stockholms rådhusrätt, Stora Sjötullen, Protokoll, A, vol. 22, Stockholms Stadsarkiv. This would the following year become the standardised practice (4 Art, 1§, 1770); 2–7 Nov 1786, 'Dombok' 1786, A1, vol. 18, Göteborgs Sjötullsrätt, Göteborgs Landsarkiv.
57 19 May 1769, & 24 May 1769, & 6 June 1769, 'Stora Siötulls Rättens Dombok' 1769, Stockholms rådhusrätt, Stora Sjötullen, Protokoll, A, vol.22, Stockholms Stadsarkiv. This would the following year become the standardised practice (4 Art, 1§, 1770); 2–7 Nov 1786, 'Dombok' 1786, A1, vol. 18, Göteborgs Sjötullsrätt, Göteborgs Landsarkiv.
58 '5, 7, 8, 9, 11, 13 Jan, 1, 4 & 8 Feb 1773, 'Dombok', 1773.
59 '-', *Götheborgs Allehanda*, February 1, 1782, no 10, 1. There had been some inflation between 1768 and 1773 and the prices are thus not exactly the same in relation to their real value. Rather than an exact comparison, the prices should be treated as indicative of the scale of the contraband hoard.
60 '-', *Götheborgska Nyheter*, March 6, 1773, no 10, 79.
61 *Stora sjö tulls rättens i Stockholm, protocoller och utslag, rörande kramhandlaren Johan Sundbeck, som d. 18 näst-ledne maji genom Skans Tulls gjordt försökt, at inpracticera åtskillige stycken utländske siden=tyger och silkes näsdukar* (Stockholm: Kongl. Tryckeriet, 1769);'-', *Dagligt Allehanda*, 29 June 1769, no 141, 2.
62 In 1785, there was a drop in his tax payments which continued until 1789 (Kronotaxeringslängder, Överståthållarämbetet för uppbördsärenden, G 1 AF, vol. 11–14, Stockholms Stadsarkiv).
63 '-', *Inrikes Tidningar*, January 27, 1801.
64 '5, 7, 8, 9, 11, 13 Jan, 1, 4 & 8 Feb 1773, 'Dombok', 1773, Kommerskollegium, Advokatfiskalskontoret, Rättsprotokoll, D, Göteborgs Sjötullsrätt, Riksarkivet.
65 '5, 7, 8, 9, 11, 13 Jan, 1, 4 & 8 Feb 1773, 'Dombok', 1773.

66 '25 & 30 April, 11 June, 20 Aug 1804', 1804, Kommerskollegium, Huvudarkivet, Justitiedivisionens protokoll, AIe, vol. 55, Riksarkivet; 'No 111 Sundbeck', 9 September 1806, Justitierevisionen, Besvärs- och Ansökningsmål, Utslagshandlingar, 1806 September 24 (II)-30, No 110–138, Riksarkivet.
67 2 - 7 Nov 1786, 'Dombok' 1786, A1, vol.18, Göteborgs Sjötullsrätt, Göteborgs Landsarkiv.
68 *Protocoller, rörande hus-visitationen d. 10 october 1786. förrättad af öfwer-inspectoren herr John. Hoffgardh, hos handelsmannen herr Erick linderoth tillika med högloft. kongl. slotts rättens ransakning öfwer de wid samma tilfälle förfallne händelser* (Göteborg: L. Wahlström, 1787), 7–8, & 27.
69 Ibid., 45.
70 'Kongl. maj:ts nådiga förordning, til förekommande af lurendrägeri och tullförsnillning gifwen Haga slott den 6 april 1799' (1799), 8 Art. 4§, 1799.
71 Ibid, 8 Art, 2–3§, 1799.
72 Johan Liljencrants and etc., *Kongl. maj:ts och rikets commerce-collegii instruction för handels= och slöjde=fiscalen, hwarefter han har at sig rätta. gifwen Stockholm den 2 augusti 1803* (Stockholm: Kongl. Tryckeriet, 1803), See f ex 8§ and 19§.
73 P. J. Junbeck, *Handels- och slöjde-fiscalen Junbecks sällsamma öden, både såsom embetsman och enskild medborgare: afskilldrade i anledning af Stockholms garfvare-embetes försök, att åtkomma sista skärfven* (Stockholm: Marquarska Tryckeriet, 1815); P. J. Junbeck, *Andra delen af handels- och slöjde- fiscalen Junbecks sällsamma öden, både såsom embetsman och enskild medborgare: afskilldrade i anledning af Stockholms garfvare-embetes försök, att åtkomma sista skär* (Stockholm: Marquarska Tryckeriet, 1817). A third volume appears to have been planned but no evidence suggests that it was ever published.
74 P. J. Junbeck, *Handels- och slöjde-fiscalen Junbecks sällsamma öden*, 27.
75 13 Dec 1803, 21 Dec 1803, 'Stora Siötulls Rättens Dombok' 1803, Stockholms rådhusrätt, Stora Sjötullen, Protokoll, A, vol.26, Stockholms Stadsarkiv, 2016–2018, 2049–2051, 2057–2059. According to Article 8, 1§ of the 1799 anti-smuggling decree, it was necessary for the fiscals to thoroughly investigate whether the goods were legal (stamped) or illegal (not stamped). See 'Kongl. maj:ts nådiga förordning, til förekommande af lurendrägeri och tullförsnillning gifwen Haga slott den 6 april 1799' (1799).
76 13 Dec 1803, 21 Dec 1803, 'Stora Siötulls Rättens Dombok' 1803, Stockholms rådhusrätt, Stora Sjötullen, Protokoll, A, vol.26, Stockholms Stadsarkiv, 2016–2018, 2049–2051, 2057–2059.
77 '25 & 30 April, 11 June, 20 Aug, 1804', 1804, Kommerskollegium, Huvudarkivet, Justitiedivisionens protokoll, AIe, vol. 55, Riksarkivet.
78 'Confiscationer I Stockholm' 1803–1807, Överdirektören vid Sjötullen, Advokatfiskalen, Liggare, D3, vol. 1–2, Riksarkivet.
79 '-', *Dagligt Allehanda*, 14 September 1810, no 251, 2.
80 '-', *Dagligt Allehanda*, 5 August 1776, no 176, 3.
81 Per Wästberg, 'Stockholm 1786', in *1786, Vitterhetsakaedmiens Jubileumssymposium* (1986), 82.
82 'Mantalslängd, Staden Södra Och Västra' 1790, Överståthållarämbetet för Uppbördsärenden, Kammarexpeditionen, Mantalslängder, BA, vol. 25/15, Riksarkivet. f. 369–370; Ek was yet another of the city's well-known merchants, mentioned in Bellman's play *Caffehuset* from 1790. See Carl Michael Bellman, *Carl Michael Bellmans Skrifter VI, dramatiska arbeten*, 1936, 169.
83 '-', *Dagligt Allehanda*, 13 November 1778, no 260, 2.
84 1 Sep 1803,'Födelse Och Dopböcker', 1803, Storkyrkoförsamlingens kyrkoarkiv, Födelse- och dopböcker, huvudserie, vol. 14 (1800–1814), Riksarkivet.
85 For Ek, see: 'Stora Siötulls Rättens Dombok', 1800, 713 & 942, For Wiberg, see 'Diarium' 1799, Överståthållarämbetet För Polisärenden 1, Äldre poliskammaren, Diarium, CIa1, vol. 26 1799, Stockholms Stadsarkiv, 878.
86 For Zetterstén and Elfving see: 'Stora Siötulls Rättens Dombok', 1800. Stockholms rådhusrätt, Stora Sjötullen, Protokoll, A, v.23, 1029, for Elfving see: 20 Feb 1804 'Confiscationer i Stockholm'.

87 7 Dec 1791, 'Johan Abraham Theel Burskap', 1791, Skråarkiv, Siden- och Klädeskramssocieteten, Siden- och klädeskramhandelssocietetens handlingar, 1787–1799, F 1, vol.3, Stockholms Stadsarkiv.
88 '-', *Stockholms Posttidningar*, 6 September 1802, no 107.
89 'Protocoll', Skråarkiv, Skråarkiv, Siden - och klädeskramhandler societeten, Protocoll, 1796–1868, A, vol.1, Stockholms Stadsarkiv.
90 'Diarium' 1799, Överståthållarämbetet För Polisärenden 1, Äldre poliskammaren, Diarium, CIa1, vol. 26 1799, Stockholms Stadsarkiv, 878.
91 'Protocoll', 1799, Kommerskollegium, Huvudarkivet, Justitiedivisionens protokoll, A I e, vol. 50 (1799), Riksarkivet, 1975–1976.
92 'Protocoll', 1800 Kommerskollegium, Huvudarkivet, Justitiedivisionens protokoll, A I e, vol. 51 (1800), Riksarkivet, 1746–1752.
93 6 Dec 1799, No. 90, 'Exporterade Lurendrejerivaror, 1799–1805', 1799. Kommerskollegiets Huvudarkiv, Särskilda utredningar och berättelser, F IV, vol.23 Utredning angående exporterade lurendrejerivaror 1799–1805. Riksarkivet.
94 No 44, 110, 111, 'Exporterade Lurendrejerivaror, 1799–1805', 1799. Kommerskollegiets Huvudarkiv, Särskilda utredningar och berättelser, F IV, vol.23 Utredning angående exporterade lurendrejerivaror 1799–1805. Riksarkivet.
95 For confiscations on board H.J. Schimd's ship in 1803 and 1804, see 'Confiscationer i Stockholm'. Äldre centrala tullarkiv, Överdirektören vid Sjötullen, Advokatfiskalen, Liggare, D3, vol. 1–2, Riksarkivet.
96 'Mantalslängd', 1800, *Överståthållarämbetet för Uppbördsärenden,* Kammarexpeditionen, Mantalslängder, BA, vol. 26/15, Riksarkivet, 408.
97 Gösta Selling, *Stockholms stads brandförsäkringskontors hus i kvarteret Aglaurus vid Mynttorget - Historik med anledning av kontorets 200-åriga tillvaro* (Stockholm, 1946), 59.
98 '-', *Stockholms Posttidningar*, 6 September 1802, no 107.
99 Tidigmoderna konkurser, http://www.tidigmodernakonkurser.se/index.php/extended, Accessed 31 October 2018.
100 Nils Lundequist, *Stockholms stadshistoria, från stadens anläggning till närwarande tid*, vol. 2 (Stockholm: Zacharias Haeggström, 1828), 247–248.
101 'Protocoll', 1796–1868, Skråarkiv, Skråarkiv, Siden - och klädeskramhandler societeten, Protocoll, A, vol. 1, Stockholms Stadsarkiv.
102 '25 & 30 April, 11 June, 20 Aug, 1804', 1804, Kommerskollegium, Huvudarkivet, Justitiedivisionens protokoll, AIe, vol. 55, Riksarkivet; No 111 Sundbeck', 9 September 1806, Justitierevisionen, Besvärs- och Ansökningsmål, Utslagshandlingar, 1806 September 24 (II)-30, No 110–138, Riksarkivet.
103 Ibid.
104 Ulf Åsén, Personal Correspondence, 12 December 2017. Svenska Frimurare Ordens Generalmatrikel ; Andreas Önnerfors, ed., *Mystiskt brödraskap – mäktigt nätverk studier i det svenska 1700-talsfrimureriet* (Lund: Lund University, 2006), 266.
105 For a discussion on freemason justice and law see: Hans Brusewitz, 'Frimurerisk straffskipning. Domstolen som försvann', *Frimuraren* 4 (2016).
106 'Fordringar Konungens Hand Cassa 1795', 1795, Statskontoret, Kammarkontoret, Furstliga personers räkningar, G2M, vol. 6, Riksarkivet.
107 From November 1799 to February 1800, Hans Axel von Fersen made at least four purchases from Théel, See 'Bill 8 March 1800' 1800, Strafsundarkivet, Ätten von Fersen, 6, Hans Axel von Fersens Samling, Räkenskaper VI, vol. 28, Riksarkivet. In January 1800, Théel entered the account books of Duke Carl and 22 separate bills were paid to Théel from 1800 until April 1803. See: Hovstatsräkenskaper Prins Karl, Räkenskaper ang. enskilda medel 1791–1800, vol. 55, Slottsarkivet; Hovstatsräkenskaper Prins Karl, Räkenskaper ang. enskilda medel 1801–1806, vol. 56, Slottsarkivet
108 Murhem and Ulväng, 'To Buy a Plate', 201.

109 Märta Helena Reenstierna, *Årstadagboken*, ed. Gunnar Broman, vol. 1, 3 vols (Stockholm: Generalstabens Litografiska Anstalts Förlag, 1946), 70.
110 Reenstierna, 103.
111 Reenstierna, 70, 81, 102, 124, 192, 275, 298, 301, 312.
112 Reenstierna seems to have been acquainted with Over-Inspector Muhr and his wife, Controller Lewin, and Lieutenant Carlén, all prominent customs officers in Stockholm. See Reenstierna, *Årstadagboken,* 274–275, 291.
113 See discussion in Chapter 5.
114 'Mantalslängd, Katarina 2' 1810, Överståthållarämbetet för Uppbördsärenden, Kammarexpeditionen, Mantalslängder, BA, vol. 27/14, Riksarkivet.
115 Gösta Selling, 'Artur Hazelius' Födelsehus I. Den fritziska sidenvävargården', *Fataburen* 65 (1926), 94.
116 'Johan Abraham Théel Bouppteckning', 1811, Justitiekollegium 1637–1856, Förmyndarkammaren 1667–1924, Rådhusrättens 1:a avdelning 1850–1924, F1 A, Bouppteckningar,1811 part 4, Stockholms Stadsarkiv. The book collection covers everything from law and tax regulation and language to philosophy, free masonry, and medicine. The previously mentioned Zetterstén makes an appearance with his history and science of trade (*Om allmänna handels historien och wetenskapen*, 1769). The list full of books on international trade and foreign languages, primarily French and notably English, indicates that Théel was also actively involved with creating and maintaining foreign trade connections.
117 'Johan Abraham Théel Bouppteckning', 680–738.
118 'Confiscationer i Stockholm'. 1803–1807, Överdirektören vid Sjötullen, Advokatfiskalen, Liggare, D3, vol. 1–2.
119 Önnerfors, *Mystiskt brödraskap,* 227 & 266.
120 P. J. Junbeck, *Handels- och slöjde-fiscalen Junbecks sällsamma öden*, 4–5, 9.
121 Junbeck, 25–27.
122 'Confiscationer I Stockholm' 1803 - 1807, Överdirektören vid Sjötullen, Advokatfiskalen, Liggare, D3, vol. 1–2, Riksarkivet.
123 Rita Bredefeldt, 'Judarna i Sverige - Invandring, ekonomi och integration', *Ekonomisk Debatt* 43, no. 4 (2015), 9.
124 Anna Brismark and Pia Lundqvist, 'A Diaspora on the Edge of Modernity? The Jewish Minority in Gothenburg in the Late Eighteenth and Early Nineteenth Centuries', in *Connecting Worlds and People. Early Diasporas*, ed. Dagmar Friest and Susanne Lachenicht (Abingdon: Routledge, 2017), 131.
125 However, this development was far from uncontested – see: Wolfgang Wilhelmius, *Juden in Vorpommern* (Schwerin: Friedrich-Ebert-Stiftung, 2007), 20.
126 C.-H. Carlsson, 'Judisk Invandring Från Aaron Isaac till Idag', in *Judarna i Sverige – En Minoritets Historia, Fyra Föreläsningar*, ed. H. Müssener, Uppsala Multiethnic Papers 53 (Uppsala: Uppsala University, 2011), 11.
127 Francesca Trivellato, *The Familiarity of Strangers: The Sephardic Diaspora, Livorno, and Cross-Cultural Trade in the Early Modern Period* (New Haven London: Yale University Press, 2009).
128 Nuala Zahedieh, 'Defying Mercantilism: Illicit Trade, Trust, and the Jamaican Sephardim, 1660–1730'. *The Historical Journal* 61, no. 1 (2018), 101–102.
129 Carlsson, 'Marstrand under Frihamnstiden 1775–1794'; Essén, *Johan Liljencrantz Som Handelspolitiker*, 94–96.
130 Bredefeldt, 'Judarna i Sverige', 9. The same Isaac later came to be the leader of the Stockholm-based Jews and he played a prominent role as a communicator between the royal court and the Jews, as can be seen in his memoirs. See Aaron Isaac, *Aaron Isaac minnen. Ett judiskt äventyr i svenskt 1700-tal*, ed. Mattias Dahlén, trans. Abraham Brody (Stockholm: Hillelförlaget, 2008), see for example 73–75, 80–82, & 94–95.
131 According to his diary, Isaac was highly resentful against the act, which he saw as putting severe limitations upon their activities. See: Isaac, *Aaron Isaac Minnen*, 94–95.

132 Rolf Nygren, 'Fördomar och ekonomisk krishantering 1815 års riksdag och frågan om judars rättsställning i Sverige', *Liber Amicorum* (2007), 452.
133 'Kongl. maj:ts och riksens commerce collegii reglemente, för them af judeska nationen, som wilja hit i riket inflytta och sig här nedsätta, 27 Maj 1782' (1782), §5–6, 12.
134 Bertil Andersson, *Göteborgs historia,* 241.
135 Andersson, 142; Eskil Olån, *Judarna på svensk mark. Historien om israeliternas invandring till Sverige* (Stockholm: Bok- o. Konstförlaget Rex, 1924), 53.
136 Bredefeldt, 'Judarna i Sverige'.
137 Hugo Valentin, *Judarna i Sverige från 1774 till 1950-talet* (Stockholm: Natur och Kultur/LTs förlag, 2004), 62; Rolf Nygren, 'Fördomar Och Ekonomisk Krishantering', 452.
138 'Commers Collegie Utslag, 26 Juli 1779' 1779, Ämnessamlingar, Miscellanea, Tullväsende, Rättegångs handlingar i tullmål 1700–1800, vol. 27, Riksarkivet. The first case I have been able to track down is David Abraham and Moses Levin Cohen who in 1780 were caught in Malmö while trying to smuggle in several "prohibited luxuries", brought along from Copenhagen.
139 'Öfver-directeuren och tullförvaltaren Mathias Fredrich Strübing angde handräckning vid visitationen anställande efter lurendregerier hos juden i Carlscrona, 5 Oct 1792', 1792. Ämnessamlingar, Personarkiv, Biographica, vol. S88. Riksarkivet.
140 Ibid.
141 For more on house peace, see Chapter 2.
142 Harry R:son Svensson, 'The Case of Fabian Philip, Karlskrona's First Jewish Entrepreneur: A Swedish Example of the Port Jews Phenomenon?', *Sjuttonhundratal* 11 (2014), 76.
143 Svensson, 77; *Kongl. maj:ts befallningshavandes beslut att förbjuda fabian philip att idka handel i karlskrona*, Familjen Rubens arkiv, Lunds Landsarkiv (translated and quoted in Harry R:son Svensson, 'The Case of Fabian Philip, Karlskrona's First Jewish Entrepreneur').
144 Janrik Bromé, *Karlskrona stads historia: Del II, 1790–1862* (Karlskrona, 1934), 122.
145 No. 7 1753, 'Födelsebok', 1753, Karlskrona tyska församlings kyrkoarkiv, Födelse- och dopböcker. Huvudserie. 1725–1797, Lund Landsarkiv; Carl Fredric Rothlieb, *Matrikel öfwer dem af Swea-Rikes ridderskap och adel: som ifrån år 1807* (Stockholm: Gadelius, 1807), 247.
146 Svensson, 'The Case of Fabian Philip', 78.
147 Svensson, 84. At the time of his report, Strübing had just been appointed Super-Inspector after 18 years of serving the Customs Office. His assiduity had been noted and he was celebrated for his work, which had dramatically increased the contraband seizures in Sweden. However, he did not shy away from adopting alternative means to his end. In January of 1793, only a few months after his appeal for a visitation order against Fabian Philip, Strübing was forced to write to the King to explain why he had been seizing goods outside of his own jurisdiction. Strübing was trying to make a name for himself and worked hard to do so. He notes: "... it becomes the unconditional duty for every Customs-Servant, to restrain the Lawbreakers' projects". Inspired by the protectionist discourse common among the burghers of Karlskrona, Strübing appears to have seen a possibility in Philip to further his own career, but this time he found himself hindered. See 'Strübing', Ämnessamlingar, Personarkiv, Biographica, vol. S 88, Riksarkivet.
148 'Kongl. maj:ts och riksens commerce collegii reglemente, för them af judeska nationen, som wilja hit i riket inflytta och sig här nedsätta, 27 maj 1782' (1782).
149 Svensson, 'The Case of Fabian Philip', 77.
150 Carlsson, 'Judisk Invandring Från Aaron Isaac till Idag'.
151 Isaac, *Aaron Isaac Minnen,* 180–182.
152 Isaac, 182.
153 Isaac, 183.
154 Valentin, *Judarna i Sverige*, 58.
155 David Hirch, 'Afskrift.', *Dagligt Allehanda*, 9 March 1799.

156 'Confiscationer i Stockholm', 1804 , Överdirektören vid Sjötullen, Advokatfiskalen, Liggare, D3, vol. 1, Riksarkivet.
157 CHC, 'Marcus, släkt', https://sok.riksarkivet.se/sbl/artikel/9079, *Svenskt biografiskt lexikon*, Accessed 2 March 2022; Isaac, *Aaron Isaac Minnen,* 307.
158 Ibid.
159 'Johan Abraham Théel Bouppteckning'.
160 Ibid.
161 'Confiscationer i Stockholm', 1803, Överdirektören vid Sjötullen, Advokatfiskalen, Liggare, D3, vol. 1 Riksarkivet.
162 16 Nov & 23 Nov 1803, 'Stora Siötulls Rättens Dombok' 1803, Stockholms rådhusrätt, Stora Sjötullen, Protokoll, A, vol.26, Stockholms Stadsarkiv; 26 June, & 3 July 1805, 'Stockholms Stora Sjötulls Rätt' 1805, Stockholms rådhusrätt, Stora Sjötullen, Protokoll, A, vol. 27, Stockholms Stadsarkiv.
163 Isaac, *Aaron Isaac Minnen,* 297.
164 'Kramhandlaren Johan Sundbeck, Handlingar' 1800–1816, vol. 4, Stockholms Stadsarkiv.
165 As already noted, Isaac Michaelson was the son-in-law of Aaron Isaac and would later take over his business, later also forming a trading house together with Bendix called Michaelson & Benedicks.
166 'Diarie No 447', 1803, Äldre centrala tullarkiv, Överdirektören för Sjötullen, Advokatfiskalens arkiv C3, vol. 24, Riksarkivet.
167 Bengt Sander, *Några bewis, att judarne äfwen på sitt sätt bidraga till den allmänna nöden i Swerige* (1809). Aaron Isaac indicated in his memoirs that Sander had previously tried to obstruct Isaac's trade at court through spreading rumours and false accusations. Isaac, *Aaron Isaac Minnen,* 106–109.
168 Anonymous, *Några ord, i anledning af en nyligen utkommen smädeskrift, kallad: några bewis att judarne äfwen på sitt sätt bidraga till den allmänna nöden i Swerige* (Stockholm: Peter Bohm, 1809), 10.
169 Ibid., 6.
170 'Letter from Robert 19 April 1793' (30 May 1793), Kommerskollegium till Kungl. Majt, 30 May 1793, vol. 252, Riksarkivet.
171 Fredric Sparre, 'Dagböcker, 1781' 1781, Ericsbergsarkivet, Enskilda arkiv, Fredric Sparres samling, vol. 5, Riksarkivet, 27.
172 Ibid., 71.
173 'Kongl. maj:ts nådige förordning, emot yppighet och öfwerflöd, gifwen Stockholm i råd-cammaren then 26 junii 1766' (1766).
174 Kungliga Arkiv, Drottning Hedvig Elisabet Charlotta, Egenhändigt förda räkenskapsböcker, K 295.
175 Kungliga Arkiv, Drottning Hedvig Elisabet Charlotta, Egenhändigt förda räkenskapsböcker, K 296; Statskontoret, Kammarkontoret, Furstliga personers räkningar, G2M, vol. 6, Riksarkivet; Lagerqvist, *Vad kostade det? Priser och löner från medeltid till våra dagar,* 133.
176 '26 Mar 1789, N.167', Allm verks skrivelser till Kungl Majt, Generaltulldirektionen till Kungl. Majt 1788–1789 v. 249, Riksarkivet.
177 1 Swedish ell = 59.38 cm.
178 '26 Mar 1789, N.167', Allm verks skrivelser till Kungl Majt, Generaltulldirektionen till Kungl. Majt 1788–1789 v. 249, Riksarkivet.
179 Hedvig Elisabeth Charlotta, *Hedvig Elisabeth Charlottas dagbok*, ed. Carl Carlson Bonde, vol. IV (P. A. Norstedt & söner, 1920), 65.
180 'Robert', 1800, Riksarkivets ämnessamlingar. Personhistoria, Biographica, Supplement, vol. R II 3, 21, Riksarkivet.
181 'Ur landshöfdingen friherre J. af Nordins hofkrönika', *Ur Svenska hofvets och aristokratiens lif. Skildringar hemtade i arkiven på Säfstaholm, Eriksberg och Sjöholm m. fl. enskilda och offentliga samlingar,* ed. Arvid Ahnfelt (Stockholm: Oscar L. Lamms förlag, 1880), vol.3, 21.

182 For a detailed study of Robert's role as an intermediary between Sweden and France, see: Charlotte Bellamy and Anna Knutsson, 'From valet to smuggler: a micro-historical study of a French intermediary in Stockholm, 1775–1832', *Revue d'histoire nordique*, no 27 (2018), 115–140.
183 'Smärre Enskilda Arkiv', Stafssundsarkivet, Vol. 15, Riksarkivet. Thank you to My Hellsing and Charlotte Bellamy for these references.
184 Ibid.
185 Murhem and Ulväng, 'To Buy a Plate', 201.
186 Lindberg, *Borgerskap och burskap,* 78–81.
187 'Undated letter' (30 May 1793), Kommerskollegium till Kungl. Maj:t, 1793, Vol 252, Riksarkivet.
188 'Letter from Robert 19 April 1793' (30 May 1793), Kommerskollegium till Kungl. Maj:t, 1793, Vol. 252, Riksarkivet.
189 'Letter 13 May 1793' (30 May 1793), Kommerskollegium till Kungl. Maj:t, 1793, Vol. 252, Riksarkivet.
190 Ibid.
191 See for example the accounts of Gustav IV Adolph: 'Fordringar Konungens Hand Cassa 1795'. Statskontoret, Kammarkontoret, Furstliga personers räkningar, G2M, v. 6; and of Duke Carl; 'Prins Karl, 1791–1800' 1791–1800, Hovstatsräkenskaper, Räkenskaper ang. enskilda medel, vol. 55, Slottsarkivet.; 'Prins Karl, 1801–1806' 1801–1806, Hovstatsräkenskaper, Räkenskaper ang. enskilda medel, vol. 56, Slottsarkivet.
192 'Note 26 July 1793' (30 May 1793), Kommerskollegium till Kungl. Maj:t, 1793, Vol. 252, Riksarkivet.; '1796', C. C. Gjörwell, Biografiska samlingar, I. 36. Kungliga Biblioteket; Robert was also referred to as *contingentborgare* in relation to his appointment as a consul to Lyon in 1796, '-', *Stockholms Posttidningar,* 21 July 1796.
193 J Lundell, *Om handtverksskrån, näringsfrihet och arbetets organisation* (Lund: C.W.K. Gleerup, 1846), 188 & 207; Anita Du Rietz, *Kvinnors entreprenörskap: under 400 år* (Stockholm: Dialogos, 2013), 224.
194 Nils Lundequist, *Stockholms stads historia, från stadens anläggning till närwarande tid*, vol. 2 (Stockholm: Zacharias Haeggström, 1828), 247–248.
195 'March 1793', Födelse och dopböcker, 1793, S:ta Eugenia Katolska församlings kyrkoarkiv, Födelse och dopböcker, Riksarkivet.
196 'Ur landshöfdingen friherre J. af Nordins hofkrönika', 45.
197 'Letter 12 August 1818', 1818, Sjöholmssamlingen, Possesamlingen, Riksarkivet.
198 Montenach, *Femmes, Pouvoir et Contrebande*, 272.

5

CONSUMING CONTRABAND

Worsteds & Coffee[1]

In the latter half of the eighteenth century, global wares and 'new' manufactured products were gaining prominence in Europe as a result of the intensification of global trade and the development of new forms of manufacturing. Few European countries welcomed the new goods into their domestic markets with open arms; on the contrary, the flows of global goods were often met with the erection of trade barriers and the introduction of protectionist legislation. As we have seen, protectionism in theory and in practice were two different things, however, and despite severe trade policies, foreign products circulated around protectionist territories. What these wares consisted of varied, over time and between regions, suggesting that in order to understand smuggling we also need to take into account the specific qualities of the goods and their 'lives' or trajectories.[2] These lives were affected by three general factors: global trade, the materiality of the objects in circulation, and the local contexts that they passed through.

There has been much debate about whether or not Sweden saw a consumer revolution in the eighteenth century: a debate that has particularly focused on manufacturing output and import numbers.[3] Quantitative studies such as these can be useful, as they point to trends, but as most foreign consumer goods were prohibited from being imported, these wares would never appear in the official trade statistics. As Eli Hecksher pointed out in his seminal work on economic history, the omission of smuggling makes the official trade statistics slightly arbitrary and can be misleading.[4] Trade statistics alone, therefore, are not enough to establish whether or not consumption trends changed within a protectionist market, particularly in regards to prohibited goods.

This chapter will therefore explore two types of contraband (worsteds and coffee) and their trajectories in order to offer a new take on how illegal global goods affected Swedish consumption. Worsted was a high-quality manufactured woollen cloth, the result of technical skill and craftsmanship.[5] Coffee, on the

DOI: 10.4324/9781003226031-5

other hand, was an exotic raw material, exclusively grown in tropical climes. They were two very distinct types of products and thus posed different types of threats to the state. Both were brought to Sweden as a consequence of the expansion of global trade and, importantly, they were smuggled in large quantities during the latter part of the eighteenth and the beginning of the nineteenth century.

Worsted and coffee also had very different social connotations. Worsted was common across the Swedish realm, in the towns as well as in the countryside, not least among the lower estates.[6] Commoners in rural areas appear to have incorporated manufactured worsteds into their traditional dress practices, while it was also the textile of choice in the new national costume used by the elite in the towns.[7] Worsted was in many ways also seen as a 'Swedish' consumer good. Woollen textiles had long been used in Scandinavia and were considered well suited to the cold climate. Climate appropriateness played a central role in many sartorial debates, as wearing inappropriate fabrics was thought to lead to disease and a weakening of the population. Crucially, worsteds were also, although to a limited extent, produced in Swedish manufactories. Worsted, a sturdy and warm textile produced by domestic manufacturers, was seen as a fitting textile both for the Scandinavian character and climate.[8] It stands in sharp contrast to the cold, less durable, and flimsy silk, which despite ardent attempts could never be produced on an industrial scale in the Nordic countries.[9] Worsted also lacked silk's elite connotations and was therefore seen as less challenging to established hierarchies.[10] In contrast to silk, which was seen as foreign, made from materials alien to the Swedish flora and fauna and thus unsuited to the Swedish body, wool, a known and familiar textile, was considered suitable for the general population.[11]

Coffee, an exotic perishable that had only relatively recently arrived in Sweden, was an altogether different matter. How widespread the use of coffee was is also much more difficult to establish, although most agree that it primarily appears to have been an urban consumer good in the eighteenth century.[12] As a relatively recent arrival on the European market, the definition, associations and consumers of coffee, were not set but a matter of continuous negotiation.[13] In Sweden, the associations of coffee went through a considerable transformation, or rather multiplication, in the course of the eighteenth century. Coffee moved from the coffee house into the female parlour where it took on increasingly feminine connotations and became linked with the emerging polite visiting culture.[14] Meanwhile, it also spread to new consumer groups such as poorer urban women, who used it as a respite from work.[15] the definition and associations, were in flux during the eighteenth century as expanding consumer groups tried to define its social and cultural role in society.

If the connotations of coffee were ambiguous, so were its effects on health. An international discourse on the health properties of coffee developed in the eighteenth century as consumers and scientists tried to come to terms with the exotic new beverage.[16] Although medical experts disagreed on its effect on health, in Sweden, an idea emerged that the reactions to coffee depended on the social standing of the individual in question. Coffee was seen as weakening for those who engaged in physical labour, but harmless for 'elite bodies' already accustomed to the beverage.[17] The dietary habits of the population were critical to eighteenth-century thinkers who saw it as affecting the character and morals not merely of the individual but the whole nation.[18] What the population ingested was thus interlinked with its very identity, both physically and morally, and the exact effects of the exotic and unfamiliar coffee were uncertain.

To consumers and legislators alike, worsted was familiar and considered compatible with Swedish bodies, whereas coffee was seen as suspect, and its exact effects on Swedish bodies uncertain. The contraband and its materiality are at the centre of this chapter, which considers how contraband came to be defined as such, how it was perceived, and received, and what effect it had on culture, society, and politics. The chapter is divided into two main parts, the first dealing with worsteds and the second with coffee. Throughout the chapter, a range of different sources are consulted from diaries, letters, governmental debates, police reports, and parish reports to material remains, and illustrations.

Norwich Worsteds: A Glimmering Sensation

A Threat to the Domestic Industry – The Ban on Worsted

Worsted derives its name from the village Worstead in Norfolk, which was one of the first places that started producing the cloth in the Middle Ages.[19] Although the production started in the countryside, it came to move into the nearby town Norwich. Worsted was first mentioned in relation to the city in 1315, but it was not until the 1560s that the trade started to flourish, after foreign weavers were allowed a special licence to settle in the city. Through the 1680s, new products like calamanco were launched, and new techniques were developed to enhance the sheen and gloss of the textiles.[20] The colour and the finish of the textiles became an important trademark and even today it is possible to identify Norwich worsteds by their quality and shine.[21] In the 1720s, the Norwich weavers stood on the brink of what would prove to be a massive and persistent challenge to their trade. With the arrival of cotton from India and the expansion of the English cotton industry, the worsted weavers found their traditional market under pressure.[22] From the 1740s onwards and particularly during the 1760s, the merchant-manufacturers started looking abroad for new international markets which could supplement the domestic market. In 1798, the wool manufacturer and Norwich resident John Taylor observed that "[t]he introduction of [Norwich worsteds] into Spain, Italy, Poland, and Russia, soon made the manufactures ample amends for the capriciousness of fashion in their own country".[23] As an extension of this trade, a port opened in Great Yarmouth in 1766 providing a direct trade link between Norwich and Northern Europe, including the Baltic Sea.[24] The Norwich worsteds appear to have spread widely, reaching as far away as South America, Siberia, and China.[25] Other markets closer to home were also explored, and Scandinavia quickly proved a lucrative one.[26] Despite these attempts to expand the market for Norwich worsteds, business dwindled during the latter half of the eighteenth century, both due to domestic competition – Yorkshire was quickly rising as a new woollen industrial centre – and due to increased competition from cotton products.[27] During this period of decline, foreign trade remained critical for the worsted manufacturers as they attempted to find new sales outlets in an increasingly globalised market.

In Sweden, the wool manufacturing industry was the largest branch of manufacturing in terms of workforce, though it was still relatively small on an international scale.[28] The output of the wool manufacturers was thus limited and the quality of Swedish wool textiles was considered inferior to that of foreign manufactures, particularly British. Some attempts were made to rectify this imbalance through tapping into the British manufacturing process. The Swedish consul to Britain, Jonas Ahlströmer, had, for example, in the 1720s, attempted to smuggle "a great quantity of wool and workmen to Stockholm and Gothenburg" in an attempt to improve the industry.[29] In the 1730s, state support for Swedish manufacturers increased, which resulted in the introduction of the 1734 import tariff that prohibited the import of most manufactured wools.[30] Swedish wool production increased, but during the economic crisis in the 1760s production decreased dramatically and production levels would not recover until the late 1770s.[31] By 1775, the British ambassador reported that Sweden could only produce two-thirds of the wool needed in the country.[32]

The situation of worsted manufacturing was particularly dire as the Swedish manufactories were unable to get the proper finish on their textiles, a crucial step in producing the worsteds' distinctive sheen and smooth texture. While the government had established a 'finishing house' next to the Barnängen wool manufactory in Stockholm back in 1748, it appears never to have been fully equipped and it burned to the ground only ten years after its construction. In 1761, the wool manufacturers applied to the government to have a new finishing house built, without result.[33] During the 1769–1770 riksdag, the issue resurfaced yet again, when it was argued that the extensive smuggling of foreign, particularly English, worsted stuffs into the Swedish realm could be directly traced back to the lack of a proper finishing house.[34]

Meanwhile, the import prohibitions on woollen and worsted textiles were renewed in 1771, 1782, and 1799.[35] Between 1785 and 1790, a complete ban on the import of worsted yarns was also in force, intended to support domestic spinning.[36] However, the Swedish worsted yarn spinning industry never properly took off due to poor payment and insufficient organisation.[37] The result was a shortage of worsted yarn, which only further injured the Swedish manufacturing industry.[38] The shortcomings of the Swedish worsted industry left the manufactories unable to cater for the domestic demand, which led to the emergence of a flourishing smuggling trade in these wares.

In the 1770s, it was believed that there were more smuggled English worsteds than legal Swedish products on the market.[39] Contemporary commentators also observed that English worsteds played a prominent role in the Swedish market despite the prohibitions. One of these, the Welsh economic and political writer and clergyman Josiah Tucker (1713–1799), noted that the Swedish attempts at strengthening their manufacturing industry represented no threat to the manufacturing powerhouse of England:

> ...every Article of [English Manufacture] ...is afforded so cheap at the Market of Stockholm, that the Swedes have lost Money in every Attempt they have made to rival them. Judge now, therefore, what little Cause there is to fear that a poor Country can ever rival a rich one in the more operose, complicated, and expensive Branches of a Manufacture: Judge also, whether a rich Country can ever lose its Trade, while it retains its Industry.[40]

Despite attempts to support and improve the Swedish manufacturing industry, in some branches, including the complex worsted production, they were unable to reach the necessary efficiency and refinement in their production to be competitive and to cater for the local demand. This opened up the door to alternative supply chains.

Concealed Cloth

Norwich worsteds arrived in Sweden through many various channels, including direct and indirect trade. Although little is yet known about how the direct trade worked in practice, it is nevertheless possible to gain some fairly unique insights through an incident that took place in 1776. Nine years previously, Jonas Krook, a well-established merchant and member of the Swedish riksdag, had ordered worsteds worth the significant sum of £508 from the Norwich-based merchant-manufacturers J. & J. Ives.[41] Although the worsteds were readily shipped, J. & J. Ives never received their due payment, prompting them to reach out to the authorities for help. This would be the start of a long and arduous process. Early on, the British ambassador Sir John Goodricke found his hands tied as the culprit was a member of the riksdag.[42] However, J. & J. Ives did not give up but with the help of Henry Howard, Lord Suffolk, the Secretary of State of the northern territories, they put pressure of Goodricke's successor Lewis de Visme to retrieve the money.[43] However, it was not possible to go through the official Swedish channels and issue a suit of law as Mr Krook "had been guilty of smuggling the English Manufactures He bought of Messers Ives into Sweden which was punishable by Swedish Laws".[44] Lord Suffolk reasoned that if Krook was convicted of smuggling he would never repay his debt. It was therefore necessary to find another way to put pressure on Krook. De Visme despaired, "Krock [sic] has an infamous Character, and will never pay this just Debt unless pressed and threatened with a Suit at Law".[45] Despite his misgivings, de Visme proceeded to threaten Krook and, finding an ally in the Swedish Chancellor of Justice

Liljenstråle, he eventually brought a suit against Krook.[46] Unfortunately, it has not been possible to locate these proceedings so the outcome of the affair remains shrouded in mystery. What the business does show is that Norwich-based manufacturers traded directly with merchants in Sweden and that credit was extended even for this type of illegal trade. It also indicates how difficult it was to interfere when something went awry, particularly for the British authorities who did not want to damage the profitable smuggling system, and attempted to work athwart Swedish legislation.

The Krook-incident does not appear to have hampered J. & J. Ives' desire to export to the Scandinavian markets, as illustrated by their export accounts from 1791 (now under the name J. & J. Ives, Son & Basely). Table 5.1 was supplied to the House of Lords hand-loom commission in 1840 by Norwich sheriff John Warden Robberds in order to illustrate how lucrative the Norwich trade once had been.[47] According to the table, Norway and Sweden make up a significant proportion of the Ives' exports, even though Norway had a population of about 800,000 and Sweden/Finland of barely 3 million in 1791, and the use of the English worsteds was strictly prohibited in the larger of the two countries. Although the calculations might be exaggerated, the export numbers were considerable in comparison to the population of these countries. Italy, for comparison, imported slightly less than Scandinavia and had a population of c. 15 million around this time. Furthermore, as we shall see, some of the Russian worsteds were also destined for Scandinavia.

The trade in worsteds was not solely conducted through direct trade but many of the worsteds passed through numerous hands, and countries, on their journey to Sweden. One of the most prominent transit areas was Norway, where the worsteds could legally be imported, before they were taken across the border. This might also be why the two countries are lumped together in Table 5.1. The extensive entrepôt and cross-border trade has already been examined in previous chapters so a few short remarks will suffice to illustrate this trade here.

TABLE 5.1 Return of the manufacturing house Messrs Ives, Basely & Robberds in the year 1791, information supplied by John Warden Robberds

	Total	*Italy*	*Spain/ America*	*Germany*	*Russia*	*Norway/ Sweden*	*Holland*	*Madeira*	*China*
Camlet	65468	9544	12816	5972	7986	8193	–	987	19970
Camletees	4423	256	–	1725	–	252	2190	–	–
Callimancoes	17693	–	742	388	15508	51	1004	–	–
Satins	11036	123	1402	6751	1457	601	702	–	–
Bombazines	1063	–	910	–	–	–	–	153	–
Lastings	4739	98	1378	245	790	1494	734	–	–
Figured Stuffs	4860	463	2425	1397	–	180	275	120	–
Total £	109282	10484	19673	16478	25741	10771	4905	1260	19970

Source: The Sessional Papers Printed by Order of the House of Lords. *Reports from Commissioners: Hand-loom Weavers* (1840), Vol. XXXVII, p. 303.

One crucial border crossing was located at Frederikshald (now Halden), a southern Norwegian border town with extensive entrepôt trade with Sweden. Norwich merchant manufacturer Philip Stannard's correspondence shows that he was already delivering worsteds to Frederikshald through Yarmouth by 1755.[48] On site in Frederikshald, the Norwegian merchant Peter Bull observed in his diary:

> From the moment when I got to know the trade of Friderichshald [sic] with the Swedes I lost my desire to establish myself there, as I took a dislike to the place, the people and the trade. Tricks, slyness, deception and almost all heavy vices were here *Grand Mode*. Cursing and swearing must be used for each piece of Camelot and Kersey, which the Swedes purchase either in exchange for iron or on credit and this trade was always subject to danger.[49]

An account by the Norwegian customs official Friedrich Wilhelm Thue gives a similar picture. He estimated with curious specificity that, in 1788, 3688 ells of Calamanco, 25,640 ells of Camlet, 40 ells of Serge, 1,110 ells of Challon, and 1,108 ells of Everlasting were illegally introduced into Sweden via Frederikshald alone (1 Norwegian ell = c. 62.75 cm).[50] Such measurements should be treated with caution, but accounts from both sides of the border bear witness to the extensive trade in the area.[51]

Fredrikshald might have been one of the most active smuggling sites when it came to worsteds, but it was far from the only one. Worsteds were brought in overland all along the Norwegian and Russia borders.[52] They were also introduced by sea. At Stockholm, worsteds were seized onboard ships from various British ports as well as Wismar, and Danzig.[53] The 'Baltic worsteds' were probably also Norwich productions, as the Norwich weavers exported textiles to various Baltic harbours including Danzig.[54] There were thus several different smuggling routes through which the worsteds could enter, both across land and by sea.

Evidence of the illegal worsted trade can also be found in Swedish museums. The Nordic Museum in Stockholm holds more than 150 worsted items of Norwich origin in their traditional costume collections.[55] Costume curator Berit Eldvik, who has studied these textiles in-depth, believes that at least 90% of the calamancoes at the Nordic Museum are Norwich creations.[56] At the Museum of Dalarna, Anna-Karin Jobs Arnberg has shown that through textile analysis it is possible to identify some of their worsted bodices not merely as originating in Norwich but also matching specimens in Ives & Baseley's 1791 sample book.[57] We shall return to these textiles later; for now, it is enough to note that the surviving material remains bear testament to the extensive illegal trade in worsteds between Norwich and Sweden.

Governmental Toleration

The government's attitude towards the contraband worsteds can be gauged from the way they treated transgressions and seized contraband. In 1778, Gustav III introduced a new national costume, which was intended to alleviate smuggling, strengthen the domestic industry, and 'reinvigorate' patriotic feeling.[58] The project's guiding star was the *esprit national.*[59] For the courtiers, the new costume would be made of plain, domestically produced fabric in two sets of colours, one for everyday use at the court, in black and "*colour* [sic] *de feu*" (a red-orange colour), and one for festive occasions in pale blue and white. Meanwhile, the burghers were prescribed a costume of a similar cut, but in a single colour, usually black.[60] It was hoped that the national costume would limit the strain posed on the manufactories by ever-changing fashions, allowing them to specialise in single wares instead of constantly lagging behind trying to copy a multitude of new foreign trends.

However, the national costume project had some unforeseen consequences. Only three months after the introduction of the costume, a member of the Privy Council, Baron Carl Sparre, pointed out that there was a universal shortage of worsteds in all shops. Sparre identified the introduction of the national costume as the main cause of this shortage. Suddenly, the demand for woollen textiles had soared as "almost everyone" needed new clothing. In order to alleviate the situation, Sparre proposed that the government ought to release seized contraband for sale, more specifically, a large contraband hoard seized a month earlier from Captain Nystrand in Nyköping.[61] The goods consisted of 100 chalons, 84 calamancoes, 10 flowered damasks, 11 camlets, 100 striped cameletees, and 30 etamins, and some silks which would not be released for re-sale.[62] The National Board of Trade was at first dismissive of the suggestion. They argued that no one was likely to buy the foreign worsteds as their quality was inferior to Swedish manufactures, although they conceded that their finish was still superior.[63] Nevertheless, the King approved of Sparre's suggestion and decided that the worsteds should stay in the kingdom and be offered for sale. A few textile samples still survive from this hoard, which illustrates what these textiles looked like.[64] A year later, the King made a general announcement that the confiscated worsteds were to be offered for sale due to the nationwide shortage.[65] The contraband worsted thus came to be incorporated into the regular market in order to sustain the regulation and to avoid removing the trade barriers to deal with the textile shortages.

The idea of aiding a struggling domestic industry with seized contraband did not disappear. In 1798, the National Board of Trade sent a report on the state of the Swedish manufacturing industry to the government. In regard to the worsted manufacturers, the Board observed that Swedish productions were just as good, although not as beautiful, as the English products. They observed that there had been a decline in domestic productions in recent years, but rejected the idea that this might be a good incentive to open up for foreign importation. Rather, they argued that the demand for worsteds was shrinking due to the increasing popularity of calico and what remained was catered for by the great quantities of smuggled worsteds on the market. Therefore, they saw no need to lift the protectionist prohibitions.[66] The government agreed, adding that the introduction of new spinning machines and the establishment of worsted factories in the countryside would eventually help to overcome the shortage of Swedish worsted stuffs.[67] Both in the 1778 and 1798 cases, the contraband worsteds were portrayed as intrinsically bound up with the continued life of the protectionist policy, covering whatever shortages occurred due to the regulations.

As previously noted, although the national costume was supposed to be universal, in practice, this was not the case. The peasants, who made up the vast bulk of the population, were excused from using it.[68] This exemption was allegedly due to that they had requested to keep using their traditional costumes made of homespun and Swedish-manufactured textiles.[69] By exempting the commoners from his dress reform, Gustav III suggested that they did not need to change. Instead, he set them up as a model for other Swedish inhabitants: controlled, simple, and patriotic in their consumer choices.[70] From a state perspective, particularly under the regime of Gustav III, the use of foreign textiles by commoners was seen not simply as unpatriotic, but even as unnatural.[71] The commoners did not conform to this elite view of their consumer habits, however, and it did not prevent them from buying foreign textiles.

An Acceptable Luxury?

The use of fashionable textiles such as the worsteds could take many forms and it is difficult to generalise their use. Drawing on examples from a few different localities, it is nonetheless possible to gauge how these fabrics *could* be used. Surviving worsted textiles in Swedish museum collections are a good place to start. As already noted, the vast majority of eighteenth-century worsteds that have survived in museums can be found in collections of traditional peasant costume.[72] The largest survival rate for Norwich worsteds is from the provinces bordering on Norway, together with the provinces of Gästrikland, Hälsingland, Halland, and southern Småland. In general, there are no striking local preferences in terms of colour, and the cuts and tailoring of the surviving clothes are so similar that nothing can be discerned about where they were used in the country.[73] There are, however, exceptions from areas in central Dalarna where the cut of the bodices reveals exactly in which parish they were sewn.[74]

One such parish was Dala-Floda. See Figure 5.1 for the Dala-Floda cut. Worsted survival rates from Dala-Floda are particularly high as local women travelled to surrounding parishes acquiring used bodices in the 1850s–1870s.[75] The bodice design was slightly longer than many from the nearby areas, and each Dala-Floda bodice required two recycled bodices. Few unaltered bodices have consequently survived from the regions around Dala-Floda.[76] Matches between Dala-Floda bodices and Norwich sample books has allowed Anna-Karin Jobs Arnberg to trace the worsteds back to England and provide dates for their production[77] (Figure 5.1). Jobs Arnberg has shown that the Norwich worsteds were being reused nearly a century after their initial production. The continued circulation and recycling of these items shows the longevity of contraband worsteds in the Swedish countryside, a sign not merely of their durable popularity

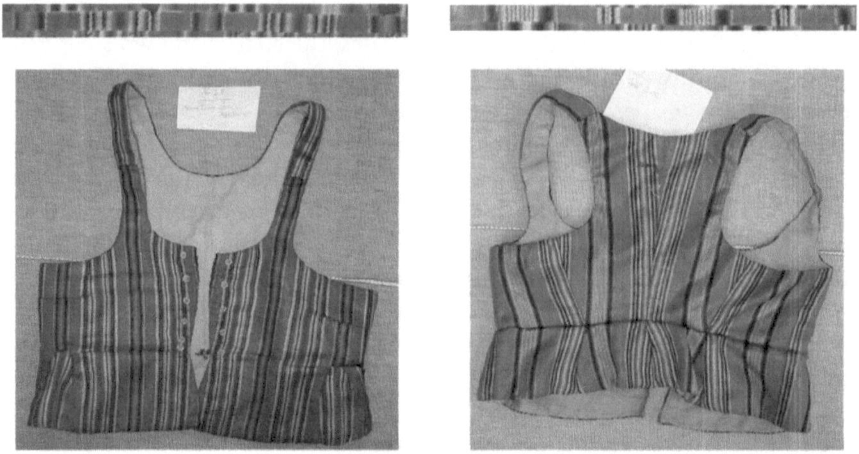

FIGURE 5.1 Bodices from Anna-Karin Jobs Arnberg's survey of bodices in Dala-Floda alongside textile samples from Ives & Baseley textile sample book.

Source: Anna-Karin Jobs Arnberg private photograph.

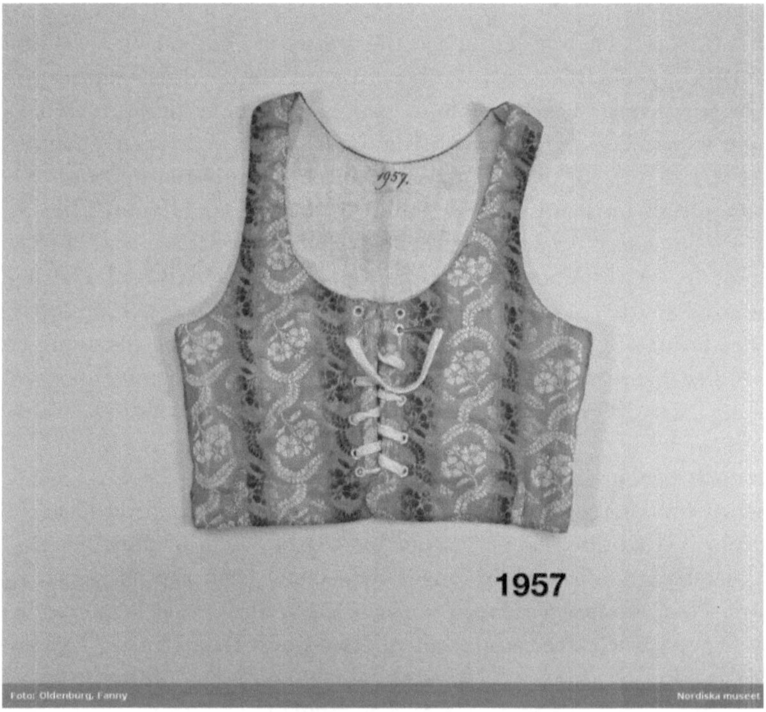

FIGURE 5.2 Taboratt bodice from Getinge parish, Halland. Cloth identified as produced in Norwich by Berit Eldvik. Textile dates from 1770 to 1790 and bodice created 1790–1810.

Source: The Nordic Museum, NM.0001957. Photo © Fanny Oldenburg/Nordiska Museet.

but also of their excellent quality. Even in Dalarna, a region famed for its use of simple traditional dress, Norwich worsteds eventually came to be incorporated into the local design.

The 1793 Parish Debates

The use of worsteds in traditional dress practices across the Swedish-Finnish territory is evident not merely from museum collections but also in the written records. Particularly useful are the 1793 parish debates, already touched upon in Chapter 2, which derived from a questionnaire sent out to all parishes. The questionnaire asked the parishes to provide descriptions of the local dress and to list the 'luxuries' the parishioners were willing to refrain from in the future. In particular, it inquired about the use of foreign cloth. The intention of the questionnaire was to gauge what goods the population was willing to do without, and their responses would form the basis of the new sumptuary law, and ensure that the law had popular approval. It was hoped that this approach would make the laws easier to enforce and maintain.[78]

Not all parishioners were included in drafting the replies, but the discussions usually only involved a small selection of male parishioners. They did, however, represent various different (male) interest groups: young and old, and various types of farmers, lay assessors, men in charge of parish order, aldermen, and occasionally even poor tenant farmers. Although men with local authority dominated the discussions with their will to maintain hierarchical order and reinforcing authority, the debates also show signs of discord. The definitions of what was unnecessary luxury could vary considerably, which underlines the necessity of thinking about consumer choice as something individually as well as locally determined. The parish replies offer insights not only into the spread of worsteds but also into how they were perceived.

The replies to the 1793 questionnaire could vary considerably between different localities and even between neighbouring parishes. One of the most contested issues was whether worsted was indeed a luxury in need of control or not. According to several parishes, including Mörskom, in the county of Nyland, in the Finnish provinces, and Gustav Adolph parish in the county of Tavastland, worsted was a dangerous luxury good in need of control.[79] By contrast, in Jämsä parish, located just north of Gustav Adolph, the parish representatives maintained that while they were willing to abandon the use of silk jackets, sweaters, skirts, aprons, and silver and gold embroidery, they wanted to keep using camlet and wool damask.[80] Similarly, in the coastal parish of Pernå, which neighboured Mörskom, it was argued that while the people in the region ought to wear homespun textiles for their everyday clothing, they should be allowed to use camlet and cotton for their best clothes.[81] Artsjö, another neighbouring parish to Mörskom, agreed with this approach, arguing that on feast days, the parish women should be allowed to wear skirts, sweaters, and bodices made of either striped and dyed wool, calamanco, satin, or cloth, depending on their wealth.[82] As a concession, some parishes offered to replace their silk usage with worsteds, which they perceived as a lesser evil.[83] Just like the legislators, the parish vestries appear to have agreed that robust fabrics like worsted, were naturally preferable to flimsy and cold silks which were unsuited to the harsh Nordic climate.[84]

In the parishes that agreed that worsteds should be banned, there was nevertheless a consensus that this ban only should apply to new textiles. Whatever worsteds the locals already owned should be free to use until they were worn out.[85] As already noted, however, these textiles had a remarkable durability. Indeed, one parish noted that as these clothes were only used sparingly, they could be passed from mother to daughter.[86] One reason for this sparse use appears to have been that fine worsteds primarily were used for festive occasions.[87]

Exactly how worsteds were used and by whom differed considerably between different localities, however. In some places, they appear to only have been used by women, either as skirts, sweaters, or bodices, while in others, worsted was only used in the cap or as hair ribbons.[88] In other locations, men wore it too, particularly in their waistcoats, and in some places, it was used by women, men, and children alike (Figures 5.2, 5.3 and 5.4).[89] The design of the local costume could

FIGURE 5.3 Worsted damask waistcoat, textile probably of Norwich origin from Getinge parish, dating from 1770 to 1790, Halland.

Source: The Nordic Museum, NM.0001999. Photo © Fanny Oldenburg/Nordiska Museet.

be very specific, at Jemsröd the parish representatives gave an elaborate account of exactly the sort of costume worn in the locality: the skirts of married women were made of fine blue wool cloth, black, red or green camlet, wool damask, or etamin. Although the costume was described as 'ancient', it incorporated many manufactured textiles.[90] There was thus not a uniform use of worsted in the country but it varied between localities, which agrees with earlier research on local dress practices.[91]

There are also some notable differences between the Swedish and the Finnish half of the country. One feature of the contraband seizures and parish records from the Finnish areas which is not present in the material from Sweden proper is the worsted belt or sash that appears to have been popular among men. This sash, either in calamanco, taboratt, wool damask, or etamin is found in several

FIGURE 5.4 Worsted damask skirt, textile probably of Norwich origin from Efra parish, Halland, dated c. 1770–1800.

Source: The Nordic Museum, NM.0001958, Nordiska Museet. Photo © Bertil Wreting/Nordiska Museet.

Finnish parish accounts and contraband seizures.[92] The worsted manufacturers in Norwich produced such sashes, especially for the Russian market.[93] This helps to explain why they are only found in the eastern half of the country, which primarily was supplied through Russia.

While certain parishes undoubtedly strove to keep their use of worsteds, this did not mean that the commoner consumers were ignorant of the concept of patriotic consumer choice. The parish vestry in Rantasalmi observed that purchasing foreign textiles was damaging to the country and drained it of money.[94] Similarly, Jämsröd parish announced that they would reject all foreign clothing as useless luxuries.[95] Even in places with easy access to cheap and good quality foreign textiles the parishioners promised to ensure that only clothes made from Swedish-made textiles were used in the future.[96] Although this was viewed as a patriotic sacrifice in some parishes, in others, they wanted something in return. While the parishioners in the coastal parish Thorshamn were willing to refrain from buying any cloth they "had misgivings about having been made in the fatherland", they also urged that more support should be given to the domestic industry to improve their manufacturing.[97] This indicates that patriotic consumer choice was not merely an idea that existed among the upper echelons of society but also among commoners in the countryside, who considered themselves quite capable of making qualified decisions about their own consumption. However, they were not merely aware of the consequences of their consumer choices but, remarkably, some even conditioned their consumption.

Although a vast array of people seem to have used worsteds, they were particularly common among the younger generation, who occur with great regularity in the records.[98] The use of foreign textiles among the young appears to have been a source of local conflict, something that is particularly evident in Lillkyro parish, just outside of Vasa. In Lillkyro, a disagreement arose between the younger farm tenants and married farmhands on one side, and the older yeomen on the other. The young farm tenants and farmhands insisted that everyone should be allowed to consume according to their income and standing, unhindered by rules and regulations.[99] A sense of a generational shift in dress practices can also be found in Jyväskyle, in Tavastland, where it was noted that the coarse cloth that had once been in common use was "now out of fashion", and instead women wore bodices of wool damask, calamanco, and camlet.[100] Complaints about youthful extravagance in dress, and deviation from older established dress traditions, was a recurring theme in commentaries on local dress across time and might say more about the relationship between generations than it does about consumer patterns.[101] The idea that there had previously been no manufactured fabrics in circulation should therefore always be approached with caution.

It is nevertheless clear that changes in dress practices and the introduction of foreign and fashionable elements could be triggered by new sources of income, both on a local and individual level. Scholars have also highlighted that disposable income varied across the life cycle, and that the last years before marriage, when expenditures were few, was a particularly lucrative period.[102] Periods of economic prosperity, either regional or national, and the introduction of new types of work, forestry, mining, or industry, were also often accompanied by shifts in the dress practice.[103]

Changes in dress could also be triggered by new encounters, and as the parishes of Frändefors, Brålanda, and Ryr, near the Norwegian border, got to experience, it was difficult to control what people wore as long as they were free to move. The parish vestries observed that while the use of "glittering Etamin and Camlet" in theory ought to be curtailed, they did not dare to place such a restriction on their servants as "the serving youth will then pour out of the Country, to such places, where the freedom to dress for pleasure had been kept".[104] The parish vestry went on to note that they were already suffering from people leaving their region and did not want to make the situation even worse. Additionally, many of the 'leavers' came back to visit after spending time in the provinces of Västergötland and Bohuslän, where they had started dressing in the ostentatious dress of those provinces. This, they believed, tempted others to leave.[105] It was therefore difficult to curb the use of luxury textiles in local parishes, as long as it was allowed elsewhere. Job migration, together with wandering pedlars, might also help to explain how the fashion of worsteds spread between different localities, although they were adapted to local dress practices.

It ought to be added that in some parish replies, worsteds are notable for their absence. This is the case for several parishes around Siljan from whence many of the worsted bodices today kept in museums originate. The parish vestries make no mention of their use of worsted, insisting instead that they wanted to continue using the costume of their forefathers.[106] In Leksand, it was even noted that: "The commoners in Dalarna have the merit, that they never ape after new fashions but are unchanging in their costume…".[107] The scarcity of surviving estate inventories from this early period makes it difficult to establish how common worsteds were in the poorer parishes in central Dalarna; however, calamanco bodices can nevertheless be observed in parishes such as Leksand and Nås around this time.[108] An absence of worsted in the vestry report does therefore not mean that they were not used in these localities.

Worsted figures in the questionnaire reply from parishes across the Swedish realm, from the Norwegian to the Russian border, north to south. Although they were present across the country, their exact use and how they were viewed differed considerably between various localities. Neighbouring parishes could view worsteds either as an unnecessary luxury or as an acceptable and suitable commodity. As this brief survey of worsteds shows, these manufactured textiles were by 1793 well-established across the Swedish realm – with distinct uses and associations. It shows how extensive the market for contraband worsteds were, even affecting commoner consumers who had a limited consumption. Even though most consumers might have purchased only a small amount of worsted, the customer base was nevertheless significant enough to have a substantial impact overall, something that is also visible in the large collections of surviving Norwich worsteds still in museums today. Because of shortages of domestic worsteds on the Swedish market, legislators not only tolerated the existence of these textiles, they even reintroduced seized contraband worsted into the market. In that way, and without having to resort to the removal of import prohibitions, the authorities were able to cover for the domestic shortfall. Contraband worsteds hence allowed untenable protectionist legislation to subsist.

Coffee: A Clandestine Desire

Coffee is something that most people are familiar with today, but in the eighteenth century, the drink was reasonably new to consumers. Coffee had first arrived in Sweden in 1680, but it was not until the eighteenth century that a larger consumer culture emerged around it. Some historians have argued that its popularity was linked to its addictive properties.[109] At the same time, as the popularity of coffee grew, knowledge about coffee and its properties was evolving.[110] There were numerous types of coffee, including Mocha, Antillean, Bourbon, and Levantine, in addition to other similar coffee products such as wild coffee and adulterated coffee; what constituted real coffee was remained uncertain.[111] Attempts were also made to find a substitute 'coffee' closer to home. Such efforts were particularly interesting to Carl Linnaeus, who expressed a dislike for the imported coffee which he considered a damaging French influence.[112]

In the eighteenth century, the definition of coffee was changing and so was its social role. Upon its arrival, coffee had first been consumed in coffee houses, which meant that it was consumed in male public spaces.[113] As the eighteenth century progressed, however, coffee increasingly came to be considered a domestic, and eventually also a female, luxury.[114] By 1761, Linnaeus was arguing in his academic treaty *Potus Coffeæ* that

> This kind of beverage, alas a novelty... has particularly won the favour of the female sex, as it is not intoxicating, and can be compared to tea, although coffee is seen as more genteel, maybe because it is more expensive than tea... if [a woman] goes to call on another lady, she will be insulted not to be received with the temptations of the coffee table, and believe me, [a person] will be considered most unrefined, if they do not offer their guests coffee after a meal.[115]

Even though it was described as a novelty in 1761, a role and an identity for coffee were clearly being demarcated, as well as a distinct set of social practices surrounding its consumption.

The Ban on Coffee

The popularity of coffee soon made the authorities aware of it as a potentially problematic addition to the Swedish market. The dangers of coffee were conceived both in terms of economy and of public health.[116] In economic terms, it was seen as incompatible with the protectionist policies that Sweden strove to uphold, the argument being that the import of coffee drained the country of its much-needed silver. It also made Sweden dependent on other nations, their trade networks and colonies. Coffee consumption consequently came to be linked to infringements on the national autonomy. During the second half of the eighteenth century, coffee import and consumption therefore came to be intermittently prohibited. The years of the prohibitions were: 1756–1761, 1766–1769, 1794–1796, 1799–1802, and 1817–1823. While it should be noted that the prohibitions normally were part of more general sumptuary decrees, the coffee prohibitions were, unlike other prohibitions, repeatedly introduced and cancelled. The regulation of coffee started back in 1747 when a proclamation announced that coffee, tea, and chocolate should henceforth be accompanied by an additional consumption tax intended to eventually suppress the use of these goods. The fines were determined by the consumer's place of residence. For example, in large cities, the consumer had to pay 8 D kmt to consume coffee, in towns 6 D kmt, in small towns 4 D kmt, and in the countryside along with the smallest towns the tax would be only 2 D kmt.[117] While this might indicate that there was a greater tolerance for these wares in the countryside, it is more likely a reflection of where the goods were consumed in any significant quantity by the middle of the century.

The first direct coffee prohibition was launched in 1756 as part of a more general sumptuary legislation. The design of the sumptuary legislation was overseen by two members of the riksdag: Carl Gustav Löwenhielm (1701–1768) and Carl Lagerberg (1708–1767). The launch was fraught with conflict, and the coffee ban had far from unanimous support. Rather, the coffee ban, propagated by Löwenhielm, had failed to gain adequate support both during the 1755/1756 riksdag and in the Secret Committee. Indeed, the Secret Committee had instead decided that the import toll on coffee should be reduced, to combat smuggling. The hesitancy to ban coffee might be related to the fact that it was considered an elite drink at this time.[118] Its prohibition could thus be considered an assault on the privileged, a group to which many members of the riksdag counted themselves. However, when Löwenhielm and Lagerberg came to be tasked with producing lists of the goods to be banned in the new sumptuary decree, they took the opportunity to pursue Löwenhielm's anti-luxury agenda, adding coffee to the list of prohibited goods, without the support of the riksdag.[119]

The second prohibition was also overseen by Löwenhielm, who had now risen to the position of President of the Chancery Department. He argued that a ban on coffee would not only bring financial gains but also health benefits, claiming that "many doctors are advising against the use of coffee, which is now a beverage spread through the whole country… it has even started being used among the peasants".[120] Löwenhielm posited that the social pressures of emulation had highly adverse economic, physical, and moral effects. The health risk was one of many lines of attack on coffee in the eighteenth century, but it had little impact in the Swedish riksdag and failed to persuade most members.[121] While the health arguments failed to be persuasive, the ongoing economic crisis of the 1760s was, and a new coffee ban was issued in 1766 to improve the trade balance.[122]

The third coffee prohibition, issued in 1794, was preceded in 1793 by a committee appointed by the Duke Regent Carl, tasked with exploring the causes of, and solutions for, the increasing luxury consumption. The committee noted that the use of coffee drained "our poor Country" of large sums of money. However, the committee also noted that a healthier type of coffee, made from chicory root, could be produced within Sweden itself and offer a solution to the dire situation.[123] 'Swedish coffee' could involve substitutes of various descriptions, including chicory root or toasted rye. Surrogates like 'Swedish coffee' were clearly used already during the earlier prohibition periods, but the term first entered the newspapers in the 1780s.[124] Privileges for making this type of coffee were awarded both by the King and the National Board of Trade.[125] Swedish coffee, at least according to their advertisements, differed little from the foreign coffee in taste and appearance, but was better for the health.[126] Although the committee considered Swedish coffee a viable alternative to the undesirable foreign coffee during the early prohibition periods in reality it proved unviable.

The reason for this can be found in a Supreme Court case, which redefined illegal coffee. In 1768, H. J. Jung stood trial for selling coffee made from burnt rye bread. During his trial, an apothecary had been called in to identify what the confiscated beverage was brewed on. While the apothecary confirmed that Jung's coffee was indeed brewed with rye bread rather than imported beans, the court decided that all types of coffee should henceforth be considered equal in the eyes of the law. The existence of coffee surrogates made it too difficult for the police, and consequently for the court, to efficiently uphold the prohibitions.[127] Prior to the Jung case, the courts had been forced to rely on oath swearing and experts, usually apothecaries, to distinguish 'real' coffee from its many copies. This made the process slow, unwieldy, and inaccurate.[128] The Jung case set a new legislative landmark for coffee, expanding its definition. It also explains why, when the third ban was launched in 1794, it also prohibited the use of so-called Swedish coffee.[129]

When the fourth coffee ban was issued in 1799, the main reason was again the bad state of the Swedish finances.[130] Throughout the period, the coffee prohibitions were used as a quick fix for dire economic situations, in theory providing an immediate stop to the silver drainage. It also needed minimal political effort as the bans could be issued without calling in the riksdag.[131]

Not everyone agreed that prohibition was the right way to improve the Swedish finances, however. In 1776, in his call to establish colonies, *Afhandling om Nyttan för Sverige af Handel och Nybyggen i Indierna och på Africa*, Ulric Nordensköld, a member of the Swedish Patriotic Society, noted that if coffee and sugar were such important wares, "[w]hy could they not be produced by a Swedish hand?". He suggested that the solution was to acquire colonies, where Swedish workers and slaves could produce these goods.[132] Nordenskköld was not alone in his views but also the State Secretary of the Trade and Finance Office Johan

Liljencrantz (1730–1815) agreed that colonies ought to be acquired in order to combat the unfavourable trade balance.[133]

In 1784, Sweden finally acquired the colony Saint Barthélemy from France, but it quickly turned out to be a disappointment for those hoping for coffee plantations. The British ambassador noted that there was scepticism towards the fecundity of the new West Indian colony already in 1784.

> It is the opinion of the best-informed people here, that for the present at least, Sweden will derive a very small advantage from this Island [St Barthélemy], considering that the whole of it's [sic] product consists only of about 20,000 Pound weight of Cotton, and tho' it be conveniently situated to carry on a smuggling Trade, no real and lasting profit could be expected from it but by planting Sugar.[134]

Indeed, while St Barthélemy turned out to be a great contraband centre for sugar in the West Indies, it does not appear to have provided Sweden with any greater quantities of coffee.[135] In 1793, the committee charged with discussing the new sumptuary decree noted that the coffee importation from St Barthélemy remained small and, "as the [import] from this island far from corresponds to the recent consumption, coffee cannot be considered a plant [existing] in the dominions of the kingdom".[136] Coffee, they argued, could not be considered a Swedish crop. Sweden was thus never able to support its own coffee needs through its colony and instead had to rely on importation from the Dutch Republic throughout the eighteenth century.[137]

Various solutions were suggested to deal with the problem of coffee consumption, but none of them were as enduring as the coffee ban. It is also notable that coffee was banned for all alike. While distinctions between those who could and those who should not be drinking coffee were made in Swedish debates, the Swedish bans eventually tarred everyone with the same brush. This stands in sharp contrast to many other types of goods in the sumptuary decrees, most prominently silk, which could only be worn by specific social groups during the second half of the eighteenth century.[138] It confirms that the main motivation for the coffee prohibitions was to safeguard the economy rather than to safeguard hierarchical consumption and that health and propriety arguments were used by the government to prop up this economic motive. While some countries might have been able to remove their sumptuary decrees and instead shape their colonial policies and production to serve domestic tastes and demands, this proved impossible for Sweden.[139]

Beans Below Board

Import statistics suggest that the coffee prohibitions had a profound effect on the legal import of coffee (see Graph 5.1). Coffee importation dropped significantly during the prohibition periods although, as can be seen in the 1790s, some

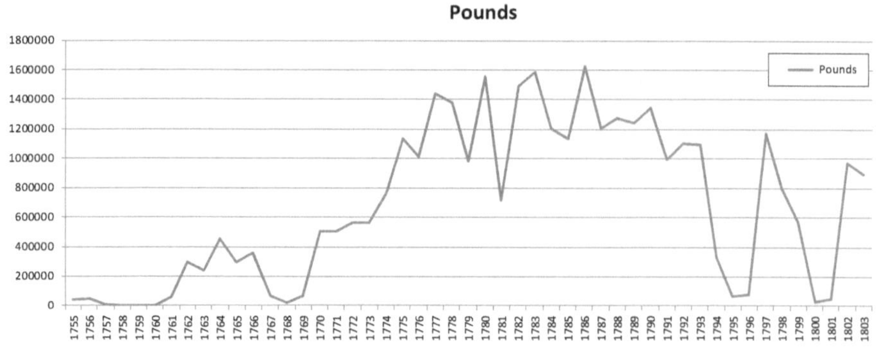

GRAPH 5.1 Legal Coffee Imports to Sweden (Pounds).
Source: Historisk Statistik För Sverige. Del 3. Utrikeshandel 1732–1970 (Stockholm: Statistiska Centralbyrån, 1972).

import was still maintained, probably for entrepôt trade. During the prohibition periods, there were also 'coffee-clearances', such as the re-export of coffee stock imported during legal times.[140] Meanwhile, the statistics also show a considerable increase in coffee importation in the second half of the century, compared to the prohibition-free first half of the century.[141] Not only is this indicative of the popularity of coffee, it is also indicative of a growing consumer base.

The intention of the coffee bans was to stop the import of coffee, but its actual effect was to push the trade underground. Already by 1756, the Burgher Estate had observed that even a slight increase in the import tax generated smuggling.[142] This is even more true for the periods when there was a complete import ban. While it is impossible to calculate the extent of illegal importation, some general observations can nevertheless be made. In the confiscation lists from the Maritime Customs Court, coffee beans appear as the second most common contraband ware, behind textiles. Looking at the 95 cases of smuggling being processed in the Stockholm Customs Court between June and December 1769, 47 of the confiscation hoards contained coffee.[143] In total, 5,257 pounds (2,234 kg) of contraband coffee was seized during this period. The lifting of the coffee prohibition in September appears to have had a limited effect on the smuggling, as 26 confiscations took place during the prohibition period and 21 after. Most confiscations were small; the largest seizure was 1,000 pounds (425 kg), but the median seizure contained only 40 pounds (17 kg). These seizures indicate a pattern of smaller private smuggling endeavours, run by sailors, mostly from Wismar (15 ships), Danzig (10), and various German provinces including Pillau and Kiel.[144]

One case from 1769 can offer some insight into what happened once the sailors had touched ground in Stockholm. On this occasion, a potential client, the Belgian envoy's cook, Ellers, was visited in his kitchen and was offered to buy coffee by a man who "by the looks of him was a sailor".[145] The asking price was 6 D kmt per pound, a considerable mark-up in comparison to the Maritime Customs Court valuation of 1.5 D kmt per pound. A servant was dispatched to collect the beans in "a yellow house" near the harbour. In this house, he had met many people, all of whom appeared to be German sailors.[146] This account supports the idea that German sailors were involved in coffee smuggling in this period, and the fact that they were selling the beans independently suggests that the trade was not part of a larger scheme but organic.

A comparison between 1769 and the end of the century suggests a distinct shift in the composition of the trade. During the six-month period from June to December 1800, there were only 43 smuggling cases processed by the Maritime Customs Court in Stockholm.[147] Only 15 of these involved coffee, considerably fewer than in the earlier period. At the same time, however, the amount of coffee seized amounted to 10,619 pounds (4,513 kg), which is more than double that seized during the same period in 1769. This calculation excludes the "several barrels of coffee" confiscated from a sailor from St Ybes, which were never weighed.[148] Extending the survey by another month, an additional 10 smuggling cases can be added, four of which concerned coffee smuggling, involving an additional 15,440 pounds (6,562 kg) of beans. The largest seizure took place on Christmas Eve and concerned a hoard of 13,050 pounds (c. 5,200 kg).[149] In contrast to the earlier period, the seized contraband coffee stashes were fewer, but considerably larger. During the seven-month period from June to January 1800, around 26,060 pounds (11,075 kg) of beans were confiscated in Stockholm. This corresponds to roughly 60% of the entire Swedish import in 1755, the year prior to the first importation ban.[150]

It is impossible to say how large the actual contraband trade in coffee was, but the increasing quantities individually seized suggest that it had expanded considerably during the last quarter of the eighteenth century. It should be borne in mind that these numbers only relate to Stockholm Maritime Customs Court, and because of patchy record survival, it is impossible to get a full idea of the annual seizures.

Although the main focus here is on Stockholm, it is worth pointing out that other towns were also partaking in the circulation and illegal consumption of coffee. In a report about the sumptuary crimes prosecuted in Linköping between 1799 and 1802, 10 out of 12 crimes involved coffee smuggling. Some of these cases concern considerable quantities, including the 900 pounds (c. 382.5 kg) of coffee seized from a coachman in August of 1800, and the 814 pounds (c. 346 kg) taken from the peasant Anders Andersson in January 1801, or the 100 pounds (42 kg) confiscated from High Bailiff Ramklou from Kalmar around the same time.[151] Linköping was in 1800 a town of 2,680 inhabitants, which means that the coffee seized solely in these three confiscations could have supplied the town's population with 0.3 kg per person.[152] Further research on other towns would likely reveal an even more extensive coffee smuggling. The demand for coffee appears to have remained high even during the prohibitions, and it was ultimately this demand that brought the prohibition periods to an end.

Governmental Despair

Along with the prohibitions came a slow realisation that such measures did not always fill their intended function. When the first prohibition was lifted in 1761, the reason given was "concerns for the kingdom".[153] To the legislators, it was clear that the continued smuggling hollowed out the prohibition. The second prohibition was lifted in 1769 as "a large amount [of coffee beans] have illegally been introduced, to a significant loss for the Crown".[154] While prohibition did not hinder the introduction of coffee, it did strip the state of the import duties, which meant that it was more financially damaging to retain the ban than to remove it.[155]

During the later prohibition periods, attempts were made to plead with the population to make them respect the prohibitions.[156] However, such efforts proved ineffective and the ongoing smuggling and consumption during the prohibition periods kept undermining the legislation. In the revocation of the coffee ban in 1796, it was sourly noted that despite the ban, the taste for coffee made it the most sought-after consumer good.[157] There is little doubt that the public taste for coffee and dislike for the coffee ban also played in when the prohibition was lifted in 1802.[158] In her diary, Duchess Hedvig Elisabeth Charlotta noted:

> [t]he king has in silence prepared some measures regarding the toll on certain goods. The importation of e.g. coffee has been prohibited, but when hardly any single person can do without this beverage, coffee has been smuggled, in large quantities.[159]

She observed that by allowing coffee to be imported, the state would at least gain some money from this insistent trade.

The prohibitions against coffee were intended to safeguard the state finances. However, the continued smuggling and consumption of coffee meant that, instead of helping the economy, prohibitions could be more financially damaging than no bans at all, since the state also lost out on potential import duties while failing to keep out coffee. The disconnect between the desired objective and the actual reality helps to explain why prohibitions were issued and withdrawn repeatedly during the eighteenth century.

Bubbling Brews and Grinding Radicals[160]

The reactions to the prohibitions were immediate and elaborate, particularly in larger towns where the coffee drinking culture was firmly established. Poems and pamphlets published in conjunction with the prohibition periods drew extensively on the perceived the connection between coffee and femininity. In the ironic poem 'Elegy when the Goddess Cofféa Fled from the Swedish Lands the 31 July 1794', coffee was equated with female godliness. In one particularly interesting stanza, the fall of the goddess is related to her selfishness and her associations with, and favouritism of, smugglers.[161] Cofféa was also accused of having stripped the poor of clothes and food, reducing their lives to suffering. The poem was part of an interactive performance in commemoration of coffee that took place on 31st July 1794 at the Royal Djurgård's Spa. This was not the only event of its kind, and the disappearance of coffee in the 1790s was lamented, or greeted, with various staged rituals and events. The newspaper reported about a celebration that had taken place at a manor just outside Åbo, in the Finnish provinces. People of all varieties had been invited to Sundholm's Manor on 31st July, where coffee had been served until the whole store had been emptied. Music and the firing of cannons accompanied the event, which ended with the coffee equipment being ceremoniously covered in crape and buried in the ground to the sound of eight cannon salutes.[162] Although the coffee ban had been celebrated at Sundholm, in Åbo, the academic H.G. Porthan observed that, "[t]he new sumptuary decree still occupies the people's attention, we will see about the observance especially where certain Articles are concerned.... no article is so much opposed as the Coffee-prohibition".[163]

One of the most spectacular commemorations of coffee took place in 1799, just before the fourth prohibition. It was recorded by the court chronicler Baron Jonas af Nordin and illustrates how high culture was summoned to arms in the lamentation for coffee. He describes how a solemn farewell and burial procession for coffee utensils was to be performed outside of Stockholm. In order to make the scene more touching and imposing, the "musical art- and perspective painter Mr Abbé Vogler [would] in his inimitable orchestration perform a, for the grievous topic, well suited lamentation music".[164] Vogler's music was to be divided up into three parts: the sound of the bubbling coffee's goodbye, the ladies' goodbye to the delicious coffee, and the ladies and the coffee's mumbling, shrieking, and crying during the burial. The tickets for this spectacle would be free but solely handed to the "amateurs of coffee and the real connoisseurs of musical paintings".[165] These types of events suggest that coffee was not only a component of genteel society, but that the prohibitions gave rise to new cultural expressions. Coffee became something to gather around, as the bans were lamented or celebrated as part of a refined culture. It is telling that only the "amateurs of coffee", or the lovers of coffee, were welcome to this display of musical invention. Af Nordin further notes,

> [o]ur present so called coffeeists and anti-coffeeists are daily passionately arguing for or against this soon to be eclipsed beverage's harmfulness or excellency, it is everywhere an almost daily discussion topic now, in all our larger and smaller circles and societies.[166]

Whether celebrating or lamenting the bans, it is clear that the events triggered a highly emotional and engaged response. The public lamentations and lampoons lay the foundations for the rejectionist culture that developed around coffee and which kept challenging the prohibitions through continued coffee consumption.

Coffee-Drinking Diarists

Rejection and protest, or acceptance and rejoicing (visual, audible, and performed), were part of the female social interaction surrounding the prohibitions. Smaller, more intimate ceremonies were also performed at home, as revealed by the diary of Märta Helena Reenstierna. On the day of the prohibition, Reenstierna, a keen coffee drinker, noted in her diary:

> Thursday. Helen's name day and the last moment of the beloved Coffee in the Swedish World. In the afternoon we drank Coffee from the small beautiful and new Coffee pot for the first and the last time down in the Solitude [a small grove on her estate], some verses authored by Molin about Helen and the Coffee were also read.[167]

While these ceremonies were intended to mark a definite end to coffee consumption, they were often followed by transgression rather than abstention. As Christina Juliana Wargetin noted in her diary, "[f]rom this day coffee was forbidden but was used secretly everywhere until its use was liberated 2.5 years later by the accession of the king".[168] Reenstierna's diary reveals that she kept drinking coffee during the prohibition although she masked the consumption behind coded terms such as 'bonbon' and 'bean drink'. Initially she chose to drink her coffee alone, sometimes even out in the grounds to avoid scents giving rise to suspicion in her home.[169]

Meanwhile, tea replaced coffee as the drink of choice at social gatherings.[170] It was with displeasure that Lisa Mullberg lamented in her diary: "Mrs Hamm:st arrived with her girls, and stayed until the evening. We spoke of coffee the whole day but never got a cup, my oh my".[171] Over time, however, the diarists started to consume coffee with others, presumably as the knowledge of who else disobeyed the decree spread.[172] When the ban was renewed in 1799, Märta Helena Reenstierna no longer bothered to use code words. Instead, she explicitly described drinking coffee with numerous individuals, including at a large gathering in the home of tradesman Mazza during Pentecost 1801, where both coffee and punch were available in abundance.[173] At this point, coffee appears to have been drunk fairly openly at various occasions. Visiting a spa town in the summer of 1800, Jacobina Charlotta Munsterhjelm described how coffee was a regular and important part of the social interaction.[174] The diary accounts show how tentative transgressions during the early prohibitions were replaced by an increasingly brazen coffee consumption in the later period, as illegal coffee consumption moved from fields and private chambers to reception parlours. Even during the prohibitions, coffee was an important instrument of urban and rural refined culture and played a central role in genteel social interaction.[175]

In the diaries, coffee appears not merely at polite social occasions but also at various festive events organised for the servants, including name day celebrations and balls.[176] This indicates that coffee was also used as a tool to create trust and show appreciation for servants. Coffee thus seems to have been a means to create amiability not just within social groups but also between them. This use of coffee would have been particularly poignant during the prohibition periods when such coffee consumption spelled a joint crime.

Although the diaries offer good insight into how the consumption of coffee developed during the prohibition periods and how consumers reacted to the prohibitions, they only shed light on the gentry, and, to a lesser extent, their servants. In order to get to other types of consumers, it is necessary to consult other sources.

Police Convictions

The coffee prohibitions were not uniform throughout the eighteenth century but they changed over time, in response to altering conditions and new information. The 1766 ban was rather simplistic. It stipulated that the fine for coffee consumption was 100 Dal smt.[177] By the 1790s, the crime had been divided into three parts, each with a different fine; to drink coffee was punished with a fine of 2 Rdr, the punishment for preparing coffee was 10 Rdr, and if the beverage was intended for sale, the fine was doubled to 20 Rdr. Intriguingly, the prohibition also featured the introduction of triple fines for those consuming coffee in open social gatherings.[178] The sale of contraband coffee beans, which was categorised as a smuggling crime rather than a consumer crime, was punished by a considerably higher fine of 50 Rdr. Such subdivisions of the coffee crime indicate an increased sensitivity towards the various individuals involved in sustaining the illegal coffee consumption but also that their culpability varied in the eyes of the legislators. While the regulations in the 1790s were considerably more complex, they should not distract from the stark decline in coffee drinking fines, which had decreased drastically between the 1760s and 1790s (100 Dal Smt in 1766 equates roughly to 33 Rdr in 1799).[179] While most monetary fines for smuggling were increasing, those for coffee consumption were plummeting.

An explanation for the decreasing fines can be found in the people convicted of consuming coffee. Early coffee consumers can be difficult to track down as the cases were generally administered by local courts, and unlike in the 1790s, there are no central police records to consult. However, a particularly notable case has been passed down to us through the Supreme Court archives. In 1770, Britta Svensdotter was appealing her conviction for coffee drinking in Varberg some years previously. She confessed that she had indulged in coffee but objected to the harsh penalty.

> [I was] sentenced to a 100 D smt fine, because I one single time for 4 öre bought and made coffee. Most merciful King! I confess my transgression… I have numerous children and have fallen into the gravest poverty which means that I could only pay the considerable fines given to me through physical labour, which due to my weak health and constitution I could not endure, but would lead to death.[180]

Unfortunately, the Supreme Court verdict is missing, but Britta Svensdotter's plea points to the difficulty of enforcing such a harsh punishment for drinking coffee as more, and poorer, consumer groups turned to coffee drinking. With an increasing number of poorer consumers, the fines were found to be disproportionate and unsuited to the task.

Before turning to the police records, it is also worth pointing out that during the third prohibition period 1794–1796, there were attempts at modernising the punishment for people sentenced for sumptuary crimes. This modernisation involved publishing the names of convicted felons in the newspapers. Unlike the later attempts to systematically name and shame smugglers, these sumptuary shamings appear not to have taken off and lists appear only in two newspapers, in 1794 and 1795.[181] While the lists contained all kinds of sumptuary crimes, coffee convictions dominate. In total, 24 culprits had their names published, 22 of them for various coffee-related crimes (brewing, selling, and drinking). Moving into the police records, it quickly becomes evident that they were only a small fraction of the people actually convicted of coffee crimes.

In total, 536 coffee-related crimes were processed by the Stockholm Police during the 1794–1796 and 1799–1802 prohibition periods.[182] There were 129 cases during the first period and 407 during the second. The majority of the culprits were female, a dominance that becomes even more evident when omitting the retailing cases and solely focusing on the consumer crimes – preparing and drinking. Women were involved in 393 consumer cases; by contrast, men were involved in a mere 26.[183] These women mainly consisted of less well-to-do women: maids and spinners, as well as the wives and widows of sailors, coachmen, porters, tailors, girdlemakers, carpenters, and even a grave-digger's wife. In some cases, the women were so poor that they were unable to pay their fines, which meant that their punishments were converted to prison sentences, on bread and water, spanning 8–28 days.[184]

It should also be noted that a significant part of the women convicted of making coffee appear to have been maids in larger households. In these instances, the end-consumers were likely their master or mistress, but it was still the maid who faced the fines. There are indications, however, that many employers took it upon themselves to pay the fines of their maids.[185] Within these households, maids could acquire the skills to make coffee but also a taste for it, which they brought with them when they left service to set up their own households.[186]

Poor women appear to mainly have consumed coffee at home either with others or in solitude. Most common was to consume coffee in the company of a female friend, indicating that coffee played an important role in social encounters not just in elite polite company but also among those with restricted means. To engage in an illegal activity like coffee consumption together probably strengthened its role as a social glue. However, the police records also show that it was mobilised against former friends when relationships deteriorated. For instance, although rare, there are examples of friends informing on each other to the police.[187] Women were also drinking coffee with their families, generally either a husband or a daughter. Such coffee sessions appear to have been intimate bonding moments, between spouses, or mothers and their daughters. In addition to social coffee consumption, women also drank coffee on their own, seemingly as a part of a break from their chores or work. This break could take place in the home or a place of work and offer a short respite and enjoyment in a day of labour.[188]

Normally, the offences were discovered when the policemen were out on patrol or on some errand and walked into a house as the act of brewing or of drinking coffee took place.[189] On one such occasion, some police officers were searching for a person in a house at Badstugegatan, when they accidentally entered the wrong door. Behind it, they found the carpenter apprentice wife Lovisa Westerberg enjoying a cup of coffee.[190] The houses of the poorer inhabitants seem to have been particularly open – their privacy was not protected nor were they forewarned of the police's arrival. This did not prevent these women from consuming, however, and some even retained their coffee habit after a conviction, such as the visitor widow Helena Lindman and her daughter who were caught with coffee when the police came to inform them about the outcome of an earlier coffee trial against them.[191]

Poor women are overrepresented in the police records, which contain a few middling consumers but hardly any elite coffee consumers at all. This is not unique to Stockholm, but evidence from Linköping points to a similar situation there.[192] The police records show that coffee was consumed by a wider range of consumers than earlier research on the prohibitions has suggested. It also had an important social role for poor consumers, who used it as part of their social intercourse. Even during the prohibition, poor women kept drinking coffee although they were particularly exposed to the police interference.

The uneven enforcement of the prohibitions attracted comment early on. In 1770, one anonymous commentator complained:

> A Law without Execution is more damaging than no Law. … one could think, that during the past years, the Distinguished and Rich have been the most Law-abiding: for all my knowledge no one of a higher estate has been accused of a crime against the Sumptuary Decrees. …Could the rich and great have been abstaining from Drinking Coffee and fine Wines? If they should err, their crime in all regards will have been more damaging, because they are Examples and can cause provocation; Does it not indicate a clear preferential treatment that they have gotten away unpunished?… everyone knows how difficult, not to say impossible it is to sue the whole gentry. The accusing party is such a small person, what can he accomplish, even if he wanted to, when he has the entire Public against him… When the execution is quite difficult and hazardous, the Prohibitions should be cancelled.[193]

Even though the legislation was theoretically egalitarian, its enforcement was not. This was most likely related to the fact that the police were mainly concerned with controlling and monitoring the lower social classes of Stockholm in general, something that probably also affected their approach to the coffee bans.[194] Most of the constables also derived from the lower part of the socio-economic spectrum and many had previously worked as manservants, journeymen, and apprentices. Consequently, they were more accustomed to, and probably comfortable with, regulating their social equals and inferiors than they were with interfering with their social superiors.

The Club

While poor women clearly make up the main group of offenders in the Stockholm police records, they were not the only group to transgress. In order to illustrate that they were not the sole target for the prohibitions, it is useful to look at an event that took place in Stockholm in 1794. At a club in Stockholm, originally founded by foreign ministers in 1785, coffee could still be drunk by the members, who were both foreign representatives and Swedish nationals.[195] The Club "[enjoyed] the immunities generally attached to the Diplomatic Character".[196] However, according to the British diplomat Henry John Spencer (1770–1795): "the general use of Coffee at the Club....was too publicly talked of and even toasted of in the presence of the Duke Regent".[197] The Duke Regent expressed his displeasure that Swedish nationals in particular were disobeying his wishes and he forbade the *maître d'hôtel* "to give Coffee to any person whatever at the Club, and threatened to shut the doors [of the Club] in case of disobedience".[198] The French Ambassador noted that this would probably be the end of the Club.[199] While the Spanish, Portuguese, and British Ambassadors handed in a protest to the government, Spencer went so far as to request to be removed from his post in Sweden.[200] As this episode shows, elite immunity from the Swedish laws only stretched so far and depended on goodwill from the establishment, in this case the Duke Regent. It indicates that even though the elite strove to find ways to circumvent the coffee prohibition, and the police were unwilling to charge them, the intention was nevertheless for the prohibitions to be universal, and transgression could be interpreted as a critique of the state and the ruler.

Depending on which sources are consulted, the answer as to who consumed coffee during the prohibitions looks very different. Diaries show that elite women maintained their consumption, police records demonstrate that poorer women joined them in their appreciation for the beverage, and letters make it clear that men hidden away in clubs found enjoyment in coffee, despite of the ban. Together, these sources suggest that by the 1790s, coffee consumption was something that most levels of society indulged in. Universal coffee drinking appears to have been primarily an urban phenomenon at this time, however, as there are few indications that coffee was in any extensive use in the countryside.[201] The unquenchable thirst for coffee in the towns is a sign of its importance as a social glue and an individual luxury. It seems likely that its illegal status actually helped to build social trust and cement relationships and probably also amplified its associations with exclusivity. Meanwhile, continued coffee smuggling and consumption caused the prohibitions to have the opposite effect of what was intended. They were not just unworkable, but even damaging as they caused the state to lose out on vital import revenues. A constant tug of war ensued between consumers and the authorities, which lasted throughout the eighteenth century.

★★★★★

When considering the reception and consumption of contraband, it is crucial to consider the characteristics of the goods themselves, how they fit into the economy and social sphere of the destination market, as well as their eventual adaptation and use. This is exemplified by the cases of worsteds and coffee, two very different types of wares with somewhat overlapping consumer markets.

Both worsteds and coffee were brought to Sweden as a result of the globalisation of trade and they were both prohibited on economic grounds. The economic grounds differed, however. While worsted was banned to protect a budding industry, coffee was prohibited to stem the flow of silver out of the kingdom for an unnecessary luxury good. Worsteds were in themselves not seen as problematic, but rather were considered to be materials suitable for Swedish consumers. The consumption of worsteds *per se* was thus not problematic, although it was clearly preferred that consumers would buy Swedish worsteds. Coffee, and its Swedish substitute 'Swedish coffee', by contrast, never came to gain the same acceptance from the authorities.

The different reasons for prohibiting worsteds and coffee are also reflected in the legislators' reactions to trespasses. Whereas contraband worsteds were used to prop up the Swedish market, coffee smuggling led to the dissolution of the prohibition itself, in order to at least salvage some state revenue. The difference lies in the expectations and the consequences of the prohibitions. In terms of worsteds, there was clearly an idea that the Swedish industry could eventually become competitive and be able to supply the domestic market; until then, some additional, albeit illegally supplied textiles were not considered overly problematic. By contrast, coffee could never be supplied from within the country and therefore there was no real solution to the issue, as import substitution was implausible at this point. Attempts to stifle the very consumption of coffee recurred through the period, but when they failed the decrees were simply dropped. This was also related to the fact that coffee, along with sugar, wine, and spirits, were the goods that contributed most to customs revenue at this time; they were the type of import wares Adam Smith referred to as "appropriate targets of taxation".[202] Contraband also affected the consumers and how they thought about their own consumption. The presence of foreign worsteds alerted the consumers to alternative cheaper options of higher quality than the textiles produced by domestic manufacturers. The illegality of coffee affected its consumption in a different way, as it appears to have been the basis of reinforcing relationships and trust. Further studies of other types of contraband would probably tell different stories, as different goods have their own specific roles in society. The cargoes hidden under the captain's floorboards thus feed into multiple narratives of material cultural exchange and development.

Notes

1 While coffee is quite straightforward, worsted needs some context. Worsted industry in the United Kingdom, came to be increasingly challenged during the eighteenth century by the import of cotton. Cotton cloth started to eat up the market, and the worsted manufacturers had to expand their export markets, at which point the Nordic countries became important markets for the worsteds. The dispersion of worsted to Sweden can thus be seen as a knock-on effect from the rise of cotton consumption in Britain.

2 Arjun Appadurai, 'Introduction: Commodities and the Politics of Value'; Anne Gerritsen and Giorgio Riello, eds., *The Global Lives of Things,* 14.

3 Olle Krantz and Lennart Schön, *Om den svenska konsumtionen under 1800- och 1900-talen* (Lund: Ekonomisk-historiska institutionen, Lund University, 1984); Christer Ahlberger and Magnus Mörner, 'Betydelsen av några latinamerikanska produkter för Sverige före 1810', *Historisk Tidskrift*, no. 1 (1993); Lars Magnusson and Klas Nyberg, *Konsumtion och industrialisering i Sverige 1820–1914. Uppsala 1995*, A Research Project (Uppsala: Ekonomisk-historiska institutionen, Uppsala University, 1995); Christer Ahlberger, *Konsumtionsrevolutionen 1 Om det moderna konsumtionssamhällets framväxt 1750–1900* (Göteborg: Humanistiska fakulteten, Göteborg University, 1996).

4 Heckscher, *Sveriges ekonomiska historia från Gustav Vasa*, 643.

5 Worsted, or stuff, is a type of woollen textile made from worsted yarn, a high-quality yarn that was combed rather than carded and tightly twisted, which together with the quality of the sheep's wool gives it a finer, harder appearance compared to carded wool, with its 'fluffier' texture. See: 'Worsted Knitting Yarn | Textile', https://www.britannica.com/technology/worsted-knitting-yarn, *Encyclopedia Britannica*, Accessed 1 March 2022.

6 Lennart Björkquist, *Jämtlands folkliga kvinnodräkter. Studier i den jämtska allmogens dräktskick under 1700-talet och 1800-talets förra hälft*, Skrifter utgifna af Kungl. Gustav Adolfs Akademien för folklivsforksning 7 (Uppsala: Appelbergs, 1941), 228 & 233; Marie Ulväng, *Klädekonomi och klädkultur. Böndernas kläder i Härjedalen under 1800-Talet* (Mörklinta: Gidlunds Förlag, 2012), 96; Seija Johnson, 'Fashion from the Ship: Life, Fashion and Fashion Dissemination in and around Kokkola, Finland in the 18th Century', in *Fashionable Encounters. Perspectives and Trends in Textile and Dress in the Early Modern Nordic World*, ed. Tove Engelhardt Mathiassen et al. (Oxford: Oxbow Books, 2014), 38–40; see also Seija Johnson, *I den folkliga modedräktens fotspår. bondekvinnors välstånd, ställning och modemedvetenhet i Gamlakarleby socken 1740–1800* (Jyväskylä: Jyväskylän yliopiston kirjasto, 2018).

7 For a discussion about the incorporation of manufactured textiles in peasant dress, see: Sigfrid Svensson, 'Svenska dräkten som bondeplagg', in *Gustavianskt. Studier kring den gustavianska tidens kulturhistoria* (Stockholm, 1932); Sigfrid Svensson, *Dräktlyx hos gotländsk allmoge 1793* (Stockholm: Ymer, 1933); Sigfrid Svensson, *Skånes folkdräkter. En dräkthistorisk undersökning 1500–1900*, Nordiska Museets Handlingar 3 (Stockholm, 1935); Svensson, *Bygd och yttervärld. Studier över förhållandet mellan nyheter och tradition.* For a discussion about the National Costume, see: Bergman, *Nationella dräkten. En studie kring Gustaf III:s dräktreform 1778*, 26.

8 Bjørn Sverre Hol Haugen, 'Virkningsfulle tekstiler - i østnorske bønders draktpraksiser på 1700-talet' (University of Oslo, 2014), 142, 153, & 181.

9 Lena Rangström, 'Gustaf III:s svenska dräktprojekt- en nationell reform i tiden', in *Nationalism och nationell identitet i 1700-talets Sverige*, ed. Åsa Karlsson and Bo Lindberg (Uppsala: Swedish Science Press, 2002). For a longer discussion about the attempts to grow silk in Sweden, see: Anders Johansson Åbonde, *Drömmen om svenskt silke* (Kungl. Skogs- och Lantbruksakademien, 2016).
10 Runefelt, *Att Hasta Mot Undergången*, 37–43 & 239–250.
11 Anonymous, *Reflexioner Wid En Anonym Auctors Tankar Om Sättet Til Wåra Swenska Manufacturers Uphjelpande* (Stockholm: Stockholm, tryckt hos Carl Stolpe, 1769), 5; '27 & 30 Jan 1794.', 1794, Kommerskollegium, Huvudarkivet, Handels- och manufaktur divisionens protokoll, A I fa, vol. 37a, Riksarkivet.
12 The contention has mainly focused on probate inventories and whether coffee use was limited to households owning coffee accessories: Ahlberger, *Konsumtionsrevolutionen 1*, 84–109; Ahlberger and Mörner, 'Betydelsen av några latinamerikanska produkter för Sverige före 1810', 102; Runefelt, *Att hasta mot undergången*, 227.
13 Emma C. Spary, *Eating the Enlightenment. Food and Sciences in Paris, 1670–1760* (Chicago & London: University of Chicago Press, 2012), 87.
14 Runefelt, *Att hasta mot undergången,* 146–147.
15 Knutsson and Hodacs, 'When coffee was banned'; Pia Lundqvist, 'Taste for Hot Drinks – the Consumption of Coffee and Tea in two Swedish Nineteenth-Century Novels', *History of Retailing and Consumption* 2, no. 3, 171–192 (2016). https://doi.org/10.1080/2373518X.2016.1241039
16 Woodruff Smith, *Consumption and the Making of Respectability, 1600–1800* (New York: Routledge, 2002), 125–126; Spary, *Eating the Enlightenment*, 77 & 80.
17 Runefelt, *Att hasta mot undergången*, 286; Annika Windal-Pontén, 'Kiär hustru, wackra barn, bodde uti ett palais- materialitet och identitet i hushållet von Linné' (Uppsala University, 2020), see chapter 2 'Medicin, moral, mode - vetenskapsidkarens formering av persona'.
18 Emma C. Spary, *Feeding France. New Sciences of Food, 1760–1815* (Cambridge: Cambridge University Press, 2014), 269.
19 K. J. Allison, 'The Norfolk Worsted Industry in the Sixteenth and Seventeenth Centuries'. *Bulletin of Economic Research*, 12 (1960), 73–83. https://doi.org/10.1111/j.1467–8586.1960.tb00007.x
20 Ursula Priestley, *The Fabric of Stuffs. The Norwich Textile Industry from 1565* (Norwich: Centre of East Anglian Studies, 1990), 7–9.
21 Berit Eldvik, Private Communication, 30 January 2017.
22 Lemire, *Fashion's Favourite*; Riello, *Cotton*.
23 John Taylor (T), 'History of Norwich Manufactures', *The Monthly Magazine* 6 (December 1798), 415; see also M. F. Lloyd Prichard, 'The Decline of Norwich', *The Economic History Review* 3, no. 3 (1951).
24 Priestley, *The Fabric of Stuffs*, 33–34.
25 Michael Nix, 'Norwich Textiles: a Global Story, 1750–1820', Norwich Castle Museum Saturday 5 December 2015; Lemire, *Global Trade,* 162.
26 Hol Haugen, 'Virkningsfulle Tekstiler', 125–140.
27 Priestley, *The Fabric of Stuffs,* 38–39.
28 Sven Gerentz, *Kommerskollegium och näringslivet, 1651–1951, minnesskrift* (Stockholm, 1951), 282.
29 Letter from Mr C Corkelke Customs House London, to Mr Tilson, 3 Apr 1729, SP 36, vol. 114, British National Archives.
30 Gerentz, *Kommerskollegium Och Näringslivet,* 240.
31 Gerentz, 267.
32 'Letter No 30, to Lord Suffolk, from De Visme, Stockholm, 1 August 1775', 1775, SP 95, vol.125, British National Archives.
33 Sven T. Kjellberg, 'Ull och ylle. Bidrag till den svenska yllemanufakturens historia' (Lund University, 1943), 414 & 417.

34 Kjellberg, 414 & 417; 'N. 69', Handels- & Manuf & Tull Deputs Betänkande För åren 1769–1770, 1769–1770, Borgareståndets arkiv, R1402, vol. 13, Riksarkivet, 4033.
35 'Kongl. maj:ts taxa, hwarefter stora sjö=tullen uppå alla inkommande waror bör erläggas och upbäras, 15 feb 1771' (1771); 'Kongl. maj:ts taxa, hwarefter stora sjö=tullen uppå alla inkommande waror bör erläggas och upbäras, 6 jun 1782' (1782); 'Kongl. maj:ts taxa, hwarefter stora sjö=tullen uppå alla inkommande waror beräknas och erlägges. gifwen Stockholm slott den 17 april 1799' (1799).
36 'Kongl. maj:ts och riksens commerce-collegii kungörelse, angående förbud emot utländskt kamulls=garns införsel. Gifwen Stockholm then 11 april 1785' (1785).
37 Kjellberg, 'Ull och ylle', 347.
38 'Letter 16 April 1798', 1798, Kollegiers m fl skrivelser till Kungl Maj:t, skrivelser från Kommerskollegiet, 9, vol. 269, Riksarkivet, 10.
39 Ibid. p.414 & 417; 'N. 69', Handels- & Manuf & Tull Deputs Betänkande För åren 1769–1770, 1769–1770, Borgareståndets arkiv, R1402, vol. 13, Riksarkivet, 4033.
40 Josiah Tucker, *Four Tracts, on Political and Commercial Subjects*, 3rd ed. (Glocester: R. Raikes, 1776), 41.
41 '25 June 1776', 1776, Justitieämbetet, Koncept, Huvudserien, BIIa:80, Riksarkivet.
42 'Letter to Lord Suffolk, from De Visme, Stockholm, 29 March 1776', 1776, SP 95, vol. 126, British National Archives.
43 'Letter to De Visme, from Lord Suffolk, 8 March 1776', 1776, SP 95, vol. 126, British National Archives.
44 'Letter to De Visme, from Lord Suffolk, 8 March 1776', 1776, SP 95, vol. 126, British National Archives.
45 'Letter to Lord Suffolk, from De Visme, Stockholm, 29 March 1776'.
46 'Letter 32, to Lord Suffolk, from De Visme, Stockholm, 2 August 1776', 1776, SP 95, vol.126, British National Archives.
47 *The Sessional Papers Printed by Order of the House of Lords. Reports from Commissioners: Hand-loom Weavers*, Vol. XXXVII (1840), 303.
48 Ursula Priestley, *The Letters of Philip Stannard, Norwich Textile Manufacturer (1751–1763)*. Vol. LVII (Norfolk Record Society, 1994), 93–97.
49 Peter Bull, 'Kjøbmand Peter Bull's optegnelser. et handelshus i Fredriksstad 1770–1800', in *Norsk tidskrift for genealogi, personalhistorie, biografi og litteraerhistorie*, ed. S.H. Finne-Grønn, vol. 1 (Christiania: Cammermeyers, 1910), 280.
50 Quoted in Hol Haugen, 'Virkningsfulle tekstiler ', 140f.
51 Hans Friedr Frick, 'Memorial 163, Götheborg, 18 Maj 1791', 1791, Äldre centrala tullarkiv, Generaltullarrendesocieteternas fullmäktige, m. fl., kansliet, Skrivelser från tullfiskaler E8, vol. 1, Riksarkivet; Ar Arvedsson, 'Memorial No 772, Uddevalla 25 Aug 1803', 1803, Äldre centrala tullarkiv, Generaltullarrendesocieteternas fullmäktige, m. fl., kansliet, Resefiskaler, E9, vol. 1, Riksarkivet. For similar accounts, see also: Frick, 'Memorial 163, Götheborg, 18 Maj 1791'.
52 See for example: 16 April 1787 & 1 Nov 1788, 'Kitee, no 578', 1788, Routsin kauppakollegion tuomiokirja-arkistoa, Rajatullioikeuksien tuomiokirjat, RTO, vol. 1, Kansallisarkisto, Finska riksarkivet.
53 Based on a compilation of cases from, 'Stora Siötulls Rättens Dombok', 1769, Stockholms rådhusrätt, Stora Sjötullen, Protokoll, A, vol.22, Stockholms Stadsarkiv.
54 Priestley, *The Fabric of Stuffs*, 34.
55 Berit Eldvik, *Möte med mode. Folkliga kläder 1750–1900 i Nordiska Museet* (Stockholm: Nordiska museets förlag, 2014), 44.
56 Berit Eldvik, Private Communication, 30 January 2017.
57 Anna-Karin Jobs Arnberg, Private Communication, 13 October 2017.
58 For a more extensive discussion about the conditions for the introduction of a national costume, see Chapter 2.
59 Bo Lindberg, 'Introduktion: nationalism och nationell identitet i 1700-talets Sverige', in *Nationalism och nationell identitet i 1700-talets Sverige*, ed. Åsa Karlsson and Bo Lindberg (Uppsala: Swedish Science Press, 2002), 12–14.

60 Lena Rangström, 'Den svenska hovdräkten - nationell och europeisk', in *Hovets dräkter*, ed. Lena Rangström (Stockholm: Livrustkammaren, 1994), 16–18.
61 '8 July 1778', 1778, Kommerskollegium, Huvudarkivet, Registratur, Huvudserie, BIa, vol. 184, Riksarkivet.
62 '9 June 1778', 1778, Kollegiers m fl skrivelser till Kongl Mayt, skrivelser från Kommerskollegium, 9, vol. 205, Riksarkivet.
63 '8 July 1778.'
64 Kollegiers m fl skrivelser till Kongl Mayt, skrivelser från Kommerskollegium, 9, vol. 205, Riksarkivet.
65 Gustav Johan Ehrensvärd, *Dagboksanteckningar förda vid Gustaf III:s hof af Friherre Gustaf Johan Ehrensvärd*, 2nd ed. Vol. 1. 2 vols (Stockholm: P.A. Norstedt & Söners förlag, 1878), 229.
66 'Letter 16 April 1798', Kollegiers m fl skrivelser till Kungl Maj:t, skrivelser från Kommerskollegium, 9, v. 269, Riksarkivet.
67 'Letter 7 Aug 1798.', Kommerskollegium, huvudarkivet, Kongliga brev och remisser huvudserie, E Ia, vol. 116, Riksarkivet.
68 In 1810, 90% of the Swedish population was living in the countryside, and the proportion would have been even larger around 1778. http://ortshistoria.se/nedladd/befolkn_txt/befolkning_1570–2000_andel.txt, accessed 24 Oct 2019.
69 Rangström, 'Den svenska hovdräkten', 18.
70 Mikael Alm, 'Making a Difference: Sartorial Practices and Social Order in Eighteenth-Century Sweden,' *Costume* 50, no. 1 (2016), 45.
71 Leif Runefelt, 'Grå bonde, blå bonde: Den globala indigomarknaden som etiskt problem på svenska landsbygden kring sekelskiftet 1800'. in *Det svenska begäret - Sekler av lyxkonsumtion*, ed. Klas Nyberg and Paula von Wachenfeldt (Stockholm: Carlsson Bokförlag, 2015), 123.
72 Eldvik, *Möte med mode*, 44; Anna-Karin Jobs Arnberg, Private Communication, 13 October 2017.
73 Eldvik, *Möte med mode*, 46.
74 Anna-Karin Jobs Arnberg, Private Communication, 13 October 2017.
75 This type of recycling of good quality fabrics was fairly common in the nineteenth century and helped to compensate for supply shortages, as discussed in Kristina Lilja and Pernilla Jonsson, 'Inadequate Supply and Increasing Demand for Textiles and Clothing: Second-Hand Trade at Auctions as an Alternative Source of Consumer Goods in Sweden, 1830–1900', *The Economic History Review* 0, no. 0 (2019).
76 Anna-Karin Jobs Arnberg, Private Communication, 13 October 2017; Anna-Karin Jobs Arnberg, 'Un-Titled' (MA thesis, Uppsala University, forthcoming).
77 Anna-Karin Jobs Arnberg, Private Communication, 13 October 2017.
78 'Sammanträde Protocoll, 7 Juni 1793' 1793, Kollegiers m fl skrivelser till Kungl. Maj:t, Skrivelser från landshövdingar, ämnesordnade handlingar, ang. Överflöd och yppighet, C, vol. 25, Riksarkivet.
79 'Mörskom', 1793, Kollegiers m fl , landshövdingars skrivelder till Kungl. Majt. Ämnesordnade, Handlingar ang. överflöd och yppighet, C, vol. 29, Riksarkivet; 'Gustav Adolph', 1793, Kollegiers m fl , landshövdingars skrivelder till Kungl. Majt. Ämnesordnade, Handlingar ang. överflöd och yppighet, C, vol. 29, Riksarkivet.
80 'Jämsä' 1793, Kollegiers m fl , landshövdingars skrivelder till Kungl. Majt. Ämnesordnade, Handlingar ang. överflöd och yppighet, C, vol.29, Riksarkivet.
81 'Pernå Och Kapellerna', 1793, Kollegiers m fl , landshövdingars skrivelder till Kungl. Majt. Ämnesordnade, Handlingar ang. överflöd och yppighet, C. vol. 29, Riksarkivet.
82 'Artsjö', 1793, Kollegiers m fl , landshövdingars skrivelder till Kungl. Majt. Ämnesordnade, Handlingar ang. överflöd och yppighet, C, vol. 29, Riksarkivet.
83 'Piexmäki', 1793, Kollegiers m fl , landshövdingars skrivelder till Kungl. Majt. Ämnesordnade, Handlingar ang. överflöd och yppighet, C, vol. 29, Riksarkivet.
84 'Rantasalmi', 1793, Kollegiers m fl , landshövdingars skrivelder till Kungl. Majt. Ämnesordnade, Handlingar ang. överflöd och yppighet, C, vol.29, Riksarkivet.

The same was observed in a parish on the other side of the Baltic Sea, in the county of Dalarna. See 'Folkärna', 1793, Kollegiers m fl skrivelser till Kungl. Maj:t, Skrivelser från landshövdingar, Ämnesordnade handlingar, ang. Överflöd och yppighet, C, vol. 28, Riksarkivet.

85 See for example, 'Gälared Socken', 1793, Kollegiers m fl skrivelser till Kungl. Maj:t, Skrivelser från landshövdingar, C, vol.26., Riksarkivet; 'Gunnarp Socken', 1793, Kollegiers m fl skrivelser till Kungl. Maj:t, Skrivelser från landshövdingar, C, vol. 26., Riksarkivet.

86 'Pernå Och Kapellerna', 1793, Kollegiers m fl , landshövdingars skrivelder till Kungl. Majt. Ämnesordnade, Handlingar ang. överflöd och yppighet, C. vol. 29, Riksarkivet.

87 'Piexmäki', 1793, Kollegiers m fl , landshövdingars skrivelder till Kungl. Majt. Ämnesordnade, Handlingar ang. överflöd och yppighet, C, vol. 29, Riksarkivet; Artsjö', 1793, Kollegiers m fl , landshövdingars skrivelder till Kungl. Majt. Ämnesordnade, Handlingar ang. överflöd och yppighet, C, vol. 29, Riksarkivet; 'Söderbärke', 1793, Kollegiers m fl skrivelser till Kungl. Maj:t, Skrivelser från landshövdingar, ämnesordnade handlingar, ang. Överflöd och yppighet, C,vol.28, Riksarkivet.

88 For some examples, see: 'Jemshög Socken', 1793, Kollegiers m fl skrivelser till Kungl. Maj:t, Skrivelser från landshövdingar, C, vol.26., Riksarkivet; 'Backaryd Socken' 1793, Kollegiers m fl skrivelser till Kungl. Maj:t, Skrivelser från landshövdingar, C, vol. 26., Riksarkivet.

89 For some examples, see: 'Slöinge Socken' 1793, Kollegiers m fl skrivelser till Kungl. Maj:t, Skrivelser från landshövdingar, C, vol.26., Riksarkivet; 'Saxe', 1793, Kollegiers m fl skrivelser till Kungl. Maj:t, Skrivelser från landshövdingar, ämnesordnade handlingar, ang. Överflöd och yppighet, C, vol. 28, Riksarkivet; 'Söderbärke' 1793, Kollegiers m fl skrivelser till Kungl. Maj:t, Skrivelser från landshövdingar, ämnesordnade handlingar, ang. Överflöd och yppighet, C, vol. 28, Riksarkivet.

90 'Jemshög Socken.', 1793, Kollegiers m fl skrivelser till Kungl. Maj:t, Skrivelser från landshövdingar, C, vol. 26., Riksarkivet.

91 Håkan Liby, *Kläderna gör upplänningen. Folkligt mode - tradition och trender* (Uppsala: Ord&Form, 1997), 5.

92 'Lappå (Brahestad)', 1793, Kollegiers m fl , landshövdingars skrivelder till Kungl. Majt. Ämnesordnade, Handlingar ang. överflöd och yppighet, C, vol. 29, Riksarkivet; Pulkkila, Piippola', 1793, Kollegiers m fl , landshövdingars skrivelder till Kungl. Majt. Ämnesordnade, Handlingar ang. överflöd och yppighet, C, vol. 29, Riksarkivet; 'Pyhäjoki', 1793, Kollegiers m fl, landshövdingars skrivelder till Kungl. Majt. Ämnesordnade, Handlingar ang. överflöd och yppighet, C, vol.29, Riksarkivet. For seizures of worsted belts, see: 'Routsin kauppakollegion tuomiokirjaarkistoa, Rajatullioikeuksien tuomiokirjat, RTO, v. 1, 'Kitee No 578, 7 Nov 1787', 'Kitee No. 580, 5 Feb 1798', Kansallisarkisto/Finska riksarkivet, Helsinki.

93 Great Britain's Parliament, House of Commons, *The Sessional Papers Printed by Order of the House of Lords. Reports from Commissioners: Hand-loom Weavers*, vol. XXXVII (1840), 302.

94 'Rantasalmi', 1793, Kollegiers m fl , landshövdingars skrivelder till Kungl. Majt. Ämnesordnade, Handlingar ang. överflöd och yppighet, C, vol. 29, Riksarkivet.

95 'Jemshög Socken.', 1793, Kollegiers m fl skrivelser till Kungl. Maj:t, Skrivelser från landshövdingar, C, vol.26., Riksarkivet.

96 'Tölö', 1793, Kollegiers m fl skrivelser till Kungl. Maj:t, Skrivelser från landshövdingar, Ämnesordnade handlingar, ang. Överflöd och yppighet, C, vol. 26, Riksarkivet.

97 'Thorhamn Socken', 1793, Kollegiers m fl skrivelser till Kungl. Maj:t, Skrivelser från landshövdingar, C, vol. 26, Riksarkivet.

98 'Mörskom', 1793, Kollegiers m fl , landshövdingars skrivelder till Kungl. Majt. Ämnesordnade, Handlingar ang. överflöd och yppighet, C, vol.29, Riksarkivet;

'Slöinge Socken' 1793, Kollegiers m fl skrivelser till Kungl. Maj:t, Skrivelser från landshövdingar, C, vol.26., Riksarkivet.

99 'Lillkyro Socken', 1793, Kollegiers m fl , landshövdingars skrivelder till Kungl. Majt. Ämnesordnade, Handlingar ang. överflöd och yppighet, C, vol.29, Riksarkivet.

100 'Jyväskyle', 1793, Kollegiers m fl , landshövdingars skrivelder till Kungl. Majt. Ämnesordnade, Handlingar ang. överflöd och yppighet, C, vol.29, Riksarkivet.

101 Björkquist, *Jämtlands folkliga kvinnodräkter,* 218.

102 John Styles, *The Dress of the People. Everyday Fashion in Eighteenth-Century England* (New Haven: Yale University Press, 2007), 9; Amanda Vickery, 'Mutton Dressed as Lamb? Fashioning Age in Georgian England,' *Journal of British Studies* 52 (October 2013), 858; Ulväng, *Klädekonomi och klädkultur,* see for example 120 & 223.

103 Sigfrid Svensson, *Bygd och yttervärld,* 80; Ulväng, *Klädekonomi och* klädkultur, 171.

104 'Frändefors, Brålanda, and Ryr Socken.', 1793 Kollegiers m fl , landshövdingars skrivelder till Kungl. Majt. Ämnesordnade, Handlingar ang. överflöd och yppighet, C, vol.27, Riksarkivet.

105 Ibid.

106 'Nås', 1793, Kollegiers m fl skrivelser till Kungl. Maj:t, Skrivelser från landshövdingar, ämnesordnade handlingar, ang. Överflöd och yppighet, C, vol.28, Riksarkivet; 'Jerna', 1793, Kollegiers m fl skrivelser till Kungl. Maj:t, Skrivelser från landshövdingar, ämnesordnade handlingar, ang. Överflöd och yppighet, C, vol.28, Riksarkivet; 'Rättvik', 1793, Kollegiers m fl skrivelser till Kungl. Maj:t, Skrivelser från landshövdingar, ämnesordnade handlingar, ang. Överflöd och yppighet, C, vol. 28, Riksarkivet.

107 'Leksand', 1793, Kollegiers m fl skrivelser till Kungl. Maj:t, Skrivelser från landshövdingar, ämnesordnade handlingar, ang. Överflöd och yppighet, C, vol.28, Riksarkivet.

108 Ten calamanco bodices have been identified in Leksand inventories 1771–1775: Personal correspondence: Johanna Gullback, 'Kalmink i Leksand', 23 February 2019. See also: Johanna Gullback, 'Karmink snörlif och wahlmars tjortil' (MA thesis, Uppsala University, 2012). In Nås parish, 12 calamanco bodices have been identified in inventories between 1758 and 1792, according to Margareta Jonth's survey of estate inventories in Nås. Anna-Karin Jobs Arberg, Personal Communication 23 February 2019; By contrast the first in Dala-Floda dates from 1840, see: Jobs Arnberg, 'Un-Titled'.

109 David T. Courtwright, *Forces of Habit: Drugs and the Making of the Modern World* (Cambridge, MA: Harvard University Press, 2009), 19–20.

110 Spary, *Eating the Enlightenment,* see Chapter 2 'From Curiosi to Consumers'.

111 Spary, 87, see also 88–90 for discussion on various coffee types.

112 Lisbet Koerner, 'Linnaeus' Floral Transplants', *Representations* 47 (Summer 1994), 157.

113 For a brief discussion about Swedish coffee houses, see: Dag Lindström, 'Leisure Culture, Entrepreneurs and Urban Space: Swedish Towns in a European Perspective, Eighteenth-Nineteenth Centuries', in *Leisure Cultures in Urban Europe, C. 1700–1870: A Transnational Perspective,* ed. Peter Borsay and Jan Hein Furnée (Oxford University Press, 2016), 149–150.

114 Runefelt, *Att hasta mot undergången,* 146–147.

115 Carl von Linné, *Kaffedrycken (Postus Coffeæ),* 1761, trans. Ejnar Haglund (Ekenäs, 1966), 13.

116 Lundqvist, 'Taste for Hot Drinks', 4.

117 'Påbud angående en consumtions-accis erläggande af thé, caffe, rök- och snus-tobak, samt puder' (1747).

118 Jacob Röding, *Tankar om de år 1756 förbudne waror, i synnerhet caffé* (Stockholm: Jör. Nyström, 1756); *Bondeståndets riksdagsprotokoll, 7, 1751–56* (Stockholm: 1963), 831; *Bondeståndets riksdagsprotokoll, 11, 1769* (Stockholm: 1975), 171.

119 Carl Gustaf Malmström, *Sveriges politiska historia från konung Karl XII:s död till statshvälfningen 1772*, 2nd ed., vol. 4 (Stockholm: P. A. Norstedt & söner, 1899), 254–255, & 287.
120 Bo Peterson, '"Yppighetens nytta och torftighets fägnad", pamflettdebatten om 1766 års överflödsförordning', *Historisk Tidskrift*, no. 1 (1981), 16.
121 Nicolas F. J. Eloy, *Af en medicinsk, så wäl som politisk fråga: om dageliga bruket at dricka caffe är nyttigt eller åtminstone oskyldigt i anseende til hälsan; om det kan förenas med statens bästa, eller om det i alla fall är skadeligt?*, trans. Unknown (Stockholm: Stolpiska Tryckeriet, 1783); 'Om Caffe', *Fahlu Weckoblad*, 25 August 1787, no 4; 'Om Caffe (Ur En Tysk Journal)', *Stockholms Posten*, 15 May 1800, no 109. On the rejection of these arguments in the riksdag: Peterson, '"Yppighetens nytta och torftighets fägnad", 16.
122 'Kongl. maj:ts nådige förordning, emot yppighet och öfwerflöd, gifwen Stockholm i råd-cammaren then 26 junii 1766' (1766).
123 'Sammanträde Protocoll, 7 Juni 1793', 1793, Kollegiers m fl skrivelser till Kungl. Maj:t, Skrivelser från landshövdingar, Ämnesordnade handlingar, ang. Överflöd och yppighet, C, vol.25, Riksarkivet.
124 For early uses of surrogates, see for example: '4 March 1768, H. J. Jung' 1768, Justitierevisionen, Besvärs- och Ansökningsmål, Utslagshandlingar, 1768 Mars, No 1/2–32, Riksarkivet. The first mention in a newspaper I have encountered occurred in *Götheborgs Allehanda*, 22 February 1782, no 16, 3.
125 *Inrikes Tidningar*, 5 July 1797, no 78, 1.
126 *Bihang till Dagligt Allehanda*, 1 February 1799, no 27; *Bihang till Dagligt Allehanda*, 18 April 1799, no 88, 8.
127 4 March 1768, H. J. Jung' 1768, Justitierevisionen, Besvärs- och Ansökningsmål, Utslagshandlingar, 1768 Mars, No 1/2–32, Riksarkivet.
128 Ibid.
129 'Kongl. maj:ts nådiga förordning, til hämmande af yppighet och öfwerflöd. Gifwen Stockholms slott den 1 januarii 1794.'; 'Kongl. maj:ts och riksens commerce-collegii kungörelse, angående förbud emot så kallat swenskt caffé. Gifwen Stockholm den 19 junii 1794.' (1794).
130 'Kong. maj:ts nådiga kungörelse, angående förnyande af det uti förordningen under den 1 januarii 1794 stadgade förbud emot caffés införsel och bruk' (1799). See also: 'Letter to Lord Grenville, from David Hailes, Stockholm 3 May 1799', FO 73, vol. 27, British National Archives.
131 'Letter to Lord Grenville, from David Hailes, Stockholm 3 May 1799', FO 73, vol. 27, British National Archives.
132 Ulric Nordensköld, *Afhandling om nyttan för Sverige af handel och nybyggen i Indierna och på Africa* (Stockholm: Peter Hesselberg, 1776), 3. See also Eric Schnakenbourg, 'Sweden and the Atlantic: The Dynamism of Sweden's Colonial Projects in the Eighteenth Century', in *Scandinavian Colonialism and the Rise of Modernity. Contributions to Global Historical Archaeology*, ed. Naum M. Nordin and et al. (New York: Springer, 2013).
133 Essén, *Johan Liljencrantz som handelspolitiker*, 6.
134 'Letter to Marquis of Carmarthen, from Charles Keene, 31 Aug 1784, Stockholm' 1784, FO 73, vol.4, British National Archives.
135 Schnakenbourg, 'Sweden and the Atlantic', 239–240f.
136 'Kommittée Ang Förordning Mot Yppighet Och Överflöd, 1793'. ÄK 817, v. 1, Riksarkivet.
137 Leos Müller, 'Kolonialprodukter i Sveriges handel och konsumtionskultur, 1700–1800', *Historisk Tidskrift* 124, no. 2 (2004), 245.
138 'Påbud angående en consumtions-accis erläggande af thé, caffe, rök- och snus-tobak, samt puder' (1747).
139 Spary, *Eating the Enlightenment*, 94.
140 In July 1799, 12,453 pounds of coffee beans (c. 5292.5 kg) were exported to Hamburg and a few months later an additional 3,457 pounds (1455kg) followed. See: '19

Aug 1799' & '30 Sep 1799', Allm. verks skrivelser till Kungl. Majt, Generaltulldirektionen, vol. 249, Riksarkivet.

141 Leos Müller, 'Kolonialprodukter i Sveriges handel och konsumtionskultur', 241.

142 *Borgarståndets Riksdagsprotokoll, 11 1755–1756, Första delen*, 359.

143 Database based on 1769 Customs Court Records, Stockholm.'Stora Siötulls Rättens Dombok', 1769, Stockholms rådhusrätt, Stora Sjötullen, Protokoll, A, v.22, Stockhollms Stadsarkiv.

144 'Stora Siötulls Rättens Dombok', 1769, Stockholms rådhusrätt, Stora Sjötullen, Protokoll, A, v.22, Stockhollms Stadsarkiv.

145 Ibid., 665–666.

146 Ibid., 625–627, 665–666.

147 'Stora Siötulls Rättens Dombok', 1800, Stockholms rådhusrätt, Stora Sjötullen, Protokoll, A, vol. 23, Stockholms Stadsarkiv.

148 23 Juli 1800, 'Stora Siötulls Rättens Dombok', 1800, Stockholms rådhusrätt, Stora Sjötullen, Protokoll, A, vol. 23, Stockholms Stadsarkiv, 398.

149 This seizure was made on the estate Rosenvik in Kongl. Djurgården. At the time of the confiscation, it is unclear who the owner of the property was, as various sources give different owners. The same thing can also be said for the coffee beans, and eventually, it was decided that the owner was Johanna Elfving, daughter of the previous owner of Rosenvik and wife of the current owner Abraham Elfving, as discussed in Chapter 4. However, in the accounts and later also in the newspapers, she went under the pseudonym Jeanette Hedengren. Johanna confessed that the beans had arrived at the estate by sea and it is possible to speculate that it was her husband who had arranged the shipping from abroad. See: 'Stora Siötulls Rättens Dombok'.1800, 1029; Arvid Ahnfelt, *Ur svenska hofvets och aristokratiens lif. skildringar hemtade i arkiven på Säfstaholm, Eriksberg och Sjöholm m. fl. enskilda och offentliga samlingar*, vol. 3, 7 vols (Norrköping, 1880), 216; 'Till underdånigste följe af kongl. maj:ts nådiga förordning till förekommande af lurendrägerier och tullförsnillning af d n 6 april 1799'.

150 'Stora Siötulls Rättens Dombok', 1769, Stockholms rådhusrätt, Stora Sjötullen, Protokoll, A, v.22, Stockhollms Stadsarkiv.

151 'Linköping 1799–1802', 1799–1803, Kommerskollegium, advokatfiskalskontoret, Årsberättelser lurendrejerimål, Cb4, vol. 1, Riksarkivet.

152 This figure has been retrieved from https://ortshistoria.se, Accessed 11 October 2018.

153 'Kongl. maj:ts nådige förordning angående wißa utrikes warors sa wäl lösgifwande ifrån förbud til införsel som beläggande med mindre manufactur fonds och andre afgifter' (1761).

154 'Kongl. maj:ts bref til hof-rätterne, commerce-collegium och gen. tull-direction, at förordningen af d. 26 julii 1766, rörande yppighets och öfwerflöds hämmande, tils widare måtte hwila, i den del, som angår införande och förtullande af caffe-bönor i riket, 23 oct 1769' (1769).

155 Ibid.

156 'Kongl. maj:ts nådiga warning, emot öfwerträdelser af deå den 1 januarii 1794 utfärdade förordning til hämmande af yppighet och öfwerflöd. Gifwen Drottningholms slott den 9 julii 1795' (1795), *Fahlu Weckoblad*, 22 August 1795, no 23.

157 'Kongl. maj:ts nådiga kungörelse, angående caffes införande och nyttjande tils widare. Gifwen Stockholms slott d 24 nov 1796' (1796).

158 'Kongl. maj:ts nådiga kungörelse om caffés införsel och bruk. Gifwen Stockholms Slott den 6 april 1802.' (1802). Although it should be noted that there was a final coffee prohibition period 1817–1823, which lies outside of the scope of this book.

159 Hedvig Elisabet Charlotta, *Hedvig Elisabeth Charlottas Dagbok.*, ed. Cecilia af Klercker, vol. 7 (Stockholm: Norstedt, 1936), 172.

160 Due to the availability of material, the following discussion looks primarily at material from Stockholm in the 1790s.

161 C. J. Hellman, *Sorge-tal då gudinnan cofféa flygtade ur Svea land den 31 julii 1794. hållet vid Kongl. djurgårds helso-frunnen i en talrik samling af bägge könen, samma dag* (Stockholm: And Jacobson Nordström, 1794), 17.
162 '-', *Stockholms Posten*, 26 August 1794, no 193, 4.
163 Henrik Gabriel Porthans, Henrik Gabriel Porthans Bref till Mathias Calonius, vol. 1, *Skrifter Utgifna Af Svenska Literatursällskapet I Finland* (Helsinki: Tidnings- & Tryckeri-Aktiebolagets Tryckeri, 1886), 61.
164 Ahnfelt, *Ur svenska hofvets och aristokratiens lif*, 120.
165 Ahnfelt, 120; Unfortunately, it has so far not been possible to confirm if this spectacular event took place.
166 Ahnfelt, 120.
167 Reenstierna, *Årstadagboken*, 75.
168 1 Aug 1794, 'Christina Juliana Wargentin dagbok' 1794, in https://stockholmskallan.stockholm.se/post/10064, *Stockholmskällan*, Accessed 11 December 2018.
169 Reenstierna, *Årstadagboken*, 75. For more coffee consumption, see 100, 107, 111, 120.
170 Reenstierna, 86, 117; 15, 23 Aug, 14 , 18 Sep 1, 22 Oct, 1794 'Fru Lisa Mullbergs Dagbok' 1794, Ämnessamlingen, Dagböcker, vol.9, Nordiska Museets Arkiv.
171 23 Sep 1794, 'Fru Lisa Mullbergs Dagbok'.
172 Reenstierna, *Årstadagboken*, 100, 107, 111, 120; 15 Dec 1794, 19 Feb 1795 and 22 Aug 1796, 'Fru Lisa Mullbergs Dagbok'. For a similar development, see also: Jacobina Charlotta Munsterhjelm, *Jacobina Charlotta Munsterhjelms Dagböcker 1799–1801 Dagbok*, ed. Bo Lönnqvist (Helsingfors: Svenska Litteratursällskapet i Finland, 1970), 29, 71, 72 & 73.
173 Reenstierna, 199, 248; 'handelsman Mazza', probably refers to the Italian trader Joseph Mazza, who was based in Rosenadlerska huset on Mynttorget together with J. A. Théel, discussed in the previous chapter.
174 Munsterhjelm, 71, 72, & 73.
175 Runefelt, *Att hasta mot undergången*, 146–147; Christer Ahlberger and Magnus Mörner, 'Betydelsen Av Några Latinamerikanska Produkter För Sverige Före 1810', 102.
176 Munsterhjelm. 84; Reenstierna, Årstadagboken, 264.
177 'Kongl. maj:ts nådige förordning, emot yppighet och öfwerflöd, Gifwen Stockholm i råd-cammaren then 26 junii 1766' (1766).
178 'Kongl. maj:ts nådiga förordning, til hämmande af yppighet och öfwerflöd. Gifwen Stockholms Slott den 1 januarii 1794.'(1794) §10.
179 100 Dal smt in 1766 corresponds roughly to 33 Rdr in 1799. See: http://historicalstatistics.org/Jamforelsepris.htm, Accessed 12 December 2018
180 '21 Feb 1770, Britta Svensdotter & Börje Svenson', 1770, Justitierevisionen, Besvärs- och Ansökningsmål, Utslagshandlingar, 1770 Feb, no 45, Riksarkivet.
181 'Förteckning på personer som förbrutit sig mot yppighet och öwerflöds förordningen', *Dagligt Allehanda*, 8 November 1794, no 256; 'Förteckning på de personer, hwilka hos öfwer=ståthållare=embetet i stockholm ytterligare blifwit sakfällde för förbrytelser emot kongl. maj:ts nådiga förordning emot yppighet och öfwerflöd af d. 1 januarii 1794', *Dagligt Allehanda*, 1 August 1795, no 172.
182 Anna Knutsson and Hanna Hodacs, 'When coffee was banned'; Anna Knutsson, and Hanna Hodacs (2019–2020), Coffee Crimes in Stockholm Police Records 1794–6, 1799–1802, [unpublished database], Uppsala University.
183 Anna Knutsson and Hanna Hodacs, 'When coffee was banned'.
184 'Diarium', 1794, vol.21, Överståthållarämbetet För Polisärenden, Äldre poliskammaren, Diarium, CIa1, 900; 'Diarium', 1795, vol.22, ibid, 28; Anna Knutsson and Hanna Hodacs, 'When coffee was banned'.
185 Anna Knutsson and Hanna Hodacs, 'When coffee was banned'.
186 Knutsson and Hodacs.
187 Knutsson and Hodacs.
188 Knutsson and Hodacs.

189 Diarium, 1794, vol. 21, Överståthållarämbetet För Polisärenden, Äldre poliskammaren, Diarium, CIa1, Stockholms Stadsarkiv, 898, 921, 938, 991, & 1051.
190 5 mar 1801, Protokoll (Askling), 1801, vol.46, Överståthållarämbetet För Polisärenden Äldre poliskammaren, Protokoll, A Ia1, Stockholms Stadsarkiv.
191 Diarium 1799, vol.26, Överståthållarämbetet För Polisärenden, Äldre poliskammaren, Diarium, CIa1, Stockholms Stadsarkiv, 807 & 987.
192 'Linköping 1799–1802'. 1799–1803, Kommerskollegium, advokatfiskalskontoret, Årsberättelser lurendrejerimål, Cb4, vol. 1, Riksarkivet.
193 '-,' *Stockholms Oordenteligheter*, vol. 8 1770, 59–60.
194 Tobias Osvald, *Stadens gränsplatser. Kungliga Poliskammaren och vardagens omstridda rum i Stockholm, 1776–1835* (Uppsala: Uppsala University Press, 2022), 69–74.
195 'Letter, n. 3, to Buchot commissaire des relations exterieur de la republique, from J. Gummer, Stockholm 10 Brumaire, L'an 3 de La Republique', 1794, Correspondance Consulaire, Stockholm 1792-Septembre 1799, vol. 3, La Courneuve, Archives des Affaires Étrangers, Paris, 115
196 'Letter to Lord Grenville, from Henry John Spencer, Stockholm 31st Oct 1794', FO 73, vol. 18, British National Archives.
197 Ibid.
198 Ibid.
199 'Letter, n. 3, to Buchot commissaire des relations exterieur de la republique, from J. Gummer, Stockholm 10 Brumaire, L'an 3 de La Republique'.
200 'Letter to Lord Grenville, from Henry John Spencer, Stockholm 31st Oct 1794'.
201 'Folkärna' 1793, Kollegiers m fl skrivelser till Kungl. Maj:t, Skrivelser från landshövdingar, ämnesordnade handlingar, ang. Överflöd och yppighet, C, vol. 28; 'Eds, Håblo, Töftedal and Nössemark Socken', 1792, Kollegiers m fl skrivelser till Kungl. Maj:t, Skrivelser från landshövdingar, ämnesordnade handlingar, ang. Överflöd och yppighet, C, vol.27, Riksarkivet; 'Högsäter', 1793, Kollegiers m fl skrivelser till Kungl. Maj:t, Skrivelser från landshövdingar, Ämnesordnade handlingar, ang. Överflöd och yppighet, C, vol.27, Riksarkivet; Among those who mention that it does not exist are: 'Alingsås', 1793, Kollegiers m fl skrivelser till Kungl. Maj:t, Skrivelser från landshövdingar, Ämnesordnade handlingar, ang. Överflöd och yppighet, C, vol. 27, Riksarkivet; 'Lena, Långared, Fullestad, Bergstena', 1792, Kollegiers m fl skrivelser till Kungl. Maj:t, Skrivelser från landshövdingar, Ämnesordnade handlingar, ang. Överflöd och yppighet, C, vol. 27, Riksarkivet.
202 Quoted in Häggqvist, 'On the Ocean of Protectionism', 152.

6

SMUGGLING AND THE PERPETUAL TRADE WAR

The second half of the eighteenth century was a period of commercial rivalry between the European states, which led to a boom in global trade and evolving manufacturing industries. It also inspired states to take control over their domestic markets, to strengthen the commercial nation, and to make it impervious to unwanted foreign competition. This could involve the erection of trade barriers and the introduction of high import duties, but it could also involve an active support of smuggling. So far, this book has explored how smuggling manifested in Sweden and the various effects it had on domestic policy, society, and culture. In this final chapter, the attention turns back to where it started, inter-state commercial competition, in order to consider how smuggling in and out of Sweden appears from an international perspective. Studying how Sweden was perceived by other states is all the more important in light of recent scholarship on the role and impact of small states on international trade competition.[1] Three states in particular will be the focus of this chapter: Sweden, Great Britain, and France. It is difficult to comprehend their perceptions of the contraband trade without first understanding how they were involved in commercial competition.

Great Britain and Sweden were significant trading partners in the middle of the eighteenth century, but the two countries had a strained relationship despite this extensive trade, something that impeded British export to Sweden.[2] Instead, Sweden's true loyalties lay with their old ally, France, another important trading partner, particularly from the 1770s onwards.[3] Meanwhile, Great Britain and France were involved in a particularly energetic trade rivalry.[4] On both sides, the trade conflict was perceived as "a kind of warfare" or a "*guerre perpétuelle*".[5] This Anglo-French trade rivalry also came to affect their various trading partners, amongst them Sweden.

Sweden had in the 1780s joined the League of Armed Neutrality, which was set up as a way to sidestep the Anglo-French battle for hegemony.[6] While this

DOI: 10.4324/9781003226031-6

contributed to making Sweden an important shipping nation, Swedish carriers never managed to exploit neutrality fully due to Sweden's relative isolation in international politics and its lack of "commercial interdependencies".[7] However, Sweden was still able to profit from the neutral trade during short periods.[8] Swedish neutrality is important to keep in mind when approaching its trade relationships, particularly during times of war, although as will be seen, neutrality in form did not always correspond to neutrality in content. While Sweden in theory was a neutral actor connecting two nations interlocked in a war, pre-existing alliances and associations affected how trade was conducted and what was seen as appropriate commercial behaviour.

In this way, Sweden was directly involved in European inter-state commercial competition, both through its neutral and normal trade activities. Swedish trade also had an indirect effect on commercial competition due to the produce it exported: iron, tar, and timber materials used to expand manufacturing industries and trading fleets in other countries, and herring to feed the slave plantations in the Americas.[9] These were goods that in various ways could be used to strengthen commercial competitiveness and attracted a governmental interest. Sweden was thus an important trading partner for Britain, as well as a French ally, which positioned the country in the middle of their perpetual trade war.

Drawing on consular and ambassadorial correspondence, this chapter asks how smuggling in and out of Sweden was perceived by Sweden's trading partners, and by representatives of the Swedish government, and how it fits into the inter-state commercial narrative. Additionally, the chapter also examines who the transnational state actors were who provided information about smuggling, and how they influenced what information was passed on.

The British Perspective – Pursuing the Fickle Trade Balance

> The country of Sweden has no considerable manufactures, and yet they have a very great trade, and are very strong in shipping; the reason is, the produce of their land, notwithstanding its northern situation and barren soil, is an immense treasure, and in a great measure, makes up for their want of manufactures. ...Their mines of copper and iron are very valuable indeed, ... and which will support Sweden, perhaps, to the end of time. ... Without this, Sweden...would not be able, on any terms, to import such great quantities of the manufactures and product of other countries as they now do: had they not copper and iron to pay with, they could never import such quantities of wine and brandy, wrought silks, and fine linens, from France and Holland; or of broad cloth, fine stuffs, wrought iron and brass, clock-work and watch-work, with other things, from England; but their copper and iron supply them with all things, and the ballance is always very much in their favour ....The interest of England, in the trade of Sweden, may be computed by the necessity of their commodities to us, and the vent of our's [sic] there.[10]

Sweden and Britain had a longstanding trade relationship, which became more intensive during the eighteenth century as exports to Britain came to dominate the Swedish trade. Two trade treaties signed in 1654 and 1661 respectively laid the foundations for these trade relations.[11] During the early eighteenth century, the British cemented their control of the Baltic and the North Sea, replacing the former Dutch dominance.[12] While Britain was establishing its trade dominance in the north, Sweden attempted to gain greater autonomy by introducing progressively stricter trade regulations. Heavy duties had already been placed on the importation of British woollen goods in the 1680s, and in 1724 the Swedish Navigation Act appeared, which caused further disturbance as it regulated the shipping in Sweden's favour.[13] Further duties were placed on manufactured goods in 1726–1727 and 1734–1735. This was the beginning of a restrictive import policy which particularly affected Britain, as Sweden's greatest trading partner. By the middle of the century, nearly all British manufactures were prohibited for import in Sweden.[14] Meanwhile, 88% of all Swedish iron export went to Britain. Although this trade declined from the middle of the century, by 1800, 78% of the Swedish iron export still went to the United Kingdom.[15] This created a highly irregular trade balance for both countries.

While this imbalance was desirable from a Swedish perspective, it caused a lot of consternation in Britain. Britain's poor trade balance against Sweden attracted much comment and there were ongoing discussions about taking action against the Swedes, although nothing ever realised.[16] At the end of the Seven Years' War, Britain attempted to free itself from its dependency on Swedish iron by scaling up its iron importation from Russia and developing iron mines in the colonies. Despite these attempts, Britain never fully managed to escape the need for the high-quality Swedish bar-iron.[17] Following the end of the Seven Years' War, Britain also gained an increasing share of the long-distance trade in exotic goods, which were in demand in Sweden, but the trade imbalance persisted.[18] According to contemporary commentators, by 1764, the adverse trade balance against Britain might have been as high as £224 000. [19]

During the 1760s, Sir John Goodricke, the British Ambassador to Sweden, attempted to secure a better trade treaty with Sweden which, it was hoped, would alleviate the situation. While Goodricke had hoped that with the Caps taking power in the Swedish riksdag in 1765/66, it might be possible to push through a more liberal trade policy, he quickly realised that this would be more difficult than he had originally envisioned.[20] Sweden had for a long time been dependent on subsidies from France which it would certainly lose if it negotiated a more favourable trade treaty with Britain. In order to secure a better trade deal with Sweden, it would therefore be necessary for Britain to pay subsidies in lieu of those from France, something they were unwilling to do. To add insult to injury, Goodricke's trade treaty also asked for the deregulation of the protectionist legislation in place to protect the Swedish manufacturers.

To the Cap Party, who were struggling to remain in power while trying to impose unpopular deflationary politics to salvage the Swedish finances, the

British trade treaty was a most unattractive offer.[21] This was not for lack of trying on Goodricke's part, and in 1765, he wrote back to Britain that his attempts to improve the British trade conditions had led to a situation whereby "[a]ll the French party and half of ours think I have a secret Design to ruin all their Manufactures".[22] Historian Michael Roberts, who has investigated these deliberations, has argued that for both Goodricke and Lord Sandwich, who was in charge of the trade negotiations on the British side, the trade treaty was important primarily as a political tool rather than in its own right.[23] While the liberation of regulation and a strengthening of Britain's position in Swedish trade might be desirable, particularly for Goodricke's career as a British ambassador, it might not, strictly speaking, have been necessary, as what was lost in legal trade could at least in part be regained through smuggling.[24] As Adam Smith would comment a few years later, the reduction of legal trade did not mean an end to trade but only that it was pushed underground.[25]

The Inestimable Smuggling

The underground trade, particularly in British manufactured goods, can be observed in reports about the state of trade submitted to the British government by diplomats and ambassadors in Sweden. In 1773, two years after the introduction of Sweden's thus-far tightest import restrictions, a questionnaire was issued to Sir Goodricke about the role of British trade in the country. He was first asked to outline a general estimate of the imports and exports to Sweden and what articles they consisted of. In his reply, Goodricke observed:

> The British Imports to Sweden are not to be learnt from any papers or accounts that can be procured in Sweden, because their [sic] manufactures which are prohibited are nevertheless Imported privately by Smuglers [sic] to a very great Value, In so much that a thousand Dozen of readymade Shirts were Smuggled into Gottenburg [sic] in one year (from Ireland) and the Swedish Ships that go from London to Stockholm are always full of contraband Goods![26]

He also took the opportunity to give reassurances that the British merchandise that did not interfere with Swedish industry would soon be received with more openness, a promise that never came to fruition. In addition, Goodricke assured the government that "French Manufactures are equally prohibited with ours".[27]

Goodricke was not the only one to supply the government with this type of report. Later in the same year, the Secretary of Legation, Charles Tullman, submitted several documents outlining the conditions of trade on the request of Henry Howard, 12th Earl of Suffolk, usually referred to in the correspondence as Lord Suffolk.[28] A little later in the period, the consuls also started to include notes about the smuggling trade in their regular reports. Such consular reports repeatedly noted that all kinds of British goods were clandestinely landed in

Sweden.[29] However, these reports about the British-Swedish contraband trade are extremely vague. They repeatedly stressed that, while smuggling was ongoing and might aid British trade, it was simply not possible to give a coherent image of the trade between the two nations. According to the reports, the smuggling trade, while inestimable, should inspire hope that the trade balance was not as bad as the official figures indicated.

The Challenges of Tea Smuggling

The British Government was particularly concerned about the tea smuggling from Sweden to the British Isles, a topic that received ample attention by contemporary writers and commentators. Most of the leaflets and books identified Sweden, and particularly Gothenburg, as the source of these illicit leaves.[30] In more recent times, this trade has also attracted the attention of historians, who have estimated the expanse of the smuggling, and explored the networks that enabled it.[31]

In contemporary Foreign Office reports, the Swedish contraband trade in tea was depicted as a threat to British economy, exacerbating the already poor trade balance. In 1763, Sir John Goodricke calculated that the illegal tea export from Sweden to Britain and the Channel Islands amounted to a staggering £800,000.[32] The "damnified teas imported from Gottenburgh" thus cost the British state considerable sums in lost revenue.[33]

In 1784, the duty on tea was finally reduced through the Commutation Act. The reason was the excessive tea smuggling, which had been exposed by the Eden Commission in 1783. The commission had deemed it impossible to stop the smuggling and suggested that the only solution was to decrease the tea duty dramatically. This would at least secure the state some import revenue on the tea trade.[34] In this way, smuggling could undermine the integrity of economic policy to the extent of making it unsustainable.

British reports about Swedish smuggling are dominated by the issue of the trade balance. Both ambassadorial and consular reports suggest that smuggling to Sweden could alleviate Britain's trading disadvantages, while the tea smuggling to Britain had the opposite effect. Consequently, the contraband trade was seen to further British interests through enabling a better trade balance, but it could also undermine British economic integrity. The ambassadors', envoys', and consuls' accounts depict Sweden as underestimated, with a latent potential to (clandestinely) expand British trade, but also as a significant threat to Britain's domestic market.

However, these accounts were far from objective. Recent research on consuls has shown them to be complex state actors, motivated by competing state interests as well as personal business concerns.[35] This naturally also played into how they chose to report on the ongoing smuggling, an activity they often participated in themselves.[36] Of course, not all consuls were involved in smuggling, but the consul could also choose to distance himself from smuggling in order to promote better trade relations between his two countries.[37] The consul's descriptions of, and interactions with, smuggling should therefore be considered not merely as a reflection of state interests but also on an individual and situational basis.

A British Consul in a Smuggling Hub – Thomas Erskine

In looking closer at Thomas Erskine (1746–1828), the British consul in Gothenburg, we can start to discern how individual interests and ambitions affected the consular reports. In the last quarter of the eighteenth-century, Gothenburg had gained an international reputation for its smuggling trade, which was an integral part of the city's economic life.[38] The city also had an extensive Scottish population, with links to the British Isles. However, that did not mean that the inhabitants felt any particular allegiance to the English government. On the contrary, many of the Scottish-owned trading houses were founded by Jacobites who had moved to Sweden to escape English persecution, particularly after the Battle of Culloden in 1746.[39] As many as 12 Jacobite merchant houses have been identified in Gothenburg alone.[40] Meanwhile, the historian Paul Monod has argued that there was a link between the Jacobite diasporas around Europe and the British contraband trade. According to Monod, the Jacobite smuggling community was based on family ties, tradition, and a drive for the common good, and crucially entailed the liberalisation of trade.[41] This connection between Jacobite expatriates and smuggling can also be observed in Gothenburg and it can help to explain how the contraband trade to Britain came to gain such traction in the town.[42]

This was the community that Thomas Erskine entered into when he at the age of 13 was sent to Gothenburg to learn a trade and secure an income.[43] Erskine had been born into the Scottish lowland clan of the same name, an aristocratic family, impoverished by the forced seizure of their property following their support of the Stuart Pretender during the Jacobite risings. He started working as an apprentice in the Gothenburg office of George Carnegie (1726–1799), a fellow Jacobite, in 1759.[44] Carnegie, who had fought at Culloden in 1746, had fled to Gothenburg following the defeat. Like many of his compatriots, Carnegie was also involved in tea smuggling to Scotland, which coincided with the period of Erskine's employment.[45] After training under Carnegie, Erskine went on to work for his friends John and Benjamin Hall, before acquiring a burghership in 1767. He eventually became part-owner in the trading company John Hall & Co., where he remained as a partner for 30 years.[46] This company became one of the most successful export companies in Gothenburg and focused on the export of iron and planks to the British market. They were also, to a lesser extent, involved in the import market, focusing on the import of salt, coal, glass, lead, and British colonial goods.[47] Over time, Erskine came to establish himself as a leading merchant in Gothenburg.

Meanwhile, Erskine also claimed an important role on Gothenburg's social scene as one of the founding members of the Royal Bachelors' Club, which was set up in 1769 with the intention of allowing its members to play billiards.[48] The club appears to have been a close-knit community with very limited recruitment between 1770 and 1813.[49] Despite their relatively small numbers, many of the members figure in Derek Janes' investigation of tea smuggling to Scotland.[50] That the Royal Bachelors' Club was secretly a dedicated smuggling ring seems unlikely, but it is certain that such a society helped to reinforce networks and create a safe space for the development of trade plans and the exchange of contacts and knowledge. Research has shown that other social societies, such as the Freemasons played an important role in making and securing contacts crucial in smuggling operations.[51] Thomas Erskine, as a founding member of the Royal Bachelors' Club and a Freemason, was thus surrounded by expatriates who were involved in the contraband trade, both in his professional and social life.[52]

When Thomas Erskine in 1775 was appointed British consul in Gothenburg, Marstrand, and other ports along the west coast of Sweden, his true allegiances were an issue of concern.[53] Intriguingly, the concern about his loyalties related to his relationship to Sweden rather than his Jacobite roots. Prior to Erskine's appointment, Lewis de Visme, the British ambassador, had written a letter to Lord Suffolk explaining that he had met Erskine, who seemed to be "a Gentleman of a very good understanding and character".[54] However, Erskine had taken an oath of fidelity to the Swedish government in order to become a Swedish burgher. In his correspondence, de Visme noted that this was a necessary procedure for merchants who wished to be competitive in Sweden, as they would otherwise labour under highly disadvantageous conditions due to the protectionist legislation that favoured Swedish traders. Further, he explained that the only two British merchant houses led by individuals who had not taken the oaths and become Swedish burghers "subsist by illicit Trade of Teas and India Goods carried on chiefly to the Coasts of Scotland and Ireland".[55] He concluded his letter:

> Your Lordship is best able to judge how far the two characters of Consul and Burgher are compatible. It is certain that merchants owe particular obedience and duty to the Government of the State in which they are settled, without renouncing their Allegiance to their natural Sovereign; and the British Subjects at Gothenburg understand that their engagements towards Sweden imply no more.[56]

Lord Suffolk was undisturbed by this news, observing that the oath of fidelity should be understood as a promise to behave peaceably in Sweden and "not as affecting his natural Allegiance in any Degree".[57] They concluded that the Swedish oath of fidelity was not so much a hindrance, as a proof of Erskine's honourable character.

It is noticeable that while Erskine's relationship to Sweden is scrutinised, no questions were raised about how his close ties with Jacobitism might have affected his "Allegiance to [his] natural Sovereign". While Erskine might not have been an active Jacobite himself, being born in the year of the last rising, he had still suffered from the persecution through his family, who had lost their property, and in Gothenburg, he found himself surrounded by a large Jacobite expatriate community, many of whom had left Scotland following the crushing of the rebellion. Nevertheless, what this might have meant for Erskine's loyalties towards the English government is never discussed.

Erskine's appointment was finalised in April 1775 but it does not appear to have been announced in Sweden until December.[58] Erskine started reporting on the trade of Gothenburg in late 1775, its exports and imports, new decrees, and various new trade developments. As part of this, he also reported on the contraband trade both in and out of Gothenburg and the other harbours under his surveillance.[59]

One of the main facets of this was the tea smuggling to Britain, which Erskine reported on and evidently also had personal links to. Whether this was known to the English government is uncertain. In June 1784, the Foreign Secretary Francis Osborne, Marquis Carmarthen (1751–1799), wrote to Charles Keene, the chargé d'affaires in Stockholm, asking him to launch an investigation into the state of this contraband trade. In his reply, Keene noted that he had asked Erskine to send him "an Account of the quantities of Tea exported from [Gothenburg] and Marstrand, and to what places during the last Twelvemonth". Keene believed that most British subjects in Gothenburg were "very deeply concerned in that dangerous tho' lucrative and illicit Commerce". However, he had no reason to believe that Erskine's reputable trading house was involved "in such dark and pernicious enterprizes [sic]".[60]

Despite Keene's beliefs, it is clear that Erskine had connections to the illicit tea trade both professionally and socially. The exact nature of Erskine's involvement in the contraband trade remains unknown. He might simply have drawn on his contacts for information about the trade. If so, he was careful to protect his sources as he never divulged any specificities or names. It is almost certain that Erskine through his various contacts sat on more information than he was willing to divulge to the government. Erskine was also involved in the tea trade himself. Two months prior to the Commutation Act, he approached Lord Carmarthen with an offer to sell Swedish East India tea to the British East India Company to cover any shortages and to provide a steady supply of tea from the continent.[61] When the Commutation Act came into force in September 1784, the duty on tea plummeted from 119% to 12.5%.[62] By January 1785, Erskine reported back to London that only a small amount of tea was still in the hands of private merchants and that smuggling had been reduced to a trifle of what it had once been.[63]

Whether Erskine himself was involved in smuggling, either in or out of Sweden, is unknown. Despite close ties to known smugglers and the seizure of a contraband shipment at Erskine's own harbour in Masthugget in 1786, no incident was ever tied directly to him.[64] It is nevertheless evident that Erskine had various allegiances both professional and personal, which affected what he chose to communicate to his superiors. Although Erskine's reports were not written with exclusively British interest in mind, they nevertheless formed a substantial part of the information available to the British government on the trade with the north. Erskine thus held a powerful sway over the image of Sweden, and Gothenburg in particular, something he could use strategically to reinforce his own interests.

The French Perspective – A Patriotic Endeavour

> The French government must energetically demand the execution of this convention [the right to an entrepôt in Gothenburg]... Indeed, the restoration of the navy requires great commercial relations with the North : The more materials of all kinds that we export to the country, the more it is in our interest to carry our merchandise and goods there... Sweden's interest commits it to the punctual execution of the convention : For its commerce, like that of France, has it not, as its mortal enemy the English commerce, which aspires to acquire a monopoly of the northern trade, a monopoly that only France can suppress through bringing Sweden all of the goods and merchandise that it lacks.[65]

The trade relationship between Sweden and France looked quite different to that with Britain. Sweden had a longstanding trade relationship with France, reaching back to at least 1499, but despite these early beginnings the trade was slow to take off. During the reign of Louis XIV, the trade eventually began to expand, and as the demand for Swedish raw materials, particularly pine and tar, increased, the King desired to build a powerful navy.[66] The 1724 Navigation Act proved another important boost for the trade. From the 1770s onwards, the trade expanded to include large quantities of iron and copper, along with the woodwares.[67] In return, salt, brandy, and wine were exported from France to Sweden. Some colonial products like indigo, coffee, and sugar were also exported to Sweden but mainly in smaller quantities.[68] Although this trade was increasing during the eighteenth century, trade statistics indicate that it was still considerably smaller in scope than the British trade.[69] However, Sweden and France were also engaged in a subsidy alliance, whereby Sweden was tied to France politically and militarily.[70] Sweden had a closer overall relationship to France than to Britain, but with considerably less ongoing trade.

The French authorities were not content with this situation, however, and in 1784, the Swedish and French governments struck a deal, whereby France would gift the Caribbean island of Saint Barthélemy to Sweden in exchange for a duty-free warehouse in Gothenburg. According to historian Pierrick Pourchasse, this deal was struck because the French authorities were concerned by the underdeveloped trade between France and Sweden and saw this as an opportunity to expand its direct trade into the Baltic area and the north.[71] This was not the first time French merchants had received special trade privileges within the Swedish dominion; already in a 1741, a treaty had granted French traders a special right to trade with the port in Wismar. While the French government might have had an interest in securing trade deals in the north, the limited expansion of trade in Wismar, and later in Gothenburg, indicates that the French merchants made very little use of this privilege and had little interest in investing in the north.[72]

From Ignorance to Ambition

The reports on Franco-Swedish trade submitted to the French government were less substantial than those that reached the British Foreign Office, and the sources generally reflect less of an active concern with the state of Swedish trade.[73] However, around 1797, the document *Notions qui résultent de l'examen de la correspondance de Suède* was submitted to the French Ministry of Foreign Affairs. This extensive document described the state of Swedish commerce and manufacturing along with other features related to the nature and the running of the kingdom. The document was in part based on material from the forthcoming trade manual *Système maritime et politique des Européens pendant le dix-huitieme siècle* by Ambroise-Marie Arnould, published in 1797, and in part on older correspondence from consuls and envoys. In *Notions,* its anonymous author pays particular attention to the ongoing trade between Great Britain and Sweden, which is compared to that between France and Sweden. Contrary to how the British themselves perceived their trade, the French report noted that the British were treated very favourably both by the Swedish government and local port officials.[74] This preoccupation with the trade between Britain and Sweden was closely linked to what was seen as a failure to fully develop the commercial potential between France and Sweden. While the British pursued their trade with Sweden with ardour the French appeared to "have an unsurmountable repugnance for the Baltic Sea" according to a letter from the chargé d'affaires in Stockholm, Jean-Pierre-François de Gaussen (1747–1845), from 1787.[75] Indeed, as the *Notions* went on to observe, it took quite a long time for the French merchants to actually understand the benefits awarded to them through the Gothenburg warehouse and to start making use of the city.[76]

This apparent disinterest in Swedish trade appears to have been replaced by a growing interest around the turn of the century. In 1802, the French consul in Gothenburg, du Goutte, submitted a list to the Ministry of Foreign Affairs, containing all French goods in demand in Gothenburg and other important cities in Sweden. It primarily appears to have been an instruction for merchants in regard to what could favourably be sold in Sweden. In-demand wares that could legally be sold included: Bordeaux wine, olive oil, fruit (such as *reinettes*), olives, Marseille soap, and capers, along with colonial goods such as coffee, sugar, indigo, and anchovies, including almost anything from the Levant. Unfortunately, du Goutte noted, the French salt was too weak to salt herring and could only be used to salt meat, which meant that French salt was in less demand than Portuguese salt.[77]

As most French wares were prohibited in Sweden, du Goutte also submitted a list of the goods that could favourably be imported into Sweden illegally. This list included a multitude of French manufactures, particularly silk, and jewels.

Such goods were in high demand on the Swedish market and this business was, as Goutte pointed out, "of great advantage to the French".[78] This trade allowed the French to expand their influence on the Swedish market, and to compete against the British smuggling trade. Johan Christian Schedel described this French smuggling trade in his 1804 trade manual *Neues und vollständiges geographisches Lexikon für Kaufleute und Geschäftsmänner*. Schedel noted that while Sweden had a positive trade balance against almost all countries, the smuggling of French luxuries and fashionable goods hollowed out Sweden's potential gains.[79] However, the French smuggling efforts were not merely focused on undermining Swedish regulation, rather the main priority appears to have been goods going *through* the country.

Eaux-de-vie Smuggling to and through Sweden

Already in 1773, the French Envoy Charles Gravier, Count of Vergennes (1717–1787), observed that large quantities of brandy and tea were imported to Sweden only to be smuggled to Ireland and Scotland, something that was also reiterated in later consular correspondence.[80] While the tea smuggling decreased after the Commutation Act in 1784 the illicit trade in French brandy continued, aided by the new Gothenburg warehouse. According to du Goutte, the warehouse played an important role in this transit trade as it allowed brandy to be imported to Sweden duty-free and stored at the entrepôt warehouse, from whence it could be illegally exported to Scotland or England at a convenient time.[81] The Swedish smuggling route to Britain was only one among many used by the French.[82] However, as will be discussed in the final section of this chapter, in Sweden, France found willing abettors for their illicit trade.

In the French foreign correspondence, the trade with Sweden is continuously intertwined with concerns about Britain, its politics, and trade. Undermining Britain is a central goal in the French correspondence, both through challenging their dominance of the Nordic markets and through compromising their economic jurisdiction at home. In both of these cases, smuggling was seen as a central tenet, it both provided the opportunity to illegally expand on the Swedish market, thus challenging the British control and allowed an opportunity to undermine British trade and their economic self-determination on their own home turf. Challenging the British dominance in the north became increasingly more pressing towards the end of the century and the outbreak of the French Revolutionary Wars. As Jean Antoine Fournier noted in 1805: "Sweden offers us various ways, not only to restore our trade with the North, but to harm our enemy".[83] The competition between France and Britain cannot merely be seen between states but as we turn back to the consuls, we can also see it playing out on the ground.

Jean Antoine and Casimir Fournier

Jean Antoine Fournier (1761–1824) was born in Grenoble, a town located at the foot of the French Alps. He arrived in Sweden in 1786 enticed by the 1784 agreement between France and Sweden which secured St Barthélemy as a Swedish colony and established a French entrepôt in Gothenburg.[84] The benefits of this deal were jealously described by Thomas Erskine in July 1787:

> I think it proper to inform your Lordship that the last Treaty or convention between France & Sweden is now first put in effect at this port. - Yesterday a French Ship *L'Espoir* Capt Louis Marai from Honfleur arrived with a Cargo of Rye, when their Consul Mr. de Lisle intimatid [sic] to the Custom house that this vessel must be admitted under all the privileges which the late treaty entitled the ships of his nation to, Viz. Not to be subject to any visitation from the custom house neither on arrival, nor on departure... & not to be liable to any duties till delivered from their magazine...[85]

A protest against this unfair treatment, Erskine added, must be submitted to Stockholm.

If Erskine's fear was that this would mark the beginning of a potent French trading community in Gothenburg, his fear was misplaced. In an undated letter from the early nineteenth century, Jean Antoine Fournier was described as "le seul français ètabli dans cette partie du Nord".[86] While the situation was not quite that severe, attracting French traders to the north proved a challenge, exasperated by a shortage of information about the Nordic markets, which discouraged merchants from involving themselves in these markets.[87]

One other French trader who managed to find his way to the north was Fournier's younger brother Casimir Fournier (1769–1841), who joined Jean Antoine in Gothenburg in 1788. While the brothers tried to benefit from the improved conditions for French merchants in the north, as foreigners, they soon ran into difficulties in such a protectionist country. In September 1789, J. A. Fournier complained that, despite the early enticements of the St Barthélemy deal, heavy taxes were starting to hurt his business and make it unprofitable.[88] Despite these issues, the brothers managed to found their own import and export company, *Les Fréres Fourniers*. The company mainly focused on importing wine and colonial goods of various types, which were sold in their shop in Domprosthuset.[89] The business was bolstered both by Jean Antoine's right to use the French warehouse and Casimir's new Swedish citizenship and *burskap*, acquired in 1791.[90] By combining the privileges of the French and the Swedish merchant, the brothers managed to establish a successful business.

How they made use of their different identities can be discerned in a smuggling case from 1792. In December 1791, a contraband cargo addressed to "J.A. Fournier à Gothenbourg" was seized just outside of Gothenburg. As Jean Antoine was in France, Casimir was brought in to the Maritime Customs Court to face the smuggling charges.[91] The total amount of contraband was calculated at 2673 Rdr Specie and included many luxury goods which appeared to be French in origin, including, among other things: black serge de reine, silk moire in various colours, black ostrich plumes, silk scarves, earrings, necklace crosses of glass, muslin scarves, gold rings, clocks, women's silk hats, and French flowers.[92]

According to Casimir, the goods must have been sent by their enemies to hurt their business and he refused to take responsibility for them. Asked by the court to swear an oath on his and his brother's innocence, Casimir refused saying that swearing such an oath might awaken suspicion. Repeated refusals to swear on their innocence instead landed the brothers with a fine for smuggling of 122 Rdr Specie.[93] The low fine was a reflection of the fact that only four of the contraband packages were marked with "J. A. Fournier", the remainder, marked "I.A.F." could not conclusively be tied to the Fourniers.

The division of duties reflected in this affair appears to be symptomatic of the early years of *Les Fréres Fourniers*. Jean Antoine organised their foreign shipping while Casimir, the Swedish burgher, was the outward face of the business, on the ground in Sweden. While the double use of French and Swedish privileges did not allow them to get away when caught with outright smuggling, it did allow them to circumvent some regulation and avoid many of the customs searches that would otherwise have been customary. The juggling of different identities became a hallmark of the Fournier brothers' time in Gothenburg.

The use of multiple identities can also be seen in Jean Antoine Fournier's journey towards becoming a consul. According to French regulations, as a representative for the King, the consul must be a French national and a Catholic and under no circumstances a merchant, to avoid any conflicts of interest. However, as French nationals could be difficult to come by in remoter areas, this regulation could be swayed for the vice-consuls.[94] This seems to have been the case when Jean Antoine Fournier in 1788 was appointed vice-consul in Gothenburg, under the long-serving consul de Lisle. As a vice-consul, Fournier was responsible for taking care of de Lisle's duties when he was indisposed or travelling.[95] It is possible that the rules about not appointing merchants changed with the fall of the monarchy, because in 1793, Fournier was appointed consul in Gothenburg. By now, he was combining not merely the French and Swedish identities but also those of merchant and state representative. Meanwhile, he managed to stay a bit removed from the Swedish side of things through his brother. Unlike Thomas Erskine, Jean Antoine thus never had to swear an oath to the Swedish state to trade in Gothenburg and remained untaintedly French in the eyes of the French government.

Competition in the North

In 1794, during the French Revolutionary Wars, one year after Jean Antoine's appointment as consul, an event took place that would test the brothers' use of identities. It sheds light on how they used their trade to advance France's interests under the cover of neutrality.

On 14 May 1794, Thomas Erskine filed a report to the British government with news of some disturbing new developments in Gothenburg. He had recently discovered that 2,000–3,000 casks of gunpowder had been purchased from private mills in Sweden by 'French Agents', "[w]ho intend to smugle [sic] it out of the Country, by puting [sic] it on board of unsuspected Ships, without entry or in such a manner as not to be known to be Powder".[96] To prevent the gunpowder from getting into French hands, Erskine, who was well acquainted with one of the manufacturers, offered to purchase the powder himself on behalf of the British government.[97] However, Erskine failed to convince the British government to purchase the Swedish gunpowder, and the sale to the 'French Agents' went ahead.[98]

The British did not sit idly by, but seized the ships on route to France. The ships were quickly identified as belonging to Casimir Fournier. In June, shortly after the seizure, the Swedish envoy in London, Laurent Engeström, wrote a letter to the Foreign Office insisting that the Court of Admiralty should not be misled by his French-sounding name: Casimir Fournier was a Swedish subject and a long-time merchant of Gothenburg.[99] His shipment should therefore not be classed as contraband of war. Despite his intervention, the vessels were not released, and in November 1794, Casimir wrote to the Swedish government to complain about the situation, noting that the goods that had been seized were *propriété neutre*, but had been treated as enemy cargo.[100] A letter from the Burgomaster of Gothenburg was consequently submitted to the British government, yet again explaining Casimir's status as a Swedish burgher.

> [H]e … neither at the time of the loading of the said Cargo nor at the time of the Capture thereof nor at the present time was or is a Partner in any Mercantile House belonging to any person or persons being Enemies of the Crown of Great Britain or Inhabiting within the Territories of France… And that he is not nor ever has been a French Consul or in any other Service under the Government of France at Gothenburg.[101]

While Casimir Fournier might not officially have been a French consul, as we have seen, his brother and close business partner certainly was.[102] The British government had also been made aware of this through Erskine's correspondence. Swedish insistences that Casimir was a neutral Swedish merchant were therefore not very convincing for the British authorities.

This also raises the question if the Swedish authorities were aware of the full situation. According to the nineteenth century historian Hugo Fröding, J. A. Fournier claimed that he had agreed with the Swedish government that a cargo of gunpowder would be shipped from Gothenburg to France but that the ship would sail under Swedish colours with a claimed destination of St Barthélemy. The Swedish government was also supposed to have taken it upon themselves to reclaim the cargo as Swedish in the case of it being seized. Swedish attempts to reclaim the ship in question continued for years without success.[103] This indicates that the Swedish authorities were willing abettors for their French allies, shielding enemy activities under the cover of neutral trade.

These cases illustrate how the Fournier brothers in various ways were actively using their contrasting identities and the cover of neutrality, not only to advance their own trade but to help their native country. They were actively involved in furthering French interests on the ground, making use of their ambiguous situation to try to elude their British rivals. However, the failed gunpowder affair spelled the end of their early trading activities in Gothenburg, as both brothers retreated from the city following this failed endeavour.[104] Although the 'Swedish' Casimir never returned, Jean Antoine reappeared again in 1799, intent to set his mark.[105]

An 'entreprise patriotique'

During his second bout in Sweden, J. A. Fournier returned to his merchant trade, but this time he made no attempts to hide his true allegiances.[106] He stayed until 1804 when he was called back to France following a breakdown in French-Swedish relations. Just a few days later, his house and all his stock were destroyed in a fire that damaged large parts of Gothenburg.[107] Despite all his setbacks, Fournier continued to have faith in the importance of the Swedish trade and continued to promote a greater French interest in Sweden. In 1805, he submitted a report about the benefits of developing trade with Sweden. He particularly stressed that developing trade with Sweden was a way to undermine Britain, arguing that Sweden would be welcoming as the British were their traditional enemies, and had often been mistreated by them in the past. Through exercising increased control over the trade in the north, Fournier argued, it would be possible to combat British dominance and advance the French political agenda.[108] The significance of establishing a trading base in the north remained an important theme in Fournier's correspondence during these years, with competition with the British being a central focus.

In 1810, after the Treaty of Paris, Fournier returned to Sweden yet again. This time he helped to secure Marshal Jean Bernadotte as heir to the Swedish throne at the Diet in Örebro.[109] Fournier had first met the Marshal in Hannover during his return trip from Gothenburg to Paris in 1804.[110] Fournier's involvement in the selection of the future Swedish monarch was his most lasting contribution to the French-Swedish relationship.

Jean Antoine Fournier cannot be accused of the *laissez-faire* attitude common among many other French consuls in the north.[111] He often referred to his stay in the north as his "entreprise patriotique".[112] Establishing a trading base and competing for the Swedish market was challenging, but according to Fournier, it was worthwhile in order to combat the influence of the British. His trading activities in Gothenburg also reveal that he practiced as he preached, as he tried not merely to establish a French trading house, even engaging in the illicit trade advocated by du Goutte but also actively sought to undermine the British, by enabling the transit of contraband of war. In contrast to many other merchant-consuls, Fournier's identities were not in conflict but compatible, reinforcing each other.

The Swedish Perspective – Pragmatic Advancement

Having looked at the British and French perspectives on smuggling in Sweden, it is necessary to consider how the Swedish viewed their trading partners, and smuggling as a tool in international trade. A central character in the Swedish context was Johan Liljencrantz, often referred to as Gustav III's minister of finance. He has already been mentioned in regard to his project to set up a freeport in Marstrand, but Liljencrantz's attempts to make Sweden into a competitive trading nation went much further. Liljencrantz believed that Sweden's ticket to commercial success might lie in smuggling, an idea he had first developed during a study trip around Europe in 1759. During this trip, he submitted a report to the National Board of Trade in which he argued that in order to develop into a strong trading nation, it was necessary for Sweden to adopt a more proactive approach to commerce.[113] He suggested that the Dutch and British business success could be traced back to the illegal commerce which the two nations conducted with the Spanish colonies.[114] State-supported smuggling, Liljencrantz argued, could also ensure commercial success for Sweden.

It was not necessary to look as far abroad as the Americas, but there were other markets closer to home ready for exploitation, most notably the British. Years later, Liljencrantz described the French brandy smuggling to Britain through Gothenburg as one of Sweden's most profitable trades, which helped to alleviate economic hardship and deserved further state support.[115] Liljencrantz was not alone in lobbying for state-supported smuggling in order to help the Swedish finances. During the riksdag proceedings in 1769/1770, the merchant Volgarth (or Volrat) von Öltcken brought up the issue of the French brandy smuggling to Britain. Von Öltcken calculated the brandy smuggling to amount to roughly 1000 hogsheads (*oxhuvud*) a year and claimed that it was highly profitable for Sweden.[116] However, von Öltken wanted Gothenburg to expand as a smuggling hub, to offer more East India goods as well as French brandy. This, von Öltcken argued, would give the city a competitive edge and would attract more British traders who would otherwise sail to Copenhagen to get hold of their East India wares.[117] As the smuggling was conducted by British smugglers, all the state had to do was to prepare favourable conditions for the smuggling, particularly the necessary storage. Von Öltcken thus called for an entrepôt to be built in Gothenburg, which would really boost this transit trade.[118] It is possible to discern a political support of the contraband trade to Britain, from both members of the riksdag and political heavyweights like Liljencrantz.

While smuggling into Sweden itself was severely condemned, encouraging smuggling through the country in order to gain a competitive advantage and improve the state finances does not appear to have been considered in the same negative light. In order to understand this difference, it is useful to consider the international trade as a mercantile power game which was, particularly in the north, dominated by the British. This dominance was seen as troubling in France and Sweden alike. While many in Sweden saw the British trade as imposing on, and damaging to, Swedish interests, particularly through the contraband it brought in, encouraging smuggling *to* Britain was seen as a way to counteract the damage done by British imports, and framed as a way of holding one's own against a mercantile empire. Furthermore, it meant that Sweden was a willing abettor for French smuggling activities. When France in 1784 received an entrepôt in Gothenburg, all was set up for this illicit trade.

British Antagonisers

A potential answer to why the British trade was deemed so dangerous can be found in some discussions that took place in 1788. That year had brought with it a new development in the shape of a looming war. Since the previous year, the Russo-Turkish War (1787–1792) had caused consternation and anxiety about expanding Russian interests in the Orient. In March 1788, Prussia, the Netherlands, and Great Britain began negotiations for an alliance to thwart Russian interests. Among other things, this led to increased support for a war in the north to distract from the southern campaigns. Gustav III, convinced that the British would support an invasion of Russia through subsidies, declared war on Russia.[119] As part of these new friendly overtures to Great Britain, in December 1788, Gustav III demanded that a commission be set up in order to explore potential changes to the trade relationship between Sweden and Britain, a move intended to show goodwill, as "none of us can foresee what connections might finally become indispensable for Us to make for the Safety of Sweden".[120]

The committee addressed questions such as: can Swedish and British trade interests be aligned, and if so how? What trade benefits could Sweden give to England without damaging its own prosperity? In the ensuing debates, it was maintained that the nature of Swedish and British trade were very different; the Swedish trade being 'passive' and the British trade being 'active'. The British dominance was deemed to be related to the strength of their trade, great capital, and seafaring skills but also due to the fact that:

> [it is] in the Character of the English Nation, to make constant intrusions on the Trade and industry of other States and despite all anticipation of difficulties and losses in the beginning, they seek with an unflinching steadfastness to expand their Own; this mindset is not only prevailing among the reigning Power, but also extends to single individual trade Enterprises.[121]

Furthermore, the commission argued that the importation of most British wares would be detrimental to the Swedish manufacturing industry and could therefore not be allowed. The only manufactured British product that was deemed acceptable for import was porter.[122] Porter was not considered a threat to Swedish beer production, but was rather thought to replace the use of wine, another imported item. The commission thus suggested that its consumption and importation should be permitted.[123] Some exceptions were also made for specific raw materials from Britain and its colonies. Even at this critical stage, when Sweden was seeking British support, it was clearly considered too big a sacrifice to open the market to British goods. The 'active' trade of the British was seen as irresistible once the floodgates were open.

While Sweden's distinctly different treatment of the two countries, France and Britain, might at first appear to be peculiar, it is worth referring back to D. C. Coleman's observation, also voiced by Michael Roberts: policy was far from solely a matter of economic logic, but politics and alliances also influenced how trade was perceived and received by various countries.[124] This is further indicated by the trade commission's discussions in 1788. While the King might have had an interest in opening up trade, the commissioners adopted the well-established view that Britain's trade was active, aggressive, and damaging. It was a persuasive notion that could not be overcome and was probably linked to old established ties of friendship and alliance as well as uncertainty about aligning themselves with a considerably more commercially driven nation. These reservations would not be overcome until the realignment of alliances in the wake of the French Revolution and the outbreak of the Napoleonic Wars.[125]

Pragmatism and Circulation of Contraband

It is worth highlighting that attitudes towards the illicit circulation of contraband were not simply the product of political ambition or alliances. Indeed, while the negotiations about import and export were ongoing, a level of pragmatism was also needed to resolve temporary shortages.

During the eighteenth century, the home distillation of spirits came to be repeatedly prohibited due to shortages of grain, particularly during years of bad harvest. This shortage naturally also gave rise to ample smuggling of spirits. [126] In 1786, the situation was pressing, Gustav III had during the winter of 1785 banned distillation due to the scarcity of corn following the crop failures of 1783–1784. This resulted in an unmanageable shortage of alcohol among the commoners and a solution was urgently sought. Two cargo ships arrived in Gothenburg from Sète loaded with *eau-de-vie* and a third was expected. However, this French brandy would still not be enough and the British ambassador, seeing a business opportunity, hurriedly wrote a letter to Francis Osborne, fifth Duke of Leeds and foreign minister under William Pitt the Younger (1783–1791):

> Having been informed that we have great quantities of these two Articles which have been seized on board Smugling [sic] Vessels [along the British coast], and now laying confiscated in His Majesty's Warehouses [in London], I thought that there might be a means of selling some of it to this Government, and yesterday I made an overture upon the Subject to Baron Liliencrants, the Minister of Finance, and who is charged with this department. I explained to Him the reason of our having these Articles in our possession, and my opinion that there might be a negotiation upon them much to the advantage of Both Parties. He seemed much pleased with the proposition, and promised to take the first opportunity of mentioning it to the King, not doubting in the least but it would meet with his Royal approbation.[127]

Ambassador Wroughton further explained that Baron Liljencrantz was ready to send a ship from Gothenburg to collect an initial 'trial' instalment of 100 000 gallons of French brandy immediately.[128] While the correspondence testifies to some difficulties over setting a price, the transaction appears to have gone ahead.[129] This episode shows a level of pragmatism in the interactions between the various countries, which allowed for a more flexible system than that officially in existence. It is highly likely that some of the spirits sold to Sweden might originally have been smuggled from Swedish harbours. The movement of goods and the reconfiguration of their usage shows how protectionist systems both could dismantle and create value. In this way, contraband could be mobilised in various ways in the international commercial competition.

The Swedish attitude to international trade is reflected in the discussions surrounding smuggling. While the official position was neutrality, in reality, it was marked by old alliances and preconceptions, but also a certain level of pragmatism. Throughout the second half of the eighteenth century, the Swedish state looked favourably on smuggling to Britain, but by the early nineteenth century, things were starting to change. Swedish relations with Britain improved as a consequence of the French Revolutionary Wars and the Napoleonic Wars, which precipitated a recalibration in the political and trade relations between Sweden, Britain, and France.[130] In terms of smuggling, this can clearly be seen during the continental blockade, 1806 to 1814, when the smuggling hub of Gothenburg was reconditioned by the British to clandestinely introduce British manufactures and colonial wares into the European market, with the consent of the Swedish state. [131]

*****

It is evident that smuggling could be an effective tool to counteract the protectionist policies of other states, to weaken the commercial sovereignty of one's enemies. All three of the countries discussed in this chapter can, to a certain extent, be considered protectionist. While the aim of any protectionist system is to enforce control and dominance over the national economic space and possibly to increase a competitive edge against other nations, undermining the protectionist system challenges a country's commercial sovereignty. Swedish smuggling was ultimately relevant to both Britain and France because Sweden played an integral part in international trade, as a neutral carrier, and as an exporter of wares crucial to building up commercial empires, most notably high-quality iron. This meant that it was necessary for Britain, and increasingly also for France, to figure out ways to relate to the Swedish market and its many and varied restrictions. Meanwhile, Britain and France were intertwined in a relentless commercial rivalry that came to shape their attitudes towards Sweden and the opportunities it offered.

The views on smuggling reflected in the foreign office correspondence were directly linked to the states' distinct trade interests and concerns. British correspondence focused on smuggling in relation to the Anglo-Swedish trade balance, which was of great concern due to Britain's large iron imports from Sweden, and their limited ability to export their own manufactures. Smuggling was described as a tool to counteract a negative trade balance. At the same time, smuggling from Sweden, to Britain was seen as a threat to the British market and as worsening the trade balance even further. By contrast, in the French correspondence, smuggling was described as a way to challenge British dominance in the north and to undermine Britain's control over its own market. This was an extension of the Anglo-Franco trade rivalry, ongoing throughout the eighteenth century, aiming to secure a French commercial advantage at the expense of the British. Swedish portrayals of international smuggling also focused on gaining a commercial advantage, but they concentrated more on extending Swedish trade than damaging that of other states. At the same time, it should be noted that Britain was seen as an appropriate 'victim' because of its own aggressive trading tactics. Smuggling thus appears to have been considered an important part of the inter-state commercial competition. The contraband trade was related to more general political and trade relationships, but as these changed with time, so did the inter-state smuggling, as new rivals appeared and alliances were struck.

Foreign office correspondence cannot merely be seen as an expression of state interests, however, it is also crucial to consider the individuals who wrote it. The ambassadors, envoys, and consuls responsible for much of the reporting on the contraband trade were transnational state actors, and while they were meant to represent the state, it is clear that their own private interests affected the way they portrayed smuggling, in particular the consuls who were also merchants. This means that it is difficult to make a clear distinction between national political interests and those of the individual, as arguments framed around the national interest might actually disguise personal concerns. In order to analyse information about the contraband trade, it is therefore necessary to consider personal motivations, shifting allegiances, and business interests that might have affected what information about the contraband trade was passed on, and how it was portrayed.

Regardless of the true motivations for sustaining or supporting smuggling, it is evident that it was an efficient tool for challenging the economic sovereignty of other states. The British Commutation Act of 1784 is one example of this, and the repeated failures of the Swedish coffee prohibitions are another. Examples can also be found in other countries, including the removal of the French ban on calico in 1759. In the long run, smuggling contributed to changing the economic system itself, as the feasibility of protectionism was questioned.

Notes

1 For a longer discussion, see Chapter 1.
2 For Sweden's extensive trade with Britain, see f ex: Andersson, *Göteborgs Historia*, 196.
3 Pierrick Pourchasse, 'Trade between France and Sweden in the Eighteenth Century', *Forum Navale* 67 (2011), 100–102.

4 Charles M Andrews, 'Anglo-French Commercial Rivalry, 1700–1750: The Western Phase I', *The American Historical Review* 20, no. 3 (April 1915); D.C. Coleman, 'Politics and Economics in the Age of Anne: The Case of the Anglo-French Trade Treaty of 1713', in *Trade, Government and Economy in Pre-Industrial England. Essays Presented to F.J. Fisher*, ed. D.C. Coleman and A.H. John (London: Weidenfeld and Nicholson, 1976); John V. C. Nye, *War, Wine, and Taxes: The Political Economy of Anglo-French Trade, 1689–1900* (Princeton: Princeton University Press, 2007); François Crouzet, *La Guerre Économique Franco-Anglaise Au XVIIIe Siècle* (Paris: Fayard, 2008). On commercial war see also: Edmond Silberner, *La guerre dans la pensée économique du XVIe au XVIIIe siècle* (Paris: Librairie du Recueil Sirey, 1939), 117–118; and more recently, Ronald Findlay and Kevin H. O'Rourke, *Power and Plenty: Trade, War, and the World Economy in the Second Millennium* (Princeton, NJ: Princeton University Press, 2007), 238–262; François Crouzet, *La guerre économique franco-anglaise au XVIIIe siècle* (Paris: Fayard, 2008), 1–2; John Shovlin, 'War and Peace: Trade, International Competition, and Political Economy,' in *Mercantilism Reimagined: Political Economy in Early Modern Britain and Its Empire*, ed. Philip J. Stern and Carl Wennerlind (Oxford: Oxford University Press, 2013).

5 Coleman, 'Politics and Economics in the Age of Anne', 204.

6 Leos Müller, 'Swedish Merchant Shipping in Troubled Times: The French Revolutionary Wars and Sweden's Neutrality 1793–1801', *The International Journal of Maritime History* 28, no. 1 (2016), 154

7 Leos Müller, 'Sweden's Neutral Trade under Gustav III: The Ideal of Commercial Independence under the Predicament of Political Isolation', in *Trade and War: The Neutrality of Commerce in the Inter-State System*, ed. Koen Stapelbroek (Helsinki: Helsinki Collegium for Advanced Studies, 2011), 160.

8 Müller. 'Sweden's Neutral Trade under Gustav III', 160; Müller, 'Swedish Merchant Shipping in Troubled Times', 148.

9 For the importance of good quality iron in British manufacturing, see: Maxine Berg, 'In Pursuit of Luxury: Global History and British Consumer Goods in the Eighteenth Century', *Past & Present* 182, no. 1 (February 1, 2004), 131–132, and for a longer discussion about Swedish iron and the industrialisation in Britain, see: B Boëthius, 'Swedish Iron and Steel, 1600–1955', *Scandinavian Economic History Review* 6, no. 2 (1958). particularly 151–157; For a discussion on the tar trade, see: H. S. K. Kent, *War and Trade in Northern Seas. Anglo-Scandinavian Economic Relations in the Mid-Eighteenth Century* (Cambridge: Cambridge University Press, 1973), 82. For the importance of Swedish timber for the French fleet, see: Pourchasse, 'Trade between France and Sweden in the Eighteenth Century', 93; Müller, *Consuls, Corsairs, and Commerce. The Swedish Consular Service and Long-Distance Shipping, 1720–1815*, 183.

10 Malachy Postlethwayt et al., *The Universal Dictionary of Trade and Commerce: With Large Additions and Improvements, Adapting the Same to the Present State of British Affairs in America, since the Last Treaty of Peace Made in the Year 1763. With Great Variety of New Remarks and Illustrations Incorporated throughout the Whole: Together with Everything Essential That Is Contained in Savary's Dictionary; Also, All the Material Laws of Trade and Navigation Relating to These Kingdoms, and the Customs and Usages to Which All Traders Are Subject*, 4th ed., vol. 2 (London: Printed for W. Strahan, J. and F. Rivington ..., 1774), 'Sweden'.

11 Müller, 'Swedish Merchant Shipping in Troubled Times', 152.

12 Ormrod, *The Rise of Commercial Empires*, 286–287.

13 The Swedish Navigation Act was modelled on earlier British Navigation Acts.

14 Kent, *War and Trade in Northern Seas*, 4–5.

15 Andersson, *Göteborgs historia*, 196.

16 Kent, *War and Trade in Northern Seas*, 11; Michael Roberts, *British Diplomacy and Swedish Politics, 1758–1773* (Minneapolis: University of Minnesota Press, 1980), 127.

17 Kent, *War and Trade in Northern Seas*, 11.

18 Kent, 101–102.
19 Roberts, *British Diplomacy and Swedish Politics, 1758–1773*, 128.
20 Roberts, 129 & 135.
21 Roberts, 136.
22 SP 95, vol. 106, 251, British National Archives, cited in Roberts 135.
23 Roberts, 129–136, & 257.
24 Kent, *War and Trade in Northern Seas*, 106–109; Roberts, *British Diplomacy and Swedish Politics, 1758–1773*, 128.
25 Adam Smith, *The Wealth of Nations* (1776), Book 3, Chapter 4 quoted in Coleman, 'Politics and Economics in the Age of Anne', 187.
26 'Heads of Observation Posed to Sr John Goodricke with Answers', August 1773. SP 95, vol. 123, British National Archives, 178.
27 Ibid., 178b.
28 Ibid., 198; Lord Suffolk was Secretary of State for the Northern Department 1771–1779.
29 'Consular Report, Gothenburg 23 Jan 1788' 1788., FO 73, vol. 7, British National Archives; 'Letter to J.B. Burges, from Mr J. Smith, Gothenburg, 23 Sep 1794', 1794, FO 73, vol. 18, British National Archives; 'Consular Report, Gothenburg 26 Jan 1799', 1799, FO 73, vol. 27, British National Archives.
30 See for example –*Seasonable advice to all smugglers of French cambricks and French lawns; with a brief state, from the honourable commissioners of his Majesty's customs, of smuggling in the year 1745; as also the destructive manner in which the smuggling trade is carried on at present; and a remedy propos'd totally to suppress it, and thereby to increase the revenue several hundred thousand pounds annually* (London, 1751); Stephen Theodore Janssen, *Smuggling laid open, in all its extensive and destructive branches; with proposals for the effectual remedy of that most iniquitous practice: comprehending among other particulars the parliamentary evidence of some of the most notorious smugglers; and a large sheet, shewing in one view, the whole state of the tea importation, consumption and revenue, from midsummer 1745 (when the reduction of two shillings per pound, took place) to new Christmas 1763* (London, 1763.), 32; *Observations on smuggling, humbly submitted to the consideration of the right honourable the House of Peers, and the honourable the House of Commons, in Parliament assembled.* [n.p.], [1779?].
31 Müller, 'The Swedish East India Trade and International Markets: Re-Exports of Teas, 1731–1813'; Janes, 'Fine Gottenburgh Teas: The Import and Distribution of Smuggled Tea in Scotland and the North of England c. 1750–1780', *History of Retailing and Consumption* 2, no. 3 (2016); Janes, '"...Of Which a Contraband Trade Makes the Basis of Their Pro t" :Tea Smuggling in the North Sea c.1750–1780', in *The New Coastal History Cultural and Environmental Perspectives from Scotland and Beyond*, ed. David Worthington (London: Palgrave Macmillan, 2017); Hanna Hodacs, 'Keeping It in the Family – the Swedish East India Company and the Irvine-Rose Family, 1733 to 1770', *Journal of World History*, 31, no. 3, Sept. 2020.
32 John Goodricke, 'England and Wales: Admiralty, Navy Office and Victualling Office: Customs: Summary of Volume of Tea Smuggled into Britain from Sweden and Denmark, and Loss to Revenue Alleged by St John Goodricke', 23 August 1763, T 1, vol. 425/199–200, British National Archives.
33 Postlethwayt et al., *The Universal Dictionary of Trade and Commerce.* See entry 'Smuggling'.
34 Hoh-Cheung Mui and Lorna Mui, 'William Pitt and the Enforcement of the Commutation Act, 1784–1788', *The English Historical Review* 76, no. 300 (July 1961), 448. See also the full report William Eden, 'First Report from the Committee Appointed to Enquire into the Illicit Practises Used in Defrauding the Revenue. Reported by the Right Honourable William Eden, 24 December 1783,' in *Reports from Committees of the House of Commons Which Have Been Printed by Order of the House*, vol. 11 (House of Commons, 1803).

35 See for example: Samuel Fettah, 'Frontières et fraudes. Les consuls de France et la contrebande dans le port franc de Livourne à l'époque du risorgimento', *Revue d'histoire Moderne et Contemporaine* 2, no. 48 (2001); M. Aglietti, M. Herrero Sánchez, F. Zamora Rodríguez (eds), *Los cónsules de extranjeros en la Edad Moderna y a principios de la Edad Contemporanea*, Ediciones Doce Calles, Madrid 2013; S. Marzagalli (ed.), *Les consuls en Méditerranée, agents d'information* (Garnier, Paris 2015); Le Gouic, 'Le consulat de France à Cadix face aux réformes carolines (1765–1788)'. For Sweden, see Müller, *Consuls, Corsairs, and Commerce;* Makko and Müller, *I främmande hamn. Den svenska och svensk-norska konsultjänsten 1700–1985.*

36 Samuel Fettah, 'Frontières et fraudes', 151. See also: Ernst Pijning, 'Passive Resistance: Portuguese Diplomacy of Contraband Trade during King John V's Reign (1706–1750)', *Arquipélago História* 2, no. II (1997); M. Aglietti, M. Herrero Sánchez, F. Zamora Rodríguez (eds.), *Los cónsules de extranjeros en la Edad Moderna y a principios de la Edad Contemporanea* (Madrid: Ediciones Doce Calles, 2013); S. Marzagalli (ed.), *Les consuls en Méditerranée, agents d'information* (Paris: Garnier, 2015); Le Gouic, 'Le consulat de France à Cadix face aux réformes carolines (1765–1788)'.

37 Anne Mézin, 'La défense des intérêts des négociants français de Cadix dans la première moitiédu xviiie siècle d'après la correspondance ministérielle', in *De l'utilité commerciale des consuls. l'institution consulaire et les marchands dans le monde méditerranéen (XVIIe–XXe Siècle)*, ed. Arnaud Bartolomei et al., Collection de l'École Française de Rome (Rome: Publications de l'École française de Rome, 2017).

38 See for example: Samuel Ricard, *Traité Général Du Commerce: Contenant Des Observations Sur Le Commerce Des Principaux Etats de l'Europe, Les Productions Naturelles, l'industrie de Chaque Païs*, vol. 1, 2 vols (Amesterdam: E. van Harrevelt, 1781), 265; this same description can be seen recounted in the trade manuals: Bohn, *Gottfried Christian Bohns Wohlerfahrner Kaufmann Herausgegeben von C.D. Ebeling, Professor Am Gymnasium Zu Hamburg Und Mitvorsteber Der Handlungsakademie, Und P. H. C. Brodhagen, Lehrer Vei Der Handlungsakademie,* 5th ed. (Hamburg: Carl Ernst Bohn, 1789), 723–724; Johann Christian Herrmann, *Allgemeiner Contorist Welcher von Allen Und Jeden Gegenständen Der Handlung Aller in Und Außer Europa Belegenen Handelsplätze Die Neuesten Und Zuverlässigsten Nachrichten Ertheilet; Theils Nach Bewährten Quellen, Theils Auch, Und Insonderheit, Nach Eigener Erfahrung Und Correspondenz Entworfen Und in Alphabetische Ordnung Gebracht*, vol. 4 (Leipzig: Schwickertschen Verlage, 1792), 375. See also the travel account: I. F. Henrik Drevon, *Voyage En Suède: Contenant Un État Detaillé de Sa Population de Son Agriculture, de Son Commerce, et de Ses Finances* (La Haye: Gosse, 1789), 310.

39 Göran Behre, 'Scots in "Little London". Scots Settlers and Cultural Development in Gothenburg in the Eighteenth Century,' *Northern Scotland* 7, no. 1 (February 2015).

40 Guy Chaussinand-Nogaret, 'Une élite insulaire au service de l'europe: Les Jacobites au xviiie siècle', *Annales. Histoire, Sciences Sociales* 28, no. 5 (1973), 1110–1112.

41 Paul Monod, 'Dangerous Merchandise: Smuggling, Jacobitism, and Commercial Culture in Southeast England, 1690–1760', *Journal of British Studies* 30, no. 2 (1991), 153.

42 Janes, 'Fine Gottenburgh Teas', 230.

43 Bengt Hildebrand, 'Thomas Erskine', *Svenskt biografiskt lexikon*, 1953, https://sok.riksarkivet.se/sbl/artikel/15455,. Accessed 25 June 2019.

44 Ibid.

45 Derek Janes, *The Business of Smuggling in South-East Scotland. John and David Nisbet and Their Associates c.1740–1790*, PhD, University of Exeter, 2020, 207.

46 Bengt Hildebrand, 'Thomas Erskine', Svenskt biografiskt lexikon.

47 Elsa-Britta Grage, 'John Hall', https://sok.riksarkivet.se/sbl/artikel/13548, Svenskt biografiskt lexikon. Accessed 18 January 2019.

48 See for example: 'Consular Report, Gothenburg 2 March 1781', 1781, FO 73, vol. 1, British National Archives; 'Consular Report, Gothenburg 21 Jan 1786', 1786., FO 73, vol. 5, British National Archives; 'Consular Report, Gothenburg 10 Feb 1787 &

Consular Report, Gothenburg 27 Nov 1787', 1787, FO 73, vol. 6, British National Archives.

49 Anders Simonsen, *Bland hederligt folk. Organiserat sällskapsliv och borgerlig formering i Göteborg 1755–1820* (Göteborg: Göteborg Universitet, 2001), 61.

50 Janes, *The Business of Smuggling in SE Scotland c.1740–1796,* 205.

51 Janes, 87.

52 For Erskine's Freemason membership, see: Önnerfors, *Mystiskt brödraskap*, 188.

53 'Thomas Erskine Consul Utnämning' 1775, Ämnessamlingar, Personarkiv, Biographica, vol. E 15, Riksarkivet.

54 'Letter No 5 to Lord Suffolk, from De Visme, Stockholm, 14th Feb 1775', 1775, SP 95, vol. 125, British National Archives.

55 Ibid.

56 Ibid.

57 'Letter from Lord Suffolk to De Visme, St James's, 28 March 1775', 1775, SP 95, vol. 125, British National Archives.

58 'Letter 15, to Lord Suffolk, from De Visme, Stockholm, 14 April 1775', 1775, SP 95, vol. 125, British National Archives; 'Thomas Erskine Consul Utnämning' 1775, Ämnessamlingar, Personarkiv, Biographica, vol. E15, Riksarkivet.

59 See for example 'Letter no 2, to Consul Erskine, from Suffolk, St James's, 4th November 1775', 1775, SP 95, vol. 125, British National Archives; 'Letter No 2, to Lord Suffolk, from Erskine, Gothenburg, 30th March 1776', 1776, SP 95, vol. 126, British National Archives.

60 'Charles Keene to Lord Carmarthen, Stockholm 8 June 1784', 1784, FO 73, vol. 4, British National Archives.

61 'Thomas Erskine to Lord Carmarthen, Gothenburg 3 July 1784', 1784, FO 73, vol. 4, British National Archives.

62 See for example: Mui and Mui, 'William Pitt and the Enforcement of the Commutation Act, 1784–1788', 452; Mui and Mui, 'The Commutation Act and the Tea Trade in Britain 1784–1793', 235; Janes, '"...Of Which a Contraband Trade Makes the Basis of Their Pro t"', 269.

63 'Thomas Erskine to Lord Carmarthen, Gothenburg 22 Jan 1785', 1785, FO 73, vol. 4, British National Archives.

64 8 Aug 1786, 'Dombok' 1786, Göteborgs Sjötullsrätt, A1, vol. 18, Göteborgs Landsarkiv.

65 'Impôte' (undated but appears to be from the 1790s), Mémoires et Documents, Suède, vol. 38, 1778–1808, Centre des Archives diplomatiques de la Courneuve.

66 Pourchasse, 'Trade between France and Sweden in the Eighteenth Century', 92–93.

67 Pourchasse, 93, 94, 101 & 104.

68 Pourchasse, 97, 99, & 106.

69 *Historisk statistik för Sverige. Del 3. Utrikeshandel 1732–1970* (Stockholm: Statistiska Centralbyrån, 1972).

70 The subsidy relationship and its effects on Sweden are currently being researched at Lund University in the project *Fransk-svensk subsidiepolitik 1631–1795: motiv och effecter.*

71 Pourchasse, 'Trade between France and Sweden in the Eighteenth Century', 109.

72 Roberts, *British Diplomacy and Swedish Politics, 1758–1773,* 134. See also Gabriella Desideri, *Les traités commerciaux de royaume de Naples avec la Hollande, le Danemark et la Suède de (1740–1790) et leurs incidences économiques* (Università degli Studi di Parma, 2020).

73 This is of course also affected by the fact that the consular correspondence from the period prior to 1793 was unavailable for consultation.

74 'Notions Qui Résultent Del'examen de La Correspondance de Suède', Mémoires et Documents, Suède, vol. 6, 1632–1814, Centre des Archives diplomatiques de la Courneuve. This information originally derives from a letter sent to the Ministry of Foreign Affairs in September 1773 by the French envoy Charles Gravier, Count of Vergennes (1717–1787).

75 Ibid.
76 Ibid.
77 This statement stands in contrast to Leos Müller's supposition that it was customary preference rather than quality that motivated the Swedish preference of Portuguese salt to British and French. See: Leos Müller, 'Swedish-Portuguese Trade and Swedish Consular Service, 1700–1800,' in *A Articulacão Do Sal Português Aos Circuitos Mundiais. Antigos e Novos Consumos. The Articulation of Portuguese Salt with Worldwide Routes. Past and New Consumption Trends* (Porto: Instituto de Historia Moderna. Universidad do Porto, 2008), 94.
78 'Relation Extérieur, Priarial an 11 (May 1802) de Goutte', 1802, Mémoires et Documents, Suède, vol. 38, 1778–1808, Centre des Archives diplomatiques de la Courneuve.
79 Johan Christian Schedel, *Neues Und Vollständiges Geographisches Lexikon Für Kaufleute Und Geschäftsmänner, Oder Alphabetisch Geordnete Beschreibung Aller Welttheile, Staaten, Länder, Plätze, Häfen, Gewässer Und Kanäle, Die Den Kaufmann Interessiren Und Wohin Gehandelt Und Verkehr Getrieben Wird*, vol. 3 (Leipzig: Schwickert, 1804), 452.
80 'Notions Qui Résultent Del'examen de La Correspondance de Suède'; B3 vol. 418, 'Remarques relatives au commerce particulier de Gothembourg (undated)', Archives Nationales de France, cited by Pourchasse, 'Trade between France and Sweden in the Eighteenth Century', 100.
81 'Relation Extérieur, Priarial an 11 (May 1802) de Goutte', 1802, Mémoires et Documents, Suède, vol. 38, 1778–1808, Centre des Archives diplomatiques de la Courneuve.
82 A large part of this illegal trade was conducted directly across the English Channel. See for example: Morieux, *The Channel*, 248–282.
83 Jean Antoine Fournier, 'À Son Excellence Le Ministre de Relations Extérieure, Mémoire', 15 January 1805, Mémoires et Documents, Suède, vol. 6, 1632–1814, Centre des Archives diplomatiques de la Courneuve. ff. 193–201.
84 'Réclamation de M. J. A. Fournier' 1808, Personnel, Première série nominative, 1700–1816, vol. 31, Centre des Archives diplomatiques de la Courneuve.
85 'Thomas Erskine to Marquis Carmarthen, Gothenburg 28 July 1787', 1787, FO 73, vol. 6, British National Archives.
86 'Rapport à son Altesse Sérénissime' Personnel, Première série nominative, 1700–1816, vol. 31, Centre des Archives diplomatiques de la Courneuve. This was not a new description; he had been described in that way already in the 1796 travelogue *Voyage de deux Française* by de Piles and Boisgelin. See: Alphonse Fortia de Piles and M. Boisgelin, *Voyage de deux Français,* vol. II (Paris: Desenne, 1796), 17.
87 Pierrick Pourchasse, 'The "Information Problem" for French Trade in the Northern Markets of the Eighteenth Century', in *Information Flows. New Approaches in the Historical Study of Business Information*, ed. Leos Müller and Jari Ojala (Helsinki: SKS/Finnish Literature Society, 2007), 241
88 Hugo Fröding, *Biografiska studier från skilda tider* (Stockholm: P.A. Norstedt & Söners förlag, 1905), 186.
89 Nils Holm, 'Jean Antoine Fournier', https://sok.riksarkivet.se/sbl/artikel/14412, Svenskt biografiskt lexikon, 1964, Accessed 24 June 2019. For information on their business and range of goods, see for example: 'Kungörelser (Fournier),' *Götheborgs Tidningar*, November 5, 1790, no 129; 'Til Salu Finnes (Fournier),' *Götheborgs Allehanda*, November 9, 1790, no 90.'Franske Skep Joseph de Le Fortrie Med Galeasen La Maire Inkommen Ifrån Havre de Grace Til Götheborg under No 206, d. 23 Maij 1791 Nederlagen Anl. Conventionen Af d. 26 Julii År 1784 - Uttagit Til Förtullning Af Cazimir Fournier', 1784, Äldre centrala tullarkiv, Generaltullarrendesocieteten, m. fl., kansliet, Skrivelser från tullfiskaler E8, vol. 1.
90 HCA 34, vol. 61, British National Archives (Thank you to Pierrick Pourchasse for this reference); Hugo Fröding, *Biografiska studier från skilda tider* (Stockholm: P.A. Norstedt & Söners förlag, 1905), 185.

91 Casimir Fournier: 29 Dec 1791, 'Dombok' 1791, Göteborgs Sjötullsrätt, A1, vol. 19, Göteborgs Landsarkiv'; This was the first of at least five court cases the two brothers would face during the subsequent 12 years: 22 April 1793, 'Dombok' 1793, Göteborgs Sjötullsrätt, A1, vol. 20, Göteborgs Landsarkiv; 'Kongl. Maj. Högsta Domstolens Utslag', *Dagligt Allehanda*, 26 April 1796. Jean Antoine Fournier: 'Konkurstvist', *Stockholms Posttidningar*, 24 August 1803, no 115.

92 Berit Eldvik, Private Communication, 30 January 2017.

93 29 Dec 1791, 'Dombok' 1791, Göteborgs Sjötullsrätt, A1, vol. 19, Göteborgs Landsarkiv; 3 Jan 1792, 5 Jan 1792, 22 Mar 1792, 26 Apr 1792, 3 Maj 1792, 22 Nov 1792, 'Dombok' 1792, Göteborgs Sjötullsrätt, A1, vol. 19, Göteborgs Landsarkiv.

94 Pierrick Pourchasse, 'The "Information Problem" for French Trade in the Northern Markets of the Eighteenth Century', in *Information Flows. New Approaches in the Historical Study of Business Information*, ed. Leos Müller and Jari Ojala (Helsinki: SKS/ Finnish Literature Society, 2007), 259.

95 Emile Taillefer, 'Contribution d'un Grenoblois à l'histoire de La Suède', *Bulletin Du Musée Bernadotte* 17 (1972), 14.

96 'Letter to Lord Grenville, from Thomas Erskine, Gothenburg 17 May 1794', 1794, FO 73, vol. 17, British National Archives.

97 Ibid.

98 'Letter to B. Burghess Downing Street, from R M Crew, Office of Ordnance, 17 June 1794,' 1794, FO 73, vol. 17, British National Archives.

99 'Letter from Laurent Engeström, 19 June 1794', 1794, FO 73, vol. 18, British National Archives.

100 'Fournier'Ämnessamlingar, Personarkiv, Biographica, vol. F II 3, Riksarkivet.

101 'Letter dated 4th of April 1795', HCA 34, vol. 61, British National Archives.

102 Müller, 'Swedish Merchant Shipping in Troubled Times', 155. Leos Müller has also discussed this case but only in terms of Swedish neutral shipping, and not in relation to the Fourniers' French allegiances.

103 Fröding, *Biografiska studier från skilda tider*, 187–188.

104 'Fournier' 1794, Ämnessamlingar, Personarkiv, Biographica, vol. F II 3, Riksarkivet.; Fröding, *Biografiska Studier Från Skilda Tider*, 187–188.

105 'Passagerare', *Inrikes Tidningar*, 17 July 1799, no 83.

106 See for example his advertisement: Jean Antoine Fournier, '-,' *Götheborgs Allehanda*, March 28, 1800.

107 'Réclamation de M. J. A. Fournier' 1808, Personnel, Première série nominative, 1700–1816, vol. 31, Centre des Archives diplomatiques de la Courneuve.

108 Jean Antoine Fournier, 'À Son Excellence Le Ministre de Relations Extérieure, Mémoire', 15 January 1805, Mémoires et Documents, Suède, vol. 6, 1632–1814, Centre des Archives diplomatiques de la Courneuve. ff. 193–201.

109 Nils Holm, 'Jean Antoine Fournier', in *Svenskt biografiskt lexikon*. Vol. 16, 1964. https://sok.riksarkivet.se/sbl/artikel/15455, Svenskt biografiskt lexikon, Accessed 25 June 2019.

110 Ibid; Emile Taillefer, 'Contribution d'un Grenoblois à l'histoire de la Suède'.

111 Pourchasse, 'The "Information Problem" for French Trade in the Northern Markets of the Eighteenth Century', 253.

112 'Réclamation de M. J. A. Fournier' 1808, Personnel, Première série nominative, 1700–1816, vol. 31, Centre des Archives diplomatiques de la Courneuve.

113 'Liljencrantz rapport 4/5 1759', 1759, Kommerskollegium, Huvudarkiv, Acta privatorum, EXVIIda, vol 3, Riksarikivet.

114 For a discussion on this smuggling, see: Scammell, 'British Smuggling in the Iberian Americas circa 1500–1750'.

115 Johan Liljencrants, 'Anteckningar Och Memorial Af Grefve Johan Liljencrantz', in *Historiska Handlingar*, vol. 5, 8 (Stockholm: Central Tryckeriet, 1878), 87.

116 This corresponds roughly to 183 000 – 235 000 litres.

117 '25 Jan 1770', Handels- & Manuf & Tull Deputs Betänkande För Åren 1769–1770', 1770, Borgareståndets arkiv, R1402, 1769–1770, vol. 6, Riksarkivet.
118 '25 Jan 1770', Handels- & Manuf & Tull Deputs Betänkande För Åren 1769–1770', 1770, Borgareståndets arkiv, R1402, 1769–1770, vol. 6, Riksarkivet.
119 E.G. Geijer, ed., *Konung Gustaf III:s efterlemnade och femtio år efter hans död öppnade papper*, vol. 3 (Uppsala: Wahlström & Låstbom, 1844), 206.
120 'Utredning Af Sveriges Och Englands Handelsförhållanden 1788–1789', 1788. ÄK 559, vol. 1. Riksarkivet.
121 Ibid.
122 Ibid.
123 Ibid.
124 Coleman, 'Politics and Economics in the Age of Anne', 205.
125 For a discussion on Swedish-British trade after the outbreak of the Napoleonic Wars, see for example: Peter Hedberg and Henric Häggqvist, 'Wartime Trade and Tariffs in Sweden from the Napoleonic Wars to World War,' in *Small and Medium Powers in Global History: Trade, Conflicts, and Neutrality from the 18th to the 20th Centuries*, ed. Jari Eloranta et al. (New York: Routledge, 2018).
126 'Memoires et Documents, Suite de l'extraie Des Négocitations Entre La France et La Suede', Mémoires et Documents, Suède, vol. 6, 1632–1814, Centre des Archives diplomatiques de la Courneuve.
127 'Letter to Lord Carmarthen (Francis Osborne), from Thomas Wroughton, Stockholm 21 July 1786', 1786, FO 73, vol. 5, British National Archives.
128 As there were several types of gallons in use at the time, it is difficult to calculate a contemporary equivalent for this, but about 382 000 litres.
129 See also: 'Franske Skep Joseph de Le Fortrie Med Galeasen La Maire Inkommen Ifrån Havre de Grace Til Götheborg under No 206, d. 23 Maij 1791 Nederlagen Anl. Conventionen Af d. 26 Julii År 1784 - Uttagit Til Förtullning Af Cazimir Fournier' , 1791, Äldre centrala tullarkiv, Generaltullarrendesocieteten, m. fl., kansliet, Skrivelser från tullfiskaler E8, vol. 1.
130 Ibid.
131 Some studies that deal with this (if only briefly) include: Marzagalli, *Boulevards de La Fraude*, 164–170; See also Häggqvist, 'On the Ocean of Protectionism', 155 & 157.

7
CONCLUSION

This book has explored smuggling in Sweden during the 40-year period 1766–1806 from five different vantage points. Together, they enable us to extend our understanding of the multifaceted and changing role that smuggling played in early modern Sweden. Rather than being a fringe phenomenon, smuggling permeated many aspects of Swedish politics, culture, and society. As this book has shown, smuggling can also be used as a prism through which we can observe numerous elements central in shaping late eighteenth-century Sweden: changing views on economy and citizenship, the reach of state authority, smuggling as a source of revenue, social attitudes towards contraband retailers, the impact of contraband, and international perceptions of smuggling as an aspect of inter-state competition. In this final chapter, attention returns to the three historical processes identified by Michael Kwass as the cause of smuggling in the eighteenth century – globalisation, state formation, and consumption – to consider what smuggling can tell us about these three processes in Sweden during this period.

Globalisation

One of the first conclusions that can be drawn is that protectionism was, at least in part, a result of globalisation. In the eighteenth century, global trade and manufacturing fuelled by inter-state competition was pursued with increasing rigour, leading to a growing volume of wares entering and circulating around Europe. These global wares were not solely imported for domestic consumption but were also supposed to be sold in rival European states through re-export, arriving there either as legal and correspondingly taxed goods or through clandestine channels and networks, with no official duties attached to them. In pursuit of a

DOI: 10.4324/9781003226031-7

positive trade balance, many European countries, including Sweden, introduced protectionist policies and trade barriers to stave off this unwanted trade.

As discussed throughout this book, the erection of trade barriers failed to ensure that the domestic market was closed to foreign influences. Smuggling enabled a continued supply of wares to enter the country. Through an examination of how porous borders and limited state authority allowed goods to circulate, it has become clear that the spread of global wares needs to be considered in relation to neighbouring territories and trading partners. In Sweden's case, the most significant foreign contraband depots appear to be Denmark-Norway, which from the 1770s onwards was undergoing a trade boom known as the period of "efflorescent trade", a boom further reinforced by the lifting of many of many trade restrictions in 1797; Pomerania, which also developed extensive long-distance trade in the 1770s and eased its protectionist legislation in 1786 and finally Britain, which was at the forefront of the European pursuit of global trade and manufacturing.[1] Meanwhile, contraband was also entering the Swedish realm over the eastern borders from Russia, a country that was participating increasingly in European trade in the eighteenth century, a development that followed its turn towards Europe and the conquest and establishment of Baltic harbours. In order to understand smuggling into Sweden, it is necessary to look both at entrepôt trade and neighbouring states with different economic legislation.

The central question, then, is perhaps not so much *when* Sweden was globalised, nor is it *whether or not* globalisation took place in eighteenth-century Sweden. Instead, globalisation should be seen as a worldwide, ongoing and unfolding process, fuelled by commercial state interests that triggered a range of various responses, reactions and counteractions shaped by dynamic national conditions. Rather than interpreting protectionism as a lack of globalisation, it should be seen as a product of the globalisation process, albeit the result of complex chains of cause and effect. Protectionism was a national response to globalisation intended to ward off the new challenges posed by global trade. Yet, the introduction of protectionist measures did not hamper the consumers' desire for global wares. The continued consumer demand fuelled smuggling, causing the effects of protectionism to be more diverse than might have been intended.

State Formation

In the eighteenth century, protectionism intensified in Sweden. While protectionist measures had been in use earlier, this period saw both an expansion and a multiplication of the protectionist legislation, particularly during the second half of the century. The intensification of protectionist policy was not merely a reaction to the expansion of global trade but also a step towards making Sweden into a homogenised economic unit, a commercial nation-state that could keep up with the challenges of increased international competition. However, as protectionism escalated, so did the dangers of smuggling, not merely because bans and duty hikes increased the incentives for smuggling but also because the supporters of protectionism defined smuggling as a threat against the state. In this way, smuggling came to highlight the limits of state authority, and its inchoate state apparatus, particularly the customs office. In the end, the state proved incapable of stamping out smuggling; Swedish protectionism was thus aspirational rather than absolute.

While smuggling challenged the state's authority and undermined its control over its own territory, inhabitants, and economy, it also came to play an important role in the development of the Swedish state. The continued access to prohibited goods led to the cancellation of certain unworkable prohibitions, most notably that on coffee, thus having a direct effect on state policy. Remarkably, contraband also allowed protectionist legislations to persist, through covering gaps in the market created by import bans and sluggishly developing domestic manufactories. In addition, smuggling and the continued access to illegal wares also led to the mobilisation of patriotism to dissuade Swedish consumers from buying contraband, and patriotic protectionism came to dominate the state's economic discourse. Through looking at smuggling, it becomes evident that the Swedish state made many attempts to enforce economic control over its territory in the latter half of the eighteenth century but also that these attempts had mixed results and that the state never succeeded in its attempts to isolate Sweden from unwanted imports.

At the same time, smuggling could also be used as a weapon against other states: to undermine their regulations and to expand export trade towards countries shielded by protectionist legislation. Indeed, if protectionist legislation was one gambit which could be used to gain an upper hand in a trade relationship, then smuggling was another. The Swedish state also appears to have used smuggling in this way to further its own trade, particularly against Britain. In this way, Sweden also contributed to the development of the British state, which eventually had to drop its extortionate tea duty as a result of the contraband trade. Smuggling could effectively both undermine and strengthen trade, and appears to have been an integrated part of domestic state formation as well as international trade relations during the eighteenth and into the nineteenth century. It should be noted that smuggling was not merely a sign of the failure of the protectionist trade, as many contemporaries posited, but it could also be seen as another feature of it.

Consumption

Smuggling also came to affect the development of Swedish consumption practices. It provided Swedish consumers from all social levels with access to foreign, exclusive items and to cheap but high-quality products. Access to these types of goods made consumers aware of what they could be consuming, increasing the demand on the manufactories to adapt and for legislation to be dropped, developments which not only show a rise in consumer awareness but also that the consumers used this knowledge to try to influence supply.

This book shows that, when studying the influence of foreign wares, attention should be paid not only to quantity, i.e. the number of imported goods, but also to the impact that these wares had on culture and society. Like other kinds of cultural transfers, some of the contraband wares came to have formative effects on Sweden and the fabrication of Swedish identity, effects which are still lingering today. Worsteds, with their superior quality, had long lives and kept being recycled and re-circulated, some for as long as a century. During this time, they became an integral part of Swedish regional and eventually national material culture, with copies of Norwich worsteds turning up, for example, in the present-day folk costume of Dala-Floda, in the Swedish heartlands of Dalarna. Coffee, meanwhile, evolved from being a Turkish-French elite luxury good in the early eighteenth century to a crucial component of popular Swedish consumer culture in the nineteenth and twentieth centuries. Both of these banned global goods eventually transformed into important elements of national identity, as symbolic markers of Swedishness, both as material expressions like the 'authentic' *folkdräkt*, and as social practices such as "Swedish fika".

Smuggling mirrors its own time, its global processes, state concerns, and consumer demands, as well as the changing political role of borders. Both the quantity of smuggling and what is being smuggled thus give insights into shifting international and national conditions and concerns. While the eighteenth century saw exotic produce and European manufactures clandestinely passing across the Swedish borders, during the twentieth century, the same borders were illicitly crossed both by individuals fleeing Nazi persecution and by prohibited alcohol, and today customs officers seize drugs, alcohol, and tobacco. Recent introductions of sugar taxes in Norway and Denmark have also led to the increasing smuggling of sweets from Sweden. At the same time, the smuggling routes remain largely the same as they were during the eighteenth century. The archipelagos around Stockholm and Gothenburg, the southern coastline, and the Norwegian borderland all still play vital parts in the contraband trade, both organised on a large-scale and for moderate private consumption.

While the western and southern borders are largely the same today as in the eighteenth century, the Swedish eastern border permanently changed in 1809 when Finland was incorporated into the larger Russian Empire, and again when in 1917 it became an independent state. Today, Sweden no longer borders on Russia but on Finland, and the border between the two countries is roughly located where the boundary between the Western and Eastern parts of the country once lay in the Torne Valley. This has also affected smuggling, as smuggling communities developed along this new border, benefitting from the meeting between two different economic jurisdictions. Indeed, until the 1960s, smuggling was referred to in the regional language Meänkieli as 'joppari', which derives from the Swedish word 'to work' (*jobba*).[2] A recent addition to these border smuggling activities is the extensive smuggling of 'snus', oral tobacco, from Sweden to Finland, where it is prohibited under EU regulation. In Sweden, exempted from this ban, snus can still be produced and sold.[3] As exemplified by the case of snus, smuggling is thus influenced both by the *longue durée* and by immediate political shifts and changes.

In exploring eighteenth and early nineteenth-century smuggling, this book has shown that global trade played a crucial role in shaping the early modern Swedish state. The state reacted to the increased globalisation with expanding protectionism, and the new legislation intended to secure economic control over Sweden's own territory was a step towards consolidating state power. Meanwhile, a domestic consumer demand for the prohibited goods meant that smuggling flourished, and illicit trade came to be formative for Swedish politics, society, and culture. This highlights the need to consider how smaller, protectionist, and less commercially advanced states, like Sweden, reacted to and interacted with the processes of globalisation. Far from being disconnected or removed from globalisation, these states were affected by and contributed to the forces that shaped eighteenth-century Europe, but this only becomes visible when we start to incorporate the illegal incarnations of global trade into our historical analyses.

Notes

1 In addition to these, there was also the important Baltic city of Danzig, which it unfortunately has not been possible to include as much as it deserves in this study; further research is therefore necessary to establish the features of the Danzig contraband trade.

2 Meänkielen sanakirja, http://meankielensanakirja.com/sana/id/79880, Accessed 15 March 2022.

Juhani Kenttämaa, 'Jopparin jokilaakso – Oliko salakuljetus järjestäytynyttä rikollisuutta vai välttämätöntä kansanhuoltoa?, *Yle Dokumentit*, https://yle.fi/aihe/artikkeli/2019/06/05/jopparin-jokilaakso-oliko-salakuljetus-jarjestaytynytta-rikollisuutta-vai, Accessed 15 March 2022.

3 European Commission Memo, Questions & Answers: New rules for tobacco products, 26 February 2014, http://europa.eu/rapid/press-release_MEMO-14–134_en.htm, Accessed 15 March 2022.

BIBLIOGRAPHY

Riksarkivet, Stockholm (Swedish National Archives)

Borgareståndets arkiv
R1402,
vol. 6.
vol. 13.
Enskilda arkiv
Ericsbergsarkivet, Enskilda arkiv, Fredric Sparres samling,
vol. 5.
Strafsundarkivet, Ätten von Fersen, 6, Hans Axel von Fersens Samling, VI räkenskaper,
vol. 28.
Sjöholmssamlingen, Possesamlingen.
1818.
Stafssundsarkivet,
vol. 15
Handels- och finansexpeditionen med finanskontoret (äldre)
Råds och konseljprotokoll i renskrift, AI,
vol. 3.
Justitierevisionen
Besvärs- och Ansökningsmål, Utslagshandlingar,
1768 January no. 4.
1768 Mars, no. 1/2–32.
1769 June no 19.
1770 February, no. 45.
1806 September (II) 30 no. 110–138.
Justitieämbetet
Koncept, Huvudserien, BIIa
vol. 80.
Kollegiers m fl, landhövdingars, hovrätters och konsistories skrivelser till Kungl Maj:t
Skrivelser från landshövdingar, Ämnesordnade, Ang handelsrörelse mellan städer och landsbygd, A,
vol. 13.

Skrivelser från landshövdingar, Ämnesordnade handlingar, ang. Överflöd och yppighet, C,
vol. 25–29.
Skrivelser från Kommerskollegiet, 9,
vol. 205.
vol. 269.
vol. 252.
Kommerskollegium
Advokatfiskalskontoret, Cb4 Årsberättelser lurendrejerimål,
vol. 1–2.
Advokatfiskalskontoret, Rättsprotokoll, D.
Gränstullsrätten norr om Värmland, 1736–1824.
Göteborgs Sjötullsrätt, 1769.
Göteborgs Sjötullsrätt, 1773.
Uleåborg Sjötullen, 1769–1794.
Huvudarkiv, Acta privatorum, EXVIIda,
Vol. 3.
Huvudarkivet, Handels- och manufakturdivisionens protokoll, A I fa,
vol. 37a.
vol. 42.
Huvudarkivet, Justitiedivisionens protokoll, A I e,
vol. 50–51
vol. 55.
Huvudarkivet, Registratur, Huvudserie, BIa,
vol. 184.
Huvudarkivet, Kungliga brev och remisser huvudserie, E Ia,
vol. 116.
Kommerskollegiets Huvudarkiv, Särskilda utredningar och berättelser, F IV
vol. 23- Utredning angående exporterade lurendrejerivaror 1799–1805.
Kungliga Arkiv
Drottning Hedvig Elisabet Charlotta, Egenhändigt förda räkenskapsböcker, K
vol. 296.
Statskontoret
Kammarkontoret, Furstliga personers räkningar, G2M,
vol. 6.
Svenskt Diplomatariums huvudkartotek över medeltidsbreven, Skännninge
SDHK-Nr: 4197
Äldre Kommittéer
559, vol. 1 'Utredning Af Sveriges Och Englands Handelsförhållanden 1788–1789'
817, vol. 1. 'Kommittée Ang Förordning Mot Yppighet Och Överflöd, 1793'.
Äldre Centrala Tullarkiv
Överdirektören för Sjötullen, Advokatfiskalens Arkiv C3,
vol. 24.
Överdirektören vid Sjötullen, Advokatfiskalen, Liggare, D3,
vol. 1–2.
Överdirektören vid Sjötullen, Huvudarkiv, Liggare över föredragna mål, D1,
vol. 7.
Överdirektören vid Sjötullen, Kansliet, Personella berättelser och anmärkningspunkter, E1,
vol. 2–3.
vol. 11–12.

vol. 16.
vol. 25–26.
vol. 38.
Generaltullarrendesocieteten, m. fl., Kansliet, Skrivelser från tullfiskaler E8,
vol. 1.
Generaltullarrendesocieteternas fullmäktige, m. fl., Kansliet, Resefiskaler, E 9,
vol. 1–2.
vol. 4–5.
Generaltullarrendesocieteternas fullmäktige, m fl, Kansliet, Skrivelser från land- och sjötullkamrarna, E10,
vol. 4.
Generaltullarrendessocieteten, Ämnesordnade handlingar F1,
vol. 1.
Generaltullförvaltningen och Överdirektören vid stora Sjötullen till kungl. majt 1670–1792.
Ämnessamlingar
Miscellanea, Tullväsende, Rättegångs handlingar i tullmål 1700–1800,
vol. 27.
Personarkiv, Biographica,
vol. B32b.
vol. E15.
vol. FII3.
vol. RII3 21.
vol. S88.
Överståthållarämbetet för Uppbördsärenden
Kammarexpeditionen, Mantalslängder, BA
25/15.
27/6.
27/14.

Kungliga Biblioteket (Swedish National Library)

Handsskriftssamlingen
Peter Adam Wallmark,
vol. 3
C. C. Gjörwell, Biografiska samlingar, I
vol. 36.

Stadsarkivet, Stockholm (Stockholm City Archives)

Borgerskapets gubbhus
Inträdesansökningar, E1,
vol. 8.
Handelskollegiet
Speciella längder och förteckningar över borgare m fl, Längder över borgare i allmänhet D II a,
vol. 6.
Justitiekollegium
Förmyndarkammaren, Rådhusrättens 1:a avdelning 1850–1924, F1A, Bouppteckningar,
1811 del. 4.

Kramhandlaren Johan Sundbeck
Handlingar, 1800–1816.
vol. 4.
Skråarkiv, Siden - och Klädeskramhandelsocieteten
Protocoll, 1796–1868, A,
vol. 1.
Siden- och klädeskramhandelssocietetens handlingar, 1787–1799, F1,
vol. 2
vol. 3.
Stockholms Rådhusrätt
Avdelning 2, avdelning för tullmål, Inneliggande handlingar, E,
vol. 1.
Stora Sjötullen, Protokoll, A,
vol. 1–8.
vol. 22–23
vol. 26–27
S:ta Eugenia Katolska församlings kyrkoarkiv
Födelse och dopböcker. 1793.
Storkyrkoförsamlingens kyrkoarkiv
Födelse- och dopböcker, huvudserie,
vol. 14.
Överståthållarämbetet För Polisärenden
Äldre poliskammaren, Protokoll, AIa1,
vol. 46
Äldre poliskammaren, Diarium, CIa1,
vol. 21
vol. 22
vol. 26
vol. 27
Överståthållarämbetet för uppbördsärenden
Register till Kronotaxeringslängd, G 1 AF,
vol. 11–14.

Landsarkivet, Lund (Regional Archives in Lund)

Karlskrona Tyska Församlings kyrkoarkiv
Födelse- och dopböcker. Huvudserie.
1725–1797.

Landsarkivet, Göteborg (Regional Archives in Gothenburg)

Göteborgs Sjötullsrätt
Domböcker, A1
vol. 7
vol. 10
vol. 18–20
Inneliggande handlingar F
vol. 7
vol. 9

Landskansliets för Göteborgs och Bohus län arkiv
'Ankomna Skrivelser Från Kungl. Maj:T m. Fl.'
Uddevalla rådhusrätt och magistrats arkiv
Bouppteckningar och arvskiften (1809–1811).

Nordiska Museets Arkiv (Archives of the Nordic Museum, Stockholm)

Ämnessamlingen
Dagböcker,
vol. 9.

Slottsarkivet (Castle Archives, Stockholm)

Hovstatsräkenskaper
Räkenskaper ang. enskilda medel,
vol. 55.
vol. 56.

Linköpings stadsbibliotek (Linköping City Library)

Lindblomska samlingen
Lindblomska brevsamlingen,
vol. 15.

Kansalliarkisto, Helsinki (Finnish National Archives)

Routsin kauppakollegion tuomiokirja-arkistoa
Rajatullioikeuksien tuomiokirjat, RTO,
vol. 1
vol. 2

British National Archives, Kew, London

Foreign Office Papers
General Correspondence from Political and Other Departments, Sweden, FO 73,
vol. 1
vol. 4–7
vol. 17–18
vol. 27
High Court of Admiralty
Prize Court: Sentences and Interlocutories, HCA 34
vol.61
HM Treasury
Treasury: Minutes, Entry-books and correspondence pre 1920, T 1,
vol. 425/199–200
State Papers Office
State Papers Domestic, George II, SP 36,
vol.114
State Papers Foreign, Sweden, SP 95,
vol. 123
vol. 125–126

Centre des Archives diplomatiques de la Courneuve, Paris

Archives du ministère des affaires étrangères
Mémoires et Documents, Suède, MD
vol. 6, 1632–1814
vol. 38, 1778–1808
Correspondance Consulaire,
vol. 3. Stockholm
Personnel,
vol. 31. Première série nominative

Printed Primary Material

Royal Decrees

Kong. Maj:ts Nådiga kungörelse, angående förnyande af det uti förordningen under den 1 januarii 1794 stadgade förbud emot caffés införsel och bruk (1799).

Kongl. Commerce-Collegii circulair til samtelige Tull=Rätter, angående widtagne anstalter emot mißbruk af den allmogen i wißa händer af Elfsborgs län tillåtne gårdfari=handel (1792).

Kongl. Maj:ts bref til Hof-Rätterne, Commerce-Collegium och Gen. Tull-Direction, at förordningen af d. 26 julii 1766, rörande yppighets och öfwerflöds hämmande, tils widare måtte hwila, i den del, som angår införande och förtullande af caffe-bönor i riket, 23 Oct 1769 (1769).

Kongl. Maj:ts Förnyade förordning emot yppighet och öfwerflöd. 15 martii 1770 (1770).

Kongl. Maj:ts Förnyade land-tulls och accis stadga, 19 sep 1776 (1776).

Kongl. Maj:ts Förnyade nådiga seglations-ordning 15 juni 1774 (1774).

Kongl. Maj:ts förordning emot lurendrägerier eller förbudne utrikes warors införsel i riket (1770).

Kongl. Maj:ts Nådiga förbud emot hus=visitationer, gifwit Ekolsund then 16 julii 1776 (1776).

Kongl. Maj:ts Nådiga förklaring öfwer wisse stycken uti förordningen af den 27 januarii 1757, angående lurendrägeriers uptäckande och hämmande (1757).

Kongl. Maj:ts Nådiga förordning til hämmande af lurendrägerier, gifwen Stockholms slott then 14 martii 1785 (1785).

Kongl. Maj:ts Nådiga förordning, til förekommande af lurendrägeri och tullförsnillning. Gifwen Haga slott den 6 april 1799 (1799).

Kongl. Maj:ts Nådiga förordning, til hämmande af yppighet och öfwerflöd. Gifwen Stockholms Slott den 1 Januarii 1794 (1794).

Kongl. Maj:ts Nådiga kungörelse angående förnyande af det uti förordningen den 1 januarii 1794 stadgade förbud emot caffés införsel och bruk (1799).

Kongl. Maj:ts Nådiga kungörelse om caffés införsel och bruk. Gifwen Stockholms slott den 6 april 1802 (1802).

Kongl. Maj:ts Nådiga kungörelse, angående afgifterne til medelhafs=handelns och sjöfartens beskydd. Gifwen Stockholms slott den 30 martii 1802 (1802).

Kongl. Maj:ts Nådiga kungörelse, angående caffes införande och nyttjande tils widare. Gifwen Stockholms slott d 24 nov 1796 (1796).

Kongl. Maj:ts Nådiga kungörelse, angående förbud emot oloflig handel och uplag af lurendrägade waror i rikets skärgårdar. Gifwen Stockholms slott den 19 junii 1798 (1798).

Kongl. Maj:ts Nådiga warning och förbud, emot gemenskap och handel med utländske kapare. Gifwen Drottningholms slott den 16 julii 1799 (1799).
Kongl. Maj:ts Nådige förordning angående wißa utrikes warors sa wäl lösgifwande ifrån förbud til införsel som beläggande med mindre manufactur fonds och andre afgifter. 21 september 1761 (1761).
Kongl. Maj:ts Nådige förordning, angående wiße öfwerflöds wahrors förbiudande til införsel i riket (4 nov 1756),
Kongl. Maj:ts Nådige förordning, emot yppighet och öfwerflöd. Gifwen Stockholm i Råd-Cammaren then 26 junii 1766 (1766).
Kongl. Maj:ts Nådige förordning, til lurendrägeriers hämmande (1766).
Kongl. Maj:ts Nådiga kungörelse, angående dels förbud emot införsel af wiße utländske waror, dels ock högre tull-afgifter derå, 1 januari 1794 (1794).
Kongl. Maj:ts Nådige kundgörelse, angående förbud emot ost-indiske sidentygers införsel och försäljande här i riket, ifrån 1755. års början, 19 februari 1754 (1754).
Kongl. Maj:ts Nådige kungörelse, angående lindring i tullen m. m. å americanske och westindiske waror, som med swenska skepp hitföras. Gifwen Stockholm slott then 6 martii 1783 (1783).
Kongl. Maj:ts Nådige resolution och förklaring, uppå de allmänna beswär, som...Städerne i Swerige och Finland... andragit (1762).
Kongl. Maj:Ts Och Rikets Commerce-Collegii Förnyade kungörelse, angående wästgöthe allmogens gårdfarihandel med hwad derwid i akt tagas bör. Gifwen Stockholm Den 8 martii 1803. Stockholm: Kongl. Tryckeriet, 1803.
Kongl. Maj:ts och Rikets Commerce-Collegii Kungörelse, angående förklaring af 5. art. 2. §. uti Kongl. Maj:ts under den 6 april 1799 utfärdade nådiga förordning til förkommande af lurendrägeri och tull=försnillning. Gifwen Stockholm den 27 julii 1801 (1801).
Kongl. Maj:ts och Rikets Commerce-Collegii Kungörelse, angående förbud för obehörige personer af judiske nationen, och italienare at til handels idkande resa omkring landet. Gifwen Stockholm den 8 februarii 1802 (1802).
Kongl. Maj:ts och Rikets Commerce-Collegii Kungörelse, angående segelfarten på utländske orter ifrån Götheborgs och Bohus, samt Hallands=läns skärgårdar (1798).
Kongl. Maj:ts och Riksens Commerce-Collegii Reglemente, för them af judeska nationen, som wilja hit i riket inflytta och sig här nedsätta, 27 Maj 1782 (1782).
Kongl. Maj:ts och Riksens Commerce-Collegii Kungörelse, Angående Förbud emot så kallat Swenskt Caffé. Gifwen Stockholm den 19 Junii 1794 (1794).
Kongl. Maj:ts och Riksens Commerce-Collegii Kungörelse, angående förbud emot utländskt kamulls=garns införsel. Gifwen Stockholm then 11 april 1785 (1785).
Kongl. Maj:ts och Riksens Commerce-Collegii Kungörelse, angående wißa omständigheter rörande Marstrands fri=hamn; Gifwen Stockholm then 20 junii 1782 (1782).
Kongl. Maj:ts Och Riksens Kammar-Collegii Kungörelse, dels angående wisza utrikes waror, hwilka til införsel i riket för thetta warit förbudne, men nu, til underdånigst följe af Hans Kongl. Maj:ts Nådige Bref under then 14 i thenna månad, til införande hädanefter blifwa låfgifne; dels ock sådane waror the uti 1771 års Siö-Tulls-Taxa utsatte afgifter, i wisza delar härmedelst blifwa ändrade (24 Sep 1776).
Kongl. Maj:ts Taxa, hwarefter Stora Sjö=Tullen uppå alla inkommande waror beräknas och erlägges. Gifwen Stockholm slott den 17 april 1799 (1799).
Kongl. Maj:ts Taxa, hwarefter Stora Sjö=Tullen uppå alla inkommande waror bör erläggas och upbäras, 6 jun 1782 (1782).
Kongl. Maj:ts Taxa, hwarefter Stora Sjö=Tullen uppå alla inkommande waror bör erläggas och upbäras, 15 feb 1771 (1771).

Kongl. Maj:ts Ytterligare nådiga förordning, till lurendrägeriers hämmande. gifwen i råd-cammaren then 18 april 1768 (1768).
Kongl. Maj:ts Ytterligare nådige förordning, angående lurendrägeriers uptäckande och hämmande (1757).
Kongl. Maj:ts Ytterligare nådige påbud, emot caffé drickande. Gifwit Stockholm i Råd-Cammaren then 24 martii 1768 (1768).
Kongl. Maj. Giästgifware=ordning, öfwersedd, förnyad och förbättrad wid riksdagen uti Stockholm (1734).
Kongl. Majts Kungörelse, angående inrättandet af en så kallad porto-franco uti Marstrand. den 15 augusti 1775 (1775).
Kongl. Seglations-ordningen af d. 28 julii 1724 (1724).
Kongl. Slotts=Canelliets Kungörelse, angående gatuköp och olaga handel samt förköp och mångleri, jämte de utfärdade taxors efterlefnad, 10 dec 1767 (1767).
Påbud angående en consumtions-accis erläggande af thé, caffe, rök- och snus-tobak, samt puder (1747).
Taxa för Wilmanstrand, Cajana, Kides- och Pelis tull-kamrar wid ryska gränsen (1738).
Taxa, hwarefter, ifrån then 1 september 1747, the på thenne förteckning upförde utrikes ifrån inkommande waror, komma at betala afgift til manufactur fonden (30 jun 1747).
Öfwer=Ståthålare Embetets Kungöresle och förbud, emot handels= manufactur- och handtwerkeri warora obehöriga afsalu, Gifwen Stockholm then 12 september 1783 (1783).
Öfwer=Ståthållare Embetets förnyade kungörelse om resandes skyldighet at med resepass sig förse. 1799 (1799).

Newspapers

'-'. *Bihang til Dagligt Allehanda*, 28 January 1783, no 22.
'-'. *Bihang till Dagligt Allehanda*, 1 February 1799, no 27.
'-'. *Bihang till Dagligt Allehanda*, 18 April 1799, no 88.
'-'. *Dagligt Allehanda*, 1 March 1800, no 50.
'-'. *Dagligt Allehanda*, 13 December 1775, no 286.
'-'. *Dagligt Allehanda*, 13 November 1778, no 260.
'-'. *Dagligt Allehanda*, 14 September 1810, no 251.
'-'. *Dagligt Allehanda*, 15 July 1780, no 158.
'-'. *Dagligt Allehanda*, 21 February 1775, no 43.
'-'. *Dagligt Allehanda*, 25 June 1788, no 145.
'-'. *Dagligt Allehanda*, 29 June 1769, no 141.
'-'. *Dagligt Allehanda*, 3 March 1775, no 52.
'-'. *Dagligt Allehanda*, 30 June 1798, no 147.
'-'. *Dagligt Allehanda*, 5 April 1792, no 81.
'-'. *Dagligt Allehanda*, 5 August 1776, no 176.
'-'. *Dagligt Allehanda*, 5 December 1775, no 279.
'-'. *Dagligt Allehanda*, 8 July 1773, no 151.
'-'. *Dagligt Allehanda*. 20 November 1771, no 261.
'-'. *Dagligt Allehanda*. 22 February 1775, no 44.
'-'. *Dagligt Allehanda*. 3 March 1775, no 52.
'-'. *Fahlu Weckoblad*, 22 August 1795, no 23.
'-'. *Fahlu Weckoblad*, 30 August 1794, no 13.

'-'. *Götheborgs Allehanda*, 1 February 1782, no 10.
'-'. *Götheborgs Allehanda*, 22 February 1782, no 16.
'-'. *Götheborgska Nyheter*, 17 August 1765, no 33.
'-'. *Götheborgska Nyheter*, 6 March 1773, no 10.
'-'. *Götheborgska Nyheter*, 6 October 1781, no 40.
'-'. *Inrikes Tidningar*, 10 September 1802, no 98.
'-'. *Inrikes Tidningar*, 23 April 1799, no 46.
'-'. *Inrikes Tidningar*, 24 April 1799, no 47.
'-'. *Inrikes Tidningar*, 27 January 1801, no 10.
'-'. *Inrikes Tidningar*, 3 December 1792.
'-'. *Inrikes Tidningar*, 5 July 1797, no 78.
'-'. *Inrikes Tidningar*, 6 November 1799, no 131.
'-'. *Inrikes Tidningar*, 1 September 1801, no 95.
'-'. *Inrikes Tidningar*, 7 July 1807, no 72.
'-'. *Inrikes Tidningar*, 9 March 1804, no 28.
'-'. *Stockholms Posttidningar*, 21 July 1796, no 80.
'-'. *Stockholms Posttidningar*, 3 January 1801, no 1.
'-'. *Stockholms Posttidningar*, 4 December 1800, no 137.
'-'. *Stockholms Posttidningar*, 6 September 1802, no 107.
'-'. *Stockholms Posten*, 26 August 1794, no 193.
'-'. *Stockholms Posten*, 8 June 1788, no 104.
'-'. *Stockholms Posten*, 10 August 1789, no 234.
'Anmärkning wid det i Dagbladet N:o 114 ugifne förslag om Landt= och Sjö=Tullarnes uphäfwande', *Dagligt Allehanda*, 13 June 1776, no 133.
'Anmärkning wid hwad i Stockholmske Dagbladet N:o 250 blifwit infördt, rörande Banco=lån och Handels=Balance', *Dagligt Allehanda*, 12 December 1778, no 285.
'Anmärkningar öfwer det, som rörande Swenske Fabrikerne', *Inrikes Tidningar*, 29 August 1797, no 101.
'Betraktelser Öfwer Några Riksdags=ämnen, Enfaldeligen Framställde Af En Profan'. *Stockholms Posten*, 3 July 1823, no 150.
'Diverse Kungörelser'. *Stockholms Post-Tidningar*, 6 September 1802, no 107.
'Enligt Högloflige Kongl. Commerce=Collegii Til Sköfdes Stads Accis=Rätt...' *Inrikes Tidningar*, 1 September 1801, no 95.
'Et Ord Til Lurendrägaren'. *Dagligt Allehanda*, 7 November 1771, no 250.
'Fabrikören Jacob Reinhold Bremers från Åbo underdånigste Tal til Hans Kongl. Maj:t, wid Nådigst lewnadt företräde på Drottningholms Slott den 4 i nästl. Månad, i anledning af Kongl. Förordningen til Lurendrägeriers hämmande, dat. Den 6 Apr 1799', *Inrikes Tidningar*, 7 August 1799, no 92.
'Fabrikören Jacob Reinhold Bremers Från Åbo Underdånigste Tal Til Hans Kongl. Maj:T, Wid Nådigst Lewnadt Företräde På Drottningholms Slott Den 4 i Nästl. Månad, i Anledning Af Kongl. Förordningen Til Lurendrägeriers Hämmande, Dat. Den 6 Apr 1799', *Inrikes Tidningar*, 7 August 1799, no 92.
'Fortsättning', *Extra Posten*, 26 February 1793, no 48.
'Fortsättning, från Gårdags=Bladet, af en Fabriqueurs Bref', *Dagligt Allehanda*, 10 March 1773, no 58.
'Frågas Herrar Såckerbruks=Idkare i Götheborg', Götheborgs Allehanda, 17 March 1775, no 22.
'Förslag om Landt= och Sjö=Tullarnes uphäfvande', *Dagligt Allehanda*, 21 May 1776, no 114.

'Förteckning På de Personer, Hwilka Hos Öfwer=Ståthållare=Embetet i Stockholm Ytterligare Blifwit Sakfällde För Förbrytelser Emot Kongl. Maj:Ts Nådiga Förordning Emot Yppighet Och Öfwerflöd Af d. 1 Januarii 1794'. *Dagligt Allehanda*, 1 August 1795, no 172.
'Förteckning På Personer Som Förbrutit Sig Mot Yppighet Och Öwerflöds Förordningen'. *Dagligt Allehanda*, 8 November 1794, no 256.
'Hjälp Gud...' *Allmänhetens Röst*, 1771.
'Huru Man Genom Snålhet Kan Blifwa Fattig Och Genom Förnuftig Hushållning Förmögen, Bewisa Twånne Ännu Lefwande Bröders Exempel'. *Fahlu Weckoblad*, 22 November 1788.
'Hwad Nytt i Staden?' *Hwad Nytt?*, 1 July 1774, nos 4 & 5.
'Kongl. Commerce Collegii underdåniga Betänkande angående Fabrikernes tilstånd, och om nödwändigheten af Visitationer efter Lurendrägade Waror. På Fabriks Societeternes anhållan utlemnadt til tryckning', *Stockholms Posten*, 15 February 1793, no 39.
'Kongl. Maj:Ts Nådiga Kungörelse, Angående Caffes Införande Och Nyttjande Tils Widare'. *Fahlu Weckoblad*, 10 December 1796, no 43.
'Kongl. Maj:Ts Nådiga Kungörelse, Angående Caffès Införande Och Nyttjande Tils Widare'. *Carlscronas Weckoblad*, 17 December 1796, no 50.
'Kongl. Maj:Ts Nådiga Warning, Emot Öfwerträdelser Af Deå Den 1 Januarii 1794 Utfärdade Förordning Til Hämmande Af Yppighet Och Öfwerflöd. Gifwen Drottningholms Slott Den 9 Julii 1795.' *Fahlu Weckoblad*, 22 August 1795.
'Kongl. Maj. Högsta Domstolens Utslag', *Dagligt Allehanda*, 26 April 1796, no 93.
'Konkurstvist', *Posttidningar*, 24 August 1803, no 115.
'Kungörelser (Fournier)'. *Götheborgs Tidningar*, 5 November 1790, no 129.
'Kungörelser'. *Götheborgs Allehanda*, 7 September 1782, no 55.
'Lista Över Folk Dömda För Lurendrägeri Och Tull-Försnillning.' *Stockholms Post-Tidningar*, 20 December 1800, no 144.
'Min Kära Broder, Jöns Krämare'. *Dagligt Allehanda*, 24 July 1770, no 164.
'Norrköpings Manufactur-Idkares Underdånigst Ingifne Skrift Til Hans Kongl. Maj:T, i Anledning Af Des Nådiga Förordning Til Lurendrägeriers Hämmande, Dat. Den 6 April 1799', *Inrikes Tidningar*, 25 June 1799, no 73.
'Något om Hus= och Hem=frid', *Extra Posten*, 13 February 1793, no 37.
'Om Caffe (Ur En Tysk Journal)'. *Stockholms Posten*, 15 May 1800, no 109.
'Om Caffe'. *Fahlu Weckoblad*, 25 August 1787, no 4.
'Om Engelska Lurendrägerierne'. *Stockholms Posten*, 24 September 1788, no 223.
'Om Yppighet.' *Sofrosyne. Ett Blad För Svenska Fruntimmer*, 8 July 1815, no 28.
'Passagerare'. *Inrikes Tidningar*, 17 July 1799, no 83.
'Passagerare'. *Inrikes Tidningar*, 4 July 1797, no 77.
'Pro Memoria för dem som skrifwa i Finance'. *Dagligt Allehanda*, 17 February 1775, no 40.
'Project, Til Hämmande Af Lurendrägerier'. *Dagligt Allehanda*, 19 June 1770, no 136.
'Strödda Tankar öfwer Swaret på Anmärkningarne emot Förslaget om Landt= och Sjötullarnes uphäfwande', *Dagligt Allehanda*, 23 August 1776, no 192.
'Svar på Stockholms Posten no 39 15 feb 1793', *Extra Posten*, 25 February 1793, no 47.
'Swar På Frågan i Dagligt Allehanda N:O 28 Om Lurendrägerie Generals=Hus'. *Dagligt Allehanda*, 12 March 1772, no 60.
'Tankar om en wiß stadgad Swensk Kläde=drägt', *Dagligt Allehanda*, 6 December 1773, no 279.
'The Herr M.---S--- i Stockholms Posten N:o 53 d 5 Martii', *Stockholms Posten*, 28 April 1794, no 95.
'Til Herr Arimaspus i Anledning Af Dagbladerne N:Ris 73 Och 74 För Innewarande År'. *Dagligt Allehanda*, 23 April 1776, no 92.

'Til Herr Arimaspus', *Dagligt Allehanda*, 7 February 1775, no 31.
'Til Herr Danaus i Dagligt Allehanda 133', *Dagligt Allehanda*, 1 July 1773, no 145.
'Til Herr Owäldig', *Dagligt Allehanda*, 2 November 1778, no 250.
'Til Herr Älskare af Rikets Wältrefnad', *Dagligt Allehanda*, 16 June 1773, no 133.
'Til Salu Finnes (Fournier)'. *Götheborgs Allehanda*, 9 November 1790, no 90.
'Till Underdånigste Följe Af Kongl. Maj:Ts Nådiga Förordning till Förekommande Af Lurendrägerier Och Tullförsnillning Af d n 6 April 1799'. *Inrikes Tidningar*, 20 October 1802, no 114.
'Till Underdånigste Följe Af Kongl. Maj:Ts Nådiga Förordning till Förekommande Af Lurendrägerier Och Tullförsnillning Af d n 6 April 1799'. *Inrikes Tidningar*, 9 March 1804, no 28.
'Till Underdånigste Följe Af Kongl. Maj:Ts Nådiga Förordning till Förekommande Af Lurendrägerier Och Tullförsnillning Af d n 6 April 1799'. *Inrikes Tidningar*, 13 March 1804, no 29.
'Till Underdånigste Följe Af Kongl. Maj:Ts Nådiga Förordning till Förekommande Af Lurendrägerier Och Tullförsnillning Af d n 6 April 1799'. *Inrikes Tidningar*, 3 May 1805, no 49.
'Till Underdånigste Följe Af Kongl. Maj:Ts Nådiga Förordning till Förekommande Af Lurendrägerier Och Tullförsnillning Af d n 6 April 1799'. *Inrikes Tidningar*, 26 November 1805, no 133.
'Till Underdånigste Följe Af Kongl. Maj:Ts Nådiga Förordning till Förekommande Af Lurendrägerier Och Tullförsnillning Af d n 6 April 1799'. *Inrikes Tidningar*, 12 June 1811, no 68.
'Utdrag Af Kongl. Maj:Ts Nådiga Kungörelse, Angående Caffes Införande Och Nyttjande Tils Widare'. *Götheborgs Tidningar*, 13 December 1796, no 143.
'Utdrag Af Kongl. Maj:Ts Nådiga Kungörelse, Angående Caffes Införande Och Nyttjande Tils Widare'. *Norrköpings Tidningar*, 21 December 1796, no 101.
'Utdrag Af Protocollet Hållit Wid Stora Sjötulls-Rätten i Stockholm Den 6 Junii 1769'. *Dagligt Allehanda*, 9 September 1773, no 205.
'Wigde i Landsorterne'. *Inrikes Tidningar*, 20 August 1764, no 65.
'Ödmjuk Memorial', *Stockholms Posten*, 6 August 1793, no 176.
Arimaspus. 'Herr Walerius Publicola'. *Dagligt Allehanda*, 29 December 1774, no 298.
Carolin. 'Swar På Dagligt Allehanda No 84, Den 11 April 1772'. *Götheborgska Nyheter*. 30 January 1773, no 5.
Fournier, Jean Antoine. '-'. *Götheborgs Allehanda*, 28 March 1800, nos 38 & 39.
Grevesmöhlen, Carl August. 'Några Svar Hafva'. *Trompeten Eller Krigsförklaring Emot Allt Ondt*, 17 March 1812, no 30.
Hirch, David. 'Afskrift.' *Dagligt Allehanda*, 9 March 1799, no 57.
Leidesdorff. '-'. *Stockholms Posten*, 15 March 1793, no 61.
Lurendrägaren (Fictional). 'Swar Til Fädernelandets=älskare'. Posten, 12 April 1769.
Lönnroth, Elias. '-'. *Helsingfors Morgonblad*, 28 July 1834.
Tertius Interveniens, (probably C.A. Grevesmöhlen). 'Några Anmärkningar Wid Grefwe C. H. Poßes Wäckta Motion Om En Förändrad Organisation of Tull=Styrelsen'. *Stockholms Posten*, 2 June 1823, no 124.
Wälment. 'Wälment Af Kärlek För Fädernelandet'. *Stockholms Posten*, 3 August 1785, no 55.

Other Printed Primary Sources

Acerbi, Giuseppe. *Travels Through Sweden, Finland, and Lapland, to the North Cape: In the Years 1798 and 1799*. London: Joseph Mawman, 1802.
'Adam Smith'. *Litteratur tidning för år 1795* 1 (1795).

Adlerbeth, Gudmund Göran, ed. *Från tredje Gustafs dagar. Anteckningar och minnen*. Vol. 2. Stockholm: F. & G. Beijer, 1893.

Anonymous. *Seasonable advice to all smugglers of French cambricks and French lawns; with a brief state, from the honourable commissioners of his Majesty's customs, of smuggling in the year 1745; as also the destructive manner in which the smuggling trade is carried on at present; and a remedy propos'd totally to suppress it, and thereby to increase the revenue several hundred thousand pounds annually*. London, 1751.

———. *Qwäde, om den gyllende tiden, då caffe war i bruk*, Stockholm: Johan Georg Lange, 1767.

———. *Reflexioner wid en anonym auctors tankar om sättet til wåra swenska manufacturers uphjelpande*. Stockholm: Stockholm, tryckt hos Carl Stolpe, 1769.

———. 'Underdån ödmjukaste memorial, upläst i Commerce-Utskottet den 26 Oct 1769', *Riksdagshandlingar*, Stockholm, 1769.

———. *Observations on smuggling, humbly submitted to the consideration of the right honourable the House of Peers, and the honourable the House of Commons, in Parliament assembled*. [n.p.], [1779?].

———. 'Review - Stockholm: undersökning om kongl. stora sjö- och gränse-tullar, samt acciser och små-tullar, med flera consumtion', edited by G.A. Silfverstolpe. *Journal för svensk litteratur* 4 (1800).

———. *Är den af tull-arrende-societetens herrar fullmäktige, i november månad år 1806, gjorda underdåniga ansökan, att till qvarblifvande i riket få försälja förbudna confiskerade manufaktur-varor, ett bevis af herrar fullmäktiges nit om de svenska manufakturernas förkofran?* Stockholm: Joh. Pehr Lindh, 1809.

———. *Några ord, i anledning af en nyligen utkommen smädeskrift, kallad: några bewis att judarne äfwen på sitt sätt bidraga till den allmänna nöden i Swerige*. Stockholm: Peter Bohm, 1809.

———. *Matrikel över svenska frimurare orden*. 1940.

Arndt, Ernst Moritz. *Resa genom Sverige år 1804*. Translated by J. M. Stjernstolpe. Vol. 3. Carlstad, 1808.

Arnould, Ambroise-Marie. *Système maritime et politique des Européens pendant le dix-huitieme siecle; fondé sur leurs traités de paix de commerce et de navigation par le citoyen Arnould chef du Bureau du commerce et de la Balance du commerce*. de l'imprimerie d'Antoine Bailleul, 1797.

Beccaria, Cesare.*An Essay on Crimes and Punishments, Translated from the Italian; with a Commentary Attributed to Mons. de Voltaire, Translated from the French*. London, 1767.

———. *Afhandling om brott och straff*. Translated by Johan Henrik Hochschild. Stockholm: Wennberg och Nordström, 1770.

Bellman, Carl Michael. *Carl Michael Bellmans skrifter standardupplaga - Fredmans Espistlar I*, Stockholm: Albert Bonniers Förlag, 1927.

———. *Carl Michael Bellmans skrifter VI. Dramatiska arbeten*, Stockholm: Albert Bonniers Förlag, 1936.

Berch, Anders. *Inledning til almänna hushålningen, innefattande grunden til politie, oeconomie och cameral wetenskaperne. til deras tiänst, som biwista de almänne föreläsningar inrättad*. Stockholm, 1747.

Bilagor till högloflige ridderskapets och adelns protocoll, vid lagtima riksdagen i Stockholm År 1823, 1823.

Biörnsson, Jonas. *Riksdagsmannens Jonas Biörnssons märkwärdiga memorial*. Stockholm, 1770.

Biurman, Georg. *Vägvisare, til och ifrån alla städer och namnkunniga orter, uti Svea- och Göta-Riken, samt stor-förstendömet Finland; jämte tvänne uti koppar stuckne väg-chartor, efter skedde vägmätningar uprättad, af georg biurman. med kongl. maj:ts allernådigste privil.* 4th ed. Stockholm: Johan Georg Lange, 1776.

Bodell, Erik Erl. *Berättelse för år 1805, afgifven till höglof.gener.tull-arrende-direktionen, ifrån Marstrands kongl. stora sjötulls-kammare: om handeln: fabriker och manufakturer: orsaken till minskning eller förhöjning i sjötulls-inkomsterna: huru tillfällen till sjötulls-uppbördens minskning måga förekommas: om lurendrägeri: och medel till en bättre sjötulls-bevakning.* Göteborg: Norberg, 1806.

———. *Anmärkningar om tull-verket, i anledning af öfver-direktören vid kgl. landtulls- och accis-verket, högädle herr C. A. Grevesmöhlens memorial i samma ämne; ingifne till rikets högloft. ständers bevillnings-utskott.* Stockholm: Henrik And. Nordström, 1809.

———. *Försök till anmärkningar öfver några punkter i stats-hushållnings och finans-ämnen.* Göteborg: Samuel Norberg, 1809.

———. *Utkast till reglemente för öfver- och under officienterna vid kgl. sjö- och gränse-tullverket.* Stockholm, 1815.

Bohn, Gottfried Christian. *Gottfried Christian Bohns Wohlerfahrner Kaufmann Herausgegeben von C.D. Ebeling, Professor Am Gymnasium Zu Hamburg Und Mitvorsteber Der Handlungsakademie, Und P. H. C. Brodhagen, Lehrer Vei Der Handlungsakademie.* 5th ed. Hamburg: Carl Ernst Bohn, 1789.

Bonde, Christer. 'Riks-rådet, presidenten i general-commerce-collegio, f.d. ambassadören vid engelska hofvet, friherre Christer Bondes Berättelse om Skånes, Hallands och Blekinges tillstånd och förbättring, strax efter desse landskapers afträdande till Sverige'. In *Handlingar Rörande Skandinaviens Historia*, Vol. 6. Stockholm: Elmén and Granberg, 1818.

Bondeståndets riksdagsprotokoll, 7, 1751–56. Stockholm: Almqvist & Wiksells, 1963.

Bondeståndets riksdagsprotokoll, 11, 1769. Stockholm: Almqvist & Wiksells, 1975.

Borgarståndets riksdagsprotokoll, 11 1755–1756, Första delen. Stockholm: Riksdagstryckeriet, 2013.

Bull, Peter. 'Kjøbmand Peter Bull's optegnelser. Et handelshus i Fredriksstad 1770–1800.' In *Norsk Tidskrift for Genealogi, Personalhistorie, Biografi og Litteraerhistorie*, edited by S.H. Finne-Grønn, Vol. 1. Christiania: Cammermeyers, 1910.

Carpelan, Carl Mauritz. 'Bilagor till pleniprotocollet för den 21 martii'. In *Bilagor till högloflige ridderskapets och adelns protocoll, vid lagtima riksdagen i Stockholm år 1823*, Vol. 2. Stockholm: Olof Grahn, 1823.

Carstèn, Eric, and Pehr Kalm. 'I Jesu namn! Historisk och œconomisk beskrifning öfwer cajanaborgslän'. Åbo Academy, 1754.

Chydenius, Anders. *Svar på den af kgl. wetenskaps academien förestälta frågan: hwad kan wara orsaken, at sådan myckenhet swenskt folk årligen flytter utur landet? Och genom hwad författningar det kan bäst förekommas? Inlemnat år 1763; men nu allmänhetens.* Stockholm: Peter Hesselberg, 1765.

———. *Politiska skrifter.* Helsinki: G. W. Edlund, 1880.

De Piles, Alphonse Fortia, & M. Boisgelin. *Voyage de deux Français.* Paris: Desenne, 1796. Vol. II.

Drevon, I. F. Henrik. *Voyage En Suède: Contenant Un État Detaillé de Sa Population de Son Agriculture, de Son Commerce, et de Ses Finances.* La Haye: Gosse, 1789.

Eden, William. 'First Report from the Committee Appointed to Enquire into the Illicit Pracitses Used in Defrauding the Revenue. Reported by the Right Honourable William Eden, 24 December 1783'. In *Reports from Committees of the House of Commons Which Have Been Printed by Order of the House*, Vol. 11. House of Commons, 1803.

Ehrensvärd, Gustaf Johan. *Dagboksanteckningar förda vid Gustaf III:s hof af friherre Gustaf Johan Ehrensvärd.* 2nd ed. Vol. 1. 2 vols. Stockholm: P.A. Norstedt & Söners förlag, 1878.

Eloy, Nicolas F. J. *Af en medicinsk, så wäl som politisk fråga: om dageliga bruket at dricka caffe är nyttigt eller åtminstone oskyldigt i anseende til hälsan; om det kan förenas med statens bästa, eller om det i alla fall är skadeligt?* Translated by Unknown. Stockholm: Stolpiska Tryckeriet, 1783.

Filangieri, Gaetano. *Lagstiftningens vetenskap.* Stängnäs: Carl Er. Ekmarck, 1814.

Flintberg, Jacob Albrecht. *Anmärkningar till Sweriges Rikes sjö-lag, jämte författningarne till närwarande tid (1815), our hwarje å utrikes om wistande swensk och norrsk consuls skylldigheter och rättigheter, i afseende på sjöfart och handel.* Stockholm: J.A.F, 1815.

Fortsättning af Kongl. Slotts-Rättens protokoller uti undersöknings-målet angående skepparen Törngrens med de fleres begångne brott. Karlskrona: Kongl. Amiralitets Boktryckeriet, 1802.

Geijer, E.G., ed. *Konung Gustaf III:s efterlemnade och femtio år efter hans död öppnade papper.* Vol. 3. Uppsala: Wahlström & Låstbom, 1844.

Granberg, Petter.A. *Staden Göteborgs historia och beskrifning.* Vol. 1. Stockholm: Elmén och Granberg, 1814.

Great Britain's Parliament, House of Commons, *Reports from Committees of the House of Commons: Repr. by Order of the House.* House of Commons, 1803.

Gustav III. *Ces Réflexions Sur La Nécessitè d'affranchir l'habillement Suédois de l'empire Des Modes Étrangères, Sont de Gustave III, Roi de Suède.* Liege, 1780.

Hall- och accis-rättens i Wästerås protocoller och utslag uti ett af tull-inspectorn derstädes Johan Brun emot 10 af handlande borgerskapet instämdt bod-visitations och confiscations måhl. Västerås: Joh. Laur. Horrn, 1770.

Hallman, Carl Israel. *Sorge-tal, då gudinnan Coffèa flygtade ur Svea Land den 31 julii 1794. hållet vid Kongl. Djurgårds helso-brunnen i en talrik samling af bägge könen, samma dag.* Stockholm: Jacobsson Nordström, 1794.

Hedenskog, Jonas. *Öfwertygad därom, at alla ledamöterne uti Stockholms Stads kämners-rätt icke kunnat wara af lika tanka med pluraliteten, som utgjordt domslutet uti den af bemälte kämners-rätt den 2 uti innewarande månad afsagde dom, emellan afledne : stads- advocaten deleen, biträdd af herr rådmannen... Qwiding å ämbetets wägnar, samt kram-handlaren här i staden Johan Sundbeck, och samme dom nu mera genom Sundbecks besörjande blifwit til trycket befordrad, så har man funnit sig : föranlåten at hos domstolen begjära, det de ledamöters meningar, som icke öfwerensstämma med domslutet, måtte til trycket utur protocollet extraderas, på det allmänheten uti et så beskaffat mål icke må sakna all uplysning, som i saken : kunnat åstadkommas.* Stockholm: Kongl. Tryckeriet, 1774.

———. *Uti det, af stads-advocaten, wälbetrodde Benjamin Delén, i lifstiden til undersökning hos rätten anmälte, samt af rådmannen... Pehr Quiding, å ämbetes wägnar, bewistade mål, angående deléns deröfwer förde klagan, at kramhandlaren Johan Sundbeck... Den 2 augusti nästledit år... wåldsamheter å Delén utöfwat.* Stockholm: Georg Lange, 1774.

Hedvig Elisabet Charlotta. *Hedvig Elisabeth Charlottas dagbok*, edited by Carl Carlson Bonde. Vol. IV. P. A. Norstedt & söner, 1920.

———. *Hedvig Elisabeth Charlottas Dagbok, edited* by Cecilia af Klercker. Vol. VII. Stockholm: Norstedt, 1936.

Hellberg, Johan Carl. *Ur minnet och dagboken om mina samtida: personer och händelser efter 1815 inom och utom fäderneslandet.* I. Haeggströms boktr., 1870.

Herrmann, Johann Christian. *Allgemeiner Contorist Welcher von Allen Und Jeden Gegenständen Der Handlung Aller in Und Außer Europa Belegenen Handelsplätze Die Neuesten Und Zuverlässigsten Nachrichten Ertheilet; Theils Nach Bewährten Quellen, Theils Auch, Und Insonderheit, Nach Eigener Erfahrung Und Correspondenz Entworfen Und in Alphabetische Ordnung Gebracht.* Vol. 4. Leipzig: Schwickertschen Verlage, 1792.

Hollertz, Magnus. *Resa omkring en mycket liten bit av jorden.* Stockholm: Albert Bonniers Förlag, 1949.

Hülper, Abraham. *Samlingar till en beskrivning öfwer Norrland, andra och tredje samlingen, Jämtland och Herjedalen*, 1775.

Hume, David. *Herr David Humes politiske afhandlingar om handel och yppighet*. Stockholm: Johan Georg Lange, 1767.

———. *Smärre afhandlingar i allämnna hushållningen*. Translated by P.J. Hjem. Stockholm: Johan A. Carlbom, 1791.

Janssen, Stephen Theodore. *Smuggling laid open, in all its extensive and destructive branches; with proposals for the effectual remedy of that most iniquitous practice: comprehending among other particulars the parliamentary evidence of some of the most notorious smugglers; and a large sheet, shewing in one view, the whole state of the tea importation, consumption and revenue, from midsummer 1745, (when the reduction of two shillings per pound, took place) to new Christmas 1763*. London, 1763.

Junbeck, P. J. *Handels- och slöjde-fiscalen Junbecks sällsamma öden, både såsom embetsman och enskild medborgare: afskilldrade i anledning af Stockholms garfvare-embetes försök, att åtkomma sista skärfven*. Stockholm: Marquarska Tryckeriet, 1815.

———. *Andra delen af handels- och slöjde- fiscalen Junbecks sällsamma öden, både såsom embetsman och enskild medborgare: afskilldrade i anledning af Stockholms garfvare-embetes försök, att åtkomma sista skär*. Stockholm: Marquarska Tryckeriet, 1817.

Kellgren, Johan Henrik. *Joh. Henr. Kellgrens samlade skrifter*. Stockholm: Johan Pehr Lindh, 1796.

Kraftman, Johan, and Johan Lagus. 'Tankar om hushållningens uphjelpande i Carelen'. Åbo Academy, 1756.

Kryger, Johan Fredrik. *Tankar wid lediga stunder*. Stockholm: Tryckt på Direct. Lars Salvii förlag, 1761.

Küttner, Carl Gottlob. *Travels Through Denmark, Sweden, Austria, and Part of Italy, in 1798 & 1799*. R. Phillips, 1805.

Lagerbring, Sven. *Sammandrag af Swea Rikes historia, ifrån de äldsta til de nyasten tiden. til ungdomens tjenst upsatt*. Vol. 1. Stockholm: Anders J. Nordström, 1778.

Leopold, Carl Gustaf af. *Samlade skrifter av Carl Gustaf Af Leopold. Senare avdelningen. andra delen. Brev 1790–1796*, edited by Knut Fredlund and Olle Holmberg. Stockholm: Svenska Vitterhetssamfundet, 1958.

Liewen, Carl Gustaf. *Wi, Carl Gustaf Liewen, friherre, ordförande, general-major... angående wåld emot en til handräckning wid tullbeslags werkställande beordrad patroull...* Kongl. Tryckeriet, 1799.

Liljencrants, Johan. 'Anteckningar och memorial af grefve Johan Liljencrantz'. In *Historiska Handlingar*, Vol. 5. 8. Stockholm: Central Tryckeriet, 1878.

Liljencrants, Johan, and etc. *Kongl. Maj:Ts och rikets commerce-collegii instruction för handels= och slöjde=fiscalen, hwarefter han har at sig rätta*. Stockholm: Kongl. Tryckeriet, 1803.

Linné, Carl von. *Almenach, för åhret, efter wår frälsares Christie födelse 1747*. Stockholm: Fabel, 1963.

———. *Kaffedrycken (Postus Coffeæ), 1761*. Translated by Ejnar Haglund. Ekenäs, 1966.

Linnerhjelm, Jonas Carl. *Brev under resor i Sverige*. Stockholm: Wahlström & Widstrand, 1932.

Locke, John. *Johan Lockes oförgripelige tankar om werldslig regerings rätta ursprung, gräntsor och ändamål*. Stockholm: Kongl. Tryckeriet, 1726.

Lundell, J. *Om handtverksskrån, näringsfrihet och arbetets organisation*. Lund: C.W.K. Gleerup, 1846.

Lundequist, Nils. *Stockholms stads historia, från stadens anläggning till närwarande tid*, vol.2. Stockholm: Zacharias Haeggström, 1828.

Marshall, Joseph. *Travels through Holland, Flanders, Germany, Denmark, Sweden, Lapland, Russia, The Ukraine, and Poland in the Years 1768, 1769, and 1770*. 2nd ed. Vol. 2. London: J. Almon, 1773.

Mason, Simon. *The Good and Bad Effects of Tea Consider'd. Wherein Are Exhibited, the Physical Virtues of Tea, Its General and Particular Use, to What Constitutions Agreeable... to Which Are Subjoined, Some Considerations on Afternoon Tea- Drinking, and the Many Subsequent Evils Attending It; with a Persuasive to the Use of Our Own Wholsome Product, Sage, &c.* London: Printed for M. Cooper, 1745.

Muller, Carl Fredric. *Uplysning, huruwida siden-fabriqueurer, kramhandlare och gördelmakare kunde komma at lida eller ej, genom den nya swenska nationella klädedrägten.* Stockholm: Anders J. Nordström, 1778.

Munsterhjelm, Jacobina Charlotta. *Jacobina Charlotta Munsterhjelms dagböcker 1799–1801 Dagbok*, edited by Bo Lönnqvist. Helsingfors: Svenska Litteratursällskapet i Finland, 1970.

———. *Bihang til samtlige riks-ståndens protcoll, innehållande de handlingar, hvilka till riks-stånden blifvit aflemnade; såsom konungens nådiga propositioner, riksens ständers utskotts betänkanden och förklaringar, samt riks-ståndens protocolls-utdrag vid lagtima riksdagen i Stockholm, 1823.* Vol. 4:6. Stockholm, 1823.

Norberg, Dan. *Kongl. Commerce Collegii underdånige relation om manufacturerne ingifwen wid riksdagen år 1769 Stockholm.* Gävle: Ernst Sundqvist, 1770.

Nordencrantz, Anders. *Bekymmerlösa stunders menlösa och owälduga tankar.* Vol. 1. Stockholm, 1767.

Nordensköld, Ulric. *Afhandling om nyttan för Sverige af handel och nybyggen i Indierna och på Africa.* Stockholm: Peter Hesselberg, 1776.

Palmstedt, Erik. *Resedagbok 1778–1780.* Uppsala: Almqvist & Wiksells A.B., 1927.

Porthans, Henrik Gabriel. *Henrik Gabriel Porthans bref till Mathias Calonius.* Vol. 1. Skrifter Utgifna Af Svenska Literatursällskapet i Finland. Helsinki: Tidnings- & Tryckeri-Aktiebolagets Tryckeri, 1886.

Posse, Carl Hindric. 'Bilaga till pleniprotocollet för den 12 martii'. In *Bilagor till högloflige ridderskapets och adelns protocoll, vid lagtima riksdagen i Stockholm År 1823*, Vol. 2. Stockholm: Olof Grahn, 1823.

Postlethwayt, Malachy, *The Universal Dictionary of Trade and Commerce : With Large Additions and Improvements, Adapting the Same to the Present State of British Affairs in America, since the Last Treaty of Peace Made in the Year 1763. With Great Variety of New Remarks and Illustrations Incorporated throughout the Whole: Together with Everything Essential That Is Contained in Savary's Dictionary; Also, All the Material Laws of Trade and Navigation Relating to These Kingdoms, and the Customs and Usages to Which All Traders Are Subject.* 4th ed. Vol. 2. London: Printed for W. Strahan, J. and F. Rivington..., 1774.

Protocoller, rörande hus-visitationen d. 10 october 1786. förrättad af öfwer-inspectoren herr John. Hoffgardh, hos handelsmannen herr Erick Linderoth tillika med högloft. kongl. slotts rättens ransakning öfwer de wid samma tilfälle förfallne händelser. Göteborg: L. Wahlström, 1787.

Register till riksdagens protokoll med bihang. Vol. 2. Stockholm: Central Tryckeriet, 1892.

Ricard, Samuel. *Traité général du commerce: contenant des observations sur le commerce des principaux etats de l'europe, les productions naturelles, l'industrie de chaque païs.* Vol. 1. 2 vols. Amesterdam: E. van Harrevelt, 1781.

Riksens hoglofl. ständers handels- och manufactur-deputations berättelse, angående de swenske manufacturers tilstånd och beskaffenhet ifrån 1764 til 1768 års slut. Stockholm: Kongl. Finska Boktryckeriet, 1769.

Röding, Jacob. *Tankar om de år 1756 förbudne waror, i synnerhet caffé.* Stockholm: Jör. Nyström, 1756.

Rothlieb, Carl Fredric. *Matrikel öfwer dem af Swea-Rikes ridderskap och adel.* Stockholm: Gadelius, 1807.

Schedel, Johan Christian. *Neues Und Vollständiges Geographisches Lexikon Für Kaufleute Und Geschäftsmänner, Oder Alphabetisch Geordnete Beschreibung Aller Welttheile, Staaten,*

Länder, Plätze, Häfen, Gewässer Und Kanäle, Die Den Kaufmann Interessiren Und Wohin Gehandelt Und Verkehr Getrieben Wird. Vol. 3. Leipzig: Schwickert, 1804.

Silverstolpe, Axel. *Skalde-stycken*. Stockholm: Kumblinska, 1801.

Smith, Adam. *Undersökning om kongl. stora sjö- och gränse- tullar, samt acciser och små-tullar, med flera consumtions- afgifter*. Translated by Bodell, Erik Erl. Stockholm, 1800.

Stockholms Oordenteligheter, vol.8 (1770).

———. *Stora sjö tulls rättens i Stockholm, protocoller och utslag, rörande kramhandlaren Johan Sundbeck, som d. 18 näst-ledne maji genom skans tulls gjordt försökt, at inpracticera åtskillige stycken utländske siden=tyger och silkes näsdukar*. Stockholm: Kongl. Tryckeriet, 1769.

———. 'Handelsbalancen', edited by G.A. Silfverstolpe. Translated by Unknown. *Läsning i Blandade Ämnen* 25 & 26 (1799).

———. *Politisk undersökning om lagar, som hindra och tvinga införseln af sådana utländska varor, som kunna alstras eller tillverkas inom landet*. Translated by Erik Erl. Bodell. Göteborg: S. Norberg, 1804.

———. *An Inquiry into the Nature and Causes of the Wealth of Nations*. Amsterdam, Lausanne, Melbourne, Milan, New York, Sao Paulo: ΜεταLibri, 2007.

Svenskt Konversations-Lexicon. Stockholm: P. G. Berg, 1847.

Sweriges Rikes lag, gillad och antagen på riksdagen 1734. Stockholm: Historiographi regni, 1736.

Taylor (T), John. 'History of Norwich Manufactures'. *The Monthly Magazine* 6 (December 1798).

Tegnér, Elof, ed. *Från tredje Gustafs dagar. Anteckningar och minnen*. Vol. 3:2. Stockholm: F. & G. Beijer, 1894.

The Sessional Papers Printed by Order of the House of Lords. Reports from Commissioners: Hand-loom Weavers, Vol. XXXVII, 1840.

Törnsten, Olof. *Undersökning, om det är möjeligt at hämma lurendrägerier igenom förbud*. Stockholm: Lars Salvius, 1766.

Tucker, Josiah. *Four Tracts, on Political and Commercial Subjects*. 3rd ed. Glocester: R. Raikes, 1776.

Tull-Styrelsen, bihang til samtlige riks-ståndens protcoll, innehållande de handlingar, hvilka till riks-stånden blifvit aflemnade; såsom konungens nådiga propositioner, riksens ständers utskotts betänkanden och förklaringar, samt riks-ståndens protocolls-utdrag vid lagtima riksdagen i Stockholm, 1823, Vol. 11. Stockholm, 1823.

Various. *Wälloflige borgare=ståndets protocoller wid riksdagen i Norrköping år 1800*. Stockholm: C. F. Marquard, 1800.

Wargentin, Christina Juliana, 'Christina Juliana Wargentin dagbok 1794', https://stockholmskallan.stockholm.se/post/10064, *Stockholmskällan*, Accessed 11 December 2018

Secondary Sources

Aglietti, Marcella, Manuel Herrero Sánchez, and Francisco Zamora Rodríguez (eds.). *Los cónsules de extranjeros en la Edad Moderna y a principios de la Edad Contemporanea*. Madrid: Ediciones Doce Calles, 2013.

Ågren, Maria. *The State as Master: Gender, State Formation and Commercialisation in Urban Sweden, 1650–1780*. Oxford: Oxford University Press, 2017.

Ahlberger, Christer. *Konsumtionsrevolutionen 1. Om det moderna konsumtionssamhällets framväxt 1750–1900*. Göteborg: Humanistiska fakulteten, Univ., 1996.

Ahlberger, Christer, and Pia Lundqvist. 'En inledning.' In *varans vägar och världar. handel och konsumtion i skandinavien ca 1600–1800*, edited by Christer Ahlberger and Pia Lundqvist. Göteborg: Historiska Institutionen i Göteborg, 2007.

Ahlberger, Christer, and Magnus Mörner. 'Betydelsen av några latinamerikanska produkter för Sverige före 1810'. *Historisk Tidskrift*, no. 1 (1993).

Ahlberger, Christer, and Eva Österberg. 'Brott och rättspraxis i det förindustriella samhället. tendenser och tolkningar i skandinavisk forskning'. *Historisk Tidskrift*, no. 1 (1993).

Ahlfors, Jens. 'Sjöfolkslöner i Göteborg 1808–1810: Presentation Av Ett Lönehistoriskt Material'. In *Handel och sjöfart under gustaviansk tid*. Göteborg: Historiska Institutionen, 1971.

Ahnfelt, Arvid. *Ur svenska hofvets och aristokratiens lif. skildringar hemtade i arkiven på Säfstaholm, Eriksberg och Sjöholm m. fl. enskilda och offentliga samlingar.* Vol. 3. 7 vols. Norrköping, 1880.

Aldman, Lili-Annè. 'Customers and Markets for "New" Textiles in Seventeenth- and Eighteenth-Century Sweden'. In *Selling Textiles in the Long Eighteenth Century. Comparative Perspectives from Western Europe*, edited by Jon Stobart and Bruno Blondé. London: Palgrave Macmillan, 2014.

———. 'En merkantilistisk början. Stockholms textila import 1720–1738'. PhD thesis, Uppsala University, 2008.

Alimento, Antonella, and Koen Stapelbroek. 'Trade and Treaties: Balancing the Interstate System'. In *The Politics of Commercial Treaties in the Eighteenth Century. Balance of Power, Balance of Trade*, edited by Antonella Alimento and Koen Stapelbroek. Palgrave Macmillan, 2017.

Alm, Mikael. 'Making a Difference: Sartorial Practices and Social Order in Eighteenth-Century Sweden'. *Costume* 50, no. 1 (2016).

Almquist, Johan Ax. *Kommerskollegium och riksens ständers manufakturkontor samt konsulsstaten*. Stockholm: P. A. Norstedt & söner, 1912.

Alvedal, Filip. 'Cesare Beccaria och Gustav III:s straffreformer'. Lund University, 2015.

Andersson, Bertil. *Göteborgs historia. Näringsliv och samhällsutveckling*. Göteborg: Nerenius & Santérus, 1996.

Andersson, Bror A. *Skepplanda socken: Från forntid till nutid i ord och bild*, edited by Sven Forsæus. Skepplanda kommunfullmäktige, 1972.

Andersson, Eva I. 'Foreign Seductions: Sumptuary Laws, Consumption and National Identity in Early Modern Sweden'. In *Fashionable Encounters. Perspectives and Trends in Textile and Dress in the Early Modern Nordic World*, edited by Tove Engelhardt Mathiassen, Marie-Louise Nosch, Maj Ringgaard, Kirsten Toftegaard, and Mikkel Venborg Pedersen. Oxford: Oxbow Books, 2014.

Andersson, Gudrun, and Klas Nyberg, eds. *Kommers. Historiska handelsformer i Norden under 1700- och 1800-talen*. Uppsala: Uppsala University, 2001.

Andrews, Charles M. 'Anglo-French Commercial Rivalry, 1700–1750: The Western Phase I'. *The American Historical Review* 20, no. 3 (April 1915).

Aneer, Cecilia. 'Skrädderi för kungligt bruk: tillverkning av kläder vid det svenska hovet ca 1600–1635'. PhD thesis, Uppsala Universitet, 2009.

Anér, Kerstin. *Läsning i Blandade Ämnen. Studier i 1790-talets svenska press- och litteraturhistoria*. Göteborg: Rundqvists, 1948.

Anners, Erik. 'Straffteorierna i svensk rättshistoria'. *Svensk Juristtidning*, 1964.

Appadurai, Arjun. 'Introduction: Commodities and the Politics of Value'. In *The Social Life of Things:Commodities in Cultural Perspective*, First published 1986. Cambridge: Cambridge University Press, 2013.

Attman, Artur. 'The Russian Market in World Trade, 1500–1860'. *Scandinavian Economic History Review* 29, no. 3 (1981).

Baghdiantz McCabe, Ina. *A History of Global Consumption 1500–1800*. London; New York: Routledge, 2015.
Behre, Göran. 'Scots in "Little London". Scots Settlers and Cultural Development in Gothenburg in the Eighteenth Century'. *Northern Scotland* 7, no. 1 (February 2015).
Bellamy, Charlotte and Anna Knutsson, 'From Valet to Smuggler: A Micro-historical Study of a French Intermediary in Stockholm, 1775–1832'. *Revue d'histoire nordique*, no. 27 (2018).
Bengtsson, Erik, Anna Missiaia, Mats Olsson, and Patrick Svensson. 'Wealth Inequality in Sweden, 1750–1900'. *The Economic History Review* 71, no. 3 (August 2018).
Bengtsson, Erik, and Patrick Svensson. 'The Wealth of the Swedish Peasant Farmer Class 1750–1900'. *Lund Papers in Economic History* 177 (2018).
Bengtsson, Rickard. *Bland smugglare, kapare och obstinata köpmän. göteborg genom tiderna ur ett tullperspektiv*. Stockholm: Carlsson Bokförlag, 2006.
———. *Ombytta roller. Om Malmö tullare som lurendrejare och tullförsnillare 1658–1850*. GRYPS 1. Elbogen, Malmö fornminnesförenings arbetsutskott, 1990.
Berg, Maxine. 'In Pursuit of Luxury: Global History and British Consumer Goods in the Eighteenth Century'. *Past & Present* 182, no. 1 (1 February 2004): 85–142.
———. *Luxury and Pleasure in Eighteenth-Century Britain*. Oxford: Oxford University Press, 2007.
———. *Markets and Manufacture in Early Industrial Europe*. Routledge, 2015.
Berg, Maxine, and Elizabeth Eger. 'Introduction'. In *Luxury in the Eighteenth Century: Debates, Desires and Delectable Goods*, edited by Maxine Berg and Elizabeth Eger. Basingstoke, Hampshire; New York: Palgrave Macmillan, 2003.
———, eds. *Luxury in the Eighteenth Century: Debates, Desires and Delectable Goods*. Basingstoke, Hampshire; New York: Palgrave Macmillan, 2003.
Berg, Maxine, Hanna Hodacs, and Chris Nierstrasz, eds. *Goods from the East, 1600–1800 Trading Eurasia*. Basingstoke, Hampshire; New York: Palgrave Macmillan, 2015.
Berggren, Jan. *Alla tiders tull i stan: historia och händelser kring Stockholms tullar*. Stockholm: Carlsson, 2000.
———. *Tullsnok - Öppna bommen! Carl Michael Bellman och tullen*. Stockholm: Carlsson Bokförlag, 2003.
Bergman, Eva. *Nationella dräkten: En studie kring Gustaf III:s dräktreform 1778*. Stockholm: Nordiska museets förlag, 1938.
Benton, Lauren, *A Search for Sovereignty: Law and Geography in European Empires, 1400–1900*. Cambridge: Cambridge University Press, 2009.
'Bidrag till Sveriges historia efter 1772', 1882. http://runeberg.org/afbtsvhi/.
Björkquist, Lennart. *Jämtlands folkliga kvinnodräkter. Studier i den jämtska allmogens dräktskick under 1700-talet och 1800-talets förra hälft*. Skrifter Utgifna Af Kungl. Gustav Adolfs Akademien För Folklivsforksning 7. Uppsala: Appelbergs, 1941.
Blondé, B. (Bruno), Peter Stabel, Jon Stobart, and Ilja van Damme. 'Introduction'. In *Buyers & Sellers : Retail Circuits and Practices in Mediaeval and Early Modern Europe*. Brepols, 2006.
Bodsten, Erik. *Politikens drivfjäder: Frihetstidens partiberättelser och den moralpolitiska logiken*. Lund: Historiska Institutionen, 2016.
Boëthius, Bertil. 'Swedish Iron and Steel, 1600–1955'. *Scandinavian Economic History Review* 6, no. 2 (1958).
Bouëdec, Gérard. 'Intra-European Costal Shipping from 1400 to 1900: A Long-Forgotten Sector of Development'. In *A Deus Ex Machina Revisited: Atlantic Colonial Trade and*

European Economic Development, edited by P.C. Emmer, O. Pétré-Grenouilleau, and Jessica V. Roitman. Leiden, Boston: Brill, 2006.

Bowen, Huw V. 'Privilege and Profit: Commanders of East Indiamen as Private Traders, Entrepreneurs and Smugglers, 1760–1813'. *International Journal of Maritime History* 19, no. 2 (December 2007).

———. '"So Alarming An Evil:" Smuggling, Pilfering and the English East India Company, 1750–1810'. *International Journal of Maritime History* 14, no. 1 (2002).

Braudel, Fernand, *The Mediterranean: and the Mediterranean World in the Age of Philip II*, trans. Siân Reynolds. Berkley: University of California Press, 1972.

Bredefeldt, Rita. 'Judarna i Sverige - Invandring, ekonomi och integration'. *Ekonomisk Debatt* 43, no. 4 (2015).

Breen, T. H. *The Marketplace of Revolution: How Consumer Politics Shaped American Independence*. Oxford, New York: Oxford University Press, 2005.

Brewer, John. 'Was the First Consumer Society Born in 18th Century Britain?' *The Independent*, 30 September 2003.

Brewer, John, and Roy Porter, eds. *Consumption and the World of Goods*. London; New York: Routledge, 1993.

Brismark, Anna. 'Hemslöjden och Stockholms textilmarknad linnehandeln i Hälsningland 1780–1846'. In *Till salu. Stockholms textila handel och manufaktur 1722–1846*, edited by Klas Nyberg. Stockholm: Stads- och Kommunhistoriska Institutet, 2010.

Brismark, Anna, and Pia Lundqvist. 'A Diaspora on the Edge of Modernity? The Jewish Minority in Gothenburg in the Late Eighteenth and Early Nineteenth Centuries'. In *Connecting Worlds and People. Early Diasporas*, edited by Dagmar Friest and Susanne Lachenicht. Abingdon: Routledge, 2017.

———. 'A Textile Web'. *Scandinavian Journal of History* 40, no. 4 (2015).

———. 'Före lanthandelns tid? Förutsättningarna för och förekomsten av handel på den svenska landsbygden före 1846'. In *Kommers. Historiska handelsformer i Norden under 1700- och 1800-talen*. Uppsala: Uppsala University, 2001.

———. 'Rural Retailing of Textiles in Early Nineteenth-Century Sweden'. In *Selling Textiles in the Long Eighteenth Century. Comparative Perspectives from Western Europe*, edited by Jon Stobart and Bruno Blondé. London: Palgrave Macmillan, 2014.

———. 'Sidensjalar och socker. judiska näringsidkares betydelse för konsumtionsrevolutionen i Sverige'. In *Från sidensjalar till flyktingmottagning. judarna i Sverige - En minoritets historia*, edited by Lars M Andersson and Carl Henric Carlsson. Uppsala: Swedish Science Press, 2013.

Bromé, Janrik. *Karlskronas stads historia*. Vol. 1. Karlskrona: K. L. Svensson, 1930.

Brown, Warren C. *Violence in Medieval Europe*. Abingdon-on-Thames:Routledge, 2014.

Brubaker, Rogers, and Frederick Cooper. 'Beyond Identity'. *Theory and Society* 29 (2000).

Brusewitz, Axel. 'Georg Adlersparre'. https://sok.riksarkivet.se/sbl/artikel/5563. *Svenskt biografiskt lexikon,* Accessed 17 August 2017.

Brusewitz, Hans. 'Frimurerisk straffskipning - Domstolen som försvann'. *Frimuraren* 4 (2016).

Carlsson, Arne. 'Marstrand under frihamnstiden 1775–1794'. In *Handel och sjöfart under gustaviansk tid*. Göteborg: Historiska Institutionen, 1971.

Carlsson, C-H. 'Judisk invandring från Aaron Isaac till idag'. In *Judarna i Sverige – En minoritets historia, fyra föreläsningar*, edited by H. Müssener. Uppsala Multiethnic Papers 53. Uppsala: Uppsala University, 2011.

Cavallin, Maria. 'I kungen och folkets tjänst. Synen på den svenske ämbetsmannen 1750–1780'. PhD thesis, Göteborgs Universitet, 2003.

Cederberg, Arno Rafael. *Pohjois-Karjalan Kauppaolot Vuosina 1721–1775*. Helsinki, 1911.

Charpentier Ljungqvist, Fredrik. *Global Nedkylning: Klimatet Och Människan under 10 000 År*. Stockholm: Nordstedts, 2009.

Chaussinand-Nogaret, Guy. 'Une élite insulaire au service de l'europe: les jacobites au xviiie siècle'. *Annales. Histoire, Sciences Sociales* 28, no. 5 (1973).

CHC, 'Marcus, släkt'. https://sok.riksarkivet.se/sbl/artikel/9079, *Svenskt biografiskt lexikon*, Accessed 23 Novemver 2018.

Christensson, Jakob. *Lyckoriket: Studier i svensk upplysning*. Stockholm: Atlantis, 1996.

Christiansen, Palle Ove. 'Peasant Adaptation to Bourgeois Culture? Class Formation and Cultural Redefinition in the Danish Countryside'. *Ethnologia Scandinavica* 8 (1978).

Clark, Peter. 'The "Mother Gin" Controversy in the Early Eighteenth Century'. *Transactions of the Royal Historical Society* 38 (1988).

Clason, Samuel. 'Talmanstafflar och ståndsklubbar'. *Svensk Tidskrift* 12, no. 1 (1922).

Clavin, Patricia. 'Defining Transnationalism'. *Contemporary European History* 14, no. 4 (November 2005).

Cole, W. A. 'Trends in Eighteenth-Century Smuggling'. *The Economic History Review* 10, no. 3 (1958).

Coleman, D. C. 'Politics and Economics in the Age of Anne: The Case of the Anglo-French Trade Treaty of 1713'. In *Trade, Government and Economy in Pre-Industrial England. Essays Presented to F.J. Fisher*, edited by D.C. Coleman and A.H. John. London: Weidenfeld and Nicholson, 1976.

Colley, Linda. *Britons: Forging the Nation 1707–1837*. New Haven, CT: Yale University Press, 1992.

Coquery, Natacha. *Tenir boutique à Paris au xviiie siècle: luxe et demi-luxe*. Paris: éditions du Comité historique et scientifique, 2011.

Courtwright, David T. *Forces of Habit: Drugs and the Making of the Modern World*. Cambridge, MA: Harvard University Press, 2009.

Cromwell, Jesse. 'Illicit Ideologies: Moral Economies of Venezuelan Smuggling and Autonomy in the Rebellion of Juan Francisco de Leon, 1749–1751'. *THE AMERICAS* 74, no. 3 (July 2017).

———. *The Smugglers' World. Illicit Trade and Atlantic Communities in Eighteenth-Century Venezuela*. Chapel Hill: The University of North Carolina Press, 2018.

Cronqvist, Marie. 'Spatialisera Alltid!: Rummets Återkomst i de Historiska Vetenskaperna'. *Scania* 74 (2008).

Crouzet, François. 'Britain's Exports and Their Markets, 1701–1913'. In *A Deus Ex Machina Revisited: Atlantic Colonial Trade and European Economic Development*, edited by P.C. Emmer, O. Pétré-Grenouilleau, and Jessica V. Roitman. Leiden, Boston: Brill, 2006.

———. *La Guerre Économique Franco-Anglaise Au XVIIIe Siècle*. Fayard, 2008.

Dahlberg, Erik. 'Suecia Antiqua et Hodierna'. https://suecia.kb.se/F/?func=find-b&local_base=sah. Accessed 13 February 2019.

Daly, Gavin. 'English Smugglers, the Channel, and the Napoleonic Wars, 1800–1814'. *Journal of British Studies* 46 (2007).

———. 'Napoleon and the "City of Smugglers", 1810–1814'. *The Historical Journal* 50, no. 2 (2007).

Davidson, Jessica. 'The Social and Cultural History of the Provincial Fair in England, c. 1750–1850'. DPhil thesis, Oxford University, 2019.

Desideri, Gabriella. 'Les traités commerciaux de royaume de Naples avec la Hollande, le Danemark et la Suède de (1740–1790) et leurs incidences économiques', PhD, Università degli Studi di Parma, 2020.

Dietze, Antje, and Katja Naumann. 'Revisiting Transnational Actors from a Spatial Perspective'. *European Review of History* 25, no. 3–4 (2018).

Dillon, Patrick. *Gin: The Much-Lamented Death of Madam Geneva*. London: Justin, Charles & Co., 2004.

Dribe, Martin, and Bart Van De Putte. 'Marriage Seasonality and the Industrious Revolution: Southern Sweden, 1690–18951'. *The Economic History Review* 65, no. 3 (1 August 2012): 1123–1146.

Du Rietz, Anita. *Kvinnors entreprenörskap: under 400 år*. Stockholm: Dialogos, 2013.

Eacott, Jonathan P. 'Making an Imperial Compromise: The Calico Acts, the Atlantic Colonies, and the Structure of the British Empire'. *The William and Mary Quarterly* 69, no. 4 (October 2012).

Eßer, Reingard, and Steven G. Ellis, eds. *Frontier and Border Regions in Early Modern Europe*. The Formation of Europe Historische Formationen Europas 7. Hannover: Wehrhahn Verlag, 2013.

Edgren, Monika. *Från rike till nation arbetskraftspolitik, befolkningspolitik och nationell gemenskapsformering i Sverige under 1700-talet*. Lund: Historisk Media, 2001.

Edvinsson, Rodney, Tor Jacobson, and Daniel Waldenström. 'The Multiple Currecies of Sweden-Finland 1534–1803'. In *Exchange Rates, Prices, and Wages, 1277–2008*. Stockholm: Ekerlids Förlag, 2010.

Edvinsson, Rodney, and Johan Söderberg. 'The Evolution of Swedish Consumer Prices 1290–2088'. In *Exchange Rates, Prices, and Wages, 1277–2008*, edited by Tor Jacobson, Daniel Waldenström, and Rodney Edvinsson. Stockholm: Ekerlids Förlag, 2010.

Edvinsson, Rodney, and Christoffer Tarek Gad. 'Assessing Trade in the Mercantilist Era: Evidence from a New Database on Foreign Trade of Sweden-Finland, 1738–1805'. *Scandinavian Economic History Review* (2018).

Eklöf Amirell, Stefan. 'Den världshistoriska vändningen. möjligheter och problem i relation till svensk historisk forskning'. *Historisk Tidskrift* 128, no. 4 (2008).

Ekstrand, Gudrun. 'Kläderna gör kungen - kungen gör kläderna'. In *Hovets Dräkter*, edited by Lena Rangström. Stockholm: Livrustkammaren, 1994.

Eldvik, Berit. *Möte med mode. Folkliga kläder 1750–1900 i Nordiska Museet*. Stockholm: Nordiska museets förlag, 2014.

Ellis, Markman, Richard Coulton, and Matthew Mauger. *Empire of Tea. The Asian Leaf That Conquered the World*. London: Reaktion Books, 2015.

Eloranta, Jari, Maria Cristina Moreira, Peter Hedberg, and Eric Golson. 'Introduction'. In *Small and Medium Powers in Global History: Trade, Conflicts, and Neutrality from the 18th to the 20th Centuries*. Oxford, New York: Routledge, 2019.

Enflo, Kerstin, and Anna Missiaia. 'Between Malthus and the Industrial Take-off: Regional Inequality in Sweden, 1571–1850'. *Lund Papers in Economic History* 168 (2017).

Essén, Åke. *Johan liljencrantz som handelspolitiker: studier i sveriges yttre handelspolitik 1773–1786*. Lund: Gleerup, 1928.

European Commission Memo, Questions & Answers: New Rules for Tobacco Products, 26 February 2014, http://europa.eu/rapid/press-release_MEMO-14-134_en.htm, Accessed 25 June 2019.

Fagan, Brian M. *The Little Ice Age: How Climate Made History 1300–1850*. New York: Basic Books, 2002.

Farrell, William. 'Silk and Globalisation in Eighteenth-Century London: Commodities, People and Connections c.1720–1800'. PhD thesis, Birkbeck, University of London, 2014.

———. 'Smuggling Silks into Eighteenth-Century Britain: Geography, Perpetrators, and Consumers'. *Journal of British Studies* 55, no. 2 (2016).

Fettah, Samuel. 'Frontières et fraudes. Les consuls de France et la contrebande dans le port franc de Livourne à l'époque du risorgimento'. *Revue d'histoire Moderne et Contemporaine* 2, no. 48 (2001).

Findlay, Ronald and Kevin H. O'Rourke. *Power and Plenty: Trade, War, and the World Economy in the Second Millennium*. Princeton, NJ: Princeton University Press, 2007.

Finlay, Robert. *The Pilgrim Art: Cultures of Porcelain in World History*. Berkley; Los Angeles; London: University of California Press, 2010.

Foghelin, Tryggve. 'Galeasen Lovisa - ett rättsfall om plundring av fartygslast, lurendrejeri och sänkning 1801'. *Forum Navale* 49 (1993).

Fontaine, Laurence. *History of Pedlars in Europe*. Translated by Vicki Whittaker, Polity Press, 1996.

Foucault, Michel. *The Punitive Society. Lectures at the College de France 1972–1973*, edited by Bernard E. Harcourt. Translated by Graham Burchell. Basingstoke, Hampshire; New York: Palgrave Macmillan, 2015.

Fredberg, C.R.A. *Det gamla Göteborg. Lokalhistoriska skildringar personalia och kulturdrag*. Vol. 3. Göteborg: Bröderna Weiss, 1922.

French, Christopher J. 'London's Overseas Trade with Europe 1700–1775'. *Journal of European Economic History* 23, no. 3 (Winter 1994).

Frängsmyr, Tore. 'Johan Fredrik Kryger'. https://sok.riksarkivet.se/sbl/artikel/11836, *Svenskt Biografiskt Lexikon*, Accessed 26 February 2018.

Fridén, Bertil. 'På tröskeln till marknaden. Makt, institutionell kontext och ekonomisk effektivitet i västsverige 1630–1800'. PhD thesis, Göteborgs Universitet, 1991.

Fröding, Hugo. *Biografiska studier från skilda tider*. Stockholm: P.A. Norstedt & Söners förlag, 1905.

Frohnert, Pär. 'Kronans skatter och bondens bröd. den lokala förvaltningen och bönderna i Sverige 1719–1775'. PhD thesis, Stockholm University, 1993.

Frykman, Niklas. 'Pirates and Smugglers: Political Economy in the Red Atlantic'. In *Mercantilism Reimagined: Political Economy in Early Modern Britain and Its Empire*, edited by Philip J. Stern and Carl Wennerlind. Oxford: Oxford University Press, 2013.

Gadd, Carl-Johan. *Den agrara revolutionen 1700–1870. Det svenska jordbrukets historia*. Borås: Natur och Kultur/LTs förlag, 2000.

———. 'The Agricultural Revolution in Sweden'. In *The Agrarian History of Sweden 4000 BC to AD 2000*. Lund: Nordic Academic Press, 2011.

Gary, Kathryn E. 'The Distinct Seasonality of Early Modern Casual Labour and the Short Durations of Individual Working Years: Sweden 1500–1800'. *Lund Papers in Economic History* 189 (2019).

Gerentz, Sven. *Kommerskollegium och näringslivet, 1651–1951, minnesskrift*, Stockholm, 1951.

Gerritsen, Anne, and Giorgio Riello, eds. *The Global Lives of Things: The Material Culture of Connections in the Early Modern World*. Abingdon-on-Thames: Routledge, 2015.

Gill, Conrad. 'The Affair of Porto Novo: An Incident in Anglo-Swedish Relations'. *The Economic History Review* 73, no. 286 (1958).

Goldthwaite, Richard A. *Wealth and the Demand for Art in Italy: 1300–1600*. Baltimore: Johns Hopkins University Press, 1993.

Gottmann, Felicia. *Global Trade, Smuggling, and the Making of Economic Liberalism, Asian Textiles in France 1680–1760*. Basingstoke, Hampshire; New York: Palgrave Macmillan, 2016.

Grage, Elsa-Britta. 'John Hall'. https://Sok.Riksarkivet.Se/Sbl/Artikel/13549, Svenskt biografiskt lexikon. Accessed 18 January 2019.

Grill, Erik. 'Den nordhalländska bondeseglationen 1645–1700'. In *Studier tillägnade Curt Weibull*, edited by Åke Holmberg. Göteborg: Elander, 1946.

Gullback, Johanna. 'Karmink snörlif och wahlmars tjortil'. MA thesis, Uppsala University, 2012.

Häggqvist, Henric. 'On the Ocean of Protectionism. The Structure of Swedish Tariffs and Trade 1780–1830'. PhD thesis, Uppsala University, 2015.

Hallberg, Peter. *Ages of Liberty: Social Upheaval, History Writing, and the New Public Sphere in Sweden, 1740–1792*. Stockholm: Statsvetenskapliga institutionen, 2003.

Hallenberg, Mats, and Magnus Linnarsson. 'Politiska rum: En introduktion'. In *Politiska rum: Kontroll, konflikt och rörelse i det förmoderna Sverige 1300–1850*, edited by Mats Hallenberg and Magnus Linnarsson. Lund: Nordic Academic Press, 2014.

Harreld, Donald J. 'An Education in Commerce'. In *Information Flows. New Approaches in the Historical Study of Business Information*, edited by Leos Müller and Jari Ojala. Helsinki: SKS/Finnish Literature Society, 2007.

Hart, Marjolein 't. 'The People and the State. Nordic Paths in State Formation, 1500–1800' *Bringing the People Back in. State Building from Below in the Nordic Countries ca. 1500–1800*, edited by Knut Dørum, Mats Hallenberg, Kimmo Katajala. Routledge, 2021.

Heckscher, Eli Filip. 'Anders Chydenius'. https://sok.riksarkivet.se/sbl/artikel/14849, *Svenskt biografiskt lexikon*, Accessed 26 February 2018.

———. *Kontinentalsystemet. Den stora handelsafspärrningen för hundra år sedan*. Stockholm: Handelshögskolan, 1918.

———. *Sveriges ekonomiska historia från Gustav Vasa: Det moderna Sveriges grundläggning, 1720–1815*. Vol. 2:2. Stockholm: Albert Bonniers förlag, 1949.

———. *The Continental System*. Translated by Harald Westergaard. Oxford: Clarendon Press, 1922.

Hedberg, Peter, and Henric Häggqvist. 'Wartime Trade and Tariffs in Sweden from the Napoleonic Wars to World War I'. In *Small and Medium Powers in Global History: Trade, Conflicts, and Neutrality from the 18th to the 20th Centuries*, edited by Jari Eloranta, Eric Golson, Peter Hedberg, and Maria Cristina Moreira. Oxford, New York: Routledge, 2019.

Hedin, Fredrik. 'Adam Smith och Sverige: Ekonomisk liberalism i frihandelsdebatten vid 1823 års riksdag'. *Umeå Papers in Economic History* 9 (1994).

Hellman, Lisa. 'Ett ensamt skepp på öppet hav? Kopplingar, kontakter och utbyten ombord svenska ostindiefarare [A Lone Ship at Open Sea? Connections, Contacts and Exchanges on Swedish East Indiamen]'. *Historisk Tidsskrift* 3 (2014).

Hertlitz, Lars. 'Anders Nordencrantz'. https://sok.riksarkivet.se/sbl/artikel/8203, *Svenskt biografiskt lexikon*, Accessed 17 February 2018.

Hildebrand, Bengt. 'Thomas Erskine'. https://sok.riksarkivet.se/sbl/artikel/15455, *Svenskt biografiskt lexikon*. Accessed 25 June 2019.

Historisk statistik för Sverige. Del 3. Utrikeshandel 1732–1970. Stockholm: Statistiska Centralbyrån, 1972.

Hodacs, Hanna. 'Keeping it in the Family – the Swedish East India Company and the Irvine-Rose Family, 1733 to 1770'. *Journal of World History* 31, no. 3 (2020).

———. *Silk and Tea in the North: Scandinavian Trade and the Market for Asian Goods in Eighteenth-Century Europe*. Palgrave Macmillan, 2016.

Hoff, Annette. *Den danske kaffehistorie*. Højbjerg & Århus: Wormianum & Den Gamle By, 2015.

Höglund, Hans. *Om sillen i Bohuslän under den stora sillfiskeperioden på 1700-talet*. Göteborg: Svenska västkustfiskarnas centralförbund, 1977.

Hol Haugen, Bjørn Sverre. 'Virkningsfulle tekstiler - I Østnorske bønders draktpraksiser På 1700-Talet'. PhD thesis, University of Oslo, 2014.

Holm, Nils. 'Jean Antoine Fournier', https://sok.riksarkivet.se/sbl/artikel/15455, *Svenskt biografiskt lexikon*. Accessed 25 June 2019.

Hont, Istvan. *Jealousy of Trade*. Cambridge, Massachusetts; London: Harvard University Press, 2005.

Hunt, E. K., and Mark Lautzenheiser. *History of Economic Thought: A Critical Perspective*. Abingdon-on-Thames: Routledge, 2015.

Hunt, Margaret. *Women in Eighteenth Century Europe*. Harlow, England; New York: Pearson Longman, 2009.

Hutchison, Ragnhild. 'An Industrious Revolution in Norway? A Norwegian Road to the Modern Market.' *Scandinavian Journal of History* 39, no. 1 (2014).

———. *In the Doorway to Development. An Enquiry into Market Oriented Structural Changes in Norway ca.1750–1830*. Leiden: Brill, 2012.

Ihalainen, Pasi. *Agents of the People: Democracy and Popular Sovereignty in British and Swedish Parliamentary and Public Debates, 1734–1800*. Leiden: Brill, 2010.

Ihalainen, Pasi, Michael Brengsbo, Karin Sennefelt, and Patrik Winton. *Scandinavia in the Age of Revolution: Nordic Political Cultures, 1740–1820*. Farnham: Ashgate, 2011.

Ihalainen, Pasi, and Karin Sennefelt. 'General Introduction'. In *Scandinavia in the Age of Revolution. Nordic Political Cultures, 1740–1820*, edited by Pasi Ihalainen, Michael Bregnsbo, Karin Sennefelt, and Patrik Winton. Farnham: Ashgate Publishing Limited, 2011.

Ilmakunnas, Johanna. 'Ståndsmässig konsumtion: Högadelns penningbruk och konsumtionsvanor i Sverige under senare delen av 1700-talet'. *Historisk Tidskrift För Finland* 86, no. 2 (2001).

———. 'The Luxury Shopping Experience of the Swedish Aristocracy in Eighteenth-Century Paris'. In *Luxury and Gender in European Towns, 1700–1914*, edited by Deborah Simonton, Marjo Kaartinen, and Anne Montenach. Abingdon-on-Thames: Routledge, 2014.

Inger, Göran, *Svensk rättshistoria*, 5th ed, Malmö: Liber, 2011.

Irwin, Douglas A. 'Free Trade and Protection in Nineteenth-Century Britain and France Revisited: A Comment on Nye'. *Journal of Economic History* 53, no. 1 (March 1993): 146–52.

Isaac, Aaron. *Aaron Isaac minnen: Ett judiskt äventyr i svenskt 1700-tal*, edited by Mattias Dahlén. Translated by Abraham Brody. Stockholm: Hillelförlaget, 2008.

Israel, Jonathan. 'Northern Varieties: Contrasting the Dano-Norwegian and the Swedish-Finnish Enlightenments'. In *Eighteenth-Century Periodicals as Agents of Change. Perspectives on Northern Enlightenment*, edited by Ellen Krefting, Aina Nøding, and Mona Ringvej. Leiden, Boston: Brill, 2015.

James, F. G. 'Irish Smuggling in the Eighteenth Century'. *Irish Historical Studies* 12, no. 48 (September 1961).

Janes, Derek Charles. 'Fine Gottenburgh Teas: The Import and Distribution of Smuggled Tea in Scotland and the North of England c. 1750–1780'. *History of Retailing and Consumption* 2, no. 3 (2016).

———. '"...Of Which a Contraband Trade Makes the Basis of Their Pro t": Tea Smuggling in the North Sea c.1750–1780'. In *The New Coastal History Cultural and Environmental Perspectives from Scotland and Beyond*, edited by David Worthington. Palgrave Macmillan, 2017.

———. *The Business of Smuggling in South-East Scotland. John and David Nisbet and their Associates c.1740–1790*. PhD, University of Exeter, 2020.

Jarrick, Arne, and Janken Myrdal. 'Globalhistoria och forkning om långa förlopp'. *Historisk Tidskrift* 130, no. 4 (2010).

Jespersen, Knud J.V. *A History of Denmark*. Translated by Ivan Hill and Christopher Wade. 3rd ed. Macmillan, 2019.

Jessup, Philip C., and Francis Deak. 'The Early Development of the Law of Contraband of War III'. *Political Science Quarterly* 48, no. 3 (1933).

Jobs Arnberg, Anna-Karin. 'Un-Titled'. MA thesis, Uppsala University, forthcoming.

Johansson, Jon. 'Min ringa kalminks väst'. MA thesis, Stockholm University, 2015.

Johnson, Seija. 'Fashion from the Ship: Life, Fashion and Fashion Dissemination in and around Kokkola, Finland in the 18th Century'. In *Fashionable Encounters. Perspectives and Trends in Textile and Dress in the Early Modern Nordic World*, edited by Tove Engelhardt Mathiassen, Marie-Louise Nosch, Maj Ringgaard, Kirsten Toftegaard, and Mikkel Venborg Pedersen. Oxford: Oxbow Books, 2014.

———. *I den folkliga modedräktens fotspår. Bondekvinnors välstånd, ställning och modemedvetenhet i Gamlakarleby socken 1740–1800.* Jyväskylä: Jyväskylän yliopiston kirjasto, 2018.

Jones, Evan T. *Inside the Illicit Economy - Reconstructing the Smugglers' Trade of Sixteenth Century Bristol.* Farnham: Ashgate Publishing Limited, 2012.

Jordaan, Han, and Victor Wilson. 'The Eighteenth-Century Danish Dutch, and Swedish Free Ports in the Northeastern Caribbean: Continuity and Change'. In *Dutch Atlantic Connections, 1680–1800: Linking Empires, Bridging Borders*, edited by Gert Oostindie and Jessica V. Roitman. Leiden: Brill, 2014.

Jorgensen, C. *The Anglo-Swedish Alliance Against Napoleonic France.* Basingstoke, Hampshire ; New York: Palgrave Macmillan, 2004.

Josephson, Ragnar. *Borgarhus i gamla Stockholm.* Stockholm: Nordiska Bokhandeln, 1916.

Kahan, Arcadius, and Richard Hellie. *The Plow, the Hammer, and the Knout: An Economic History of Eighteenth-Century Russia.* Chicago: University of Chicago Press, 1985.

Kaiser, Wolfgang. 'Penser la frontière. notions et approches'. *Histoire Des Alpes* 3 (1998).

Karlsson, Rickard. *Svensk-franska förhandlingar. Bland sprätthökar och franska flugor i svenskt 1700-tal.* Linköping: LiU Tryck, 2007.

Kent, H. S. K. *War and Trade in Northern Seas: Anglo-Scandinavian Economic Relations in the Mid-Eighteenth Century.* Cambridge: Cambridge University Press, 1973.

Kenttämaa, Juhani. 'Jopparin jokilaakso – Oliko salakuljetus järjestäytynyttä rikollisuutta vai välttämätöntä kansanhuoltoa?, *Yle Dokumentit*, https://yle.fi/aihe/artikkeli/2019/06/05/jopparin-jokilaakso-oliko-salakuljetus-jarjestaytynytta-rikollisuutta-vai, Accessed 25 June 2019.

Kjellberg, Sven T. 'Ull och ylle: Bidrag till den svenska yllemanufakturens historia'. PhD thesis, Lund University, 1943.

Knutsson, Anna. 'Clandestine Commerce. Retailing Contraband Textiles in Late Eighteenth-Century Sweden', *History of Retailing and Consumption* 5, no. 3 (2019), doi: 10.1080/2373518X.2019.1703323.

Knutsson, Anna and Hanna Hodacs. 'When Coffee Was Banned: Strategies of Labour and Leisure among Stockholm's Poor Women, 1794–1796 and 1799–1802'. *Scandinavian Economic History Review* (2021), doi: 10.1080/03585522.2021.2000489.

Koerner, Lisbet. 'Linnaeus' Floral Transplants'. *Representations* 47 (Summer 1994).

———. *Linnaeus: Nature and Nation.* Harvard University Press, 1999.

Kopytoff, Igor. 'The Cultural Biography of Things'. In *The Social Life of Things. Commodities in Cultural Perspective*, edited by Arjun Appadurai. Cambridge: Cambridge University Press, 1986.

Krantz, Olle, and Lennart Schön. *Om den svenska konsumtionen under 1800- och 1900-talen.* Lund, 1984.

Kümin, Beat. 'Useful to Have, but Difficult to Govern. Inns and Taverns in Early Modern Bern and Vaud'. *Journal of Early Modern History* 3, no. 2 (1999).

Kwass, Michael. *Contraband: Louis Mandrin and the Making of a Global Underground.* Cambridge, Massachusetts: Harvard University Press, 2014.

Lagerqvist, Lars O. *Vad kostade det? Priser och löner från medeltid till våra dagar.* Lund: Historisk Media, 2015.

Larson, Alf. 'Kaffe, alkohol m.m'. *Svensk Kemisk Tidskrift*, 1914.
'*Läsning i Blandade Ämnen*', http://www.ne.se/uppslagsverk/encyklopedi/lång/läsning-i-blandade-ämnen, Nationalencyklopedin, Accessed 17 August 2017.
Le Gouic, Olivier. 'Le consulat de France à Cadix face aux réformes carolines (1765–1788)'. In *De l'utilité Commerciale Des Consuls. L'institution Consulaire et Les Marchands Dans Le Monde Méditerranéen (XVIIe–XXe Siècle)*, edited by Arnaud Bartolomei and et al. Collection de l'École Française de Rome. Rome: Publications de l'École française de Rome, 2017.
Lemire, Beverly. *Cotton*. Oxford: Berg Publishers, 2011.
———. *Fashion's Favourite: The Cotton Trade and the Consumer in Britain, 1660–1800*. Oxford: Oxford University Press, 1991.
———. *Global Trade and the Transformation of Consumer Cultures*. Cambridge: Cambridge University Press, 2018.
———. 'Peddling Fashion: Salesmen, Pawnbrokers, Taylors, Thieves and the Second-Hand Clothes Trade in England, 1680–1800'. *Textile History* 22, no. 1 (1991): 67–82.
Levander, Lars. *Landsväg, krog & marknad*. Mörklinta: Gidlunds Förlag, 1976.
Liby, Håkan. *Kläderna gör upplänningen. Folkligt mode - tradition och trender*. Uppsala: Ord&Form, 1997.
Liedman, Sven-Eric. *Den synliga handen. Anders Berch och ekonomiämnena vid 1700-talets svenska universitet*. Göteborg & Stockholm: Arbetarkultur, 1986.
Lilja, Kristina, and Pernilla Jonsson. 'Inadequate Supply and Increasing Demand for Textiles and Clothing: Second-Hand Trade at Auctions as an Alternative Source of Consumer Goods in Sweden, 1830–1900'. *The Economic History Review* 0, no. 0 (2019).
Lilja, Sven. 'Klimat och skördar ca 1530–1820'. In *Fiske, jordbruk och klimat i östersjöregionen under förmodern tid*, edited by Sven Lijla. Stockholm: Södertörns högskola, 2012.
Lindberg, Bo. 'Introduktion: Nationalism och nationell identitet i 1700-talets Sverige'. In *Nationalism Och Nationell Identitet i 1700-Talets Sverige*, edited by Åsa Karlsson and Bo Lindberg. Uppsala: Swedish Science Press, 2002.
Lindberg, Erik. *Borgerskap och burskap: Om näringsprivilegier och borgerskapets institutioner i Stockholm 1820–1846*. Uppsala: Acta Universitatis Upsaliensis, 2001.
Lindgrén, S., and J. Neumann. 'Crossings of Ice-Bound Sea Surfaces in History'. *Climatic Change* 4, no. 1 (1 March 1982).
Lindström, Dag. 'Leisure Culture, Entrepreneurs and Urban Space: Swedish Towns in a European Perspective, Eighteenth-Nineteenth Centuries'. In *Leisure Cultures in Urban Europe, C. 1700–1870: A Transnational Perspective*, edited by Peter Borsay and Jan Hein Furnée. Oxford University Press, 2016.
Linnarsson, Magnus. 'Contested Customs. Swedish Towns and the Private Customs Company, 1726–1762', *Bringing the People back in. State Building from Below in the Nordic Countries ca. 1500–1800*, edited by Knut Dørum, Mats Hallenberg, Kimmo Katajala. Routledge, 2021.
Lloyd Prichard, M. F. 'The Decline of Norwich'. *The Economic History Review* 3, no. 3 (1951).
Lundén, Thomas. *Pommern ett gränsfall i tid och rum*. Slavica Lundensia 27. Lund: Lund University, 2016.
Lundqvist, Pia. 'Förbjudna tyger – Textilsmuggling till Sverige under 1700- Och 1800-talen'. In *Dolda innovationer. Textila produkter och ny teknik under 1800-talet*, edited by Klas Nyberg and Pia Lundqvist. Stockholm: Kulturhistoriska Bokförlaget, 2013.
———. 'Hemslöjden och Stockholms textilmarknad. Den västgötska gårdfarihandeln 1790–1846'. In *Till salu. Stockholms textila handel och manufaktur 1722–1846*, edited by Klas Nyberg. Stockholm: Stads- och Kommunhistoriska Institutet, 2010.

———. *Marknad på väg. Den västgöta gårdfarihandeln 1790–1864*. Göteborg: Göteborg Universitet, 2008.

———. 'Taste for Hot Drinks - the Consumption of Coffee and Tea in Two Swedish Nineteenth-Century Novels'. *History of Retailing and Consumption*, 2, no.3, 2016.

MacKenzie, Brian R., Jürgen Alheit, Daniel J. Conley, Poul Holm, and Carl Christian Kinze. 'Ecological Hypotheses for a Historical Reconstruction of Upper Trophic Level Biomass in the Baltic Sea and Skagerrak'. *Canadian Journal of Fisheries and Aquatic Sciences* 59, no. 1 (2002).

Magnusson, Lars. *An Economic History of Sweden*. London: Routledge, 2000.

———. Äran, korruptionen och den borgerliga ordningen, essäer från svensk ekonomihistoria. Stockholm: Atlantis, 2001.

———. 'Den ekonomiska diskussionen under frihetstiden – Ett framlängesperspektiv'. In *Riksdag, kaffehus och predikstol. frihetstidens politiska kultur 1766–1772*, edited by Marie-Christine Skuncke and Henrietta Tandefelt. Stockholm: Atlantis, 2003.

———. 'Försnillning, smyghandel och fusk. Förlagssystem och hantverkskultur i Eskilstuna vid början av 1800-talet'. *Historisk Tidskrift*, no. 2 (1986).

———. 'Mercantilism and "Reform" Mercantilism: The Rise of Economic Discourse in Sweden during the Eighteenth Century'. *History of Political Economy* 19, no. 3 (1987).

———. *Merkantilism: Ett ekonomiskt tänkande formuleras*. Stockholm: S N S Forlag, 1999.

———. 'Merkantilismens teori och praktik: utrikeshandel: och manufakturpolitik i sitt idéhistoriska sammanhang'. In *Till salu. Stockholms textila handel och manufaktur 1722–1846*, edited by Klas Nyberg. Stockholm: Stads- och Kommunhistoriska Institutet, 2010.

———. *The Tradition of Free Trade*. Abingdon: Routledge, 2004.

Magnusson, Lars, and Klas Nyberg. *Konsumtion och industrialisering i Sverige 1820–1914. Uppsala 1995*. A Research Project. Uppsala, 1995.

Makko, Aryo, and Leos Müller, eds. *I främmande hamn. Den svenska och svensk-norska konsultjänsten 1700–1985*. Malmö: Universus Academic Press, 2015.

Malmström, Carl Gustaf. *Sveriges politiska historia från konung Karl XII:s död till statshvälfningen 1772*. 2nd ed. Vol. 4. Stockholm: P. A. Norstedt & söner, 1899.

Mann, Michael E. 'Little Ice Age'. In *Encyclopedia of Global Environmental Change*, edited by Michael C MacCracken and John S Perry, Vol. 1. The Earth System: Physical and Chemical Dimensions of Global Environmental Change. Chichester, West Sussex, Malden, MA: John Wiley & Sons, 2002.

Marjanen, Jani. 'Den ekonomiska patriotismens uppgång och fall. finska hushållningssällskapet i europeisk, svensk och finsk kontext 1720–1840'. PhD thesis, Helsingfors universitet, 2013.

———. 'Moral Economy and Civil Society in Eighteenth Century Europe: The Case of Economic Societies and Business of Improvement'. *Journal of Global Ethics* 11, no. 2 (2015).

Martens, Vibe Maria. 'Indian Textiles in Seventeenth- and Eighteenth- Century Denmark. Trade and the Rise of a Global Consumer Culture. Vol 1'. PhD thesis, European University Institute, 2017.

———. 'The Theft of Fashion: Circulation of Fashionable Textiles and Garments in 18th-Century Copenhagen'. In *Fashionable Encounters. Perspectives and Trends in Textile and Dress in the Early Modern Nordic World*, edited by Tove Engelhardt Mathiassen, Marie-Louise Nosch, Maj Ringgaard, Kirsten Toftegaard, and Mikkel Venborg Pedersen. Oxford: Oxbow Books, 2014.

Marzagalli, Silvia. *Boulevards de La Fraude: Le Negoce Maritime Et Le Blocus Continental, 1806–1813: Bordeaux, Hambourg, Livourne*. Villeneuve- d'Ascq: Presses Univ. Septentrion, 1999.

———. (ed.), *Les consuls en Méditerranée, agents d'information*. Paris: Garnier, 2015.

Maxwell, Alexander. *Patriots against Fashion: Clothing and Nationalism in Europe's Age of Revolutions*. Palgrave Connect. Houndmills, Basingstoke, Hampshire, UK; New York: Palgrave Macmillan, 2014.

McKendrick, Neil, John Brewer, and John Harold Plumb. *The Birth of a Consumer Society: The Commercialization of Eighteenth-Century England*. New York: Europa Publications, 1982.

Melkersson, Martin. 'Staten, ordningen och friheten. En studie av den styrande elitens syn på statens roll mellan stormaktstiden och 1800-talet'. PhD thesis, Uppsala University, 1997.

Merovuo, Jenni, 'Local Space Building as State Building? Mediating Clergy on the Russo-Swedish Borderland.' In *Bringing the People back in. State Building from Below in the Nordic Countries ca. 1500–1800*, edited by Knut Dørum, Mats Hallenberg, Kimmo Katajala. Routledge, 2021.

Meyer Spacks, Patricia. *Privacy: Concealing the Eighteenth-Century Self*. Chicago: The University of Chicago Press, 2003.

Mézin, Anne. 'La défense des intérêts des négociants français de Cadix dans la première moitié du xviiie siècle d'après la correspondance ministérielle'. In *De l'utilité commerciale des consuls. L'institution consulaire et les marchands dans le monde méditerranéen (XVIIe–XXe Siècle)*, edited by Arnaud Bartolomei, Guillaume Calafat, Mathieu Grenet, and Jörg Ulbert. Collection de l'École Française de Rome. Rome: Publications de l'École française de Rome, 2017.

Mickwitz, Joachim. 'Om wanans werkan. Konsumtion av lyxbetonade kolonialvaror i de bottniska småstäderna under sent 1700-tal'. In *Global historia från periferin, Norden 1600–1850*, edited by Leos Müller, Göran Rydén, and Holger Weiss. Lund: Studentlitteratur, 2010.

Midgley, Clare. 'Slave Sugar Boycotts, Female Activism and the Domestic Base of British Anti-slavery Culture'. *Slavery & Abolition* 17, no. 3 (1 December 1996).

Mintz, Sidney Wilfred. *Sweetness and Power: The Place of Sugar in Modern History*. New York; London: Penguin Books, 1986.

Möller, Peter von. *Halländska herregårdar*. Stockholm, 1871.

Monod, Paul. 'Dangerous Merchandise: Smuggling, Jacobitism, and Commercial Culture in Southeast England, 1690–1760'. *Journal of British Studies* 30, no. 2 (2016).

Montenach, Anne. 'Conflict, Terriotor and the Frontier Economy: Smuggling in the Alps of Dauphiné During the 18th Century'. *Journal of Alpine Research | Revue de Géographie Alpine* 104, no. 1 (2016).

———. *Femmes, Pouvoir et Contrebande Dans Les Alpes Au XVIIIe Siècle*. Grenoble: Presses Universitaires de Grenoble, 2017.

———. 'Gender and Luxury in Eighteenth Century Grenoble: From Legal Exchanges to Shadow Economy'. In *Luxury and Gender in European Towns, 1700–1914*, edited by Deborah Simonton, Marjo Kaartinen, and Anne Montenach. New York: Routledge, 2015.

———. 'Une économie du secret. Le commerce clandesitin de viande en Carême'. *Rives Méditerranéennes* 17 (2004).

Montgomery, Arthur. 'Svensk tullpolitik 1816–1911'. PhD thesis, Uppsala University, 1921.

Morieux, Renaud. 'Chapitre VIII. Le jeu des identités: Fraude et contrebande'. In *Une Mer Pour Deux Royaumes : La Manche, Frontière Franco-Anglaise (XVIIe–XVIIIe Siècles)*, 241–73. Histoire. Rennes: Presses universitaires de Rennes, 2015.

———. *The Channel: England, France and the Construction of a Maritime Border in the Eighteenth Century*. Cambridge University Press, 2016.

Morrisette, Annie Tock. '"They Would Have a Law of Their Own": The Discourse on Smuggling at the Old Bailey, 1736–1814'. MA thesis, East Carolina University, 2013.

Mui, Hoh-Cheung, and Lorna H. Mui. *Shops and Shopkeeping in Eighteenth-Century England*. Montreal: McGill-Queen's University Press, 1989.

———. 'Smuggling and the British Tea Trade before 1784'. *The American Historical Review* 74, no. 1 (October 1968).

———. 'The Commutation Act and the Tea Trade in Britain 1784–1793'. *The Economic History Review* 16, no. 2 (1963).

———. *The Management of Monopoly. A Study of the East India Company's Conduct of Its Tea Trade, 1784–1833*. Vancouver: The University of British Columbia Press, 1984.

———. 'Trends in Eighteenth-Century Smuggling Reconsidered'. *The Economic History Review* 28 (1975).

———. 'William Pitt and the Enforcement of the Commutation Act, 1784–1788'. *The English Historical Review* 76, no. 300 (July 1961).

Müller, Leos. *Consuls, Corsairs, and Commerce. The Swedish Consular Service and Long-Distance Shipping, 1720–1815*. Acta Universitatis Upsaliensis 213. Uppsala: Uppsala University, 2004.

———. 'Kolonialprodukter i Sveriges handel och konsumtionskultur, 1700–1800'. *Historisk Tidskrift* 124, no. 2 (2004).

———. *Neutrality in World History*. Abingdon-on-Thames: Routledge, 2019.

———. 'Peace: Sweden's Neutrality and the Eighteenth-Century Inter-State System'. In *Sweden in the Eighteenth-Century World: Provincial Cosmopolitans*, edited by Göran Rydén. Farnham: Ashgate, 2013.

———. 'Svensk sjöfart, neutralitet och det väpnade neutralitetsförbundet'. *Sjuttonhundratal* 9, 2012.

———. *Sveriges Första globala århundrade. En 1700-talshistoria*. Stockholm: Dialogos, 2018.

———. 'Sweden's Neutral Trade under Gustav III: The Ideal of Commercial Independence under the Predicament of Political Isolation'. In *Trade and War: The Neutrality of Commerce in the Inter-State System*, edited by Koen Stapelbroek. Helsinki: Helsinki Collegium for Advanced Studies, 2011.

———. 'Swedish Consular Reports as a Source of Business Information, 1700–1800'. In *Information Flows. New Approaches in the Historical Study of Business Information*, edited by Leos Müller and Jari Ojala. Helsinki: SKS/Finnish Literature Society, 2007.

———. 'Swedish Merchant Shipping in Troubled Times: The French Revolutionary Wars and Sweden's Neutrality 1793–1801'. *The International Journal of Maritime History* 28, no. 1 (2016).

———. 'Swedish-Portuguese Trade and Swedish Consular Service, 1700–1800'. In *A Articulacão Do Sal Português Aos Circuitos Mundiais. Antigos e Novos Consumos. The Articulation of Portuguese Salt with Worldwide Routes. Past and New Consumption Trends*. Porto: Instituto de Historia Moderna. Universidad do Porto, 2008.

———. 'The Swedish East India Trade and International Markets: Re-Exports of Teas, 1731–1813'. *Scandinavian Economic History Review* 51, no. 3 (2003).

———. 'Under svensk flagg i medelhavet. Algeriska sjöpass 1770–1800'. In *Från Afrikakompaniet till Tokyo. En vänbok till György Nováky*, edited by Marie Lennersand and Leos Müller. Exkurs, 2017.

Müller, Leos, Göran Rydén, and Holger Weiss. 'Global historia - Något för nordiska historiker?' In *Global historia från periferin. Norden 1600–1850*, edited by Leos Müller, Göran Rydén, and Holger Weiss. Lund: Studentlitteratur, 2009.

Murdoch, Steve, Leos Müller, Simon Ekström, and Leos Müller. 'Neutral före neutraliteten. Svensk sjöfart i krigens skugga, cirka 1650–1800'. In *Angöringar. Berättelser och kunskap från havet*. Göteborg: Makadam Förlag, 2017.

Murhem, Sofia, and Göran Ulväng. 'To Buy a Plate: Retail and Shopping for Porcelain and Faience in Stockholm during the Eighteenth Century'. In *A Taste for Luxury in Early Modern Europe*, edited by Johanna Ilmakunnas and Jon Stobart. London: Bloomsbury, 2017.

Murray, John J. 'Baltic Commerce and Power Politics in the Early Eighteenth Century'. *Huntington Library Quarterly* 6, no. 1 (1 January 1942).

Muskett, Paul. 'English Smuggling in the Eighteenth Century.' PhD thesis, Open University, 1996.

Nash, Catherine, Lorraine Dennis, and Brian Graham. 'Putting the Border in Place: Customs Regulation in the Making of the Irish Border, 1921–1945'. *Journal of Historical Geography* 36 (2010).

Nash, R. C. 'South Carolina Indigo, European Textiles, and the British Atlantic Economy in the Eighteenth Century'. *The Economic History Review* 63, no. 2 (2010).

Nilsson, Lars, and Erik Lönnroth. 'Det stora sillfisket 1752–1808'. In *Bohusläns historia*. Stockholm: Almqvist & Wiksells A.B., 1963.

Nilsson, Rasmus. 'När kaffet kom till staden. Uppsalabornas te- och kaffekonsumption från 1750 till 1850'. B-Uppsats, Uppsala University, 2014.

Nordin, Christina. *Oordning. Torghandel i Stockholm 1540–1918*. Stockholm: Sekel Bokförlag, 2009.

Nordin, Jonas. *Ett fattigt men fritt folk. Nationell och politisk självbild i Sverige från sen stormaktstid till slutet av frihetstiden*. Stockholm: Brutus Östlings Bokförlag Symposium, 2000.

'Nordisk familjebok/Uggleupplagan. 16. Lee - Luvua', 1912. http://runeberg.org/nfbp/.

Norton, Macy. 'Tasting Empire: Chocolate and the European Internalization of Mesoamerican Aesthetics'. *The American Historical Review* 111, no. 3 (2006).

Nyberg, Klas. '1700-talets textilmanufaktur i Stockholm. Centraliserad fabrik eller hemindustri?' In *Till salu. Stockholms textila handel och manufaktur 1722–1846*, edited by Klas Nyberg. Stockholm: Stads- och Kommunhistoriska Institutet, 2010.

———. 'Anti-lyx : En samtida bildberättelse om fersenska mordet den 20 juni 1810'. In *Det svenska begäret - Sekler av lyxkonsumtion*, edited by Klas Nyberg and Paula von Wachenfeldt. Stockholm: Carlsson Bokförlag, 2015.

———. 'Köpes: ull, säljes: kläde. Yllemanufakturens företagsformer i 1780-talets Stockholm'. PhD thesis, Uppsala University, 1992.

———. 'Staten, manufakturerna och hemmamarknadens framväxt'. In *Till salu. Stockholms textila handel och manufaktur 1722–1846*, edited by Klas Nyberg. Stockholm: Stads- och Kommunhistoriska Institutet, 2010.

———. 'Stockholms handlande borgerskap och manufakturister'. In *Till salu. Stockholms textila handel och manufaktur 1722–1846*, edited by Klas Nyberg. Stockholm: Stads- och Kommunhistoriska Institutet, 2010.

———. 'Stockholms textila handel och manufaktur'. In *Till salu. Stockholms textila handel och manufaktur 1722–1846*, edited by Klas Nyberg. Stockholm: Stads- och Kommunhistoriska Institutet, 2010.

Nyberg, Klas, and Paula von Wachenfeldt. 'Introduktion'. In *Det svenska begäret - Sekler av lyxkonsumtion*, edited by Klas Nyberg and Paula von Wachenfeldt, 1st ed. Stockholm: Carlsson Bokförlag, 2015.

Nye, John V. C. 'Reply to Irwin on Free Trade'. *The Journal of Economic History* 53, no. 1 (March 1993).

———. *War, Wine, and Taxes: The Political Economy of Anglo-French Trade, 1689–1900 John V. C. Nye Princeton: Princeton University Press, 2007*. Princeton: Princeton University Press, 2007.

Nygren, Rolf. 'Fördomar och ekonomisk krishantering 1815 års riksdag och frågan om judars rättsställning i Sverige'. *Liber Amicorum*, 2007.

Olàn, Eskil. *Judarna på svensk mark. Historien om israeliternas invandring till Sverige*. Stockholm: Bok- o. Konstförlaget Rex, 1924.

Oliver, Lisi. *The Beginnings of English Laws*. Toronto: Toronto University Press, 2002.

Olofsson, Sven. 'Till ömsesidig nytta. Entreprenörer, framgång och sociala relationer i centrala Jämtland ca 1810–1850'. Uppsala University, 2011.

Önnerfors, Andreas. 'Gränser och gemenskaper. Hur svenskt var svenska Pommern?' In *Vid gränsen. Integration och identitet i det förnationella Norden*, edited by Harald Gustafsson and Hanne Sanders. Göteborg & Stockholm: Makadam Förlag, 2006.

———, ed. *Mystiskt brödraskap – Mäktigt nätverk studier i det svenska 1700-talsfrimureriet*. Lund: Lund University, 2006.

———. *Svenska Pommern: Kulturmöten och identifikation 1720–1815*. Lund: Lund University, 2003.

Opsahl, Erik. 'Jemtland fra dansk til svensk i 1645? Staten, riket og nasjonen som identitets- og lojalitetsgrunnlag i Norden i tidlig nytid'. In *Jämtland och den jämtländska världen 1000–1645*, edited by Olof Holm. Stockholm: Kungl. Vitterhets Historie och Antikvitets Akademien, 2011.

Ormrod, David. *The Rise of Commercial Empires. England and the Netherlands in the Age of Mercantilism, 1650–1770*. Cambridge: Cambridge University Press, 2003.

Oscarsson, Ingemar. '1700-talets periodiska press'. In *Det offentliga språkbruket och dess vilkor i Sverige under 1700-talet*, edited by Ulf Teleman. Nordund Småskrifter Från Institutionen För Nordiska Språk i Lund. Lund: Nordund, 1985.

———. 'Med tryckfrihet som tidig tradition'. In *Den svenska pressens historia: I begynnelsen (tiden före 1830)*, edited by Karl Erik Gustafsson and Per Rydén. Stockholm: Ekerlids Förlag, 2000.

Östman, Anna-Catrin, and Hanna Lindberg. 'Försäljning och försörjning i marginalen'. In *Rum för eftertanke, en antologi om att utmana det invanda*, edited by Mio Lindman and Jonas Ahlskog. Åbo: Folkets bildningsförbund rf., 2017.

Osvald, Tobias, *Stadens gränsplatser. Kungliga Poliskammaren och vardagens omstridda rum i Stockholm, 1776–1835*, Uppsala University Press, 2022.

Påhlman, Axel. 'Adam Smiths Wealth of Nations. Spridda Bibliografiska Anteckningar'. *Ekonomisk Tidskrift* 35, no. 5/6 (1933).

Parker, Charles H. 'Entrepreneurs, Families, and Companies'. In *The Cambridge World History. The Construction of a Global World, 1400–1800 CE.*, edited by Jerry H. Bentley, Sanjay Subrahmanyam, and Merry E. Weisner-Hanks, Vol. 2. Patterns of Change. Cambridge: Cambridge University Press, 2015.

Peterson, Bo. '"Yppighetens nytta och torftighets fägnad", Pamflettdebatten om 1766 års överflödsförordning'. *Historisk Tidskrift*, no. 1 (1984).

Pieterse, Jan Nederveen. 'Oriental Globalization'. *Theory, Culture & Society* 23, no. 2–3 (May 2006).

Pihlaiamäki, Heikki. *Conquest and the Law in Swedish Livonia*. Leiden: Brill, 2017.

Pijning, Ernst. 'Passive Resistance: Portuguese Diplomacy of Contraband Trade during King John V's Reign (1706–1750)'. *Arquipélago História* 2, no. II (1997).

Pomeranz, Kenneth, and Steven Topik. *The World That Trade Created. Society, Culture, and the World Economy 1400 to the Present*. 2nd ed. Armonk, New York; London, England: M.E Sharpe, 2006.

Ponce Vàzquez, Juan José. *Islanders and Empire: Smuggling and Political Defiance in Hispaniola, 1580–1690.* Cambridge: Cambridge University Press, 2020.

Pourchasse, Pierrick. *Le commerce du Nord: Les échanges commerciaux entre la France et l'Europe septentrionale au XVIIIe siècle.* Histoire. Rennes: Presses universitaires de Rennes, 2015.

———. 'The "Information Problem" for French Trade in the Northern Markets of the Eighteenth Century'. In *Information Flows. New Approaches in the Historical Study of Business Information*, edited by Leos Müller and Jari Ojala. Helsinki: SKS/Finnish Literature Society, 2007.

———. 'Trade between France and Sweden in the Eighteenth Century'. *Forum Navale* 67 (2011).

Price, Jacob M. 'What Did Merchants Do? Reflections on British Overseas Trade, 1660–1790'. *Journal of Economic History* 49, no. 2 (June 1989).

Priestley, Ursula. *The Fabric of Stuffs. The Norwich Textile Industry from 1565.* Norwich: Centre of East Anglian Studies, 1990.

———, ed. *The Letters of Philip Stannard, Norwich Textile Manufacturer (1751–1763).* Vol. LVII. Norfolk Record Society, 1994.

Rangström, Lena. 'Den svenska hovdräkten - nationell och europeisk'. In *Hovets dräkter*, edited by Lena Rangström. Stockholm: Livrustkammaren, 1994.

———. 'Gustaf II:s svenska dräktprojekt. En nationell reform i tiden'. In *Nationalism och nationell identitet i 1700-talets Sverige*, edited by Åsa Karlsson and Bo Lindberg. Uppsala: Swedish Science Press, 2002.

———. *Kläder för tid och evighet: Gustaf III sedd genom sina dräkter.* Stockholm: Livrustkammaren, 1997.

———. *Modelejon. Manligt Mode 1500-Tal, 1600-Tal, 1700-Tal.* 2nd ed. Stockholm: Livrustkammaren/Atlantis, 2002.

Rasmussen, Pernilla. *Skräddaren, sömmerskan och modet: Arbetsmetoder och arbetsdelning i tillverkningen av kvinnlig dräkt 1770–1830.* Stockholm: Nordiska museets förlag, 2010.

Rau, Susanne. *Räume: Konzepte, Wahrnehmungen, Nutzungen.* Frankfurt am Main: Campus Verlag, 2013.

Reenstierna, Märta Helena. *Årstadagboken*, edited by Gunnar Broman. Vol. 1. 3 vols. Stockholm: Generalstabens Litografiska Anstalts Förlag, 1946.

Reinert, Sophus A. 'Rivalry: Greatness in Early Modern Political Economy'. In *Mercantilism Reimagined: Political Economy in Early Modern Britain and Its Empire*, edited by Philip J. Stern and Carl Wennerlind. Oxford: Oxford University Press, 2013.

Reinert, Sophus A., and Jani Marjanen. 'Patriotism, Cosmopolitanism, and Political Economy in the Accademia Dei Pugni in Austrian Lombardy, 1760–1780'. In *The Rise of Economic Societies in the Eighteenth Century: Patriotic Refom in Europe and North America*, edited by Koen Stapelbroek and Jani Marjanen. Basingstoke, Hampshire; New York: Palgrave Macmillan, 2012.

Ressel, Magnus. 'Swedish Pomeranian Shipping in the Revolutionary Age (1776–1815)'. *Forum Navale* 68 (2012).

Ribeiro, Aileen. *Dress in Eighteenth-Century Europe, 1715–1789.* 2nd ed. New Haven: Yale University Press, 2002.

Riello, Giorgio. *Cotton: The Fabric That Made the Modern World.* Cambridge: Cambridge University Press, 2013.

Robert, Dhyana. 'La contrebande à Montréal, 1729–1752: Passages, pratiques et protagonistes'. MA thesis, University of Sherbrooke, 2016.

Roberts, Michael. *British Diplomacy and Swedish Politics, 1758–1773.* Minneapolis: University of Minnesota Press, 1980.

Roche, Daniel. *The Culture of Clothing: Dress and Fashion in the 'ancien Régime'*. Translated by Jean Birrell. Cambridge: Cambridge University Press, 1996.

Roeck, Bernd, and Herman Roodenburg. 'Introduction'. In *Cultural Exchange in Early Modern Europe: Forging European Identities, 1400–1700*, Vol. 4. Cambridge: Cambridge University Press, 2007.

Rönnbäck, Klas. 'An Early Modern Consumer Revolution in the Baltic?' *Scandinavian Journal of History* 35, no. 2 (2010).

———. ''Balancing the Baltic Trade: Colonial Commodities in the Trade on the Baltic, 1773–1856'. *Scandinavian Economic History Review* 58, no. 3 (November 2010).

Rosander, Göran. *Gårdfarihandel i Norden. En översikt av en gammal handelsform*. LTs förlag i samarbete med Institutet för folklivsforskning, 1980.

Runefelt, Leif. *Att hasta mot undergången. Anspråk, flyktighet, föreställning i debatten om konsumtion i Sverige 1730–1830*. Lund: Nordic Academic Press, 2015.

———. 'Från yppighets nytta till dygdens försvar. Den frihetstida debatten om lyx'. *Historisk Tidskrift* 124, no. 2 (2004).

———. 'Grå bonde, blå bonde: Den globala indigomarknaden som etiskt problem på svenska landsbygden kring sekelskiftet 1800'. In *Det svenska begäret. Sekler av lyxkonsumtion*, edited by Klas Nyberg and Paula von Wachenfeldt. Stockholm: Carlsson Bokförlag, 2015.

Ryckbosch, Wouter. 'Early Modern Consumption History. Current Challenges and Future Perspectives'. *Low Countries Historical Review* 130, no. 1 (2015).

Rydén, Göran. 'Eskilstuna Fristad: The Beginnings of an Urban Experiment'. In *Sweden in the Eighteenth-Century World: Provincial Cosmopolitans*, edited by Göran Rydén. Farnham: Ashgate Publishing Limited, 2013.

———, ed. *Sweden in the Eighteenth-Century World: Provincial Cosmopolitans*. Farnham: Ashgate, 2013.

Sack, Robert David. *Human Territoriality: Its Theory and History*. Cambridge: Cambridge University Press, 1986.

Sahlin, Peter, *Boundaries. The Making of France and Spain in the Pyrenees*. Berkley; Los Angeles; London: University of California Press, 1989.

Salvemini, Biagio. 'The "Intervention Practices" of the Late Ancient Régime: Notes on the Institutional and Mercantile Spheres of Eighteenth-Century Europe'. In *War, Trade and Neutrality. Europe and the Mediterranean in the Seventeenth and Eighteenth Centuries*, edited by Antonella Alimento. Milano: Franco Angeli, 2011.

Samuelsson, Kurt. 'De stora köpmanshusen i Stockholm 1730–1815. En studie i den svenska handelskapitalismens historia.' PhD thesis, Stockholms Högskola, 1951.

Sander, Bengt, *Några bewis, att judarne äfwen på sitt sätt bidraga till den allmänna nöden i Swerige*. 1809.

Sandklef, Albert. *Allmogesjöfart på Sveriges västkust 1575–1850*. Lund: C. W. K. Gleerup, 1973.

Sandvik, Einar. 'Levangermartnan', 93 1992. http://www.marsimartnan.no/Marsimartnan%202008/DKS/LEVANGERMARTNAN.pdf., Accessed 26 December 2017.

Saunier, Pierre-Yves. 'Circulations, connexions et espaces transnationaux'. *Genèses* 57, no. 4 (2004).

———. *Transnational History*. New York: Palgrave Macmillan, 2013.

Scammell, G.V. 'British Smuggling in the Iberian Americas circa 1500–1750'. *Itinerario* 24, no. 3/4 (2000).

Schaffer, Simon, Lissa Roberts, Kapil Raj, and James Delbourgo, eds. *The Brokered World. Go-Betweens and Global Intelligence, 1770–1820*. Sagamore Beach: Science History Publications, U.S.A., 2009.

Schendel, Willem van, and Itty Abraham. 'Introduction'. In *Illicit Flows and Criminal Things. States, Borders, and the Other Side of Globalization*, edited by Willem van Schendel and Itty Abraham. Indiana University, 2005.

Schnakenbourg, Eric. 'Sweden and the Atlantic: The Dynamism of Sweden's Colonial Projects in the Eighteenth Century.' In *Scandinavian Colonialism and the Rise of Modernity. Contributions to Global Historical Archaeology*, edited by Naum M. Nordin and et al. New York: Springer, 2013.

Schön, Lennart. *Sweden's Road to Modernity: An Economic History*. Translated by Ken Schubert. Stockholm: S N S Forlag, 2010.

Scott, Hamish. *The Oxford Handbook of Early Modern European History, 1350–1750: Volume I: Peoples and Place*. Oxford: OUP Oxford, 2015.

Selling, Gösta. 'Artur Hazelius' födelsehus I. Den Fritziska sidenvävargården'. *Fataburen* 65 (1926).

———. *Stockholms stads brandförsäkringskontors hus i kvarteret Aglaurus vid Mynttorget. Historik med anledning av kontorets 200-åriga tillvaro*. Stockholm, 1946.

Sennefelt, Karin. *Politikens Hjärta. Medborgarskap, manlighet och plats i frihetstidens Stockholm*. 2nd ed. Stockholm: Stockholmia Förlag, 2015.

Shovlin, John. 'War and Peace: Trade, International Competition, and Political Economy'. In *Mercantilism Reimagined: Political Economy in Early Modern Britain and Its Empire*, edited by Philip J. Stern and Carl Wennerlind. Oxford University Press, 2013. Ebook.

Sicking, Louis. 'A Wider Spread of Risk: A Key to Understanding Holland's Domination of Eastward and Westward Seafaring'. In *The Dynamics of Economic Culture in the North Sea- and Baltic Regions*, edited by Hanno Brand and Leos Müller. Hilversum: Verloren, 2007.

Silberner, Edmond. *La guerre dans la pensée économique du XVIe au XVIIIe siècle*, Paris: Librairie dú Recueil Sirey, 1939.

Simonsen, Anders. *Bland hederligt folk. Organiserat sällskapsliv och borgerlig formering i Göteborg 1755–1820*. Göteborg: Göteborg Universitet, 2001.

Sjöding, Allan. 'Gästgivargården i svensk 1700-talslitteratur'. *Svensk Litteraturtidskrift* 42, no. 1 (1978).

Skunke, Marie-Christine. 'Press and Political Culture in Sweden at the End of the Age of Liberty'. In *Enlightenment, Revolution and the Periodical Press*, edited by Hans-Jürgen Lüsebrink and Jeremy D. Popkin. Oxford: Voltaire Foundation, 2004.

Smart, Alan, and Filippo M. Zrilli. 'Extralegality'. In *Companion to Urban Anthropology*, edited by Donald M. Nonini. Chichester, West Sussex, Malden, MA: Wiley Blackwell, 2014.

Smith, David Chan. 'Fair Trade and the Political Economy of Brandy Smuggling in Early Eighteenth-Century Britain' *Past & Present*, 251, no. 1 (May 2021), https://doi.org/10.1093/pastj/gtaa008.

Smith, Joshua M. *Borderland Smuggling: Patriots, Loyalists, and Illicit Trade in the Northeast, 1783–1820*. Gainesville: University Press of Florida, 2006.

Smith, Woodruff. *Consumption and the Making of Respectability, 1600–1800*. New York: Routledge, 2002.

Söderberg, Johan. 'Long-Term Trends in Real Wages of Labourers'. In *Exchange Rates, Prices, and Wages, 1277–2008*, edited by Rodney Edvinsson, Tor Jacobson, and Daniel Waldenström. Stockholm: Ekerlids Förlag, 2010.

Söderberg, Johan, Ulf Jonsson, and Christer Persson. *A Stagnating Metropolis. The Economy and Demography of Stockholm, 1750–1850*. Cambridge: Cambridge University Press, 1991.

Soen, Violet, Bram De Riddler, Alexander Soetaert, Werner Thomas, Johan Verberckmoes, and Sophie Verreyken. 'How to Do Transregional History: A Concept, Method and Tool for Early Modern Border Research'. *Journal of Early Modern History* 21 (2017).

Somaini, Francesco. 'Territory, Territoralisation, Territoriality: Problems of Definiton and Historical Interpretation'. *Plurimondi* 10 (2012).

Spary, Emma C. *Eating the Enlightenment. Food and Sciences in Paris, 1670–1760*. Chicago & London: University of Chicago Press, 2012.

———. *Feeding France. New Sciences of Food, 1760–1815*. Cambridge: Cambridge University Press, 2014.

Stapelbroek, Koen, and Jani Marjanen. 'Political Economy, Patriotism and the Rise of Societies'. In *The Rise of Economic Societies in the Eighteenth Century. Patriotic Reform in Europe and North America*, edited by Koen Stapelbroek and Jani Marjanen. Basingstoke, Hampshire ; New York: Palgrave Macmillan, 2012.

Stare, Jacqueline, ed. *Judiska gårdfarihandlare i Sverige*. Stockholm: Judiska museet, 1996.

Stern, Philip J., and Carl Wennerlind. 'Introduction'. In *Mercantilism Reimagined: Political Economy in Early Modern Britain and Its Empire*. Oxford: Oxford University Press, 2013.

Stobart, Jon. *Sugar and Spice. Grocers and Groceries in Provincial England, 1650–1830*. Oxford: Oxford University Press, 2013.

Stobart, Jon, I. Van Damme, and Ilja Van Damme. *Modernity and the Second-Hand Trade: European Consumption Cultures and Practices, 1700–1900*. New York: Springer, 2010.

Stobart, Jon, and Andrew Hann. 'Retailing Revolution in the Eighteenth Century? Evidence from North-West England'. *Business History* 46, no. 2 (1 April 2004).

'Stockholms hamnar'. Accessed 12 February 2019. https://www.stockholmshamnar.se/historia/epoker/1850-1899/.

Storå, Nils. '"Rucksack Russians" in Finland Peddling and Culture Contact'. Translated by Michele McNabb. *Ethnologia Scandinavica* 21 (1991).

Strandberg, Åsa. '650 Stycken Citroner, 120 Stycken Påmerantzer, 200 Stycken Apellisiner. Vägledning till tullarkiven på landsarkivet i Uppsala'. MA thesis, Uppsala University, 2011.

Struck, Bernhard, Kate Ferris, and Jacques Revel. 'Introduction: Space and Scale in Transnational History'. *The International History Review* 33, no. 4 (2011).

Styles, John. *The Dress of the People: Everyday Fashion in Eighteenth-Century England*. New Haven: Yale University Press, 2007.

Subrahmanyam, Sanjay, ed. *Merchant Networks in the Early Modern World*. London; New York: Routledge, 1996.

Svensson, Harry R:son. 'The Case of Fabian Philip, Karlskrona's First Jewish Entrepreneur: A Swedish Example of the Port Jews Phenomenon?' *Sjuttonhundratal* 11 (17 August 2014).

Svensson, Sigfrid. *Bygd och yttervärld. Studier över förhållandet mellan nyheter och tradition*. Nordiska Museets Handlingar 15. Stockholm, 1942.

———. *Dräktlyx hos gotländsk allmoge 1793*. Stockholm: Ymer, 1933.

———. *Skånes folkdräkter. En dräkthistorisk undersökning 1500–1900*. Nordiska Museets Handlingar 3. Stockholm, 1935.

———. 'Svenska dräkten som bondeplagg'. In *Gustavianskt. Studier kring den gustavianska tidens kulturhistoria*. Stockholm: Nordisk rotogravyr, 1932.

Swensson, Margareta. 'Bondehamnar i nordvästra Skåne och Blekinge under 1600-talet'. *Historisk Tidsskrift* 12 (1 January 1970).

Sylwan, Otto. *Svenska pressens historia till statshvälfningen 1772*. Lund: Gleerup, 1896.

Taillefer, Emile. 'Contribution d'un Grenoblois à l'histoire de La Suède'. *Bulletin Du Musée Bernadotte* 17 (1972).

Tengroth Ulväng, Marie. *Klädekonomi och klädkultur. Böndernas kläder i Härjedalen under 1800-talet*. Mörklinta: Gidlunds Förlag, 2012.

———. 'Kattunspår i Härjedalen 1750 till 1850'. In *Dolda innovationer. Textila produkter och ny teknik under 1800-talet*, edited by Klas Nyberg and Pia Lundqvist. Stockholm: Kulturhistoriska Bokförlaget, 2013.

Tesdahl, Eugene Richard Henry. 'The Price of Empire: Smuggling between New York and New France, 1700–1754'. PhD thesis, University of Colorado, 2012.

Tracy, James D. *The Political Economy of Merchant Empires: State Power and World Trade, 1350–1750*. Cambridge: Cambridge University Press, 1997.

Trentmann, Frank. 'Materiality in the Future of History: Things, Practices, and Politics'. *Journal of British Studies* 48, no. 2 (April 2009).

Trivellato, Francesca. *The Familiarity of Strangers: The Sephardic Diaspora, Livorno, and Cross-Cultural Trade in the Early Modern Period*. New Haven London: Yale University Press, 2009.

———. 'The Historical and Comparative Study of Cross-Cultural Trade'. In *Religion and Trade: Cross-Cultural Exchange in World History*, edited by Francesca Trivellato, Leor Halevi, and Catia Antunes. Oxford: Oxford University Press, 2014.

Tveite, Stein. 'Den norske tekstilmarknaden på 1700-talet'. *Historiallinen Arkisto*, 1967.

Ukers, William. *All About Tea*. Lulu.com, 2017.

Ulväng, Göran, Sofia Murham, and Kristina Lilja. *Den glömda konsumtionen. Auktionshandel i Sverige under 1700- och 1800-talen*. Mörklinta: Gidlunds Förlag, 2013.

Valentin, Hugo. *Judarna i Sverige från 1774 till 1950-talet*. Stockholm: Natur och Kultur/ LTs förlag, 2004.

Vallinder, Torbjörn. 'Adam Smiths genombrott i Sverige'. *Ekonomisk Debatt* 3 (1987).

Veluwenkamp, Jan, and Maarten Draper. 'Sound Toll Registers Online and the Eighteenth-Century Baltic Coffee Commerce.' *Groniek Historisch Tijdschrift* 46, no. 199 (2014).

Verley, Patrick. 'From One International Trade to Another: Changes in European Trade during the Nineteenth Century'. In *A Deus Ex Machina Revisited: Atlantic Colonial Trade and European Economic Development*, edited by P.C. Emmer, O. Pétré-Grenouilleau, and Jessica V. Roitman. Leiden, Boston: Brill, 2006.

Vickery, Amanda. 'Mutton Dressed as Lamb? Fashioning Age in Georgian England'. *Journal of British Studies* 52 (October 2013).

Vries, Jan de. 'Between Purchasing Power and the World of Goods: Understanding the Household Economy in Early Modern Europe'. In *Consumption and the World of Goods*, edited by John Brewer and Roy Porter. London; New York: Routledge, 1993.

———. 'Luxury in the Dutch Golden Age in Theory and Practice'. In *Luxury in the Eighteenth Century: Debates, Desires and Delectable Goods*, edited by Maxine Berg and Elizabeth Eger. Basingstoke, Hampshire; New York: Palgrave Macmillan, 2003.

Waggen, Lars. 'Gamaltids marknadsliv i Inntrøndelag'. *Årbok for 1952, Nord-Trøndelag Historielag*, 1952.

Walsh, Claire. 'Shop Design and the Display of Goods in Eighteenth-Century London'. *Journal of Design History* 8, no. 3 (1995): 157–76.

———. 'Shops, Shopping, and the Art of Decision-Making in Eighteenth-Century England'. In *Gender, Taste, and Material Culture in Britain and North America, 1700–1830*, edited by John Styles and Amanda Vickery. Yale University Press, 2006.

Warner, Jessica, Minghao Her, Gerhard Gmel, and Jürgen Rehm. 'Can Legislation Prevent Debauchery? Mother Gin and Public Health in 18th-Century England'. *American Journal of Public Health* 91, no. 3 (March 2001).

Warner, Jessica, and Frank Ivis. '"Damn You, You Informing Bitch." Vox Populi and the Unmaking of the Gin Act of 1736'. *Journal of Social History* 33, no. 2 (Winter 1999).

Wassholm, Johanna, and Anna Sundelin. 'Emotions, Trading Practices and Communication in Transnational Itinerant Trade: Encounters between "Rucksack Russians" and Their Customers in the Late Nineteenth- and Early Twentieth-Century Finland'. *Scandinavian Economic History Review* 66, no. 2 (2018).

Wästberg, Per. 'Stockholm 1786'. In *1786, Vitterhetsakaedmiens Jubileumssymposium*, 1986.

Welch, Evelyn S. *Shopping in the Renaissance: Consumer Cultures in Italy, 1400–1600*. 2nd Printing edition. New Haven Conn.; London: Yale University Press, 2009.

Wendland, Anna Veronika. 'Cultural Transfer'. In *Travelling Concepts for the Study of Culture*, edited by Birgit Neumann and Ansgar Nünning. Berlin: Walter de Gruyter, 2012.

Wennerlind, Carl. 'Theatrum Œconomicum: Anders Berch and the Dramatization of the Swedish Improvement Discourse'. In *New Perspectives on the History of Political Economy*, edited by R. Fredona and S.A. Reinert, 2018.

———. 'Atlantis Restored: Natural Knowledge and Political Economy in Early Modern Sweden.' *American Historical Review*. 2022. Vol. 127. No. 4.

Westin, Gunnar T. 'Olavus Petri', https://sok.riksarkivet.se/sbl/artikel/7688, *Svenskt biografiskt lexikon*. Accessed 20 October 2018.

Westrin, Thomas. 'John Holyoaks Goodricke'. In *Nordisk Familjebok - Uggleupplagan*. Vol. 9. Stockholm: Nordisk Familjebok förlag, 1908.

Wigton Smith, Chloe. '"Callico Madams": Servants, Consumption, and the Calico Crisis'. *Eighteenth-Century Life* 31, no. 2 (Spring 2007).

Wikberg, Karin. *Alla dessa tullar - en Arkivguide. En vägledning till tullarkiv och tullhandlingar i riksarkivet*. Stockholm: Riksarkivet, 2006.

———. '"Skogarnas Wilda Innevånare" Tull och smuggling i 1800-talets Jämtland'. *Argus*, no. 8 (1994).

Wiking-Faria, Pablo. 'Freden, friköpen och järnplogarna: drivkrafter och förändringsprocesser under den agrara revolutionen i Halland 1700–1900'. PhD thesis, Göteborgs Universitet, 2009.

Wilhelmius, Wolfgang. *Juden in Vorpommern*. Schwerin: Friedrich-Ebert-Stiftung, 2007.

Wilson, Victor. *Commerce in Disguise: War and Trade in the Caribbean Free Port of Gustavia, 1793–1815*. Åbo: Åbo Akademis förlag, 2015.

Windahl Pontén, Annika. 'Sorgdräkt och engelska kläder. Två av familjen von Linnés kvitton'. In *Svenska Linnésällskapets Årsbok*. Uppsala: Svenska Linnéesällskapet, 2012.

———. 'Kiär Hustru, Wackra Barn, Bodde Uti Ett Palais- Materialitet Och Identitet i Hushållet von Linné'. Uppsala University, Unpublished Doctoral Dissertation.

Winslow, Cal. 'Sussex Smugglers'. In *Albion's Fatal Tree. Crime and Society in Eighteenth-Century England*, First American Edition. New York: Pantheon Books, 1975.

Winther, Nils-Erik, Rolf Wändel, and Matz Jörgensen. *Gästgifwerier, Krogar och skjutshåll*. Löddeköpinge: Harjager härads fornminnes- och hembygdsförening, 2003.

———. 'Sweden and the Seven Years War, 1757–1762: War, Debt and Politics', *War in History*, 19 (2012).

———. 'The Political Economy of Swedish Absolutism, 1789–1809'. *European Review of Economic History* 16, no. 4 (November 2012).

Winton, Patrik. 'Parliamentary Control, Public Discussion and Royal Autonomy: Sweden, 1750–1780'. *Histoire & Mesure* XXX, no. 2 (2015).

Wolff, Charlotta. 'Sveriges representation i Paris: Sändebuden och beskickningen under frihetstiden och den gustavianska tiden'. *Historisk Tidskrift För Finland* 2, no. 86 (2001).

———. *Vänskap och makt. Den svenska politiska eliten och upplysningstidens Frankrike*. Helsinki: Svenska litteratursällskapet i Finland, 2005.

'Worsted Knitting Yarn | Textile'. Encyclopedia Britannica, https://www.britannica.com/technology/worsted-knitting-yarn, Accessed 5 December 2018.

Wottle, Martin. *Det lilla ägandet. Korporativ formering och sociala relationer inom Stockholms minuthandel 1720–1810*. Stockholm: Stads- och Kommunhistoriska Institutet, 2000.

———. 'Detaljhandeln med kläder och tyger, 1734–1834'. In *Till salu. Stockholms textila handel och manufaktur 1722–1846*, edited by Klas Nyberg. Stockholm: Stads- och Kommunhistoriska Institutet, 2010.

Yun Casalilla, Bartollomé. 'Transnational History. What Lies behind the Label? Some Reflections from the Early Modernist's Point of View.' *Culture & History Digital Journal* 3, no. 2 (December 2014).

Zahedieh, Nuala. 'Defying Mercantilism: Illicit Trade, Trust, and the Jamaican Sephardim, 1660–1730'. *The Historical Journal* 61, no. 1 (2018): 77–102.

Other Secondary Sources

Online Databases

Borgmästare och råd i Stockholm, Utdrag ur Taxor för år 1620 (ryggtitel), see https://stockholmskallan.stockholm.se/post/7896, Accessed 29 March 2018.

Edvinsson, Rodney. 'Prisomräknare Från Medeltiden till 2100', http://www.historicalstatistics.org/Jamforelsepris.htm., Accessed on numerous occasions 2018–2019.

Meänkielen sanakirja, http://meankielensanakirja.com/sana/id/79880, Accessed 25 June 2019.

Orts historia, https://ortshistoria.se, Accessed 11 October 2018

Sound Toll Registers Online, http://www.soundtoll.nl/index.php/en/over-het-project/str-online, Accessed 20 April 2017.

'STR Online - Shipmaster Names', http://dietrich.soundtoll.nl/public/names.php?id=258070, Accessed 20 April 2017.

Tidigmoderna Konkurser, http://www.tidigmodernakonkurser.se/index.php/extended, Accessed 31 October 2018.

Presentations

Bull, Ida. 'Immigrating Merchants to Trondheim in the 18th Century – Intermediaries between Europe and the Trondheim Hinterland', IEHC Congress, Helsinki 2006, Session 16: *Merchant Settlements as Intermediaries for European Influences in the Baltic North, or Elsewhere 1650–1850. Economic, Social and Cultural Aspecs.*

Clark, Gregory. 'The Consumer Revolution: Turning Point in Human History, or Statistical Artifact?' Munich Personal RePEc Archive, 2010.

Dalhede, Christina. 'Early Modern Merchant Families. Foreign Intermediaries in Swedish Cities. The Gothenburg Market in the 17th Century', IEHC Congress, Helsinki 2006, Session 16: *Merchant Settlements as Intermediaries for European Influences in the Baltic North, or Elsewhere 1650–1850. Economic, Social and Cultural Aspects.*

Nix, Michael, 'Norwich Textiles: a Global Story, 1750–1820', Norwich Castle Museum Saturday 5 December 2015.

Nyberg, Klas. 'Financial Networks, Migration and the Transformation of the Merchant Elite in 18th Century Stockholm', IEHC Congress, Helsinki 2006, Session 16: *Merchant Settlements as Intermediaries for European Influences in the Baltic North, or Elsewhere 1650–1850. Economic, Social and Cultural Aspects.*

Waldinger, Maria. 'Drought and the French Revolution: The Effects of Adverse Weather Conditions on Peasant Revoluts in 1789', n.d.

Personal Correspondence

Åsén, Ulf. Personal Correspondence, 12 December 2017.
Eldvik, Berit. Private Communication, 30 January 2017.
Gullback, Johanna. 'Kalmink i Leksand', 23 February 2019.
Jobs Arnberg, Anna-Karin. Private Communication, 13 October 2017, 23 February 2019.

INDEX

Note: Page numbers followed by "n" denote endnotes.

Taylor & Francis Group
an informa business

Taylor & Francis eBooks

www.taylorfrancis.com

A single destination for eBooks from Taylor & Francis with increased functionality and an improved user experience to meet the needs of our customers.

90,000+ eBooks of award-winning academic content in Humanities, Social Science, Science, Technology, Engineering, and Medical written by a global network of editors and authors.

TAYLOR & FRANCIS EBOOKS OFFERS:

- A streamlined experience for our library customers
- A single point of discovery for all of our eBook content
- Improved search and discovery of content at both book and chapter level

REQUEST A FREE TRIAL

support@taylorfrancis.com

Routledge
Taylor & Francis Group

CRC Press
Taylor & Francis Group